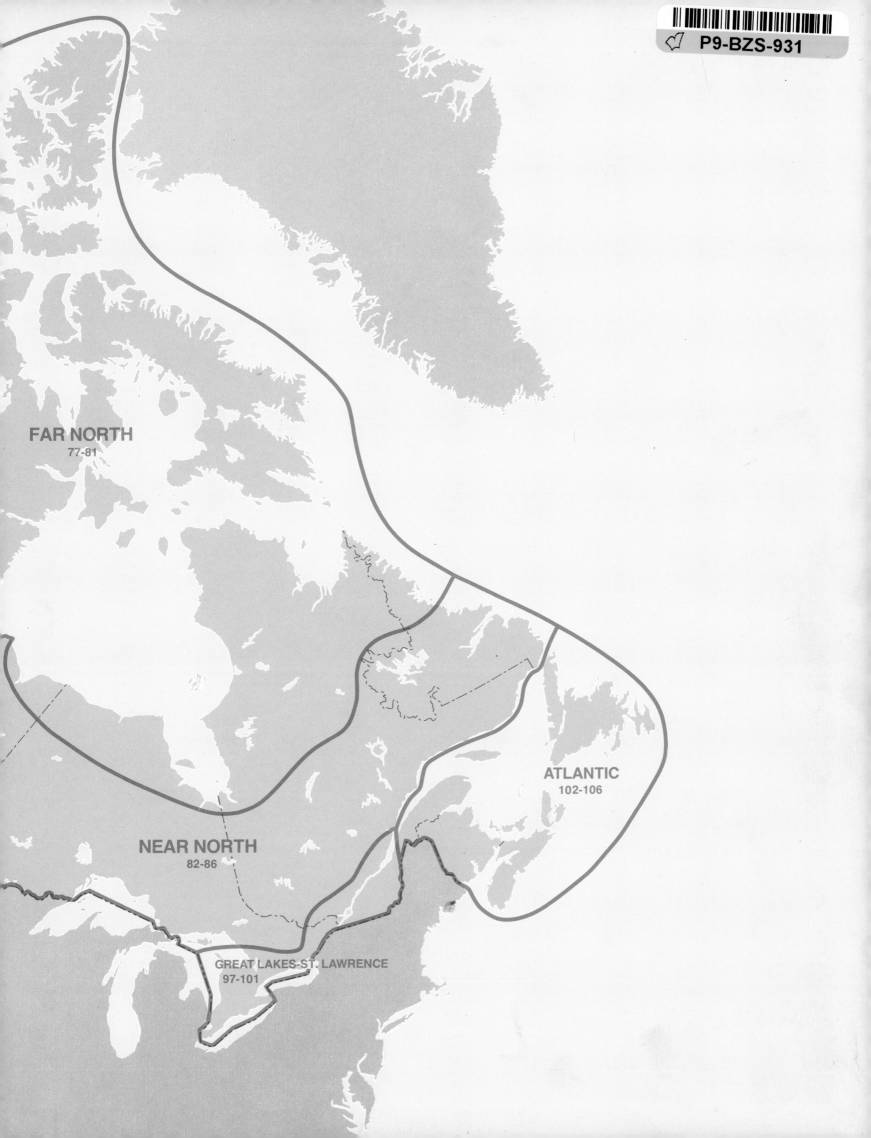

FAR NORTH
77-81

NEAR NORTH
82-86

ATLANTIC
102-106

GREAT LAKES-ST. LAWRENCE
97-101

CANADA
and the World

AN ATLAS RESOURCE

Geoffrey J. Matthews
Chief Cartographer
Department of Geography
University of Toronto

Robert Morrow, Jr.
Co-ordinator of Social and Environmental Studies
Wentworth County Board of Education

Prentice-Hall Canada Inc., Scarborough, Ontario

To Amanda, Lori,
and Michael

Canadian Cataloguing in Publication Data

Matthews, Geoffrey J., 1932–
    Canada and the world : an atlas resource

Bibliography: p.
Includes index.
ISBN 0-13-113986-X (school ed.). — ISBN 0-13-113846-4 (trade ed.).

1. Canada – Maps.   2. Atlases, Canadian.   I. Morrow, Robert, 1942–
II. Title.

G1115.M37 1984   912'.71   C83-099125-5

Reprinted with updates, 1986
Prentice-Hall, Inc., Englewood Cliffs, New Jersey
Prentice-Hall International, Inc., London
Prentice-Hall of Australia, Pty., Ltd., Sydney
Prentice-Hall of India, Pvt., Ltd., New Delhi
Prentice-Hall of Japan, Inc., Tokyo
Prentice-Hall of Southeast Asia (Pte.) Ltd., Singapore
Editora Prentice-Hall do Brasil Ltda., Rio de Janeiro
Prentice-Hall Hispanoamericana, S.A., Mexico

ISBN 0-13-113986-X (school ed.)   ISBN 0-13-113846-4 (trade ed.)

 Metric Commission Canada has granted permission for use of the National Symbol for Metric conversion.

Project Editor: Rebecca Vogan
Production Editor: Paula Pettitt
Design of Cover: The Dragon's Eye Press
Design of Front and Back Matter: Steven Boyle
Production: Monika Heike
Cartography: Department of Geography, University of Toronto
Photomechanical Services and Colour Proofs: Northway-Gestalt Corporation, Toronto
Composition: Cooper and Beatty Limited; Q Composition Inc. (front and back matter)

Printed and bound in Canada by The Bryant Press Limited

6 7 8 9 BP 93 92 91 90

PHOTO CREDITS

pp. 2, 40 courtesy of NASA. pp. 23 (centre left, bottom centre), 82, 85 (bottom right) courtesy of Ronald Fulton. pp. 23 (bottom left, bottom right), 24 (centre right), 83 (centre, bottom), 84, 85 (centre left), 88, 90 (bottom), 91, 92, 93, 101, 102, 104 courtesy of Gary Birchall. pp. 24 (top left), 51, 52, 75 (bottom left, bottom centre), 77, 78, 83 (top), 87, 90 (top left, top right), 95, 97, 98, 103 Landsat imagery courtesy of the Canada Centre for Remote Sensing. p. 24 (top centre) courtesy of K. Forbes. pp. 35, 36 (bottom) courtesy of Ontario Hydro. p. 36 (top) courtesy of Société d'Énergie de la Baie James. p. 39 courtesy of Environment Canada, Meteorological Branch. p. 55 courtesy of Macmillan-Bloedel Limited. p. 56 courtesy of Energy, Mines and Resources Canada. p. 81 courtesy of Ian Reid. p. 86 courtesy of Corporation de promotion industrielle, commerciale et touristique de Sept-Îles inc. p. 94 courtesy of Wolfgang Ziegler.

Name in the Atlas	Page No.	Official Québec Place Name
Appalachians	20	Les Appalaches
Chaleur Bay	103	Baie des Chaleurs
La Grande Basin	35	La Grande Rivière Basin
La Grande	35-36	La Grande Rivière
Gulf of St. Lawrence	20, 22, 34, 58, 84, 103, 106	Golfe du Saint-Laurent
Hudson Bay	8, 20, 78, 134	Baie d'Hudson
Hudson Strait	20, 78, 134	Détroit d'Hudson
James Bay	20, 35, 78	Baie James
Laurentians	20	Les Laurentides
Lièvre (River)	98	Rivière du Lièvre
Ottawa (River)	20, 84, 98	Rivière des Outaouais
Rouge (River)	98	Rivière Rouge
St-Jean	74, 98	Saint-Jean-sur-Richelieu
St. Lawrence (River)	20, 58, 84, 98, 103	Fleuve Saint-Laurent
Ungava Bay	20, 78	Baie d'Ungava

PREFACE

ACKNOWLEDGEMENTS

Canada and the World: An Atlas Resource is designed to provide a current, accurate, and detailed view of Canada in its world setting.

The Canadian coverage begins with a thematic approach to history and geography, and to the social, economic, and cultural fabric. The plates in this section cover the basic topics of exploration, population distribution, physiography, climate, energy, industry, economics, transportation, and urbanization. Topics of special interest, such as provincial and federal politics, consumerism, the labour force, and social issues, are also explored.

In addition, Canada is presented from a regional perspective. The introductory plate for each region defines the physical area, shows the population distribution, and briefly describes the social and economic situation. Important aspects of the region are emphasized on the second plate. A topographic map focuses on a representative section of each region. Photographs and satellite images illustrate most of these plates.

Canada and the World: An Atlas Resource also provides a concise but comprehensive view of the world. The regional plates depict political boundaries, major cities, major bodies of water, and transportation routes. A series of thematic plates examines basic topics such as relief, climate, agriculture, and population. Critical issues of the contemporary world — inflation, nuclear arms development, living standards, and military power — are also considered. The Canadian situation, described extensively in the first section of the atlas, comes into perspective within the global context.

As an atlas resource, *Canada and the World* provides significant information on a wide range of subjects. The technique of complementing maps with text, graphs, tables, photographs, satellite images, and illustrations is used to present the information in the most effective way possible. This combination of abundant data and imaginative design encourages the reader to actively interpret information and to consider regional, national, and international issues. When plates are examined and compared, patterns emerge, and relationships between the physical environment and human activity become more clear.

Additional sections in the atlas give supplementary data and interpretive aids. Separate statistical sections for Canada and for the world expand on the information on the plates. The gazetteer allows the reader to locate places in Canada and the world easily, and the glossary defines all key terms. In addition, the sources for all information are listed.

Canada and the World: An Atlas Resource is dedicated to those who enjoy the challenge of finding information, ordering it, and then using it to gain insight into their world.

It is impossible to acknowledge all the people who have contributed to *Canada and the World: An Atlas Resource*. Our first thought is to thank those who provided inspiration in the learning and teaching of geography: James Forrester, Kenneth A. Stanley, and Gordon E. Carswell. Special thanks must also go to many others who contributed valuable insight and information, often without the advantage of seeing the project as a whole. Their generous donation of time and skill is greatly appreciated.

Next, we would like to thank those people involved in the actual design and production of the atlas. Rob Greenaway, Executive Editor at Prentice-Hall, conceived the project. Rebecca Vogan, Project Editor, and Paula Pettitt, Production Editor, provided boundless enthusiasm and guided the project through the many complex stages of production. Monika Heike, Production Assistant, and Rand Paterson, Assistant Vice-President, Manufacturing, are responsible for the fine quality of the physical specifications. Len Ugarenko of Northway-Gestalt Corporation guaranteed the project exceptional filmwork.

Finally, *Canada and the World: An Atlas Resource* is the product of three years of meticulous work by a dedicated team of professionals from the Department of Geography at the University of Toronto. It is impossible to exaggerate the contribution that cartographers Chris Grounds, Hedy Later, Shelley Laskin, Dorothy Gunther, Byron Moldofsky, Daniel Poirier, Julia Sandquist, Jane Davie, Roddie McNeil, and Ada Cheung have made to this project, and we cannot thank them enough. We would like to give special thanks to Chris for his organizational skills and to Hedy for her elegant illustrations.

The beauty, clarity, and utility of this atlas are the result of a vision, hard work, and fine cartographic skills.

Geoffrey J. Matthews

Robert Morrow, Jr.

CONTENTS

[Handwritten note:]
• Urbanization
• Prairies 92 & 93/94 & 95/96
• Population distribution - 117/118
• Population characteristics
• Economy
• Living standards

WORLD—THEMATIC

WORLD—REGIONAL

The following maps all show political boundaries, countries, cities, transportation features including major roads, railways, and international airports, and bodies of water with the 200 m depth line identified.

CANADA AND THE WORLD

This photograph was taken from the Apollo 17 spacecraft. It shows a clear image of Africa, the Middle East, and Antarctica.

CANADA

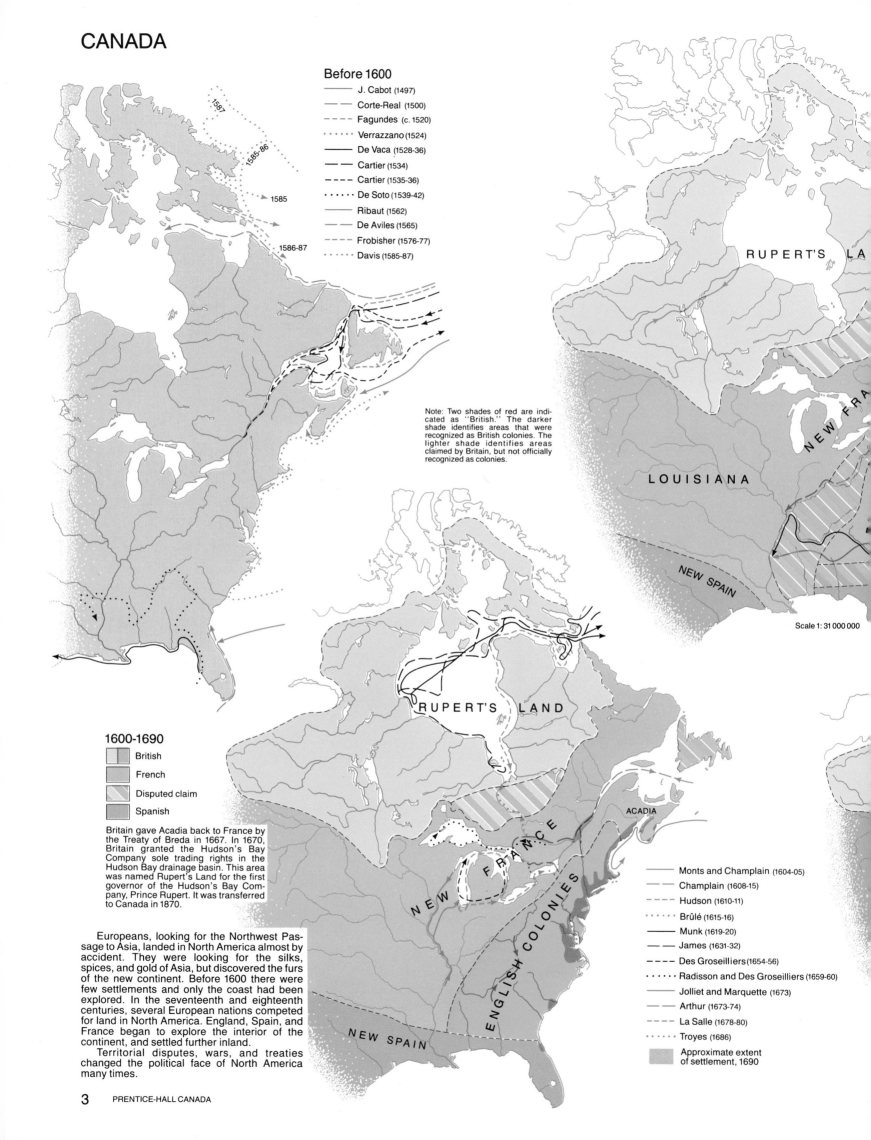

Before 1600

——	J. Cabot (1497)
– –	Corte-Real (1500)
- - -	Fagundes (c. 1520)
······	Verrazzano (1524)
——	De Vaca (1528-36)
— —	Cartier (1534)
- - -	Cartier (1535-36)
······	De Soto (1539-42)
——	Ribaut (1562)
– –	De Aviles (1565)
- - -	Frobisher (1576-77)
······	Davis (1585-87)

Note: Two shades of red are indicated as "British." The darker shade identifies areas that were recognized as British colonies. The lighter shade identifies areas claimed by Britain, but not officially recognized as colonies.

Scale 1: 31 000 000

1600-1690

▨	British
▨	French
▨	Disputed claim
▨	Spanish

Britain gave Acadia back to France by the Treaty of Breda in 1667. In 1670, Britain granted the Hudson's Bay Company sole trading rights in the Hudson Bay drainage basin. This area was named Rupert's Land for the first governor of the Hudson's Bay Company, Prince Rupert. It was transferred to Canada in 1870.

Europeans, looking for the Northwest Passage to Asia, landed in North America almost by accident. They were looking for the silks, spices, and gold of Asia, but discovered the furs of the new continent. Before 1600 there were few settlements and only the coast had been explored. In the seventeenth and eighteenth centuries, several European nations competed for land in North America. England, Spain, and France began to explore the interior of the continent, and settled further inland.

Territorial disputes, wars, and treaties changed the political face of North America many times.

——	Monts and Champlain (1604-05)
– –	Champlain (1608-15)
- - -	Hudson (1610-11)
······	Brûlé (1615-16)
——	Munk (1619-20)
— —	James (1631-32)
- - -	Des Groseilliers (1654-56)
······	Radisson and Des Groseilliers (1659-60)
——	Jolliet and Marquette (1673)
– –	Arthur (1673-74)
- - -	La Salle (1678-80)
······	Troyes (1686)
▨	Approximate extent of settlement, 1690

1690-1713

British
French
Disputed claim
Spanish
Disputed claim

France gave up Nova Scotia, claims to the Hudson Bay territories, and interests in Newfoundland to Britain by the Treaty of Utrecht in 1713.

NOVA SCOTIA

Kelsey (1690-92)
Viele (1692)
Couture (1696-1700)
Welch (1698)
Approximate extent of settlement, 1713

1763-1784

British
American
Disputed claim
Spanish

The second Treaty of Paris (1783) established the independence of the United States of America. Britain granted the new nation a vast territory east of the Mississippi, and south of the Great Lakes and the St. Lawrence. In British North America, New Brunswick and Cape Breton became colonies separate from Nova Scotia.

RUPERT'S LAND

NEWFOUNDLAND

1778 1779 1779
1780
1769-70 1767-68 1781

QUÉBEC

ST. JOHN'S ISLAND
CAPE BRETON ISLAND
N.B.
NOVA SCOTIA

LOUISIANA

UNITED STATES

Tomison (1767-70)
Hearne (1770-71)
Turnor (1778-81)
Approximate extent of settlement, 1784

RUPERT'S LAND

1739
1741
1731
1738

NEWFOUNDLAND

TERRITORY

QUÉBEC

NOVA SCOTIA

INDIAN

BRITISH COLONIES

LOUISIANA

1713-1763

British
Spanish

In 1763, at the end of the Seven Years' War, Britain, France and Spain signed the Treaty of Paris. France gave up the eastern part of North America to Britain, and the territory called Louisiana to Spain.

Stuart (1715)
P. la Vérendrye (1731-41)
Pierre and Paul Mallet (1738-41)
Middleton (1741)
L.-J. and F. la Vérendrye (1742-43)
Gist (1750-52)
Approximate extent of settlement, 1763

Approximate extent of settlement, 1825

1784-1825

British
American
Joint occupation
Spanish
Russian

ALASKA
THE NORTH-WESTERN TERRITORY

OREGON TERRITORY

RUPERT'S LAND

LOWER CANADA
UPPER CANADA
N.B.
P.E.I.
N.S.

MEXICO

UNITED STATES

Scale 1: 67 000 000

British North America's international border was extended along the 49th parallel of latitude to the Rocky Mountains in 1818. Cape Breton rejoined Nova Scotia in 1820. Britain and the United States both occupied the Oregon territory, and in 1824 Britain agreed with Russia on the position of the Alaska boundary.

Bering (1741)
Cook (1778-79)
Vancouver (1792-94)

CANADA

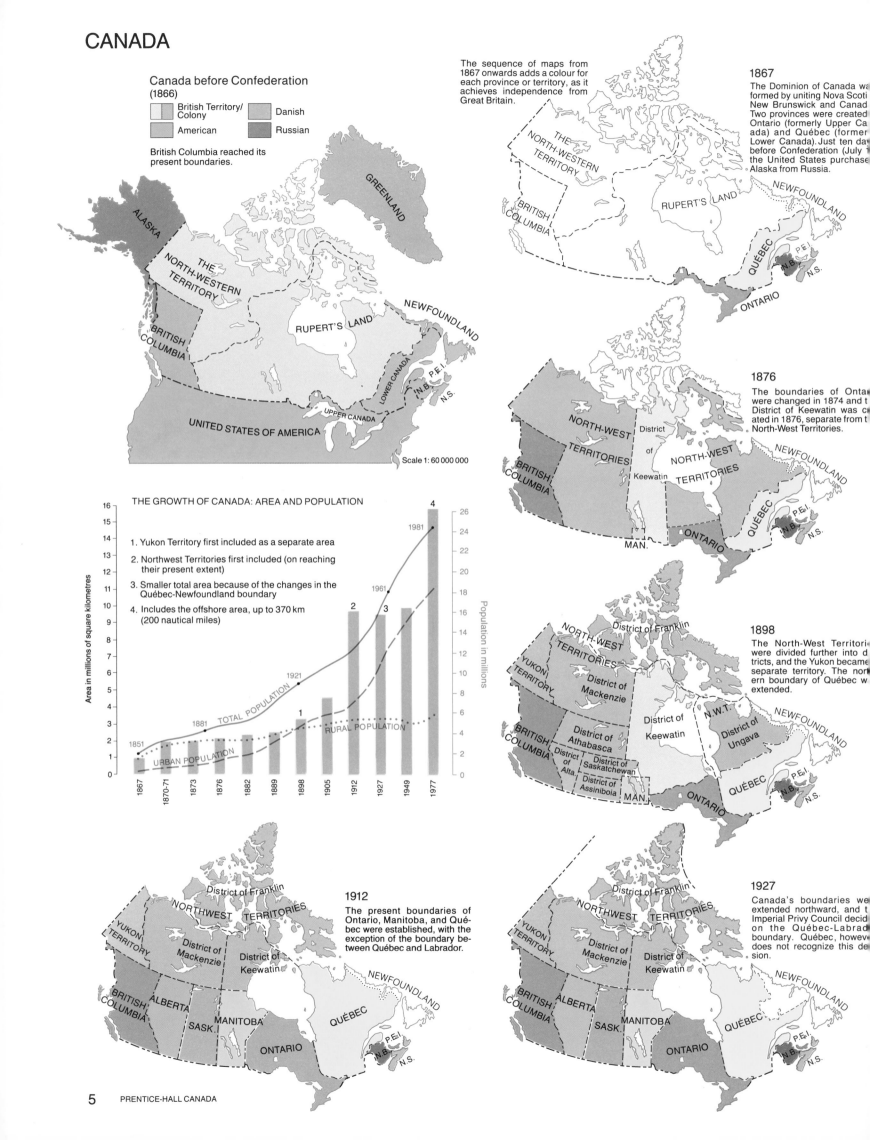

Canada before Confederation
(1866)

- British Territory/Colony
- American
- Danish
- Russian

British Columbia reached its present boundaries.

GREENLAND

ALASKA

THE NORTH-WESTERN TERRITORY

BRITISH COLUMBIA

RUPERT'S LAND

NEWFOUNDLAND

LOWER CANADA

P.E.I.

N.B.

N.S.

UNITED STATES OF AMERICA

UPPER CANADA

Scale 1: 60 000 000

THE GROWTH OF CANADA: AREA AND POPULATION

1. Yukon Territory first included as a separate area

2. Northwest Territories first included (on reaching their present extent)

3. Smaller total area because of the changes in the Québec-Newfoundland boundary

4. Includes the offshore area, up to 370 km (200 nautical miles)

Area in millions of square kilometres

Population in millions

TOTAL POPULATION

RURAL POPULATION

URBAN POPULATION

1851 1867 1870-71 1873 1876 1882 1889 1898 1905 1912 1927 1949 1977

1881 1921 1961 1981

The sequence of maps from 1867 onwards adds a colour for each province or territory, as it achieves independence from Great Britain.

1867

The Dominion of Canada wa formed by uniting Nova Scoti New Brunswick and Canad Two provinces were created Ontario (formerly Upper Ca ada) and Québec (former Lower Canada). Just ten day before Confederation (July 1 the United States purchase Alaska from Russia.

THE NORTH-WESTERN TERRITORY

BRITISH COLUMBIA

RUPERT'S LAND

NEWFOUNDLAND

QUÉBEC

P.E.I.

N.B.

N.S.

ONTARIO

1876

The boundaries of Ontar were changed in 1874 and t District of Keewatin was c ated in 1876, separate from t North-West Territories.

NORTH-WEST TERRITORIES

District of Keewatin

NORTH-WEST TERRITORIES

BRITISH COLUMBIA

NEWFOUNDLAND

MAN.

ONTARIO

QUÉBEC

P.E.I.

N.B.

N.S.

1898

The North-West Territori were divided further into d tricts, and the Yukon became separate territory. The nor ern boundary of Québec w extended.

NORTH-WEST TERRITORIES

District of Franklin

YUKON TERRITORY

District of Mackenzie

District of Keewatin

N.W.T.

District of Ungava

NEWFOUNDLAND

BRITISH COLUMBIA

District of Athabasca

District of Alta.

District of Saskatchewan

District of Assiniboia

MAN.

QUÉBEC

P.E.I.

N.B.

N.S.

ONTARIO

1912

The present boundaries of Ontario, Manitoba, and Québec were established, with the exception of the boundary between Québec and Labrador.

District of Franklin

NORTHWEST TERRITORIES

YUKON TERRITORY

District of Mackenzie

District of Keewatin

NEWFOUNDLAND

BRITISH COLUMBIA

ALBERTA

SASK.

MANITOBA

QUÉBEC

ONTARIO

P.E.I.

N.B.

N.S.

1927

Canada's boundaries we extended northward, and t Imperial Privy Council decid on the Québec-Labrad boundary. Québec, howeve does not recognize this de sion.

District of Franklin

NORTHWEST TERRITORIES

YUKON TERRITORY

District of Mackenzie

District of Keewatin

NEWFOUNDLAND

BRITISH COLUMBIA

ALBERTA

SASK.

MANITOBA

QUÉBEC

ONTARIO

P.E.I.

N.B.

N.S.

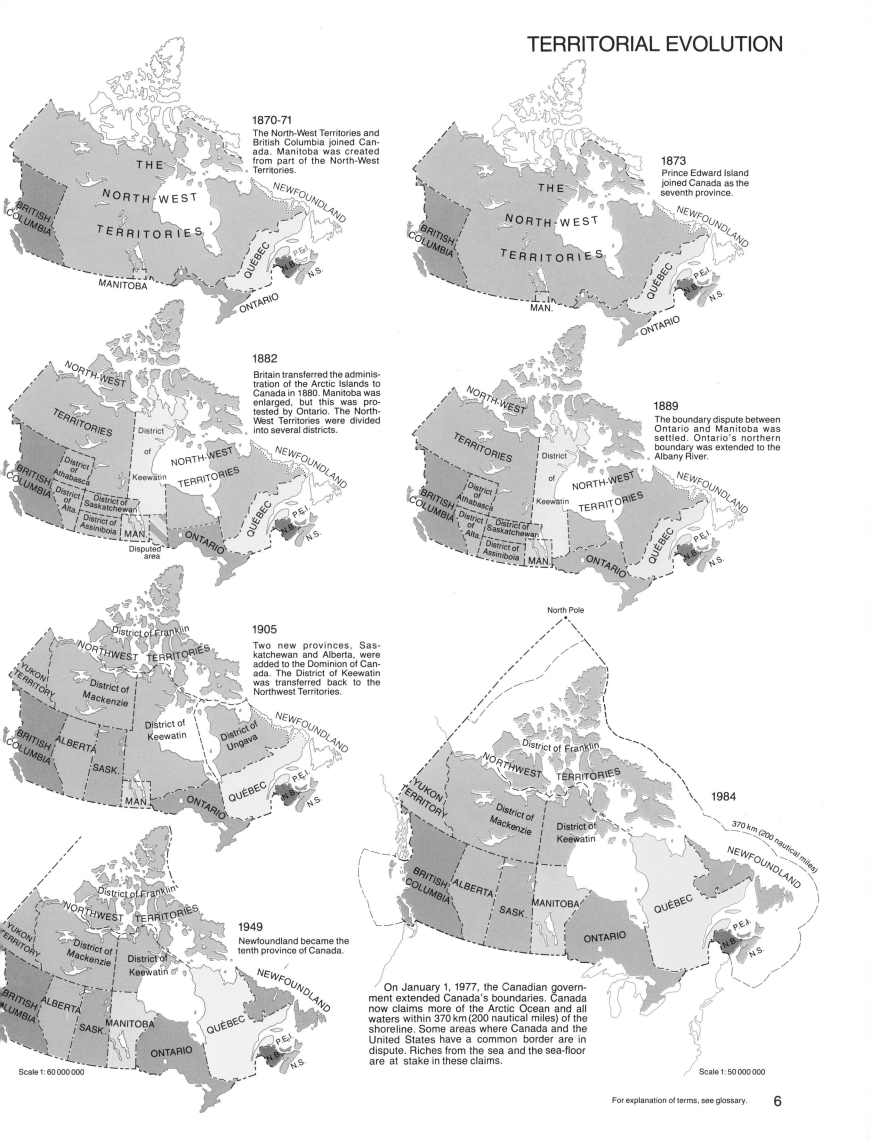

1870-71
The North-West Territories and British Columbia joined Canada. Manitoba was created from part of the North-West Territories.

1873
Prince Edward Island joined Canada as the seventh province.

1882
Britain transferred the administration of the Arctic Islands to Canada in 1880. Manitoba was enlarged, but this was protested by Ontario. The North-West Territories were divided into several districts.

1889
The boundary dispute between Ontario and Manitoba was settled. Ontario's northern boundary was extended to the Albany River.

1905
Two new provinces, Saskatchewan and Alberta, were added to the Dominion of Canada. The District of Keewatin was transferred back to the Northwest Territories.

1949
Newfoundland became the tenth province of Canada.

1984

On January 1, 1977, the Canadian government extended Canada's boundaries. Canada now claims more of the Arctic Ocean and all waters within 370 km (200 nautical miles) of the shoreline. Some areas where Canada and the United States have a common border are in dispute. Riches from the sea and the sea-floor are at stake in these claims.

Scale 1: 60 000 000

Scale 1: 50 000 000

For explanation of terms, see glossary. **6**

CANADA

YUKON TERRITORY
Entered Confederation:
June 13, 1898
Capital: Whitehorse
Area: 531 844 km²
Population: 23 153
(0.1% of Canada)
Population density: 0.04/km²
Urban population: 64.0%

BRITISH COLUMBIA
Entered Confederation:
July 20, 1871
Capital: Victoria
Area: 892 677 km²
Population: 2 744 467
(11.3% of Canada)
Population density: 3.1/km²
Urban population: 78.0%

ALBERTA
Entered Confederation:
September 1, 1905
Capital: Edmonton
Area: 638 233 km²
Population: 2 237 724
(9.2% of Canada)
Population density: 3.5/km²
Urban population: 77.2%

"The strength of Canada's Constitution lies not in the words it contains but in the foundation upon which it rests, the desire of the people of Canada that their country remain strong and united."

QUEEN ELIZABETH II

The Canadian Constitution was patriated from Great Britain on April 17, 1982. The Constitution Act, 1982, gives Canada the power to amend its own constitution. Canada is now completely independent from Great Britain.

SASKATCHEWAN
Entered Confederation:
September 1, 1905
Capital: Regina
Area: 570 113 km²
Population: 968 313
(4.0% of Canada)
Population density: 1.7/km²
Urban population: 58.2%

MANITOBA
Entered Confederation:
July 15, 1870
Capital: Winnipeg
Area: 547 704 km²
Population: 1 026 241
(4.2% of Canada)
Population density: 1.9/km²
Urban population: 71.2%

ONTARIO
Entered Confederation:
July 1, 1867
Capital: Toronto
Area: 916 734 km²
Population: 8 625 107
(35.4% of Canada)
Population density: 9.4/km²
Urban population: 81.7%

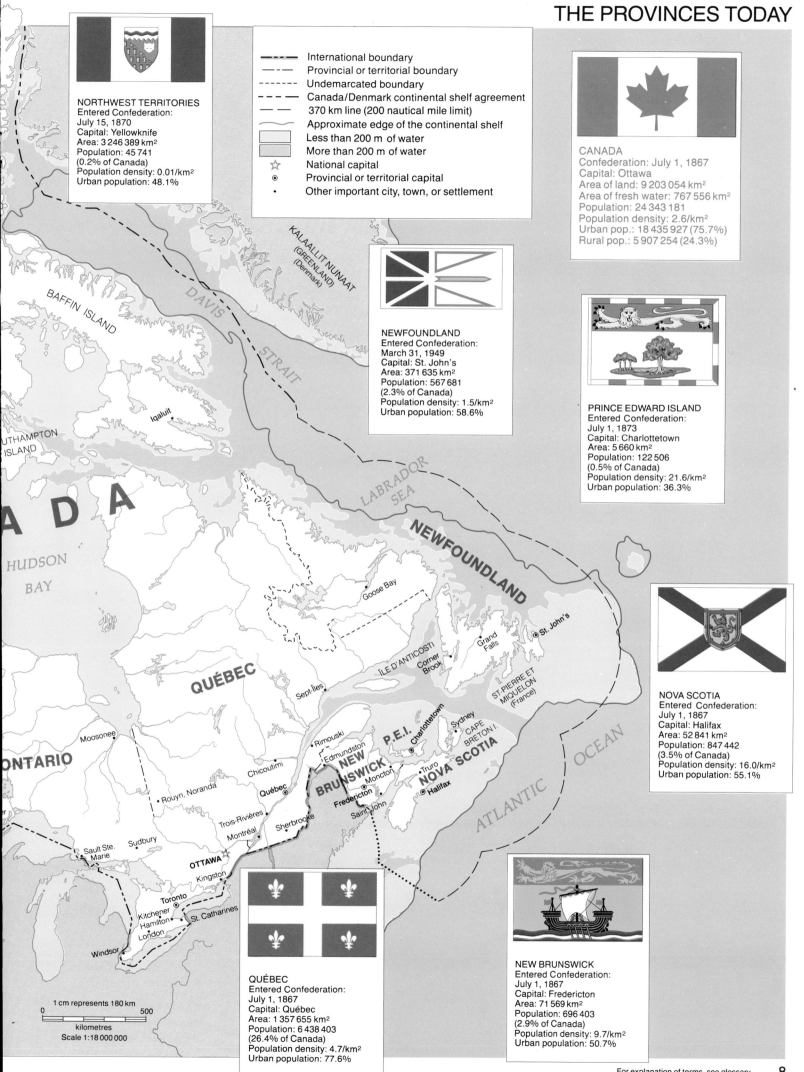

NORTHWEST TERRITORIES
Entered Confederation:
July 15, 1870
Capital: Yellowknife
Area: 3 246 389 km²
Population: 45 741
(0.2% of Canada)
Population density: 0.01/km²
Urban population: 48.1%

----- International boundary
---·--- Provincial or territorial boundary
------- Undemarcated boundary
--- --- Canada/Denmark continental shelf agreement
--- --- 370 km line (200 nautical mile limit)
〜〜〜 Approximate edge of the continental shelf
▢ Less than 200 m of water
▢ More than 200 m of water
☆ National capital
⦿ Provincial or territorial capital
• Other important city, town, or settlement

CANADA
Confederation: July 1, 1867
Capital: Ottawa
Area of land: 9 203 054 km²
Area of fresh water: 767 556 km²
Population: 24 343 181
Population density: 2.6/km²
Urban pop.: 18 435 927 (75.7%)
Rural pop.: 5 907 254 (24.3%)

NEWFOUNDLAND
Entered Confederation:
March 31, 1949
Capital: St. John's
Area: 371 635 km²
Population: 567 681
(2.3% of Canada)
Population density: 1.5/km²
Urban population: 58.6%

PRINCE EDWARD ISLAND
Entered Confederation:
July 1, 1873
Capital: Charlottetown
Area: 5 660 km²
Population: 122 506
(0.5% of Canada)
Population density: 21.6/km²
Urban population: 36.3%

NOVA SCOTIA
Entered Confederation:
July 1, 1867
Capital: Halifax
Area: 52 841 km²
Population: 847 442
(3.5% of Canada)
Population density: 16.0/km²
Urban population: 55.1%

QUÉBEC
Entered Confederation:
July 1, 1867
Capital: Québec
Area: 1 357 655 km²
Population: 6 438 403
(26.4% of Canada)
Population density: 4.7/km²
Urban population: 77.6%

NEW BRUNSWICK
Entered Confederation:
July 1, 1867
Capital: Fredericton
Area: 71 569 km²
Population: 696 403
(2.9% of Canada)
Population density: 9.7/km²
Urban population: 50.7%

1 cm represents 180 km
0 ───── 500
kilometres
Scale 1:18 000 000

For explanation of terms, see glossary. **8**

CANADA

POPULATION PROFILES

Thousands of people

1200 1000 800 600 400 200 0 | 0 200 400 600 800 1000 1200

| 0-4 |
| 5-9 |
| 10-14 |
| 15-19 |
| 20-24 |
| 25-29 |
| 30-34 |
| 35-39 |
| 40-44 |
| 45-49 |
| 50-54 |
| 55-59 |
| 60-64 |
| 65-69 |
| 70-74 |
| 75-79 |
| 80-84 |
| 85-89 |
| 90 + |

MALE   FEMALE

1981

Thousands of people

400 200 0 | 0 200 400

| 0-4 |
| 5-9 |
| 10-14 |
| 15-19 |
| 20-24 |
| 25-29 |
| 30-34 |
| 35-39 |
| 40-44 |
| 45-49 |
| 50-54 |
| 55-59 |
| 60-64 |
| 65-69 |
| 70-74 |
| 75-79 |
| 80-84 |
| 85-89 |
| 90 + |

MALE   FEMALE

1911

Thousands of people

400 200 0 | 0 200 400

| 0-4 |
| 5-9 |
| 10-14 |
| 15-19 |
| 20-24 |
| 25-29 |
| 30-34 |
| 35-39 |
| 40-44 |
| 45-49 |
| 50-54 |
| 55-59 |
| 60-64 |
| 65-69 |
| 70 + |

MALE   FEMALE

1871

Population profiles show the structure of the population according to age and sex. Many factors affect the number of births and deaths, including war, economic depression, health care, birth control, and the role of the family.

YUKON TERRITORY

NORTHWEST TERRITORIES

BRITISH COLUMBIA

ALBERTA

SASKATCHEWAN

MANITOBA

Edmonton

Victoria

Vancouver

Calgary

Saskatoon

Regina

Winnipeg

B.C. & MAN. — ┌ N.W.T.

N.S.

N.B.

ONT.

QUÉ.

Percent population, 1871

Population distribution, 1871

One dot represents 200 people

Scale 1: 50 000 000

COMPONENTS OF POPULATION GROWTH IN CANADA

100 000 000

Total population

Number of people (Logarithmic scale)

10 000 000

Natural increase

1 000 000

In-migration

Out-migration

100 000

1871 1881 1891 1901 1911 1921 1931 1941 1951 1961 1971 1981

POPULATION DISTRIBUTION

Population distribution,
1911

∴ One dot represents 200 people

Percent population, 1911

Scale 1: 40 000 000

Percent population, 1981

NEWFOUNDLAND

QUÉBEC

ONTARIO

NEW BRUNSWICK

P.E.I.

NOVA SCOTIA

St. John's

Chicoutimi-Jonquière

Québec

Montréal

Trois-Rivières

Ottawa-Hull

Sudbury

Halifax

Saint John

der Bay

Hamilton

Oshawa

Kitchener

St. Catharines-Niagara

London

Toronto

Windsor

Scale 1:15 000 000

POPULATION DISTRIBUTION, 1981

∴ One dot represents 200 people

Ecumene *

* The Ecumene is considered the area of
Canada that supports a large population and an integrated transportation
system.

POPULATION OF CENSUS METROPOLITAN AREAS, 1981

oronto	2 998 947
ontréal	2 828 349
ancouver	1 268 183
ttawa-Hull	717 978
dmonton	657 057
algary	592 743
innipeg	584 842
uébec	576 075
amilton	542 095
. Catharines-Niagara	304 353
itchener	287 801
ondon	283 668
alifax	277 727
indsor	246 110
ictoria	233 481
egina	164 313
t. John's	154 820
shawa	154 217
askatoon	154 210
udbury	149 923
hicoutimi-Jonquière	135 172
hunder Bay	121 379
aint John	114 048
rois-Rivières	111 453

Where Canadians live is the final
expression of the country's geography.
One half of the population lives in twenty
large urban areas. People usually settle
where physical and economic conditions
are best. Landforms, climate, and economic activity keep most of the population in the south. One out of every two
Canadians lives in a highly industrialized
corridor between Windsor and Québec.
Only one province, Prince Edward
Island, is completely settled. Some
regions have never been settled.

CENSUS METROPOLITAN AREAS

Greater than
2 000 000 people

1 000 000 – 2 000 000

500 000 – 999 999

100 000 – 499 999

Note: Circles are proportional
to the 1981 C.M.A. population

For explanation of terms, see glossary.

10

CANADA

POPULATION DENSITIES– SELECTED COUNTRIES

Persons per square kilometre

BANGLADESH– 644	
SOUTH KOREA– 395	
JAPAN– 317	
GREAT BRITAIN– 235	
SWITZERLAND– 153	
FRANCE– 99	
BULGARIA– 80	
TURKEY– 59	
UNITED STATES– 25	
TANZANIA– 20	
BRAZIL– 14	
U.S.S.R.– 12	
ARGENTINA–10	
SAUDI ARABIA– 5	
CANADA–2.6	
AUSTRALIA– 2	

The population density of a country is determined by comparing the total area to the total population. Density figures can be deceiving. In countries such as Canada, U.S.S.R., and Japan, large areas are uninhabited and other areas contain many people. The population density figure cannot express these variations.

YUKON TERRITORY

NORTHWEST TERRITORIES

BRITISH COLUMBIA

ALBERTA

SASKATCHEWAN

MANITOBA

AUSTRALIA
7 686 810 km²
14 800 000 people

P.E.I population Density is 21.6 people per km²

NORTHWEST TERRITORIES–0.01	
YUKON TERRITORY–0.04	
NEWFOUNDLAND–1.5	
SASKATCHEWAN–1.7	
MANITOBA–1.9	
BRITISH COLUMBIA–3.1	
ALBERTA–3.5	
QUÉBEC–4.7	
ONTARIO–9.4	
NEW BRUNSWICK–9.7	
NOVA SCOTIA–16.0	
P.E.I.–21.6	

Persons per square kilometre

POPULATION DENSITIES–PROVINCES AND TERRITORIES

TANZANIA
945 087 km²
19 200 000 people

POPULATION DENSITY

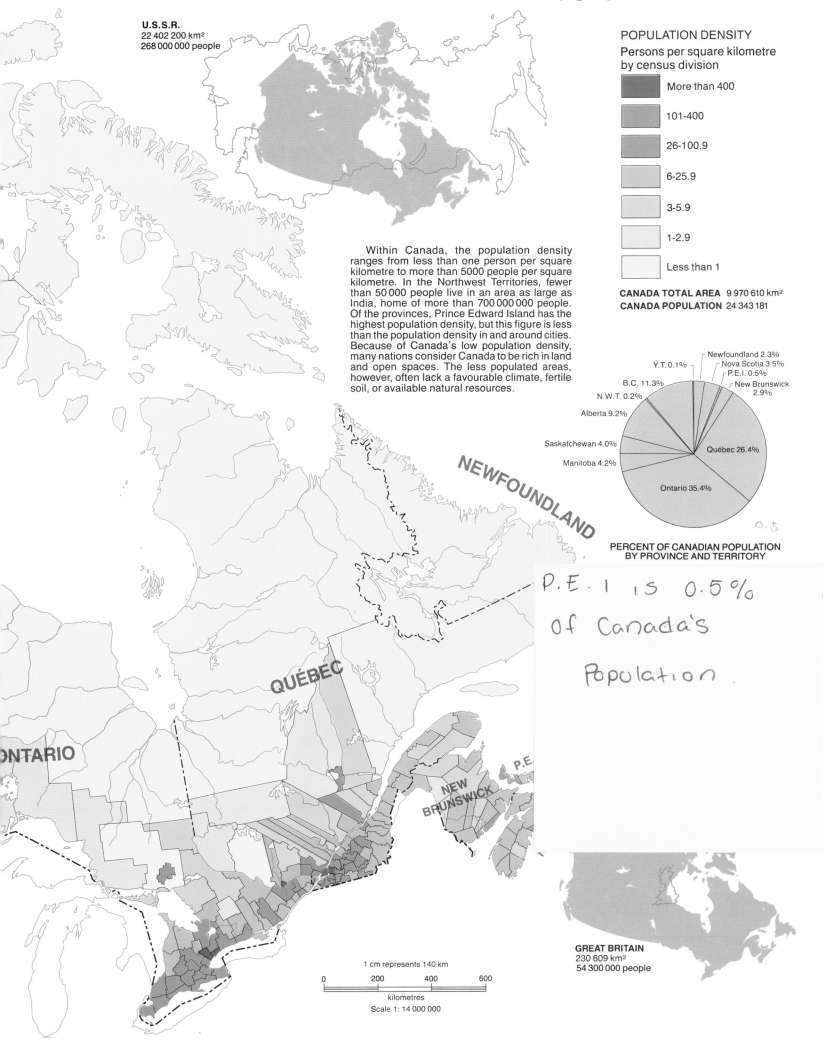

U.S.S.R.
22 402 200 km²
268 000 000 people

POPULATION DENSITY
Persons per square kilometre
by census division

	More than 400
	101-400
	26-100.9
	6-25.9
	3-5.9
	1-2.9
	Less than 1

CANADA TOTAL AREA 9 970 610 km²
CANADA POPULATION 24 343 181

Within Canada, the population density ranges from less than one person per square kilometre to more than 5000 people per square kilometre. In the Northwest Territories, fewer than 50 000 people live in an area as large as India, home of more than 700 000 000 people. Of the provinces, Prince Edward Island has the highest population density, but this figure is less than the population density in and around cities. Because of Canada's low population density, many nations consider Canada to be rich in land and open spaces. The less populated areas, however, often lack a favourable climate, fertile soil, or available natural resources.

Y.T. 0.1%
Newfoundland 2.3%
Nova Scotia 3.5%
P.E.I. 0.5%
New Brunswick 2.9%
B.C. 11.3%
N.W.T. 0.2%
Alberta 9.2%
Saskatchewan 4.0%
Manitoba 4.2%
Québec 26.4%
Ontario 35.4%

0.5

**PERCENT OF CANADIAN POPULATION
BY PROVINCE AND TERRITORY**

P.E.1 is 0.5%
of Canada's
Population.

NEWFOUNDLAND

QUÉBEC

ONTARIO

NEW BRUNSWICK

P.E.

1 cm represents 140 km

0   200   400   600

kilometres

Scale 1: 14 000 000

GREAT BRITAIN
230 609 km²
54 300 000 people

CANADA

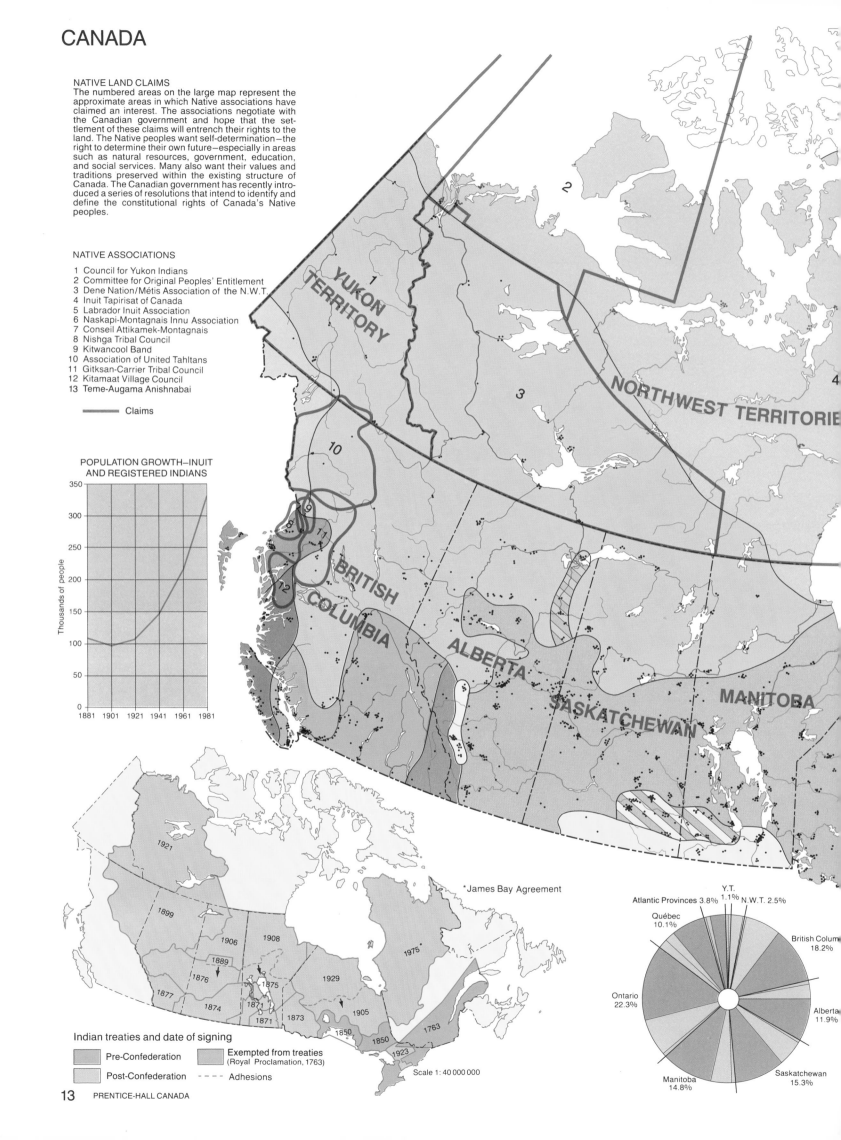

NATIVE LAND CLAIMS
The numbered areas on the large map represent the approximate areas in which Native associations have claimed an interest. The associations negotiate with the Canadian government and hope that the settlement of these claims will entrench their rights to the land. The Native peoples want self-determination—the right to determine their own future—especially in areas such as natural resources, government, education, and social services. Many also want their values and traditions preserved within the existing structure of Canada. The Canadian government has recently introduced a series of resolutions that intend to identify and define the constitutional rights of Canada's Native peoples.

NATIVE ASSOCIATIONS

1. Council for Yukon Indians
2. Committee for Original Peoples' Entitlement
3. Dene Nation/Métis Association of the N.W.T.
4. Inuit Tapirisat of Canada
5. Labrador Inuit Association
6. Naskapi-Montagnais Innu Association
7. Conseil Attikamek-Montagnais
8. Nishga Tribal Council
9. Kitwancool Band
10. Association of United Tahltans
11. Gitksan-Carrier Tribal Council
12. Kitamaat Village Council
13. Teme-Augama Anishnabai

——— Claims

POPULATION GROWTH—INUIT AND REGISTERED INDIANS

YUKON TERRITORY

NORTHWEST TERRITORIES

BRITISH COLUMBIA

ALBERTA

SASKATCHEWAN

MANITOBA

*James Bay Agreement

Indian treaties and date of signing

- Pre-Confederation
- Post-Confederation
- Exempted from treaties (Royal Proclamation, 1763)
- – – – Adhesions

Scale 1: 40 000 000

Y.T. 1.1%
Atlantic Provinces 3.8%
N.W.T. 2.5%
Québec 10.1%
British Columbia 18.2%
Ontario 22.3%
Alberta 11.9%
Manitoba 14.8%
Saskatchewan 15.3%

During the ice ages, lower sea levels created a land bridge between Siberia and Alaska. Probably because game migrated, people from Siberia crossed into North America, and moved south and east. They adapted to the new and often harsh environment by making clothing, tools, weapons, and shelter from animal skins and bones, trees, rocks, and snow.

According to one theory, the first inhabitants arrived about 40 000 a (years) ago, and spread across the continent and into Central and South America. Over such a long period of time and such a large land area (one in which the climate was changing), many different customs and languages evolved.

The Inuit, who live in the Canadian tundra, traditionally have hunted and fished for survival. Indian cultural groups in southern Ontario and Québec hunted, fished, and raised crops such as beans, maize, squash, and tobacco. In the forested areas and on the prairies, nomadic tribes survived by hunting. Indians along both coasts also hunted, but fished for most of their food.

Since contact with Europeans, many Native peoples have lost these more traditional ways of earning a living. Finding new and suitable sources of income remains a major problem.

MAJOR LINGUISTIC GROUPS AND POPULATION DISTRIBUTION

- Algonquian
- Athapaskan
- Haidan
- Iroquoian
- Kutenaian
- Salishan
- Siouan
- Tlingit
- Tsimshian
- Wakashan
- Inuktituk

One dot represents 100 Indians
One dot represents 100 Inuit

MAJOR LINGUISTIC GROUPS BY PERCENT

CANADA TOTAL 329 533
(Indians and Inuit)

Inuktituk 5.7%
Wakashan 3.0%
Tsimshian 3.0%
Tlingit 0.2%
Siouan 2.5%
Salishan 7.5%
Kutenaian 0.1%
Iroquoian 7.9%
Haidan 0.5%
Athapaskan 8.6%
Algonquian 61.0%

Native peoples include registered Indians, non-registered Indians, Métis, and Inuit, collectively. The term "Native" describes the aboriginal people after the period of contact with the Europeans. Before this period, the aboriginal people were either Indian or Inuit.

No linguistic group is shown for the island section of Newfoundland. The Beothuks, a separate group found in Newfoundland, were destroyed by disease and several years of conflict with the new settlers and the Algonquian Indians.

Note:
Treaty lands do not include the James Bay Agreement land area.

NEWFOUNDLAND

QUÉBEC

ONTARIO

NEW BRUNSWICK

P.E.I.

NOVA SCOTIA

When the first Europeans arrived, the Indian and Inuit inhabited much of the land area of Canada. The population density was very low because many aboriginal groups were nomadic. As the European population grew and spread, the area occupied by the aboriginal peoples decreased. Often with little choice, various Indian groups signed treaties and turned over large tracts of land to the government of Canada. More than 2000 reserves have been set aside for the Indians, but the area of these reserves is less than one quarter of one percent of Canada's total land area. Today, most of the 300 000 registered Indians live on reserves. Nearly 700 000 non-status Indians, Métis, and Inuit live off reserves.

REGISTERED INDIANS
- Living on reserve
- Living off reserve
- Living on crown land

Scale 1:15 000 000

A disappearing heritage
- Present reserves
- Treaty lands prior to 1929
- Original ownership

For explanation of terms, see glossary.

CANADA

Canada is called a "cultural mosaic". It has many cultures and has two official languages. Customs and traditions from many countries enrich Canada's cultural environment.

According to the latest research, the ancestors of the North American Indian and Inuit may have arrived approximately 40 000 a (years) ago. Some authorities suggest even earlier dates. Europeans began to settle in Canada in the early sixteenth century. Different ethnic groups often lived in clusters. They have given certain regions of Canada distinct cultural characteristics.

Today, the historical pattern of cultural groups is changing. People move within provinces and to different parts of the country, often because of job availability. However, Canadians have preserved many of their cultural differences.

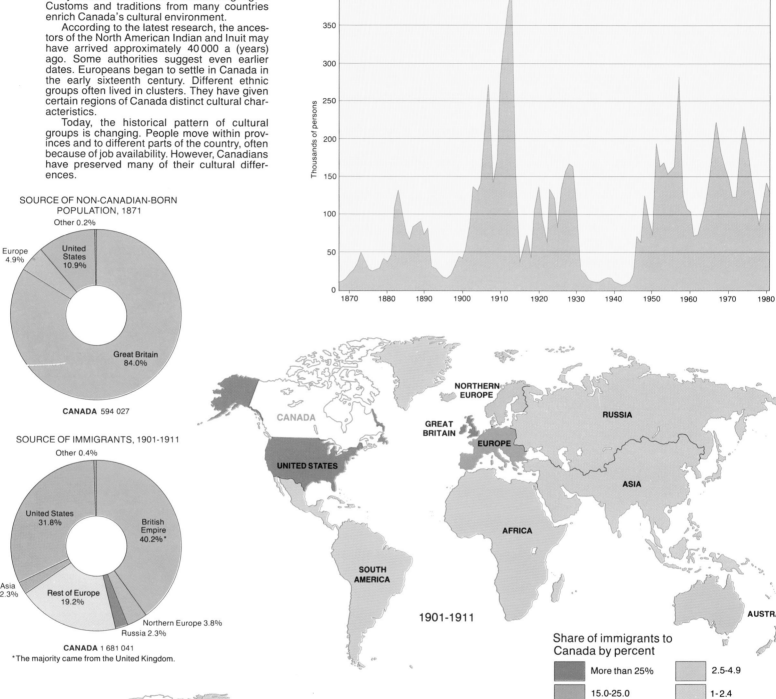

IMMIGRATION BY CALENDAR YEAR, 1867-1981

SOURCE OF NON-CANADIAN-BORN
POPULATION, 1871

Other 0.2%
Europe 4.9%
United States 10.9%
Great Britain 84.0%

CANADA 594 027

SOURCE OF IMMIGRANTS, 1901-1911

Other 0.4%
United States 31.8%
British Empire 40.2% *
Asia 2.3%
Rest of Europe 19.2%
Russia 2.3%
Northern Europe 3.8%

CANADA 1 681 041
*The majority came from the United Kingdom.

1901-1911

Share of immigrants to Canada by percent

More than 25%	2.5-4.9
15.0-25.0	1-2.4
5.0-14.9	Less than 1%

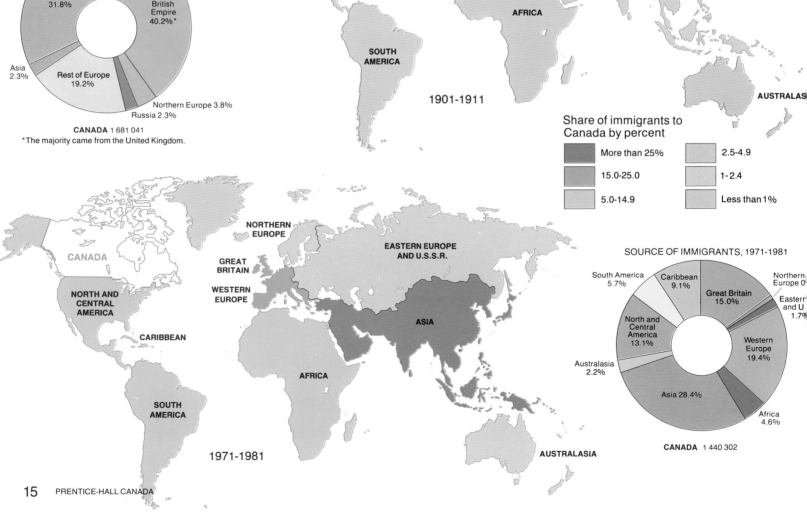

1971-1981

SOURCE OF IMMIGRANTS, 1971-1981

South America 5.7%
Caribbean 9.1%
Great Britain 15.0%
Northern Europe 0
Eastern and U 1.7%
North and Central America 13.1%
Australasia 2.2%
Asia 28.4%
Western Europe 19.4%
Africa 4.6%

CANADA 1 440 302

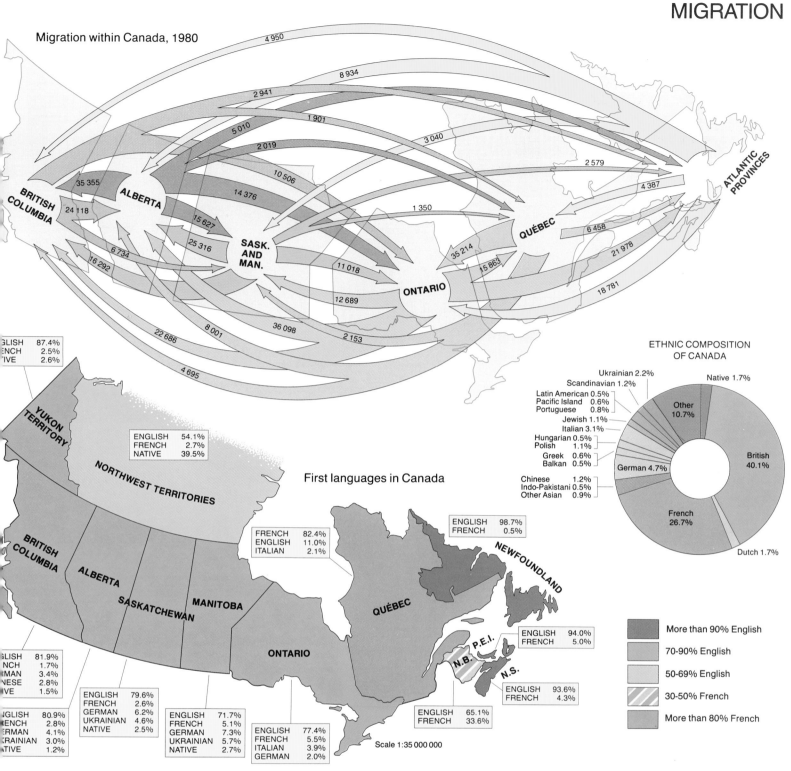

Migration within Canada, 1980

ETHNIC COMPOSITION
OF CANADA

Ukrainian 2.2%
Scandinavian 1.2%
Latin American 0.5%
Pacific Island 0.6%
Portuguese 0.8%
Jewish 1.1%
Italian 3.1%
Hungarian 0.5%
Polish 1.1%
Greek 0.6%
Balkan 0.5%
Chinese 1.2%
Indo-Pakistani 0.5%
Other Asian 0.9%

Native 1.7%
Other 10.7%
British 40.1%
German 4.7%
French 26.7%
Dutch 1.7%

YUKON
TERRITORY

ENGLISH	54.1%
FRENCH	2.7%
NATIVE	39.5%

NORTHWEST TERRITORIES

First languages in Canada

ENGLISH	87.4%
FRENCH	2.5%
NATIVE	2.6%

BRITISH
COLUMBIA

ENGLISH	81.9%
FRENCH	1.7%
GERMAN	3.4%
CHINESE	2.8%
NATIVE	1.5%

ALBERTA

ENGLISH	80.9%
FRENCH	2.8%
GERMAN	4.1%
UKRAINIAN	3.0%
NATIVE	1.2%

SASKATCHEWAN

ENGLISH	79.6%
FRENCH	2.6%
GERMAN	6.2%
UKRAINIAN	4.6%
NATIVE	2.5%

MANITOBA

ENGLISH	71.7%
FRENCH	5.1%
GERMAN	7.3%
UKRAINIAN	5.7%
NATIVE	2.7%

ONTARIO

ENGLISH	77.4%
FRENCH	5.5%
ITALIAN	3.9%
GERMAN	2.0%

QUÉBEC

FRENCH	82.4%
ENGLISH	11.0%
ITALIAN	2.1%

NEWFOUNDLAND

| ENGLISH | 98.7% |
| FRENCH | 0.5% |

P.E.I.

| ENGLISH | 94.0% |
| FRENCH | 5.0% |

N.B.

| ENGLISH | 65.1% |
| FRENCH | 33.6% |

N.S.

| ENGLISH | 93.6% |
| FRENCH | 4.3% |

Scale 1:35 000 000

More than 90% English
70-90% English
50-69% English
30-50% French
More than 80% French

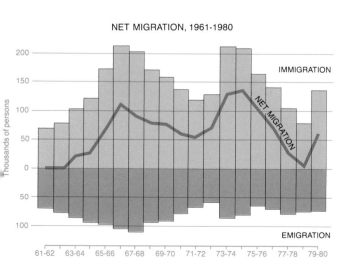

NET MIGRATION, 1961-1980

Thousands of persons

IMMIGRATION

NET MIGRATION

EMIGRATION

61-62 63-64 65-66 67-68 69-70 71-72 73-74 75-76 77-78 79-80

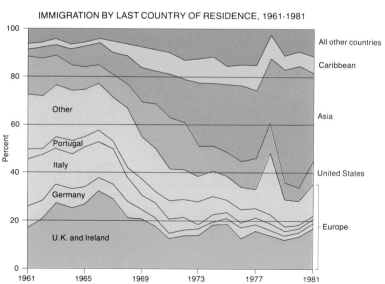

IMMIGRATION BY LAST COUNTRY OF RESIDENCE, 1961-1981

Percent

All other countries
Caribbean
Asia
United States
Europe

Other
Portugal
Italy
Germany
U.K. and Ireland

1961   1965   1969   1973   1977   1981

CANADA

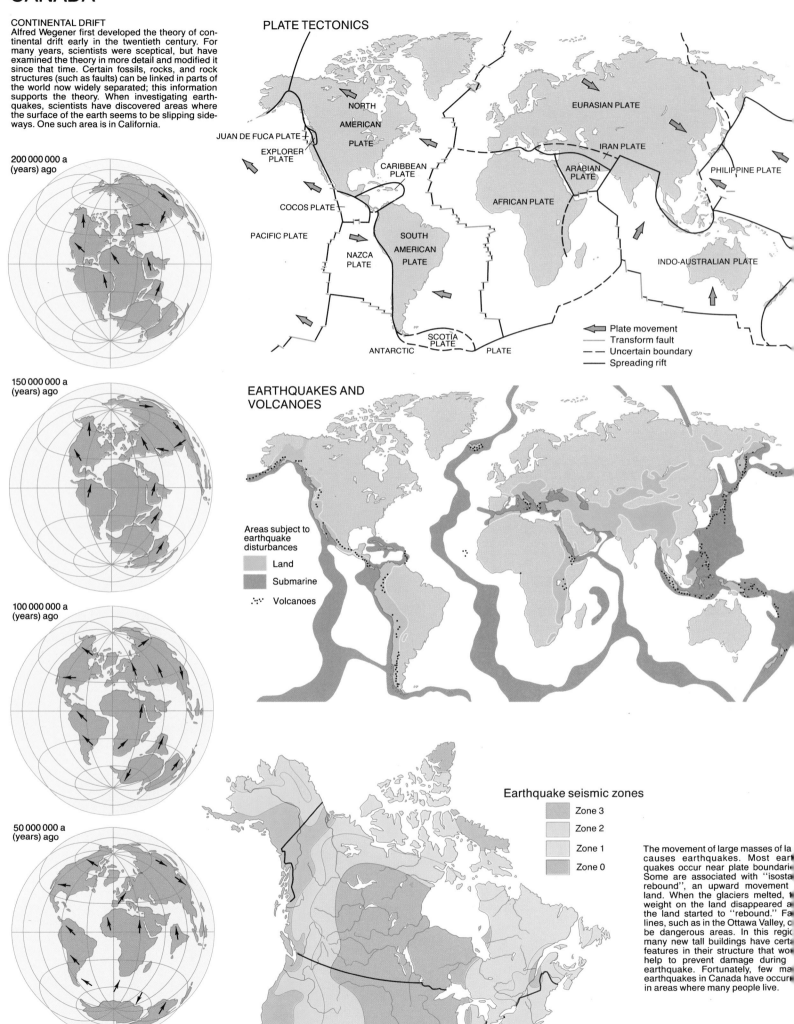

CONTINENTAL DRIFT

Alfred Wegener first developed the theory of continental drift early in the twentieth century. For many years, scientists were sceptical, but have examined the theory in more detail and modified it since that time. Certain fossils, rocks, and rock structures (such as faults) can be linked in parts of the world now widely separated; this information supports the theory. When investigating earthquakes, scientists have discovered areas where the surface of the earth seems to be slipping sideways. One such area is in California.

200 000 000 a (years) ago

150 000 000 a (years) ago

100 000 000 a (years) ago

50 000 000 a (years) ago

PLATE TECTONICS

NORTH AMERICAN PLATE

EURASIAN PLATE

JUAN DE FUCA PLATE

EXPLORER PLATE

IRAN PLATE

CARIBBEAN PLATE

ARABIAN PLATE

PHILIPPINE PLATE

COCOS PLATE

AFRICAN PLATE

PACIFIC PLATE

SOUTH AMERICAN PLATE

NAZCA PLATE

INDO-AUSTRALIAN PLATE

SCOTIA PLATE

ANTARCTIC PLATE

Plate movement
Transform fault
Uncertain boundary
Spreading rift

EARTHQUAKES AND VOLCANOES

Areas subject to earthquake disturbances

Land

Submarine

Volcanoes

Earthquake seismic zones

Zone 3

Zone 2

Zone 1

Zone 0

The movement of large masses of la causes earthquakes. Most eart quakes occur near plate boundari Some are associated with "isosta rebound", an upward movement land. When the glaciers melted, weight on the land disappeared a the land started to "rebound." Fa lines, such as in the Ottawa Valley, c be dangerous areas. In this regic many new tall buildings have cert features in their structure that wo help to prevent damage during earthquake. Fortunately, few ma earthquakes in Canada have occur in areas where many people live.

According to the most recent theories on continental drift, the earth's lithosphere is divided into large, rigid sections called plates. Convection currents flow in the asthenosphere and cause the plates above them to shift. Plate movements can cause earthquakes and volcanoes. If one plate rides over another, the lower plate can be pushed down into the molten interior of the earth. Scientists believe that movement around the Pacific Plate caused Mount St. Helens and other volcanoes in that area. The collision of two plates may produce mountain ranges—the Andes Mountains, for example, have developed along the contact line between the Nazca Plate and the South American Plate. The separation of two plates often creates ridges. These are formed by the upwelling of volcanic material along the line of separation.

Sedimentary layer

CONTINENTAL CRUST

LITHOSPHERE OR UPPER MANTLE

Convection currents

ASTHENOSPHERE

LOWER MANTLE

LIQUID CORE

SOLID CORE

340 km   10 km

2530 km

2260 km

1230 km

The temperature of the solid core is 4000°C.

The layers of the earth are diagrammatic and are not drawn to scale.

THE EARTH'S CORE

HE ATLANTIC OCEAN FLOOR

A crack runs from north to south through the Atlantic Ocean beneath the thin layer of the ocean crust. Volcanic material, pushed through this crack, forms the new sea floor and a ridge called the Mid-Atlantic Ridge. The sea floor spreads away from the ridge. Scientists use matching rock bands on either side of the ridge to measure how quickly the sea floor spreads.

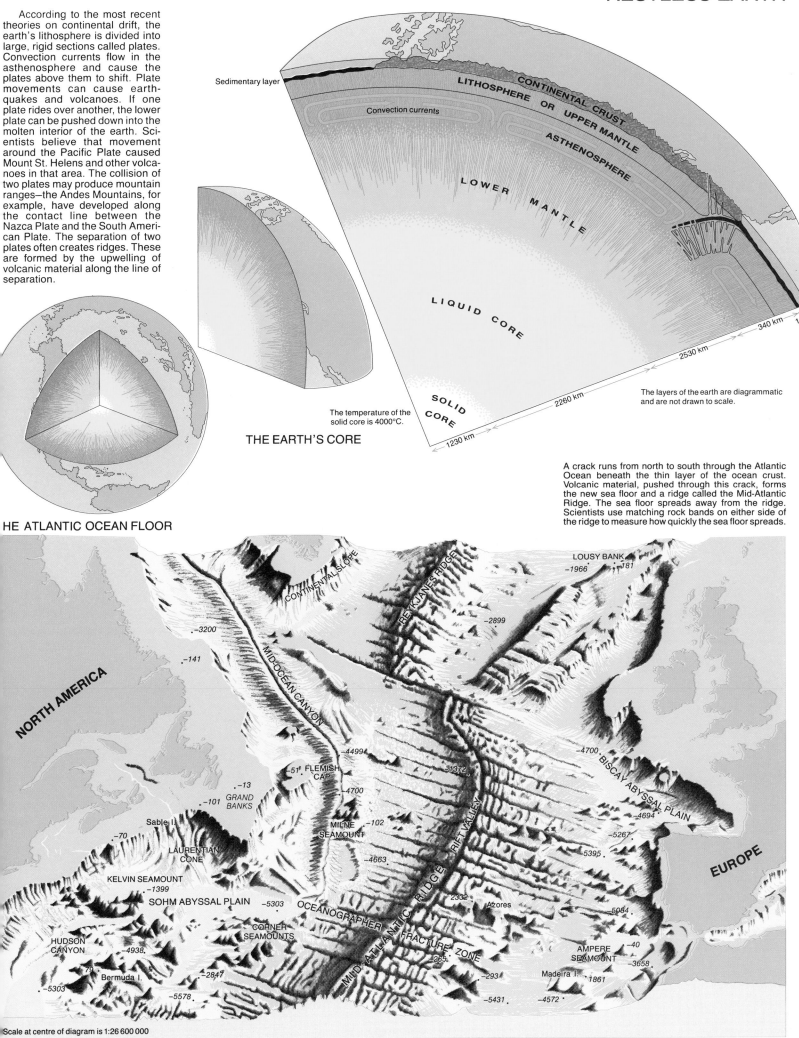

CONTINENTAL SLOPE

REYKJANES RIDGE

LOUSY BANK
-1966   -181

-2899

-3200

-141

MID-OCEAN CANYON

NORTH AMERICA

-4499

-5372

-4700 BISCAY ABYSSAL PLAIN

-51 FLEMISH CAP

-13

-101 GRAND BANKS

-4700

-4694

MILNE SEAMOUNT

-102

-5267

Sable I.

-70

-4663

RIFT VALLEY

-5395

LAURENTIAN CONE

KELVIN SEAMOUNT
-1399

SOHM ABYSSAL PLAIN   -5303

OCEANOGRAPHER

2332

Azores

MID-ATLANTIC RIDGE

EUROPE

-5084

CORNER SEAMOUNTS

FRACTURE ZONE

AMPERE SEAMOUNT

-40

HUDSON CANYON

-4938

-265

-293

Madeira I.
1861

-3658

79

Bermuda I.

-2847

-5431

-4572

-5303

-5578

Scale at centre of diagram is 1:26 600 000

CANADA

ELLESMERE ISLAND

90°
80°
60°
50°
40°
30°
20°

ICELAND

Arctic Circle

20°

DEVON ISLAND

KALAALLIT NUNAAT
(GREENLAND)
(Denmark)

BAFFIN

BAY

30°

BAFFIN ISLAND

DAVIS STRAIT

Nettilling Lake

Foxe
Basin

Amadjuak Lake

LABRADOR

SEA

50°

40°

SOUTHAMPTON
ISLAND

Hudson Strait

ATLANTIC

Ungava
Bay

HUDSON

Rivière aux Feuilles

OCEAN

BAY

Smallwood Reservoir

Churchill

BELCHER
ISLANDS

La Grande Rivière

ILE D'ANTICOSTI

ST PIERRE
ET MIQUELON
(France)

Lac
Sakami

Gulf of
St. Lawrence

Cabot Strait

James
Bay

Riv. de Rupert

Lac Mistassini

LAURENTIANS

CAPE
BRETON
ISLAND

Reservoir
Gouin

of
Woods

Sévern

Attawapiskat

Winisk

APPALACHIANS

Lac
St-Jean

Lake
Nipigon

Natashquan

Riv. St-Maurice

St. John

Lac Seul

Albany

Moose

of
Woods

Lake Superior

Ottawa

St. Lawrence

Bay of Fundy

Mississippi

Lake
Huron

Lake
Champlain

Lake Michigan

Lake Ontario

Hudson

Lake Erie

90°
80°
40°
70°
60°

Scale 1:17 000 000

Longitude west of Greenwich

CANADA

CROSS SECTION FROM PRINCE RUPERT TO MITTIMATALIK

Vertical scale

Metres: 2500, 2000, 1500, 1000, 500, Sea level, −500

Labels: Prince Rupert, Skeena River, Rocky Mountains, Liard River, Mackenzie River, Horn Plateau, Coppermine River, Arctic Circle, Bathurst Inlet, Victoria Island, Larsen Sound, Boothia Peninsula, Gulf of Boothia, Admiralty Inlet, Baffin Island, Mittimatalik

BRITISH COLUMBIA   **NORTHWEST TERRITORIES**

The map and cross sectional diagrams provide a general view of the surface of Canada. Areas with many colours, such as the Cordillera, have a varied pattern of relief. In large areas with one colour, the vertical differences in elevation are less, although local variations may occur. For example, areas in the Canadian Shield and the Maritime Provinces, shown on the map as between 300 m and 600 m in elevation, may have some very rough, rugged, and steep-sloped sections.

PRINCE RUPERT

156

156

213

50°

217

The distance across Canada from east to west is more than 5000 km. The difference between the highest and lowest points in Canada is approximately 6000 *metres*. The vertical scale has been exaggerated greatly to emphasize these small vertical differences.

CROSS SECTION ALONG 50° NORTH

Vertical scale

Metres: 3000, 2500, 2000, 1500, 1000, 500, Sea level, −500

Labels: Strait of Georgia, Jervis Inlet, Fraser River, Mount Findlay, Kootenay River, Tornado Mountain, Medicine Hat, Red River

BRITISH COLUMBIA   **ALBERTA**   **SASKATCHEWAN**   **MANITOBA**

RELIEF

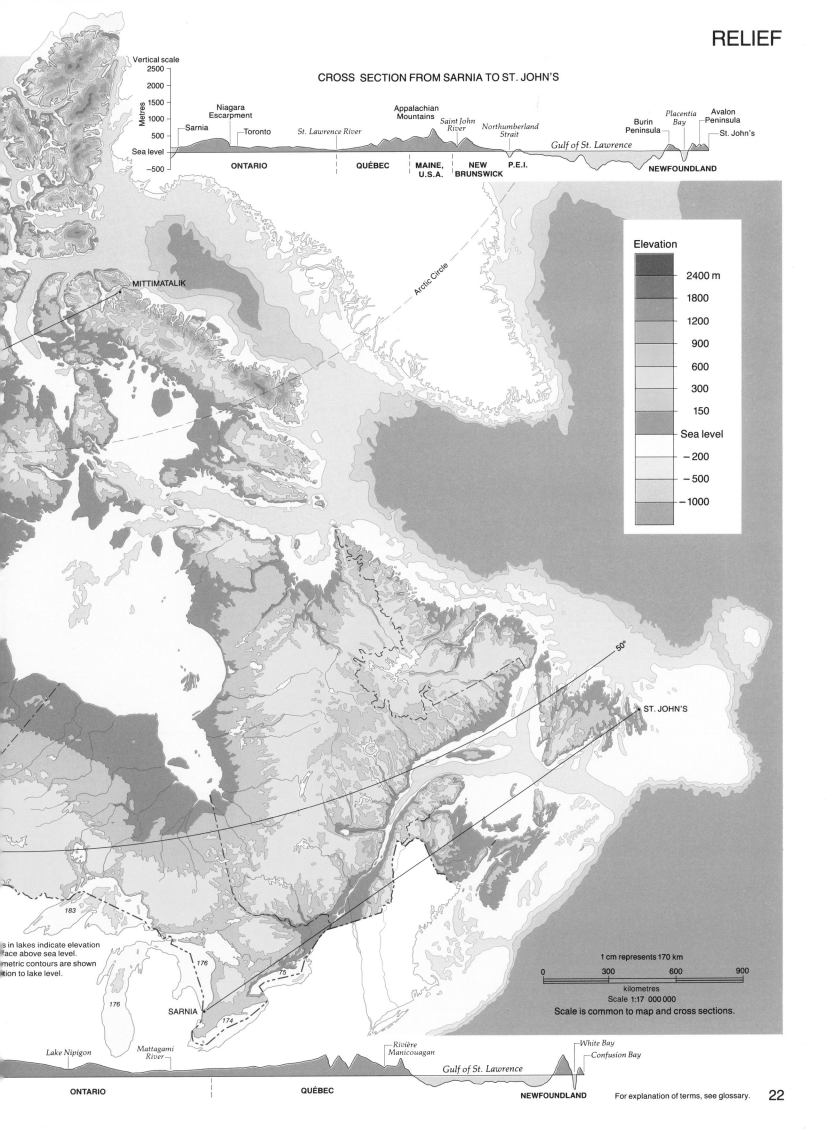

CROSS SECTION FROM SARNIA TO ST. JOHN'S

Vertical scale

Elevation

2400 m
1800
1200
900
600
300
150
Sea level
−200
−500
−1000

1 cm represents 170 km

0   300   600   900

kilometres

Scale 1:17 000 000

Scale is common to map and cross sections.

For explanation of terms, see glossary.   22

CANADA

RETREAT OF THE WISCONSIN ICE SHEET

Approximate time in years before present

- 15 000
- 13 000
- 10 000
- 7000
- Present
- No glaciation

Over the past 2 000 000 a (years), four distinct continental ice sheets covered much of Canada. They carried and later dumped many unsorted glacial materials. The latest ice sheet, the Wisconsin, began to retreat about 15 000 a (years) ago. Glacial melt-waters flooded low-lying areas in Ontario and southern Manitoba, reworking the glacial materials. Rocks were rounded and sorted by size and weight; glacial materi-als filled the valleys, flattening the landscape. When the glaciers receded and the glacial melt-waters dropped to their present levels, these materials formed the basis for excellent soils.

Scale 1:60 000 000

INNUITIAN REGIO

This region contains a variety of phy features, including glacier-clad mount and broad, flat plains. The arctic loca unites these different land forms. Feat such as permafrost, pack-ice, glaciers, rock deserts cover much of the A Islands. In future, this region may yiel gas, and other minerals.

CORDILLERAN REGION

Mountain ranges which run parallel to the coast dominate this region. Between the Coast Mountains and the Rocky Mountains lies a series of plateaus, dissected by deep river valleys. Because of the rugged topog-raphy, people tend to live in the valley areas, particularly near the mouth of the Fraser River.

INTERIOR PLAINS

This region increases in elevation from east to west. Three prairie levels are separated by escarpments. The Manitoba lowland, once covered by a glacial lake, is very flat. The glaciated Saskatchewan plain is more rolling. The third prairie level, in southern Alberta, has flat plains, dry badlands, and gentle hills. This region is one of Canada's most important agricul-tural areas.

THE CANADIAN SHIELD

Rugged, rocky, mountainous, picturesque – all of these terms describe the physical features of a region that covers almost half of Canada's land area. This region is rich in resources: forests for the pulp and paper industry; nickel, iron, and copper for the mining industry; and water for hydro-electric power.

ST. LAWRENCE LOWLAND

Sedimentary rock underlies this hea populated region. Glaciers and their m waters have made the surface of the l flat to rolling; transportation is easy farming is good. The Niagara Escarpm in southern Ontario and the Montereg Hills in southern Québec are distinc features of the landscape.

Physiography is the study of the earth's surface. It describes the major features of the earth that are influenced by bedrock, and the landforms produced by erosion.

Flat-lying sedimentary rocks form plains, and ranges of folded mountains make up the Western Cordillera. Glaciers have greatly affected the surface of many areas. Glacial erosion is most significant in the Canadian Shield where the land was scraped bare and areas were gouged out, later forming lakes. Farther south, moraines, drumlins, and till-covered plains were created by glacial deposition. Beaches along the edges of post-glacial lakes can also be found.

People can alter the physiography of an area. For example, the Holland Marsh in southern Ontario has been drained for agricultural uses. Hills have been levelled for urban development and strip mining purposes. Even some of the rivers, such as the Nechako in British Columbia, have been diverted for specific purposes.

ARCTIC LOWLANDS

This is a land of rock deserts, permafrost, mosses, and lichens. The region seems forbidding, but hosts many migrating birds and large concentrations of wildlife: seals, whales, caribou, polar bears, and musk oxen. Few people live in this area today; the potential for intensive use of the land by man is limited because of the fragile environment.

GLACIAL EFFECT ON PHYSIOGRAPHY

- Existing glaciers
- Generally unglaciated areas
- Areas of glacial erosion and deposition
- Areas once covered by seas
- Areas once covered by lakes
- Eskers
- End moraines
- Direction of flow during the retreat of the Wisconsin ice sheet

Scale 1:24 000 000

APPALACHIAN REGION

While these uplands are mostly forest covered, the broad Saint John River valley, the Annapolis Valley, and the flat-lying sandstone region of Prince Edward Island have agricultural potential. The varied landscape, the ocean setting, and the distinctive traditions of the people attract tourists to this region.

PHYSIOGRAPHIC REGIONS

- Innuitian Region
- Arctic Lowlands
- Cordilleran Region
- Interior Plains
- The Canadian Shield
- Hudson Bay Lowlands
- St. Lawrence Lowlands
- Appalachian Region

PHYSIOGRAPHIC REGIONS

Canada can be divided into seven physiographic regions. These regions are based on the age and type of rock, the forces that have molded the rock, and the surface features. The Canadian Shield is the oldest region. Shield rocks underlie the lowlands surrounding the Shield, but sedimentary rock and other materials have been deposited on top. On the outer edge of the lowlands are mountain ranges. The Appalachians, 400 000 000 a (years) old, are much older than the Western Cordillera and Innuitian ranges, which are less than 100 000 000 a (years) old.

Scale 1:40 000 000

CANADA

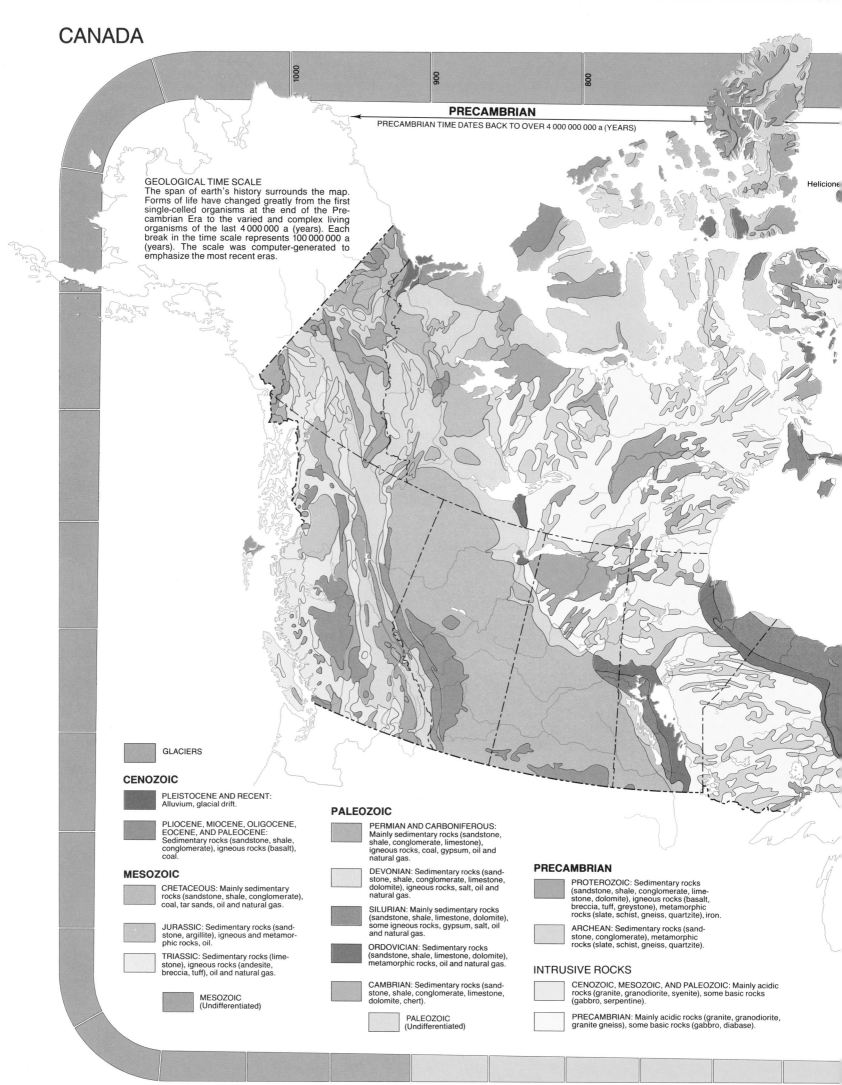

PRECAMBRIAN TIME DATES BACK TO OVER 4 000 000 000 a (YEARS)

1000   900   800

Helicione

GEOLOGICAL TIME SCALE
The span of earth's history surrounds the map.
Forms of life have changed greatly from the first
single-celled organisms at the end of the Precambrian Era to the varied and complex living
organisms of the last 4 000 000 a (years). Each
break in the time scale represents 100 000 000 a
(years). The scale was computer-generated to
emphasize the most recent eras.

GLACIERS

CENOZOIC

PLEISTOCENE AND RECENT:
Alluvium, glacial drift.

PLIOCENE, MIOCENE, OLIGOCENE,
EOCENE, AND PALEOCENE:
Sedimentary rocks (sandstone, shale,
conglomerate), igneous rocks (basalt),
coal.

MESOZOIC

CRETACEOUS: Mainly sedimentary
rocks (sandstone, shale, conglomerate),
coal, tar sands, oil and natural gas.

JURASSIC: Sedimentary rocks (sandstone, argillite), igneous and metamorphic rocks, oil.

TRIASSIC: Sedimentary rocks (limestone), igneous rocks (andesite,
breccia, tuff), oil and natural gas.

MESOZOIC
(Undifferentiated)

PALEOZOIC

PERMIAN AND CARBONIFEROUS:
Mainly sedimentary rocks (sandstone,
shale, conglomerate, limestone),
igneous rocks, coal, gypsum, oil and
natural gas.

DEVONIAN: Sedimentary rocks (sandstone, shale, conglomerate, limestone,
dolomite), igneous rocks, salt, oil and
natural gas.

SILURIAN: Mainly sedimentary rocks
(sandstone, shale, limestone, dolomite),
some igneous rocks, gypsum, salt, oil
and natural gas.

ORDOVICIAN: Sedimentary rocks
(sandstone, shale, limestone, dolomite),
metamorphic rocks, oil and natural gas.

CAMBRIAN: Sedimentary rocks (sandstone, shale, conglomerate, limestone,
dolomite, chert).

PALEOZOIC
(Undifferentiated)

PRECAMBRIAN

PROTEROZOIC: Sedimentary rocks
(sandstone, shale, conglomerate, limestone, dolomite), igneous rocks (basalt,
breccia, tuff, greystone), metamorphic
rocks (slate, schist, gneiss, quartzite), iron.

ARCHEAN: Sedimentary rocks (sandstone, conglomerate), metamorphic
rocks (slate, schist, gneiss, quartzite).

INTRUSIVE ROCKS

CENOZOIC, MESOZOIC, AND PALEOZOIC: Mainly acidic
rocks (granite, granodiorite, syenite), some basic rocks
(gabbro, serpentine).

PRECAMBRIAN: Mainly acidic rocks (granite, granodiorite,
granite gneiss), some basic rocks (gabbro, diabase).

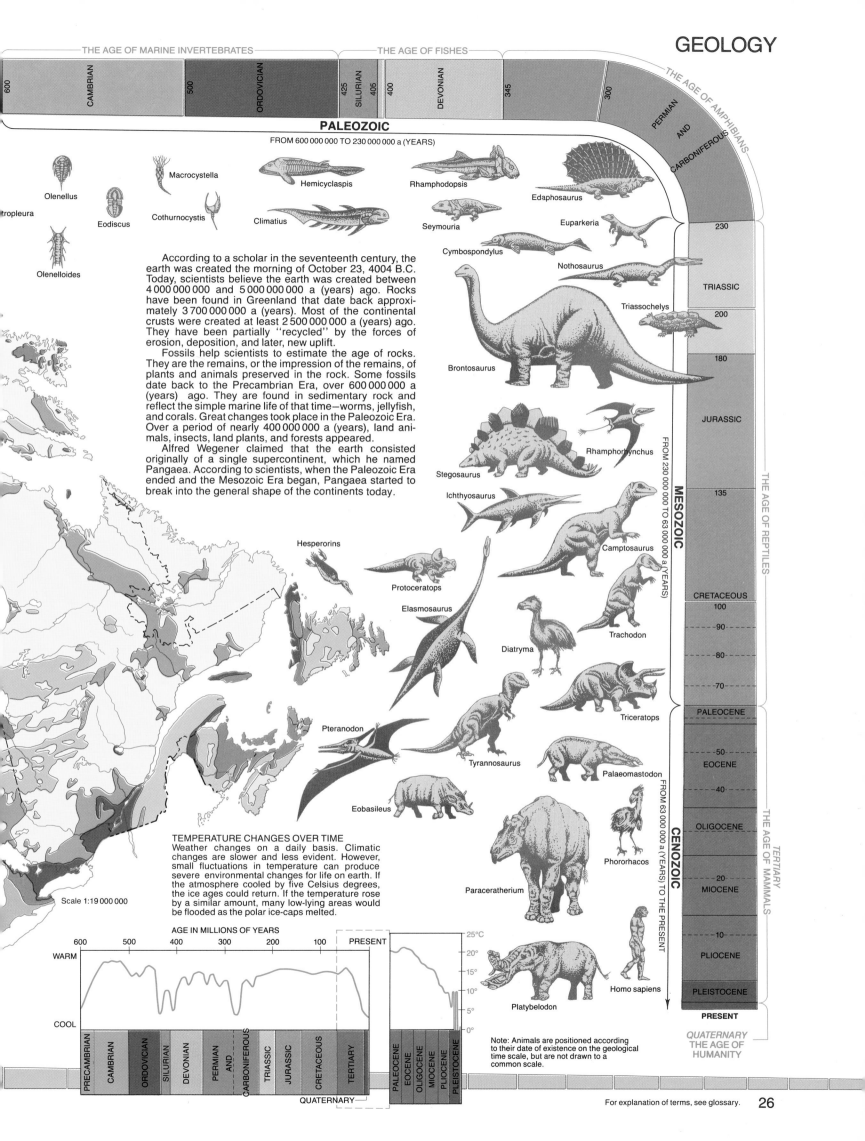

THE AGE OF MARINE INVERTEBRATES

THE AGE OF FISHES

THE AGE OF AMPHIBIANS AND CARBONIFEROUS

| 600 | CAMBRIAN | 500 | ORDOVICIAN | 425 SILURIAN | 405 | DEVONIAN | 345 | PERMIAN | 300 |

PALEOZOIC
FROM 600 000 000 TO 230 000 000 a (YEARS)

Olenellus
tropleura
Eodiscus
Olenelloides

Macrocystella
Cothurnocystis

Hemicyclaspis
Climatius

Rhamphodopsis
Seymouria

Edaphosaurus
Cymbospondylus
Euparkeria
Nothosaurus
Triassochelys

Brontosaurus

Stegosaurus
Ichthyosaurus
Rhamphorhynchus

Hesperorins
Protoceratops
Elasmosaurus
Diatryma
Camptosaurus
Trachodon
Triceratops

Pteranodon
Tyrannosaurus
Eobasileus

Paraceratherium
Palaeomastodon
Phororhacos

Platybelodon
Homo sapiens

According to a scholar in the seventeenth century, the earth was created the morning of October 23, 4004 B.C. Today, scientists believe the earth was created between 4 000 000 000 and 5 000 000 000 a (years) ago. Rocks have been found in Greenland that date back approximately 3 700 000 000 a (years). Most of the continental crusts were created at least 2 500 000 000 a (years) ago. They have been partially "recycled" by the forces of erosion, deposition, and later, new uplift.

Fossils help scientists to estimate the age of rocks. They are the remains, or the impression of the remains, of plants and animals preserved in the rock. Some fossils date back to the Precambrian Era, over 600 000 000 a (years) ago. They are found in sedimentary rock and reflect the simple marine life of that time—worms, jellyfish, and corals. Great changes took place in the Paleozoic Era. Over a period of nearly 400 000 000 a (years), land animals, insects, land plants, and forests appeared.

Alfred Wegener claimed that the earth consisted originally of a single supercontinent, which he named Pangaea. According to scientists, when the Paleozoic Era ended and the Mesozoic Era began, Pangaea started to break into the general shape of the continents today.

TEMPERATURE CHANGES OVER TIME
Weather changes on a daily basis. Climatic changes are slower and less evident. However, small fluctuations in temperature can produce severe environmental changes for life on earth. If the atmosphere cooled by five Celsius degrees, the ice ages could return. If the temperature rose by a similar amount, many low-lying areas would be flooded as the polar ice-caps melted.

Scale 1:19 000 000

AGE IN MILLIONS OF YEARS

| 600 | 500 | 400 | 300 | 200 | 100 | PRESENT |

WARM

COOL

| PRECAMBRIAN | CAMBRIAN | ORDOVICIAN | SILURIAN | DEVONIAN | PERMIAN AND CARBONIFEROUS | TRIASSIC | JURASSIC | CRETACEOUS | TERTIARY |

QUATERNARY

| PALEOCENE | EOCENE | OLIGOCENE | MIOCENE | PLIOCENE | PLEISTOCENE |

25°C
20°
15°
10°
5°
0°

Note: Animals are positioned according to their date of existence on the geological time scale, but are not drawn to a common scale.

MESOZOIC
FROM 230 000 000 TO 63 000 000 a (YEARS)

230	TRIASSIC
200	
180	JURASSIC
135	CRETACEOUS
100	
90	
80	
70	

CENOZOIC
FROM 63 000 000 a (YEARS) TO THE PRESENT

PALEOCENE	
50	EOCENE
40	
OLIGOCENE	
20	MIOCENE
10	
PLIOCENE	
PLEISTOCENE	

PRESENT

THE AGE OF REPTILES

TERTIARY THE AGE OF MAMMALS

QUATERNARY THE AGE OF HUMANITY

CANADA

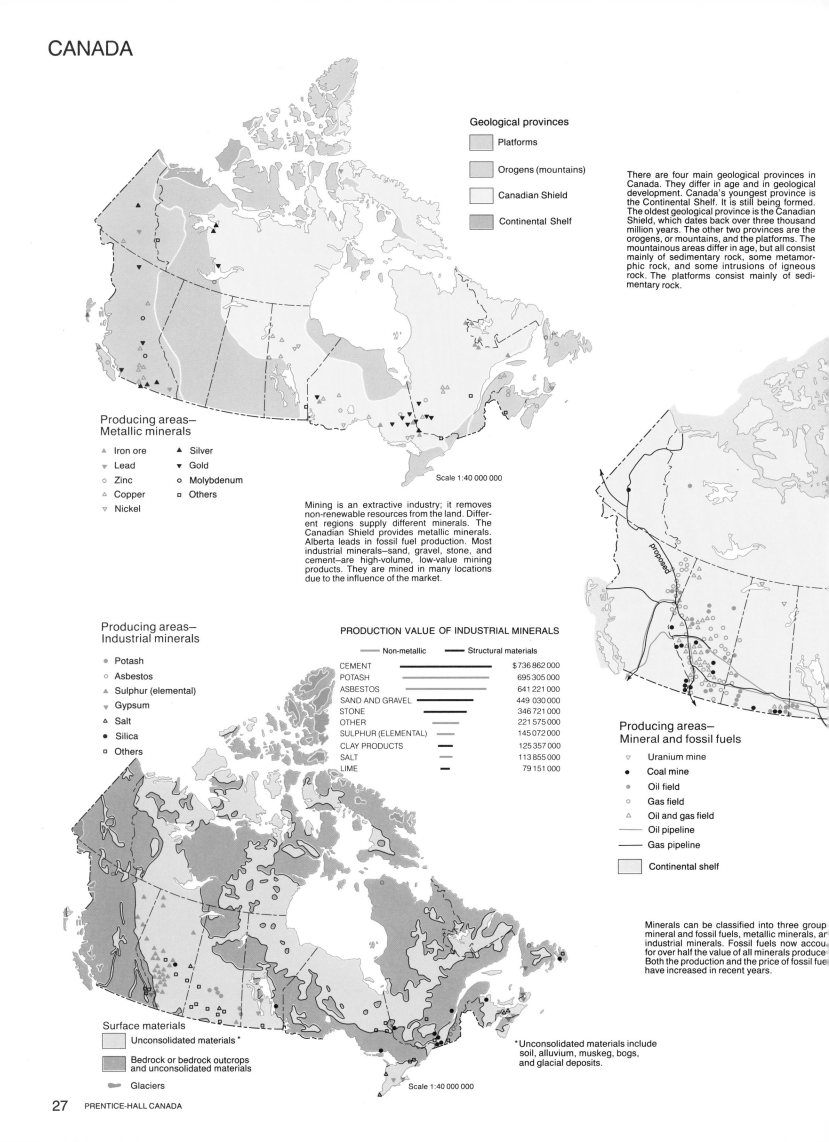

Geological provinces

- Platforms
- Orogens (mountains)
- Canadian Shield
- Continental Shelf

There are four main geological provinces in Canada. They differ in age and in geological development. Canada's youngest province is the Continental Shelf. It is still being formed. The oldest geological province is the Canadian Shield, which dates back over three thousand million years. The other two provinces are the orogens, or mountains, and the platforms. The mountainous areas differ in age, but all consist mainly of sedimentary rock, some metamorphic rock, and some intrusions of igneous rock. The platforms consist mainly of sedimentary rock.

Producing areas— Metallic minerals

- ▲ Iron ore
- ▼ Lead
- ○ Zinc
- △ Copper
- ▽ Nickel
- ▲ Silver
- ▼ Gold
- ○ Molybdenum
- □ Others

Scale 1:40 000 000

Mining is an extractive industry; it removes non-renewable resources from the land. Different regions supply different minerals. The Canadian Shield provides metallic minerals. Alberta leads in fossil fuel production. Most industrial minerals—sand, gravel, stone, and cement—are high-volume, low-value mining products. They are mined in many locations due to the influence of the market.

Producing areas— Industrial minerals

- ● Potash
- ○ Asbestos
- ▲ Sulphur (elemental)
- ▼ Gypsum
- △ Salt
- ● Silica
- □ Others

PRODUCTION VALUE OF INDUSTRIAL MINERALS

—— Non-metallic ▬▬ Structural materials

CEMENT	$736 862 000
POTASH	695 305 000
ASBESTOS	641 221 000
SAND AND GRAVEL	449 030 000
STONE	346 721 000
OTHER	221 575 000
SULPHUR (ELEMENTAL)	145 072 000
CLAY PRODUCTS	125 357 000
SALT	113 855 000
LIME	79 151 000

Producing areas— Mineral and fossil fuels

- ▽ Uranium mine
- ● Coal mine
- ● Oil field
- ○ Gas field
- △ Oil and gas field
- —— Oil pipeline
- ▬▬ Gas pipeline
- Continental shelf

Minerals can be classified into three group mineral and fossil fuels, metallic minerals, an industrial minerals. Fossil fuels now accou for over half the value of all minerals produce Both the production and the price of fossil fue have increased in recent years.

Surface materials

- Unconsolidated materials *
- Bedrock or bedrock outcrops and unconsolidated materials
- Glaciers

*Unconsolidated materials include soil, alluvium, muskeg, bogs, and glacial deposits.

Scale 1:40 000 000

Canada has a large mining industry that produces nearly 60 different types of minerals — more than any other nation in the world. Canada ranks first in the world production of zinc, second in asbestos, nickel and potash, and third in silver and gold. The mining industry employs many people directly and many more indirectly in related industries.

The rich rewards of mining come only after many risks and huge investment. The cost of exploration is high. Before production begins, environmental studies and years of planning take place. Remote areas need transportation links, a skilled labour force, and services for the new mining community.

The health of the mining industry depends on many factors. Some of these are mineral prices, production costs, availability of skilled labour, demand for minerals in Canada and abroad, competition from other nations, and government trade policies around the world.

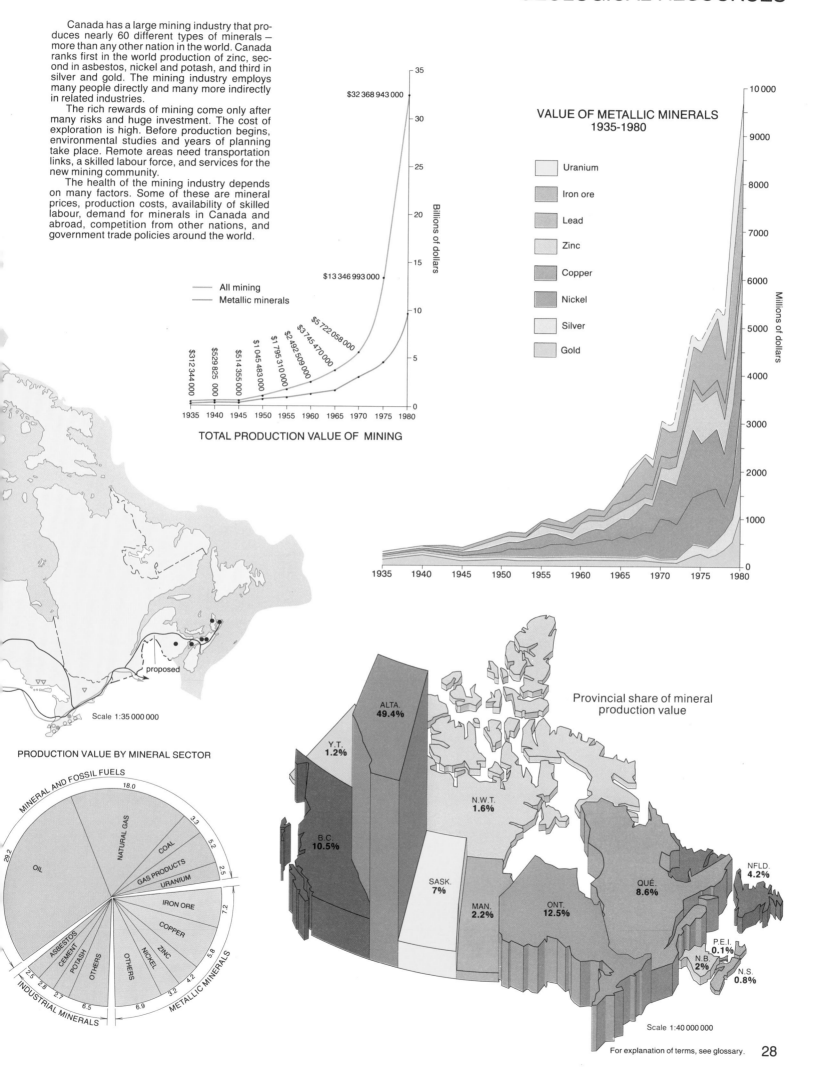

VALUE OF METALLIC MINERALS
1935-1980

- Uranium
- Iron ore
- Lead
- Zinc
- Copper
- Nickel
- Silver
- Gold

$32 368 943 000

$13 346 993 000

$5 722 058 000

$3 745 470 000

$2 492 509 000

$1 795 310 000

$1 045 483 000

$514 355 000

$529 825 000

$312 344 000

All mining
Metallic minerals

Billions of dollars

Millions of dollars

TOTAL PRODUCTION VALUE OF MINING

Scale 1:35 000 000

proposed

PRODUCTION VALUE BY MINERAL SECTOR

MINERAL AND FOSSIL FUELS

OIL 29.2
NATURAL GAS 18.0
COAL 3.3
GAS PRODUCTS 5.2
URANIUM 2.5
IRON ORE
COPPER 7.2
ZINC 5.8
NICKEL 4.2
OTHERS 3.2
OTHERS 6.9
POTASH 6.5
CEMENT 2.7
ASBESTOS 2.8
2.5

INDUSTRIAL MINERALS

METALLIC MINERALS

Provincial share of mineral
production value

ALTA. **49.4%**
Y.T. **1.2%**
B.C. **10.5%**
N.W.T. **1.6%**
SASK. **7%**
MAN. **2.2%**
ONT. **12.5%**
QUÉ. **8.6%**
NFLD. **4.2%**
P.E.I. **0.1%**
N.B. **2%**
N.S. **0.8%**

Scale 1:40 000 000

For explanation of terms, see glossary.

28

In Canada, the major sources of electrical energy are fossil fuels, moving water, and uranium. New power projects are being planned or developed to produce electrical energy in the right place at the right price. These projects include large-scale coal-powered stations, nuclear power plants, and hydro-electric mega-projects such as the James Bay power development. Canada, in spite of its small population, produces more hydro-electric power than any country except the United States or the U.S.S.R.

TOTAL ELECTRICITY DEMAND

Losses*
Industrial
Commercial
Residential and Farm

Yukon and N.W.T., B.C., Alta., Sask., Man., Ont., Qué., N.B., N.S., P.E.I., Nfld.

Percent: 0 10 20 30 40 50 60 70 80 90 100

*Some energy is lost in the form of heat through transmission lines and transformers.

MONTHLY RESIDENTIAL ELECTRICITY COSTS *

Charlottetown	$78.78
Yellowknife	55.87
Halifax	49.15
Moncton	48.62
Whitehorse	48.48
St. John's	42.80
Vancouver	36.63
Toronto	35.70
Calgary	33.74
Edmonton	33.60
Ottawa	32.60
Regina	31.67
Winnipeg	30.86
Montréal	30.40

* Average cost per residential unit

ELECTRICAL ENERGY MOVEMENT (GWh)

36 039   10 967   6438   3487   1217

Total exports: 33 875

WORLD COAL PRODUCTION

U.S.S.R. and Eastern Europe 31.2%
China 19.0%
United States 23.4%
Western Europe 9.9%
Others 9.3%
Australia 3.0%
South Africa 3.0%
Canada 1.2%

EXPORTERS

United States 26.3%
South Africa 3.7%
U.S.S.R. and Eastern Europe 37.1%
Australia 16.2%
Canada 6.7%
Other 10.0%

IMPORTERS

Japan 32.4%
Canada 8.1%
Other 29.8%
E.E.C. 29.7%

PRIMARY ENERGY SOURCES

Hydro-electric 24.5%
Coal 9.8%
Nuclear 3.9%
Natural gas 18.2%
Petroleum 43.6%

Rising oil and gas prices, and the uncertain future of the nuclear power industry may make coal a more popular source of electrical energy in the future. People who are concerned that the mining and burning of coal might harm the environment will probably oppose this trend.

YUKON TERRITORY
NORTHWEST TERRITORIES
BRITISH COLUMBIA
ALBERTA
SASKATCHEWAN
MANITOBA

Coal and uranium

- Anthracite
- Bituminous coal
- Subbituminous coal and lignite
- Areas favourable for uranium

Coal exports from Vancouver 15 126 000 t

Coal exports from Sydney 579 000 t

Coal imports from U.S. 14 836 000 t

Scale 1:35 000 000

COAL PRODUCTION AND EXPORT

Millions of tonnes: 0 20 40 60 80 100 120 140 160 180 200

Actual / Projection
Production
Export

1900 1920 1940 1960 1980

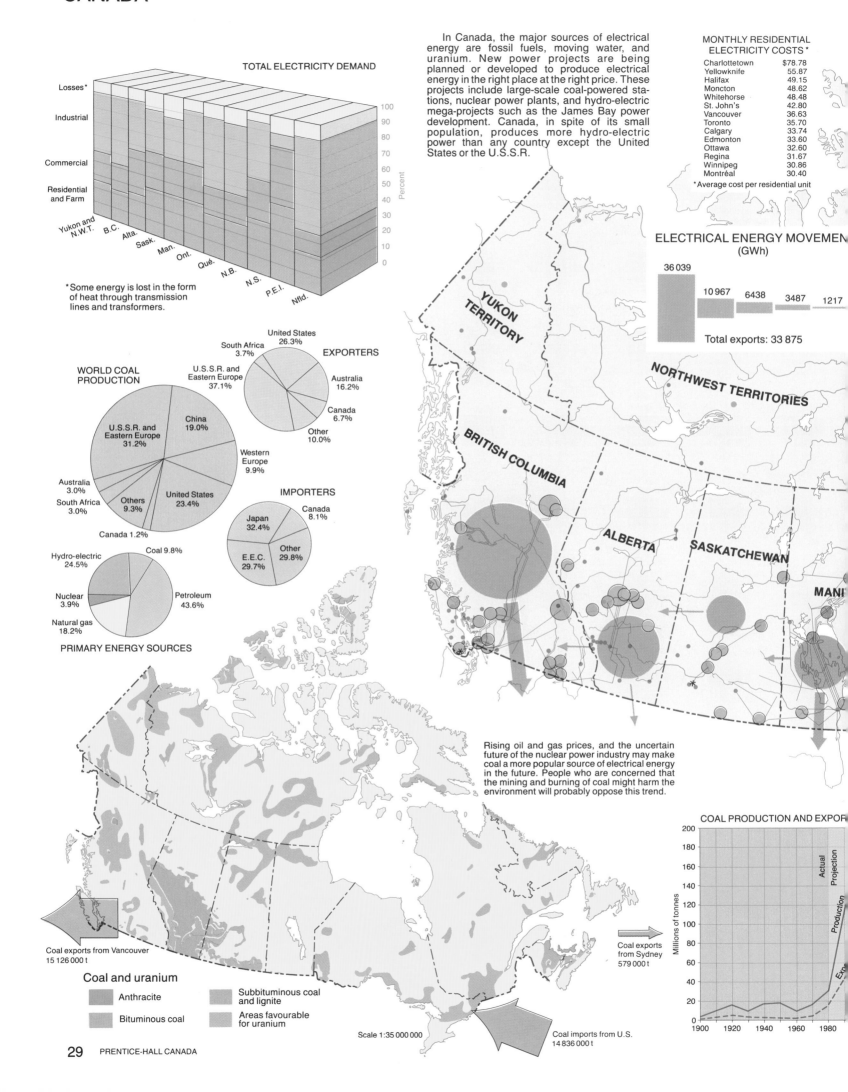

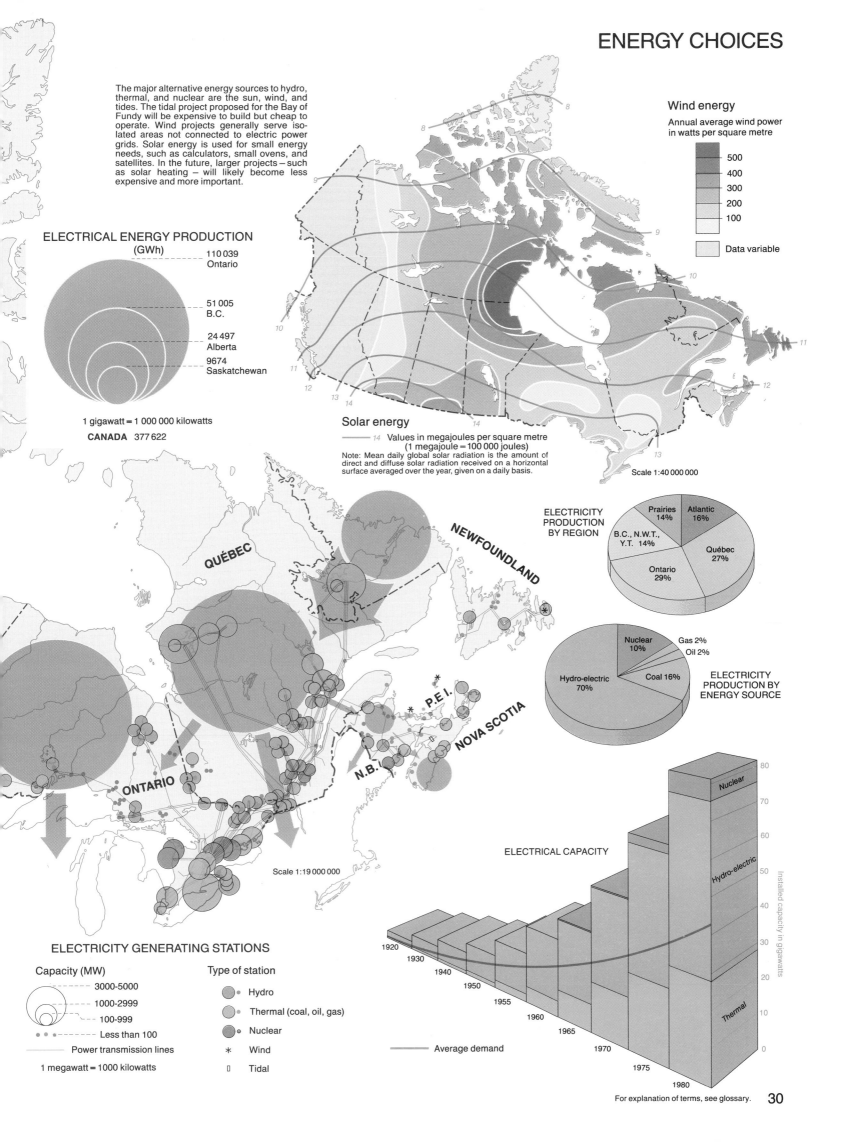

ENERGY CHOICES

The major alternative energy sources to hydro, thermal, and nuclear are the sun, wind, and tides. The tidal project proposed for the Bay of Fundy will be expensive to build but cheap to operate. Wind projects generally serve isolated areas not connected to electric power grids. Solar energy is used for small energy needs, such as calculators, small ovens, and satellites. In the future, larger projects – such as solar heating – will likely become less expensive and more important.

Wind energy

Annual average wind power in watts per square metre

- 500
- 400
- 300
- 200
- 100

Data variable

ELECTRICAL ENERGY PRODUCTION
(GWh)

110 039 Ontario

51 005 B.C.

24 497 Alberta

9674 Saskatchewan

1 gigawatt = 1 000 000 kilowatts

CANADA 377 622

Solar energy

_14_ Values in megajoules per square metre
(1 megajoule = 100 000 joules)

Note: Mean daily global solar radiation is the amount of direct and diffuse solar radiation received on a horizontal surface averaged over the year, given on a daily basis.

Scale 1:40 000 000

QUÉBEC

NEWFOUNDLAND

P.E I.

NOVA SCOTIA

N.B.

ONTARIO

Scale 1:19 000 000

ELECTRICITY PRODUCTION BY REGION

- Prairies 14%
- Atlantic 16%
- B.C., N.W.T., Y.T. 14%
- Québec 27%
- Ontario 29%

ELECTRICITY PRODUCTION BY ENERGY SOURCE

- Nuclear 10%
- Gas 2%
- Oil 2%
- Hydro-electric 70%
- Coal 16%

ELECTRICAL CAPACITY

Nuclear

Hydro-electric

Thermal

Installed capacity in gigawatts

80
70
60
50
40
30
20
10
0

1920 1930 1940 1950 1955 1960 1965 1970 1975 1980

—— Average demand

ELECTRICITY GENERATING STATIONS

Capacity (MW)

- 3000-5000
- 1000-2999
- 100-999
- Less than 100
- —— Power transmission lines

1 megawatt = 1000 kilowatts

Type of station

- Hydro
- Thermal (coal, oil, gas)
- Nuclear
- * Wind
- Tidal

CANADA

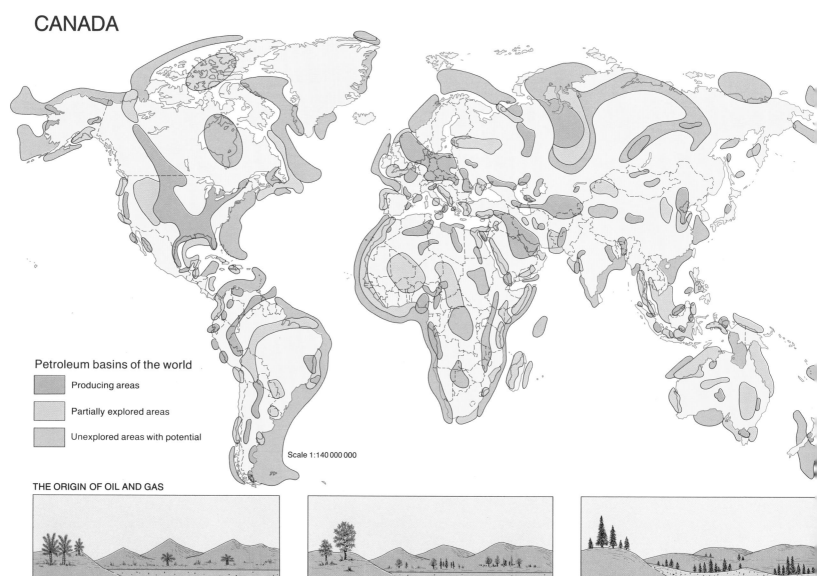

Petroleum basins of the world

- ▨ Producing areas
- ▨ Partially explored areas
- ▨ Unexplored areas with potential

Scale 1:140 000 000

THE ORIGIN OF OIL AND GAS

Plant and animal organisms died; their remains settled on the seabed.

Layers of mud, silt, and sand accumulated on top of these materials.

Heat, bacterial action, and the pressure of upper layers changed the remains of marine plants and animals into oil and natural gas.

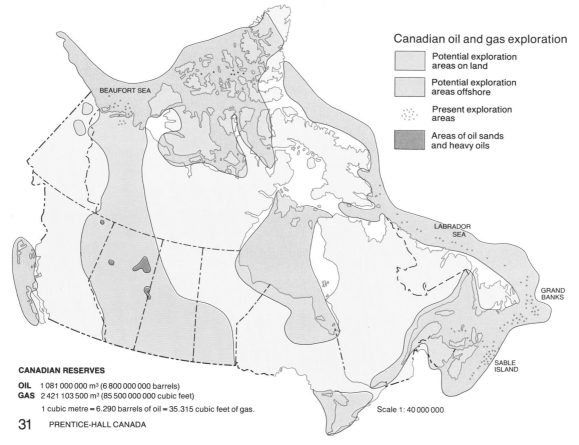

Canadian oil and gas exploration

- ▨ Potential exploration areas on land
- ▨ Potential exploration areas offshore
- ⋯ Present exploration areas
- ▨ Areas of oil sands and heavy oils

BEAUFORT SEA

LABRADOR SEA

GRAND BANKS

SABLE ISLAND

Scale 1:40 000 000

CANADIAN RESERVES

OIL 1 081 000 000 m³ (6 800 000 000 barrels)
GAS 2 421 103 500 m³ (85 500 000 000 cubic feet)

1 cubic metre = 6.290 barrels of oil = 35.315 cubic feet of gas.

Reservoirs of oil and gas are found in rock dating back to the Cambrian Period (600 000 000 a(years) ago). In Canada, the most productive periods appear to have been the Mississippian and Devonian Periods (350 000 000 a(years) ago).

Scientists believe that heat, pressure, and bacterial action changed organic matter to gaseous and liquid hydrocarbons. Changes in the earth's crust squeezed out much oil and gas, but some remained trapped inside the crust; this is the oil and gas that geologists search for today.

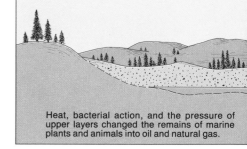

WORLD OIL RESERVES

	Millions of cubic metres	(Milli of ba
MIDDLE EAST	58 215	(366
EASTERN EUROPE/ASIA	15 581	(98
AFRICA	9436	(59
CENTRAL/SOUTH AMERICA	6418	(40
NORTH AMERICA	5644	(35
WESTERN EUROPE	4588	(28
ASIA/PACIFIC	2981	(18

WORLD GAS RESERVES

	Billions of cubic metres	(Billio cubic
EASTERN EUROPE/ASIA	27 043	(955
MIDDLE EAST	20 379	(719
NORTH AMERICA	7589	(268
AFRICA	5876	(207
WESTERN EUROPE	3913	(138
ASIA/PACIFIC	3475	(122
CENTRAL/SOUTH AMERICA	3075	(108

THE PIPELINE NETWORK

- Oil field
- Gas field
- Oil and gas field
- Oil pipeline
- Gas pipeline
- Pipeline proposed or under construction

A L A S K A

C A N A D A

U N I T E D   S T A T E S

1 cm represents 300 km

| 0 | 300 | 600 | 900 |

kilometres

Scale 1 : 30 000 000

SOLINE CONSUMPTION

	Kilograms/ person
ITED STATES	1346
EENLAND	1204
NADA	1118
STRALIA	701
W ZEALAND	520
EDEN	513
XEMBOURG	507
TED KINGDOM	282
VIET UNION	280
AN	192

rages for—

VELOPED NATIONS	582
VELOPING NATIONS	33
MMUNIST NATIONS	75
RICA	26
RTH AMERICA	1324
STERN EUROPE	255

CE OF GASOLINE
(erage price as of May 1983)

	Cents per litre
GENTINA	$0.33
STRALIA	0.46
LIVIA	0.22
AZIL	0.85
NADA	0.46
LOMBIA	0.30
BA	0.40
YPT	0.17
SALVADOR	0.81
ANCE	0.76
NGARY	0.48
LY	0.91
PAN	0.84
XEMBOURG	0.60
XICO	0.08
GERIA	0.40
RU	0.28
JDI ARABIA	0.04
UTH KOREA	1.22
S.S.R.	0.26
EDEN	0.65
ITZERLAND	0.68
ITED KINGDOM	0.67
ITED STATES	0.40
NEZUELA	0.08

PICAL FORMS OF OIL AND GAS TRAPS

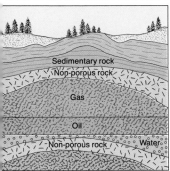

NTICLINE: Folding causes an upward
ch in the rock strata. Gas and oil collect
tween the non-porous rock layers above
d below.

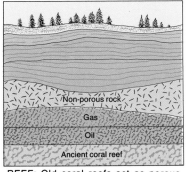

REEF: Old coral reefs act as porous
"sponges" for oil and gas deposits.

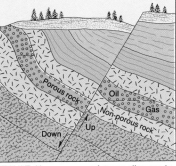

FAULT: Non-porous rock traps oil or gas in
permeable (porous) rock such as
sandstone. The rock layers "slip" sealing
in the oil- or gas-bearing rock.

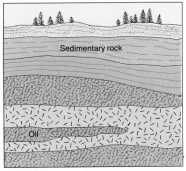

STRATIGRAPHIC: These traps are porous
rocks that lie between non-porous layers of
undisturbed sedimentary rock.

For explanation of terms, see glossary. 32

CANADA

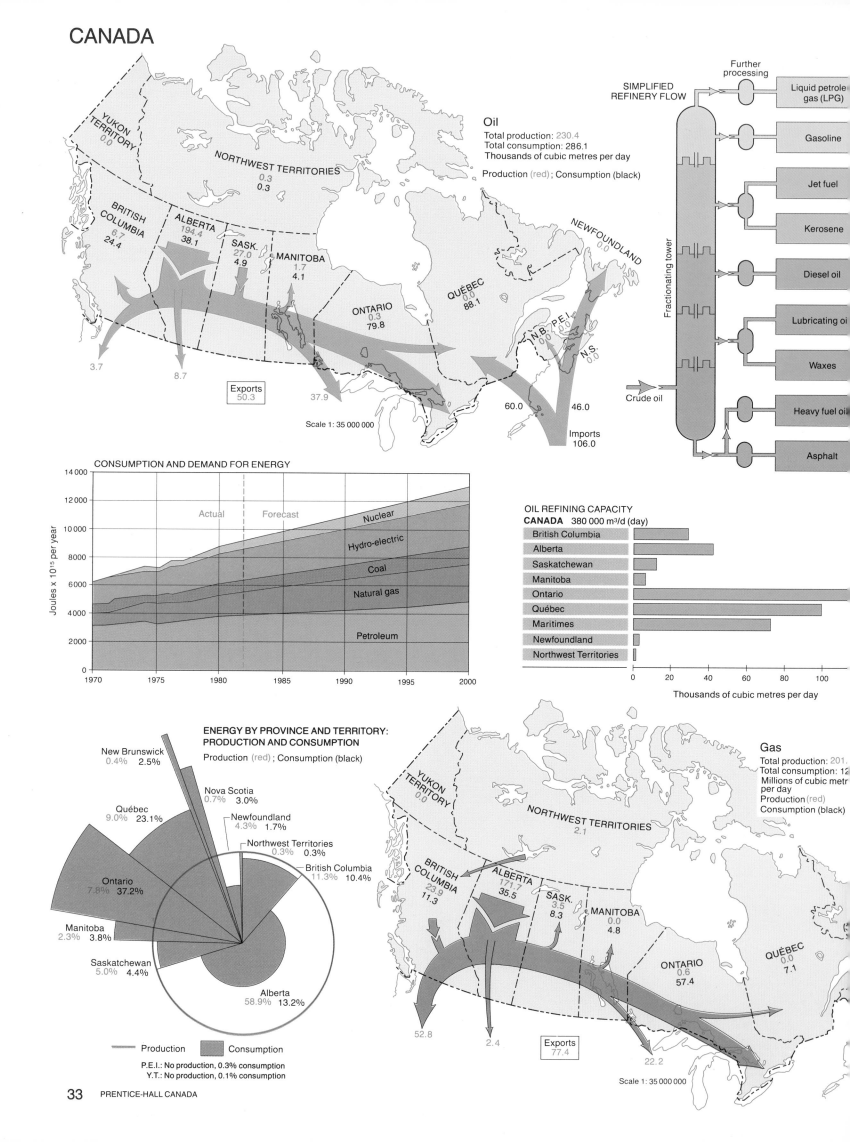

Oil

Total production: 230.4
Total consumption: 286.1
Thousands of cubic metres per day

Production (red) ; Consumption (black)

YUKON TERRITORY
0.0

NORTHWEST TERRITORIES
0.3
0.3

BRITISH COLUMBIA
6.7
24.4

ALBERTA
194.4
38.1

SASK.
27.0
4.9

MANITOBA
1.7
4.1

ONTARIO
0.3
79.8

QUÉBEC
0.0
88.1

NEWFOUNDLAND
0.0

N.B.
0.0

P.E.I.
0.0

N.S.
0.0

3.7

8.7

37.9

Exports
50.3

60.0

46.0

Imports
106.0

Scale 1: 35 000 000

SIMPLIFIED REFINERY FLOW

Further processing

Liquid petrole gas (LPG)

Gasoline

Jet fuel

Kerosene

Diesel oil

Lubricating oi

Waxes

Heavy fuel oi

Asphalt

Fractionating tower

Crude oil

CONSUMPTION AND DEMAND FOR ENERGY

Joules x 10^{15} per year

Actual | Forecast

Nuclear

Hydro-electric

Coal

Natural gas

Petroleum

1970 1975 1980 1985 1990 1995 2000

OIL REFINING CAPACITY
CANADA 380 000 m³/d (day)

British Columbia
Alberta
Saskatchewan
Manitoba
Ontario
Québec
Maritimes
Newfoundland
Northwest Territories

0 20 40 60 80 100

Thousands of cubic metres per day

ENERGY BY PROVINCE AND TERRITORY: PRODUCTION AND CONSUMPTION

Production (red) ; Consumption (black)

New Brunswick
0.4%   2.5%

Nova Scotia
0.7%   3.0%

Québec
9.0%   23.1%

Newfoundland
4.3%   1.7%

Northwest Territories
0.3%   0.3%

British Columbia
11.3%   10.4%

Ontario
7.8%   37.2%

Manitoba
2.3%   3.8%

Saskatchewan
5.0%   4.4%

Alberta
58.9%   13.2%

Production | Consumption

P.E.I.: No production, 0.3% consumption
Y.T.: No production, 0.1% consumption

Gas

Total production: 201.
Total consumption: 12
Millions of cubic metr
per day
Production (red)
Consumption (black)

YUKON TERRITORY
0.0

NORTHWEST TERRITORIES
2.1

BRITISH COLUMBIA
23.9
11.3

ALBERTA
171.7
35.5

SASK.
3.5
8.3

MANITOBA
0.0
4.8

ONTARIO
0.6
57.4

QUÉBEC
0.0
7.1

52.8

2.4

Exports
77.4

22.2

Scale 1: 35 000 000

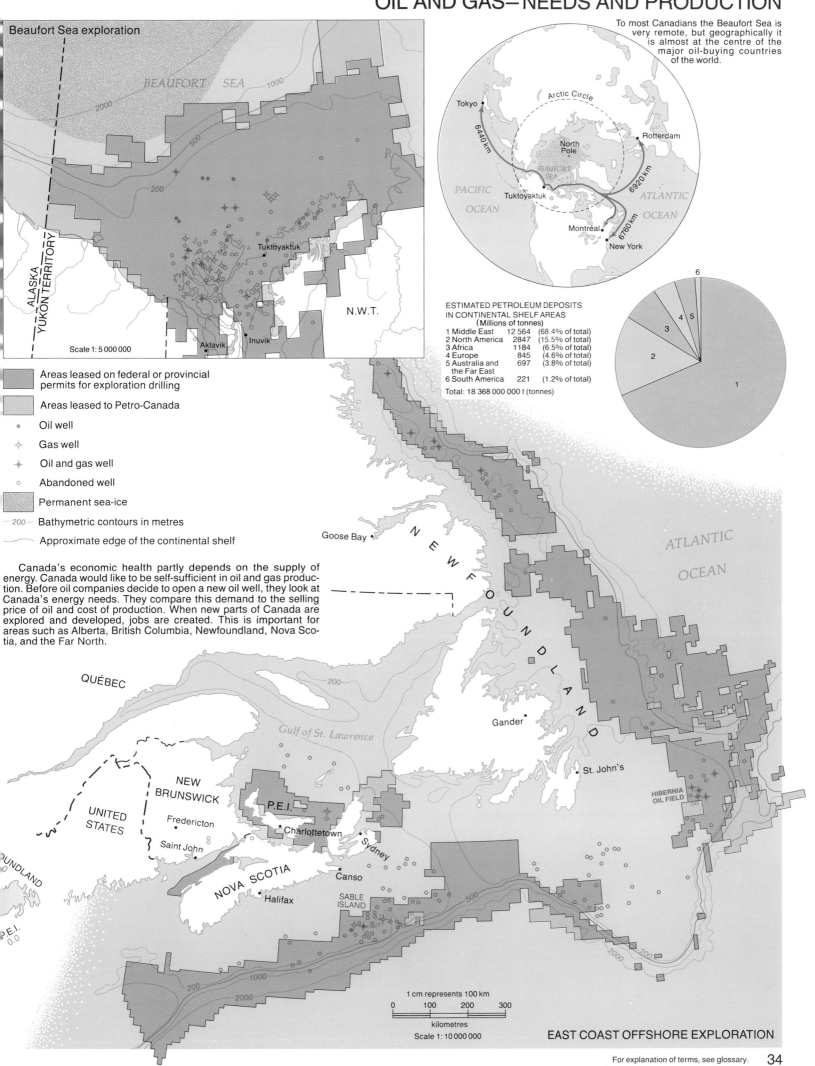

Beaufort Sea exploration

BEAUFORT SEA
1000
2000
500
200
ALASKA
YUKON TERRITORY
Tuktoyaktuk
N.W.T.
Aklavik
Inuvik
Scale 1: 5 000 000

To most Canadians the Beaufort Sea is very remote, but geographically it is almost at the centre of the major oil-buying countries of the world.

Arctic Circle
Tokyo
6440 km
North Pole
Rotterdam
BEAUFORT SEA
PACIFIC OCEAN
6920 km
ATLANTIC OCEAN
Tuktoyaktuk
Montréal
6760 km
New York

ESTIMATED PETROLEUM DEPOSITS
IN CONTINENTAL SHELF AREAS
(Millions of tonnes)

1 Middle East	12 564	(68.4% of total)
2 North America	2847	(15.5% of total)
3 Africa	1184	(6.5% of total)
4 Europe	845	(4.6% of total)
5 Australia and the Far East	697	(3.8% of total)
6 South America	221	(1.2% of total)

Total: 18 368 000 000 t (tonnes)

Areas leased on federal or provincial permits for exploration drilling

Areas leased to Petro-Canada

• Oil well

✧ Gas well

✦ Oil and gas well

○ Abandoned well

Permanent sea-ice

—200— Bathymetric contours in metres

Approximate edge of the continental shelf

Canada's economic health partly depends on the supply of energy. Canada would like to be self-sufficient in oil and gas production. Before oil companies decide to open a new oil well, they look at Canada's energy needs. They compare this demand to the selling price of oil and cost of production. When new parts of Canada are explored and developed, jobs are created. This is important for areas such as Alberta, British Columbia, Newfoundland, Nova Scotia, and the Far North.

Goose Bay
NEWFOUNDLAND
ATLANTIC OCEAN
QUÉBEC
200
Gulf of St. Lawrence
Gander
St. John's
HIBERNIA OIL FIELD
NEW BRUNSWICK
P.E.I.
UNITED STATES
Fredericton
Charlottetown
Saint John
Sydney
NOVA SCOTIA
Canso
Halifax
SABLE ISLAND
500
2000
1000
200
500
2000

1 cm represents 100 km
0 100 200 300
kilometres
Scale 1: 10 000 000

EAST COAST OFFSHORE EXPLORATION

CANADA

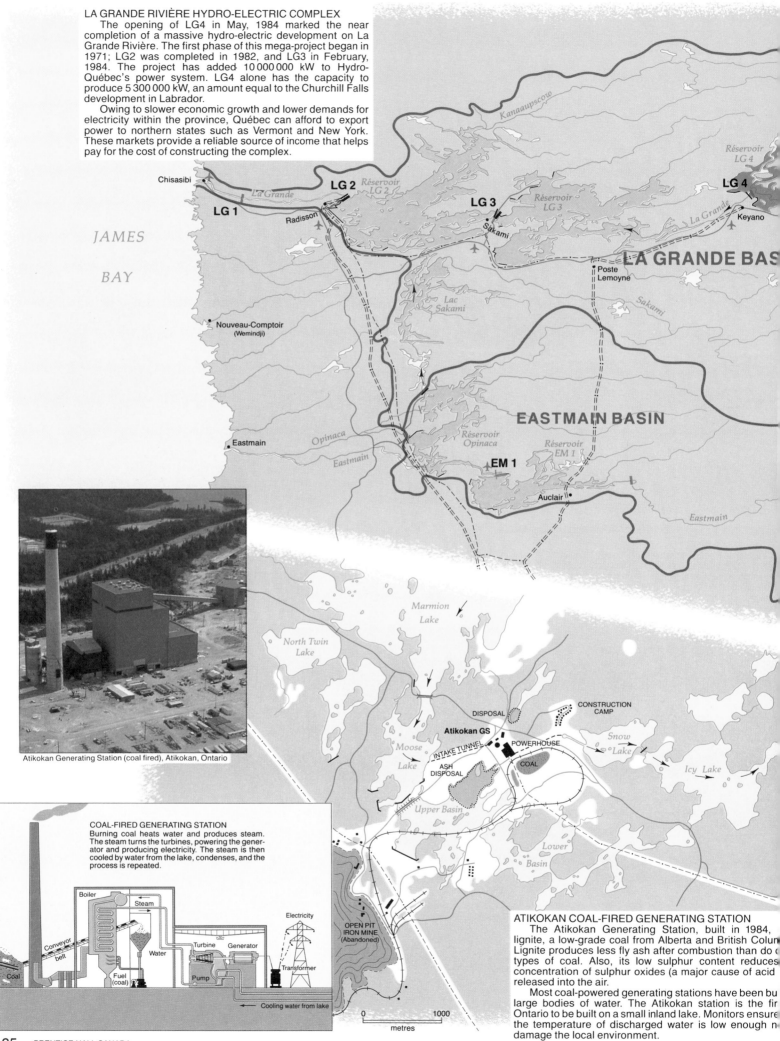

LA GRANDE RIVIÈRE HYDRO-ELECTRIC COMPLEX

The opening of LG4 in May, 1984 marked the near completion of a massive hydro-electric development on La Grande Rivière. The first phase of this mega-project began in 1971; LG2 was completed in 1982, and LG3 in February, 1984. The project has added 10 000 000 kW to Hydro-Québec's power system. LG4 alone has the capacity to produce 5 300 000 kW, an amount equal to the Churchill Falls development in Labrador.

Owing to slower economic growth and lower demands for electricity within the province, Québec can afford to export power to northern states such as Vermont and New York. These markets provide a reliable source of income that helps pay for the cost of constructing the complex.

Kanaaupscow

Chisasibi

La Grande

LG 1

LG 2

Réservoir LG 2

LG 3

Réservoir LG 3

Réservoir LG 4

LG 4

Radisson

Sakami

La Grande

Keyano

JAMES

BAY

Poste Lemoyne

LA GRANDE BAS

Nouveau-Comptoir (Wemindji)

Lac Sakami

Sakami

Eastmain

Opinaca

Eastmain

EASTMAIN BASIN

Réservoir Opinaca

Réservoir EM 1

EM 1

Auclair

Eastmain

Atikokan Generating Station (coal fired), Atikokan, Ontario

Marmion Lake

North Twin Lake

DISPOSAL

CONSTRUCTION CAMP

Atikokan GS

POWERHOUSE

Snow Lake

Moose Lake

INTAKE TUNNEL

ASH DISPOSAL

COAL

Icy Lake

Upper Basin

Lower Basin

COAL-FIRED GENERATING STATION

Burning coal heats water and produces steam. The steam turns the turbines, powering the generator and producing electricity. The steam is then cooled by water from the lake, condenses, and the process is repeated.

Boiler

Steam

Electricity

Conveyor belt

Water

Turbine

Generator

Coal

Fuel (coal)

Pump

Transformer

Cooling water from lake

OPEN PIT IRON MINE (Abandoned)

0   1000

metres

ATIKOKAN COAL-FIRED GENERATING STATION

The Atikokan Generating Station, built in 1984, lignite, a low-grade coal from Alberta and British Colum Lignite produces less fly ash after combustion than do types of coal. Also, its low sulphur content reduces concentration of sulphur oxides (a major cause of acid released into the air.

Most coal-powered generating stations have been bu large bodies of water. The Atikokan station is the fir Ontario to be built on a small inland lake. Monitors ensure the temperature of discharged water is low enough n damage the local environment.

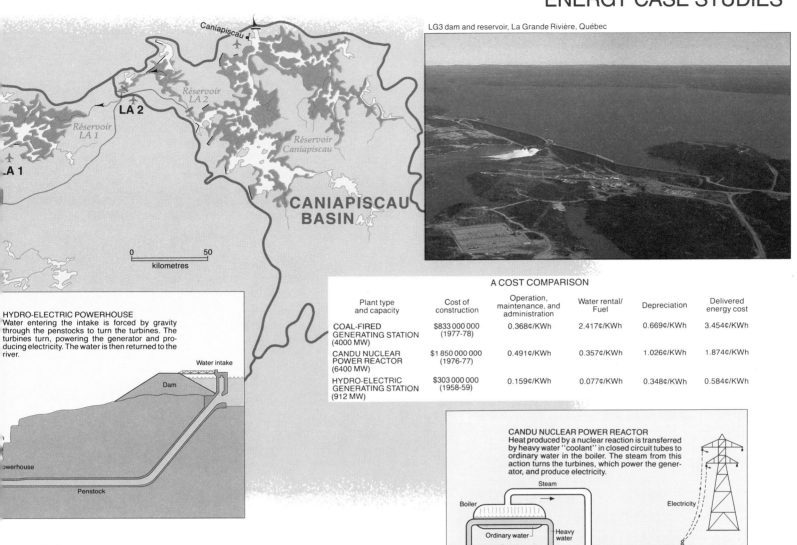

LG3 dam and reservoir, La Grande Rivière, Québec

HYDRO-ELECTRIC POWERHOUSE
Water entering the intake is forced by gravity through the penstocks to turn the turbines. The turbines turn, powering the generator and producing electricity. The water is then returned to the river.

(Labels: Water intake, Dam, Powerhouse, Penstock)

A COST COMPARISON

Plant type and capacity	Cost of construction	Operation, maintenance, and administration	Water rental/ Fuel	Depreciation	Delivered energy cost
COAL-FIRED GENERATING STATION (4000 MW)	$833 000 000 (1977-78)	0.368¢/KWh	2.417¢/KWh	0.669¢/KWh	3.454¢/KWh
CANDU NUCLEAR POWER REACTOR (6400 MW)	$1 850 000 000 (1976-77)	0.491¢/KWh	0.357¢/KWh	1.026¢/KWh	1.874¢/KWh
HYDRO-ELECTRIC GENERATING STATION (912 MW)	$303 000 000 (1958-59)	0.159¢/KWh	0.077¢/KWh	0.348¢/KWh	0.584¢/KWh

CANDU NUCLEAR POWER REACTOR
Heat produced by a nuclear reaction is transferred by heavy water "coolant" in closed circuit tubes to ordinary water in the boiler. The steam from this action turns the turbines, which power the generator, and produce electricity.

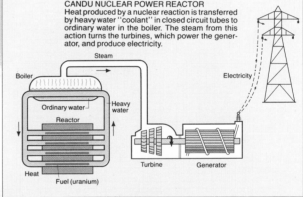

(Labels: Steam, Boiler, Electricity, Ordinary water, Heavy water, Reactor, Heat, Fuel (uranium), Turbine, Generator)

Legend
- • Settlement
- ✈ Airport
- — Dyke
- ▬ Power dam
- — Dam
- ▬ Proposed power dam
- ▬ Proposed dam
- ---- Transmission line
- ——— Road
- ++++ Railway
- ——➤ Direction of water flow
- ——— Drainage basin
- ▨ Flooded area
- ▨ Area to be flooded
- ▨ Forested area

Note: Legend common to all maps.

(Map labels: Caniapiscau, Réservoir LA 2, Réservoir LA 1, LA 2, LA 1, CANIAPISCAU BASIN, 0 50 kilometres)

BRUCE NUCLEAR GENERATING STATION
The Bruce Nuclear Power Development near Kincardine on Lake Huron includes three nuclear generating stations — Douglas Point, Bruce A, and Bruce B. Also included are two heavy water plants, an oil-fired steam plant, a bulk steam system, waste storage facilities, and training and information centres. An "energy centre", proposed for nearby, would operate on steam from the complex and include greenhouses and other facilities.

Douglas Point, the first commercial nuclear generating station, was built in 1967 but closed in 1984. It could generate 200 000 kW of electricity. Both Bruce A and Bruce B have four units with a capacity of 750 000 kW each. Bruce B will be completed in the late 1980's. The contribution of nuclear power to Ontario's electricity supply is expected to increase from the present 37 percent to 60 percent by the 1990's.

(Map labels: Bruce A NGS, LAKE HURON, SWITCH YARD, CONSTRUCTION CAMP, HEAVY WATER PLANTS, STEAM PLANT, Douglas Point GS (Abandoned), Bruce B NGS, SWITCH YARD, RADIOACTIVE WASTE INCINERATOR, RADIOACTIVE WASTE MANAGEMENT AREA, INVERHURON PARK, 0 1000 metres)

WORLD NUCLEAR ENERGY USE

Generating capacity (MW)		Plants in use
61 916	United States	80
21 626	France	30
16 615	Japan	25
15 886	U.S.S.R.	38
9 832	West Germany	15
7 597	United Kingdom	33
6 415	Sweden	9
5 494	Canada	11
3 110	Taiwan	4
2 160	Finland	4
1 973	Spain	4
1 940	Switzerland	4
1 694	East Germany	5
1 675	Belgium	4
1 232	Italy	3
1 224	Bulgaria	3
840	Czechoslovakia	2
808	India	4
632	Yugoslavia	1
626	Brazil	1
564	South Korea	1
499	Netherlands	2
408	Hungary	1
335	Argentina	1
125	Pakistan	1

Bruce Nuclear Power Station, Douglas Point (near Kincardine), Ontario

CANADA

TEMPERATURE

The average January and July temperatures are affected by several factors. The most important of these are latitude and continentality. The isotherms (lines that join points of equal temperature) reflect the influence of both factors. A continental climate occurs when there is little effect on temperature by a large body of water. A comparison between the two maps shows the wide temperature range that interior parts of Canada experience. This wide range is a characteristic of a continental climate.

July temperature
°C
20
10

January temperature
°C
0
−10
−20
−30

KAUJUITOQ
136 mm

DAWSON
326 mm

THUNDER BAY
738 mm

CALGARY
437 mm

CHURCHILL
397 mm

MONTRÉAL
999 mm

PRINCE RUPERT
2414 mm

REGINA
398 mm

WINNIPEG
535 mm

WINDSOR
836 mm

VANCOUVER
1068 mm

Solar radiation
MJ/m²
13
11
9

• Climograph station

Kaujuitoq
Dawson
Iqaluit
Prince Rupert
Churchill
Nitchequon
St. John's
Calgary
Vancouver
Regina
Winnipeg
Thunder Bay
Halifax
Montréal
Windsor

Bright sunshine hours
hours
2200
1800
1400

RADIATION / BRIGHT SUNSHINE

The pattern of solar radiation on the map reflects the influence of latitude and the angle of the sun's rays as they enter the atmosphere and penetrate to the surface of the earth. A combination of factors affects the number of hours of bright sunshine in a given area each year. These factors include air masses, cyclonic storms, and the number of daylight hours.

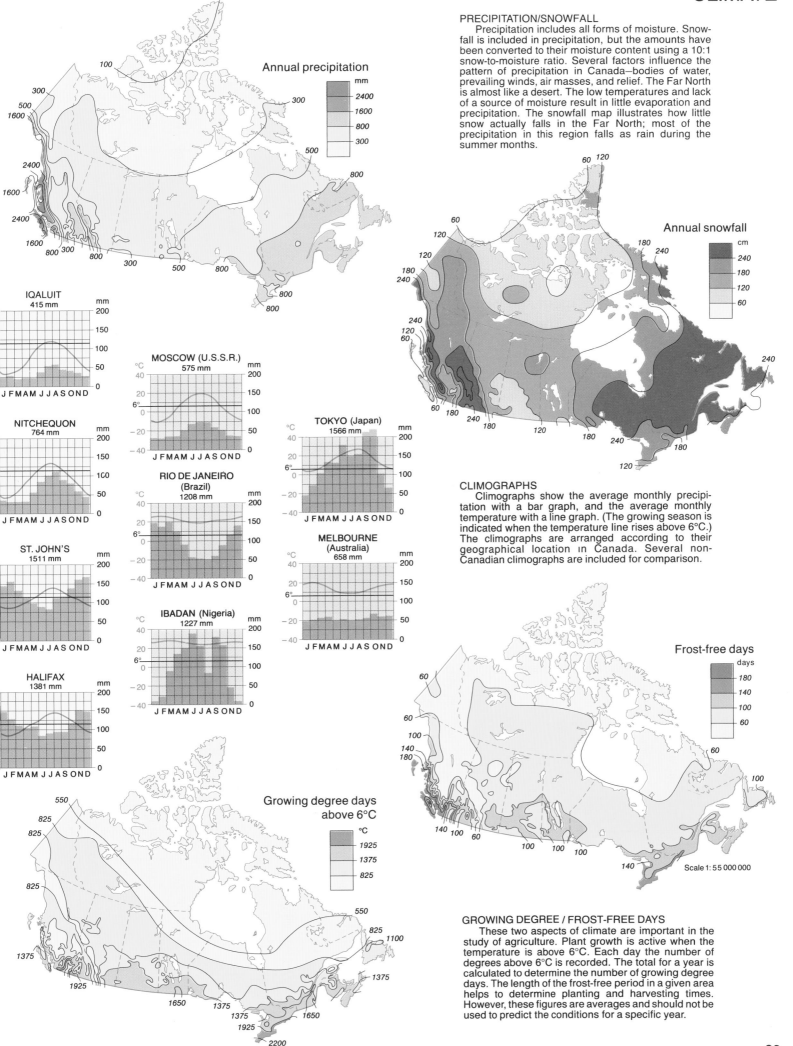

Annual precipitation

mm
2400
1600
800
300

IQALUIT
415 mm

mm
200
150
100
50
0

J F M A M J J A S O N D

NITCHEQUON
764 mm

mm
200
150
100
50
0

J F M A M J J A S O N D

ST. JOHN'S
1511 mm

mm
200
150
100
50
0

J F M A M J J A S O N D

HALIFAX
1381 mm

mm
200
150
100
50
0

J F M A M J J A S O N D

MOSCOW (U.S.S.R.)
575 mm

°C
40
20
6°
0
-20
-40

mm
200
150
100
50
0

J F M A M J J A S O N D

RIO DE JANEIRO
(Brazil)
1208 mm

°C
40
20
6°
0
-20
-40

mm
200
150
100
50
0

J F M A M J J A S O N D

IBADAN (Nigeria)
1227 mm

°C
40
20
6°
0
-20
-40

mm
200
150
100
50
0

J F M A M J J A S O N D

TOKYO (Japan)
1566 mm

°C
40
20
6°
0
-20
-40

mm
200
150
100
50
0

J F M A M J J A S O N D

MELBOURNE
(Australia)
658 mm

°C
40
20
6°
0
-20
-40

mm
200
150
100
50
0

J F M A M J J A S O N D

PRECIPITATION/SNOWFALL

Precipitation includes all forms of moisture. Snowfall is included in precipitation, but the amounts have been converted to their moisture content using a 10:1 snow-to-moisture ratio. Several factors influence the pattern of precipitation in Canada—bodies of water, prevailing winds, air masses, and relief. The Far North is almost like a desert. The low temperatures and lack of a source of moisture result in little evaporation and precipitation. The snowfall map illustrates how little snow actually falls in the Far North; most of the precipitation in this region falls as rain during the summer months.

Annual snowfall

cm
240
180
120
60

CLIMOGRAPHS

Climographs show the average monthly precipitation with a bar graph, and the average monthly temperature with a line graph. (The growing season is indicated when the temperature line rises above 6°C.) The climographs are arranged according to their geographical location in Canada. Several non-Canadian climographs are included for comparison.

Frost-free days

days
180
140
100
60

Scale 1: 55 000 000

Growing degree days above 6°C

°C
1925
1375
825

GROWING DEGREE / FROST-FREE DAYS

These two aspects of climate are important in the study of agriculture. Plant growth is active when the temperature is above 6°C. Each day the number of degrees above 6°C is recorded. The total for a year is calculated to determine the number of growing degree days. The length of the frost-free period in a given area helps to determine planting and harvesting times. However, these figures are averages and should not be used to predict the conditions for a specific year.

For explanation of terms, see glossary.

CANADA

Air masses

An air mass is a large body of air in which temperature and moisture conditions are relatively similar throughout. It takes on the characteristics of the surface over which it forms. An air mass forming over northern Canada in winter will be cold and dry; over the Gulf of Mexico, it will be warm and moist. The air mass then carries these characteristics to "invaded" areas. This invasion is preceded by a front which marks the leading edge of the air mass.

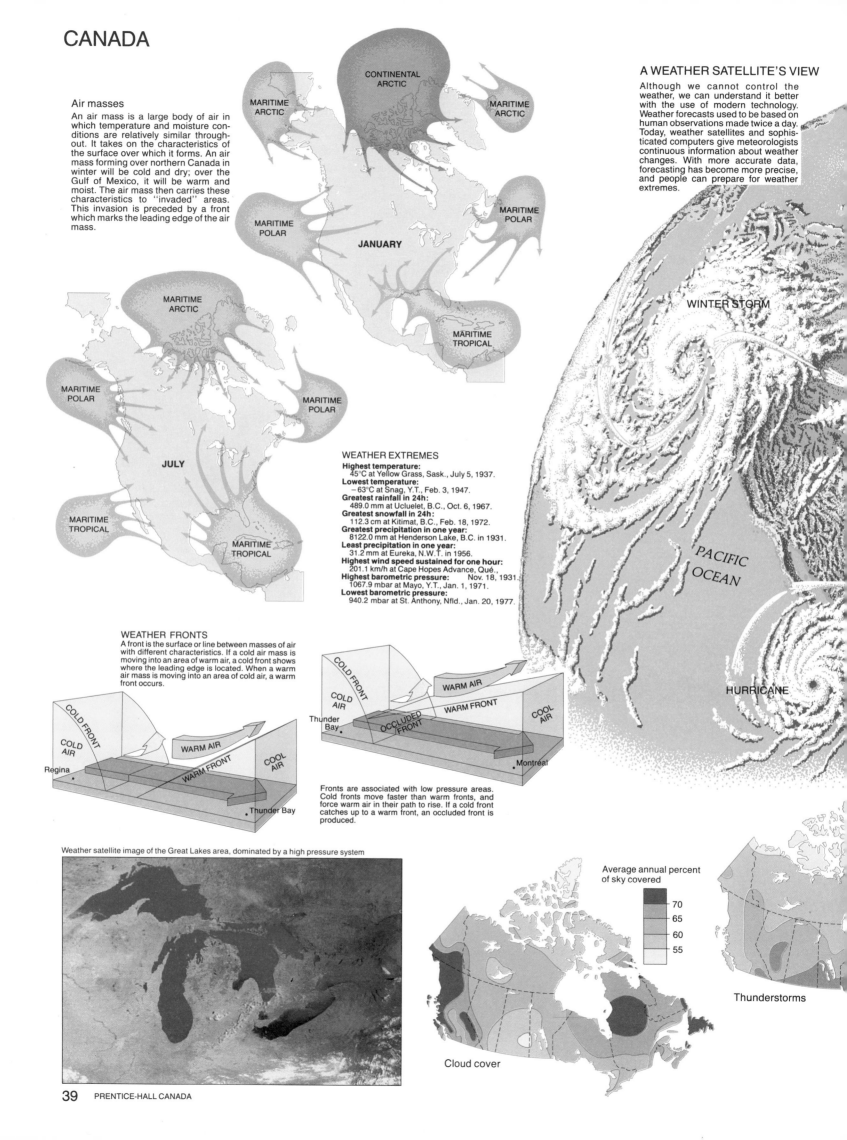

CONTINENTAL ARCTIC

MARITIME ARCTIC

MARITIME ARCTIC

MARITIME POLAR

MARITIME POLAR

JANUARY

MARITIME TROPICAL

MARITIME ARCTIC

MARITIME POLAR

MARITIME POLAR

JULY

MARITIME TROPICAL

MARITIME TROPICAL

A WEATHER SATELLITE'S VIEW

Although we cannot control the weather, we can understand it better with the use of modern technology. Weather forecasts used to be based on human observations made twice a day. Today, weather satellites and sophisticated computers give meteorologists continuous information about weather changes. With more accurate data, forecasting has become more precise, and people can prepare for weather extremes.

WINTER STORM

PACIFIC OCEAN

HURRICANE

WEATHER EXTREMES

Highest temperature:
45°C at Yellow Grass, Sask., July 5, 1937.
Lowest temperature:
−63°C at Snag, Y.T., Feb. 3, 1947.
Greatest rainfall in 24h:
489.0 mm at Ucluelet, B.C., Oct. 6, 1967.
Greatest snowfall in 24h:
112.3 cm at Kitimat, B.C., Feb. 18, 1972.
Greatest precipitation in one year:
8122.0 mm at Henderson Lake, B.C. in 1931.
Least precipitation in one year:
31.2 mm at Eureka, N.W.T. in 1956.
Highest wind speed sustained for one hour:
201.1 km/h at Cape Hopes Advance, Qué., Nov. 18, 1931.
Highest barometric pressure:
1067.9 mbar at Mayo, Y.T., Jan. 1, 1971.
Lowest barometric pressure:
940.2 mbar at St. Anthony, Nfld., Jan. 20, 1977.

WEATHER FRONTS

A front is the surface or line between masses of air with different characteristics. If a cold air mass is moving into an area of warm air, a cold front shows where the leading edge is located. When a warm air mass is moving into an area of cold air, a warm front occurs.

COLD FRONT

COLD AIR

WARM AIR

WARM FRONT

COOL AIR

Regina

Thunder Bay

COLD FRONT

COLD AIR

Thunder Bay

OCCLUDED FRONT

WARM AIR

WARM FRONT

COOL AIR

Montréal

Fronts are associated with low pressure areas. Cold fronts move faster than warm fronts, and force warm air in their path to rise. If a cold front catches up to a warm front, an occluded front is produced.

Weather satellite image of the Great Lakes area, dominated by a high pressure system

Average annual percent of sky covered

70
65
60
55

Cloud cover

Thunderstorms

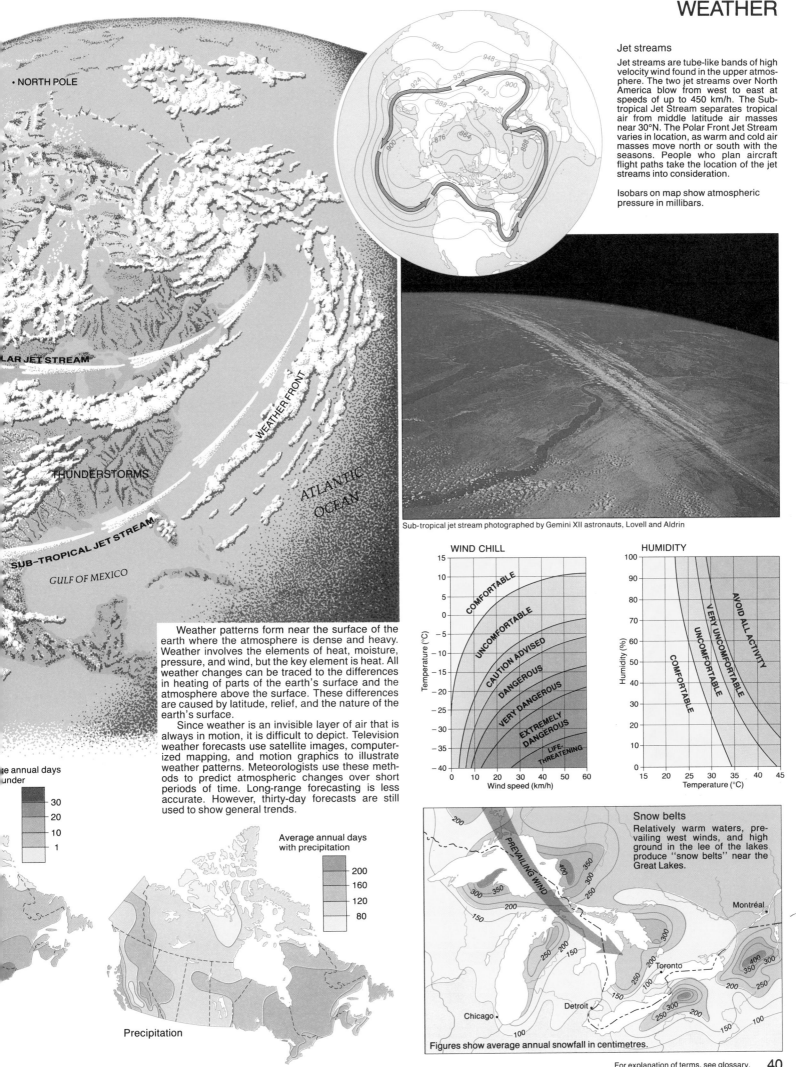

Jet streams

Jet streams are tube-like bands of high velocity wind found in the upper atmosphere. The two jet streams over North America blow from west to east at speeds of up to 450 km/h. The Sub-tropical Jet Stream separates tropical air from middle latitude air masses near 30°N. The Polar Front Jet Stream varies in location, as warm and cold air masses move north or south with the seasons. People who plan aircraft flight paths take the location of the jet streams into consideration.

Isobars on map show atmospheric pressure in millibars.

Sub-tropical jet stream photographed by Gemini XII astronauts, Lovell and Aldrin

Weather patterns form near the surface of the earth where the atmosphere is dense and heavy. Weather involves the elements of heat, moisture, pressure, and wind, but the key element is heat. All weather changes can be traced to the differences in heating of parts of the earth's surface and the atmosphere above the surface. These differences are caused by latitude, relief, and the nature of the earth's surface.

Since weather is an invisible layer of air that is always in motion, it is difficult to depict. Television weather forecasts use satellite images, computerized mapping, and motion graphics to illustrate weather patterns. Meteorologists use these methods to predict atmospheric changes over short periods of time. Long-range forecasting is less accurate. However, thirty-day forecasts are still used to show general trends.

NORTH POLE

LAR JET STREAM

WEATHER FRONT

THUNDERSTORMS

ATLANTIC OCEAN

SUB-TROPICAL JET STREAM

GULF OF MEXICO

WIND CHILL

COMFORTABLE
UNCOMFORTABLE
CAUTION ADVISED
DANGEROUS
VERY DANGEROUS
EXTREMELY DANGEROUS
LIFE-THREATENING

Temperature (°C) / Wind speed (km/h)

HUMIDITY

AVOID ALL ACTIVITY
VERY UNCOMFORTABLE
UNCOMFORTABLE
COMFORTABLE

Humidity (%) / Temperature (°C)

e annual days
under

30
20
10
1

Average annual days with precipitation

200
160
120
80

Precipitation

Snow belts

Relatively warm waters, prevailing west winds, and high ground in the lee of the lakes produce "snow belts" near the Great Lakes.

PREVAILING WIND

Montréal
Toronto
Detroit
Chicago

Figures show average annual snowfall in centimetres.

CANADA

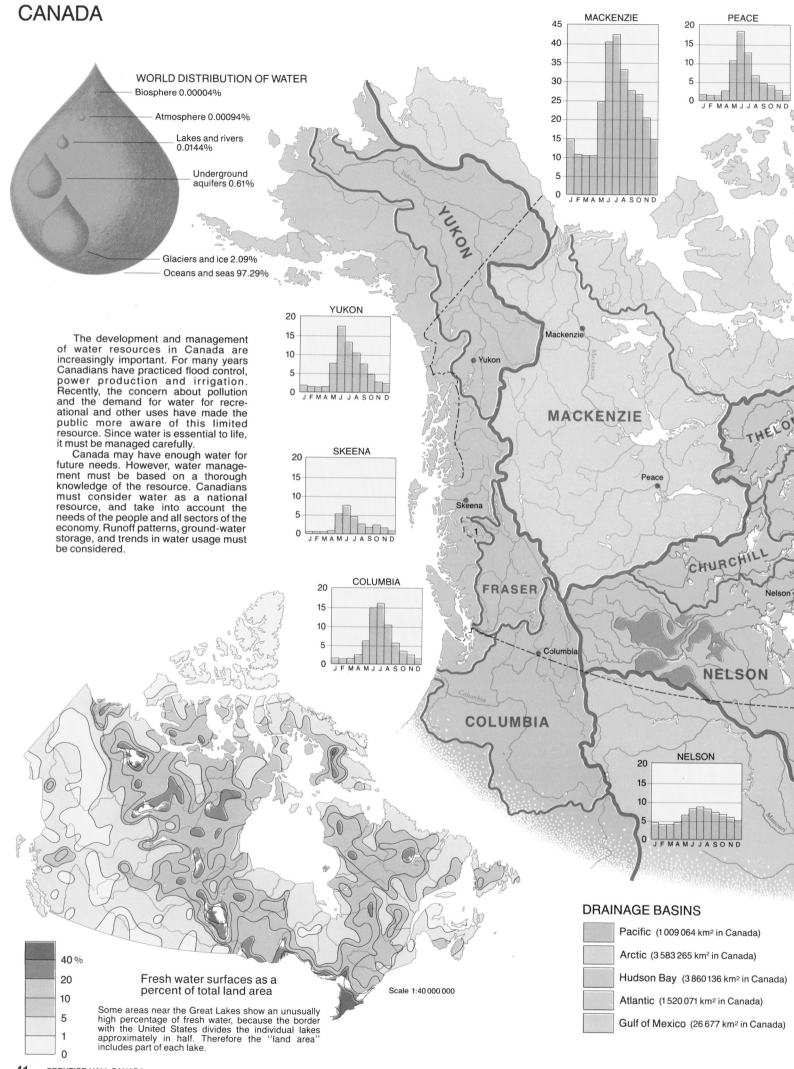

WORLD DISTRIBUTION OF WATER

- Biosphere 0.00004%
- Atmosphere 0.00094%
- Lakes and rivers 0.0144%
- Underground aquifers 0.61%
- Glaciers and ice 2.09%
- Oceans and seas 97.29%

The development and management of water resources in Canada are increasingly important. For many years Canadians have practiced flood control, power production and irrigation. Recently, the concern about pollution and the demand for water for recreational and other uses have made the public more aware of this limited resource. Since water is essential to life, it must be managed carefully.

Canada may have enough water for future needs. However, water management must be based on a thorough knowledge of the resource. Canadians must consider water as a national resource, and take into account the needs of the people and all sectors of the economy. Runoff patterns, ground-water storage, and trends in water usage must be considered.

Fresh water surfaces as a percent of total land area

40 %
20
10
5
1
0

Some areas near the Great Lakes show an unusually high percentage of fresh water, because the border with the United States divides the individual lakes approximately in half. Therefore the "land area" includes part of each lake.

Scale 1:40 000 000

DRAINAGE BASINS

- Pacific (1 009 064 km² in Canada)
- Arctic (3 583 265 km² in Canada)
- Hudson Bay (3 860 136 km² in Canada)
- Atlantic (1 520 071 km² in Canada)
- Gulf of Mexico (26 677 km² in Canada)

WATER RESOURCES

Precipitation can evaporate, sink below ground level, or run down the surface of the land. Moisture that sinks into the ground becomes ground water; the amount of ground water varies with slope, vegetation, temperature, and the porous nature of the soil or rock. Water that runs down the surface of the land and flows into streams and rivers is called runoff.

Average annual runoff

	200 cm
	100
	50
	10
	0

Scale 1:40 000 000

In parts of Canada and the United States, acid rain and snow are affecting the land and water. Fossil-fuelled power plants and smelters in Canada and the United States, and automobile exhaust fumes, produce more than two-thirds of the acid rain. Toxic wastes, primarily sulphur dioxide and nitrogen oxides, mix with moisture in the upper atmosphere and fall to earth as a mild acid. The acid kills plants and animals in lakes, hurts crop production, and damages timber stands. Acid rain affects the lakes of the Canadian Shield most strongly. Lakes found in areas of limestone bedrock are harmed less because limestone can neutralize some of the acid. The causes and prevention of acid rain concern both Canada and the United States, and the importance of this environmental problem will probably increase in the next few years.

Acid rain
(pH level)

	Alkaline
	6.5
	6.0
	5.5
	5.0
	4.5
	Acidic

Areas that are potentially sensitive to acid rain

Scale 1:50 000 000

Scale 1:21 000 000

BACK

CANIAPISCAU

MOOSE

CHURCHILL

SAINT JOHN

ST. LAWRENCE

Billions of m³

The bar graphs indicate the volume of flow by month at gauging stations on selected rivers.

Major drainage basin

Minor drainage basin

Artificially diverted drainage area
  1 Nechako
  2 Lake St. Joseph
  3 Ogoki
  4 Long Lake

Internal drainage area

Gauging station

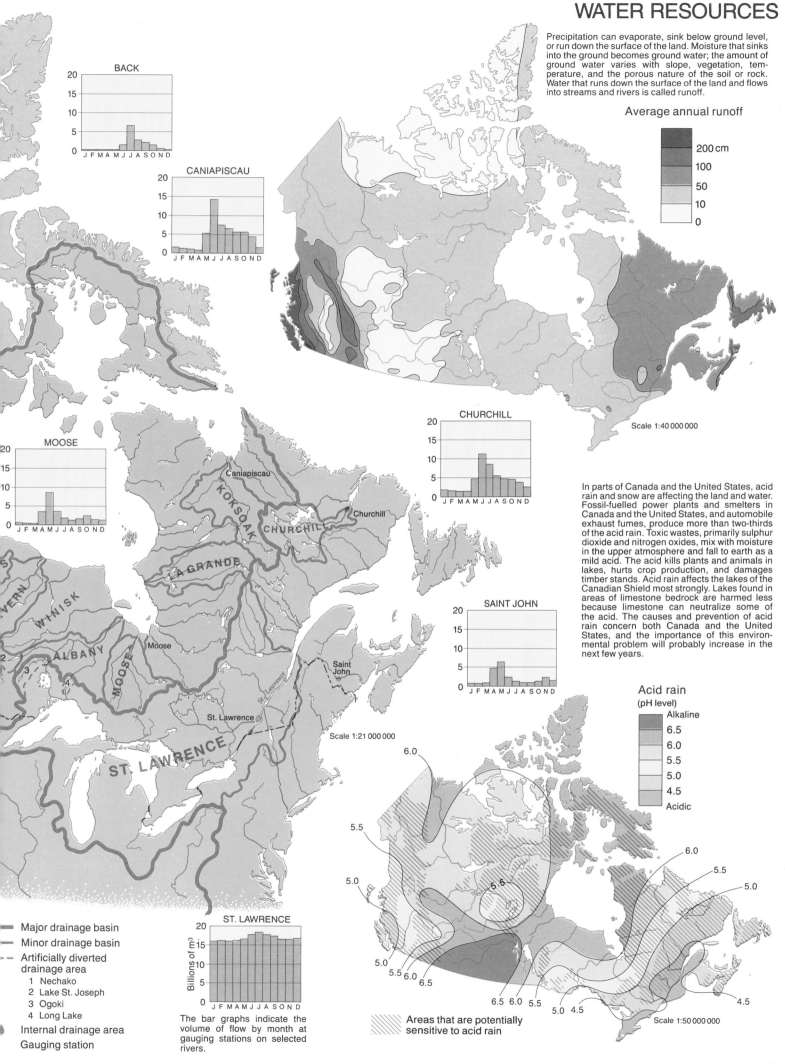

For explanation of terms, see glossary. 42

CANADA

SOIL PROFILES

ORGANIC LAYERS
Organic layers may consist of well drained plant litter, or poorly drained peat and moss layers in stages of decomposition.

A HORIZON
The A horizon consists of plant and animal litter. The most recent deposits lie on top of decomposing material. At the bottom is a modified zone in which water, percolating down, has removed soluble minerals.

B HORIZON
The B horizon contains the deposited soluble minerals from the A horizon. It is often possible to identify different layers within this horizon.

C HORIZON
The C horizon consists mainly of weathered parent material (bedrock). In many areas of Canada, the bedrock has been covered by glacial deposits; these deposits are the "parent material" for the soil's development.

The profile above illustrates the general structure of soil. Individual profiles of some soil groups shown on the map are given below.

Technically, soil is a natural body consisting of organic and inorganic materials, and capable of supporting plant growth. The inorganic materials include rock fragments, liquids, and gases. The liquids are in the form of complex solutions, and the gases, similar to those found in the atmosphere, are released by chemical activity in the soil. The organic matter consists of plant or animal materials, both living and dead. The most important living organisms are the bacteria and fungi which assist in the decaying process. They also produce soluble nitrogen, important for plant growth.

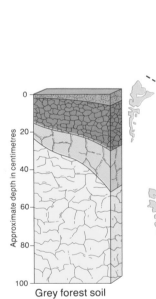

Alluvial soil

Grey forest soil

Dark brown soil

Black chernozem

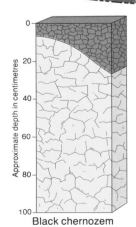

Areas of excessive stoniness and/or rock outcrops

Scale 1:60 000 000

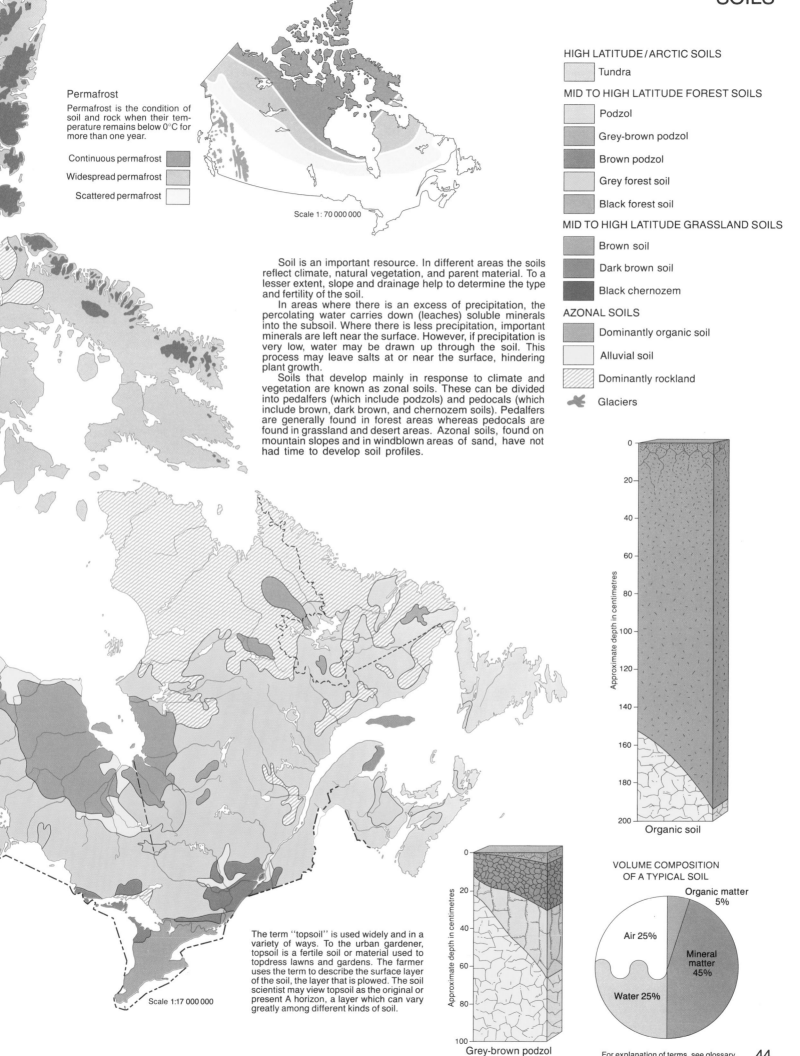

Permafrost

Permafrost is the condition of soil and rock when their temperature remains below 0°C for more than one year.

Continuous permafrost

Widespread permafrost

Scattered permafrost

Scale 1: 70 000 000

HIGH LATITUDE / ARCTIC SOILS

Tundra

MID TO HIGH LATITUDE FOREST SOILS

Podzol

Grey-brown podzol

Brown podzol

Grey forest soil

Black forest soil

MID TO HIGH LATITUDE GRASSLAND SOILS

Brown soil

Dark brown soil

Black chernozem

AZONAL SOILS

Dominantly organic soil

Alluvial soil

Dominantly rockland

Glaciers

Soil is an important resource. In different areas the soils reflect climate, natural vegetation, and parent material. To a lesser extent, slope and drainage help to determine the type and fertility of the soil.

In areas where there is an excess of precipitation, the percolating water carries down (leaches) soluble minerals into the subsoil. Where there is less precipitation, important minerals are left near the surface. However, if precipitation is very low, water may be drawn up through the soil. This process may leave salts at or near the surface, hindering plant growth.

Soils that develop mainly in response to climate and vegetation are known as zonal soils. These can be divided into pedalfers (which include podzols) and pedocals (which include brown, dark brown, and chernozem soils). Pedalfers are generally found in forest areas whereas pedocals are found in grassland and desert areas. Azonal soils, found on mountain slopes and in windblown areas of sand, have not had time to develop soil profiles.

Scale 1:17 000 000

The term "topsoil" is used widely and in a variety of ways. To the urban gardener, topsoil is a fertile soil or material used to topdress lawns and gardens. The farmer uses the term to describe the surface layer of the soil, the layer that is plowed. The soil scientist may view topsoil as the original or present A horizon, a layer which can vary greatly among different kinds of soil.

Approximate depth in centimetres

Organic soil

Approximate depth in centimetres

Grey-brown podzol

VOLUME COMPOSITION OF A TYPICAL SOIL

Organic matter 5%

Air 25%

Mineral matter 45%

Water 25%

For explanation of terms, see glossary.

CANADA

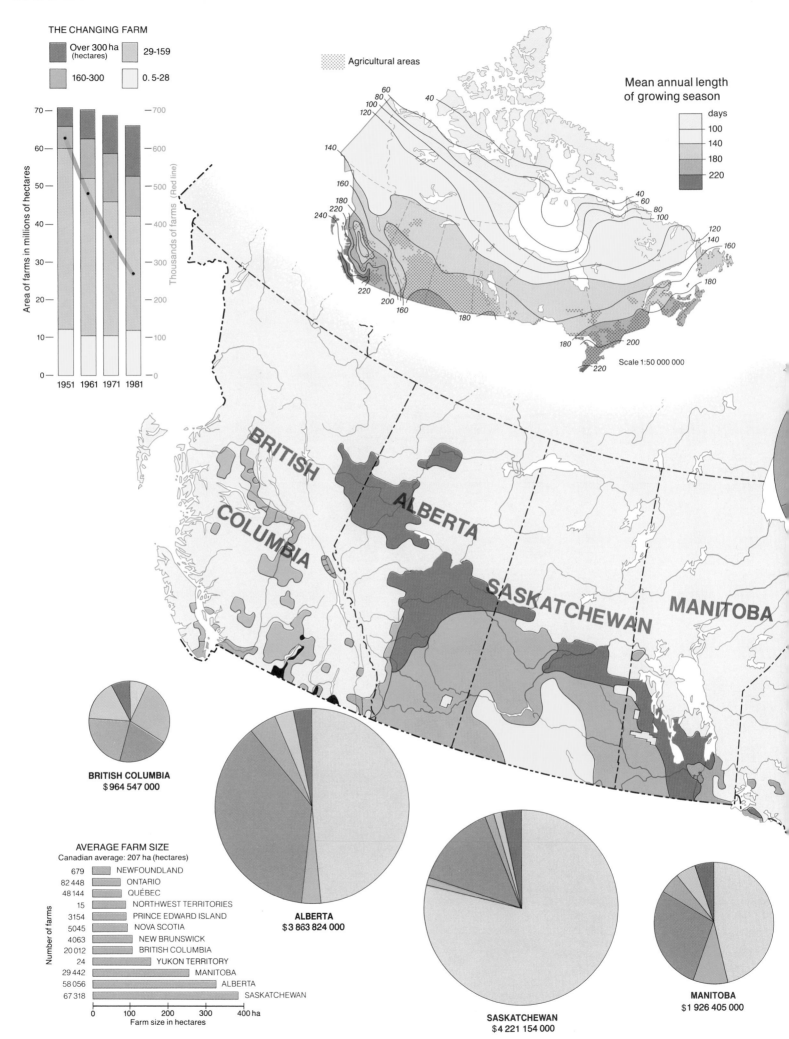

THE CHANGING FARM

- Over 300 ha (hectares)
- 160-300
- 29-159
- 0.5-28

Area of farms in millions of hectares

Thousands of farms (Red line)

1951 1961 1971 1981

Agricultural areas

Mean annual length of growing season

days
- 100
- 140
- 180
- 220

Scale 1:50 000 000

BRITISH COLUMBIA

COLUMBIA

ALBERTA

SASKATCHEWAN

MANITOBA

BRITISH COLUMBIA
$ 964 547 000

AVERAGE FARM SIZE
Canadian average: 207 ha (hectares)

Number of farms

679		NEWFOUNDLAND
82 448		ONTARIO
48 144		QUÉBEC
15		NORTHWEST TERRITORIES
3154		PRINCE EDWARD ISLAND
5045		NOVA SCOTIA
4063		NEW BRUNSWICK
20 012		BRITISH COLUMBIA
24		YUKON TERRITORY
29 442		MANITOBA
58 056		ALBERTA
67 318		SASKATCHEWAN

0   100   200   300   400 ha
Farm size in hectares

ALBERTA
$ 3 863 824 000

SASKATCHEWAN
$ 4 221 154 000

MANITOBA
$ 1 926 405 000

Most productive agriculture in Canada (90 percent by value) is found in the southern part of the prairie provinces and in southern Ontario and Québec. Other productive areas include southern British Columbia, lowlands in the Atlantic provinces, and the clay belts in Northern Ontario and Québec.

Some products are associated with certain regions — wheat with Saskatchewan, tobacco with southwestern Ontario, potatoes with Prince Edward Island, and cattle with interior British Columbia. However, many areas of Canada practice "mixed" farming, producing combinations of crops and animals.

Like other sectors of the Canadian economy, agriculture is constantly changing. The amount of land farmed has been decreasing as marginal areas have been abandoned. The number of active farms has also decreased but the average size of farms has grown. These changes reflect the fact that farming is big business in Canada. To be financially successful, a farm must either be large, or highly mechanized, or both.

FARMS CLASSIFIED BY PRODUCT TYPE

Poultry 2.0%
Wheat 20.5%
Beef cattle and hogs 26.7%
Other small grains 19.2%
Dairy products 15.4%
Other field crops 2.8%
Fruits and Vegetables 3.8%
Miscellaneous specialty 4.3%
Mixed farms 5.3%

CANADA 271 604 farms

VALUE OF PROVINCIAL AGRICULTURAL PRODUCTION

Poultry and Eggs
Dairy products
Other
Crops
Fruit and Vegetables
Livestock

CANADA $20 051 554 000

TYPES OF FARMING

- Wheat
- Beef cattle
- Beef cattle/Grain
- Grain/Mixed livestock
- Dairying/Mixed livestock
- Dairying/Beef cattle
- Potatoes/Mixed livestock
- Forest products from farms
- Tree fruits
- Tobacco
- Vegetables
- Non-agricultural areas

TOTAL LAND IN FARMS 65 940 000 ha
TOTAL CROPLAND 31 000 000 ha

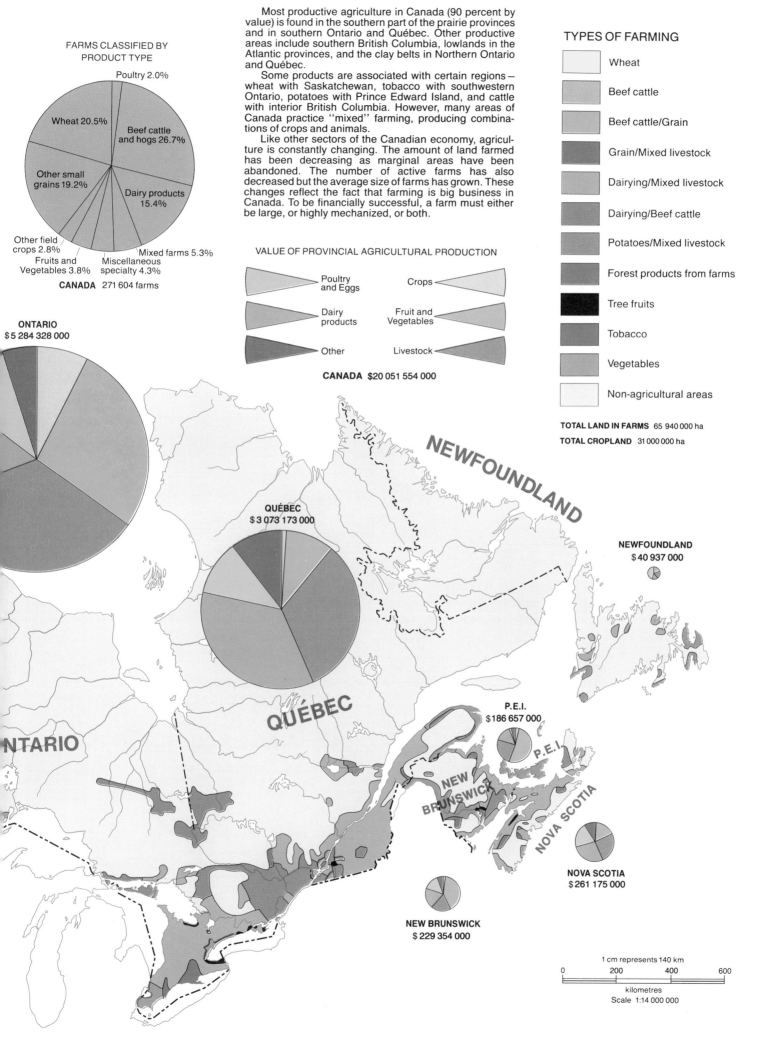

ONTARIO
$5 284 328 000

QUÉBEC
$3 073 173 000

NEWFOUNDLAND
$40 937 000

P.E.I.
$186 657 000

NOVA SCOTIA
$261 175 000

NEW BRUNSWICK
$229 354 000

1 cm represents 140 km
0   200   400   600
kilometres
Scale 1:14 000 000

CANADA

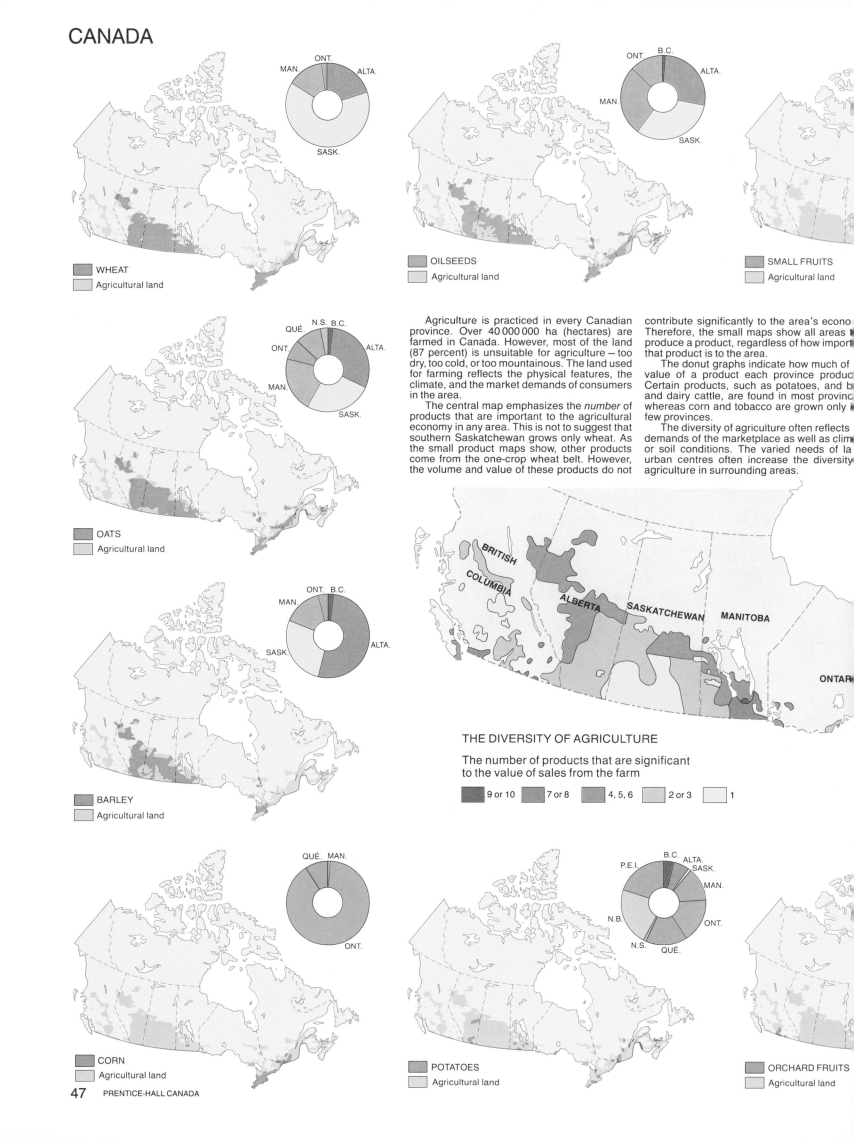

WHEAT
Agricultural land

OILSEEDS
Agricultural land

SMALL FRUITS
Agricultural land

OATS
Agricultural land

BARLEY
Agricultural land

CORN
Agricultural land

POTATOES
Agricultural land

ORCHARD FRUITS
Agricultural land

Agriculture is practiced in every Canadian province. Over 40 000 000 ha (hectares) are farmed in Canada. However, most of the land (87 percent) is unsuitable for agriculture — too dry, too cold, or too mountainous. The land used for farming reflects the physical features, the climate, and the market demands of consumers in the area.

The central map emphasizes the *number* of products that are important to the agricultural economy in any area. This is not to suggest that southern Saskatchewan grows only wheat. As the small product maps show, other products come from the one-crop wheat belt. However, the volume and value of these products do not contribute significantly to the area's econo Therefore, the small maps show all areas produce a product, regardless of how impor that product is to the area.

The donut graphs indicate how much of value of a product each province produc Certain products, such as potatoes, and b and dairy cattle, are found in most provinc whereas corn and tobacco are grown only few provinces.

The diversity of agriculture often reflects demands of the marketplace as well as clim or soil conditions. The varied needs of la urban centres often increase the diversity agriculture in surrounding areas.

THE DIVERSITY OF AGRICULTURE

The number of products that are significant to the value of sales from the farm

9 or 10   7 or 8   4, 5, 6   2 or 3   1

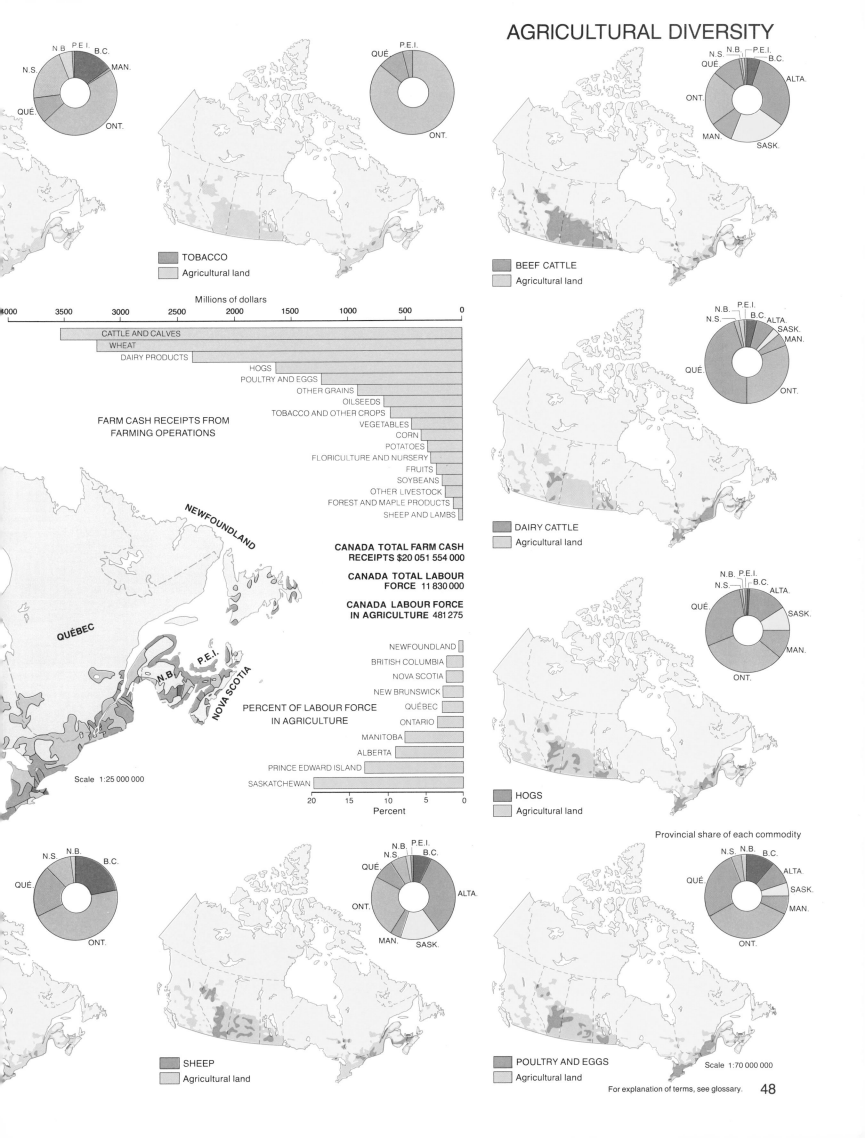

TOBACCO
Agricultural land

BEEF CATTLE
Agricultural land

Millions of dollars

4000   3500   3000   2500   2000   1500   1000   500   0

CATTLE AND CALVES
WHEAT
DAIRY PRODUCTS
HOGS
POULTRY AND EGGS
OTHER GRAINS
OILSEEDS
TOBACCO AND OTHER CROPS
VEGETABLES
CORN
POTATOES
FLORICULTURE AND NURSERY
FRUITS
SOYBEANS
OTHER LIVESTOCK
FOREST AND MAPLE PRODUCTS
SHEEP AND LAMBS

**FARM CASH RECEIPTS FROM
FARMING OPERATIONS**

NEWFOUNDLAND

QUÉBEC

P.E.I.

N.B.

NOVA SCOTIA

Scale 1:25 000 000

**CANADA TOTAL FARM CASH
RECEIPTS $20 051 554 000**

**CANADA TOTAL LABOUR
FORCE 11 830 000**

**CANADA LABOUR FORCE
IN AGRICULTURE 481 275**

NEWFOUNDLAND
BRITISH COLUMBIA
NOVA SCOTIA
NEW BRUNSWICK
QUÉBEC
ONTARIO
MANITOBA
ALBERTA
PRINCE EDWARD ISLAND
SASKATCHEWAN

**PERCENT OF LABOUR FORCE
IN AGRICULTURE**

20   15   10   5   0
Percent

DAIRY CATTLE
Agricultural land

HOGS
Agricultural land

Provincial share of each commodity

SHEEP
Agricultural land

POULTRY AND EGGS
Agricultural land

Scale 1:70 000 000

For explanation of terms, see glossary.   48

CANADA

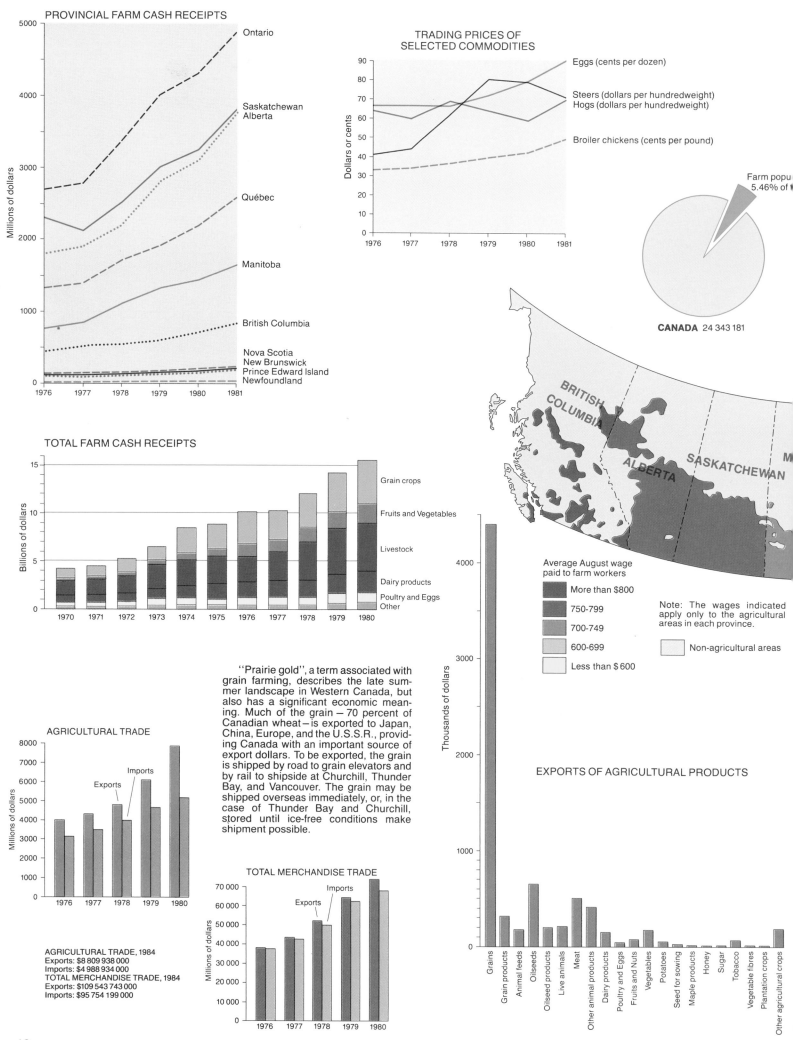

PROVINCIAL FARM CASH RECEIPTS

Millions of dollars

Ontario
Saskatchewan
Alberta
Québec
Manitoba
British Columbia
Nova Scotia
New Brunswick
Prince Edward Island
Newfoundland

1976 1977 1978 1979 1980 1981

TRADING PRICES OF SELECTED COMMODITIES

Dollars or cents

Eggs (cents per dozen)
Steers (dollars per hundredweight)
Hogs (dollars per hundredweight)
Broiler chickens (cents per pound)

1976 1977 1978 1979 1980 1981

Farm popu
5.46% of

CANADA 24 343 181

TOTAL FARM CASH RECEIPTS

Billions of dollars

Grain crops
Fruits and Vegetables
Livestock
Dairy products
Poultry and Eggs
Other

1970 1971 1972 1973 1974 1975 1976 1977 1978 1979 1980

Average August wage paid to farm workers

More than $800
750-799
700-749
600-699
Less than $ 600

Note: The wages indicated apply only to the agricultural areas in each province.

Non-agricultural areas

''Prairie gold'', a term associated with grain farming, describes the late summer landscape in Western Canada, but also has a significant economic meaning. Much of the grain — 70 percent of Canadian wheat — is exported to Japan, China, Europe, and the U.S.S.R., providing Canada with an important source of export dollars. To be exported, the grain is shipped by road to grain elevators and by rail to shipside at Churchill, Thunder Bay, and Vancouver. The grain may be shipped overseas immediately, or, in the case of Thunder Bay and Churchill, stored until ice-free conditions make shipment possible.

AGRICULTURAL TRADE

Millions of dollars

Imports
Exports

1976 1977 1978 1979 1980

AGRICULTURAL TRADE, 1984
Exports: $8 809 938 000
Imports: $4 988 934 000
TOTAL MERCHANDISE TRADE, 1984
Exports: $109 543 743 000
Imports: $95 754 199 000

TOTAL MERCHANDISE TRADE

Millions of dollars

Imports
Exports

1976 1977 1978 1979 1980

EXPORTS OF AGRICULTURAL PRODUCTS

Thousands of dollars

Grains
Grain products
Animal feeds
Oilseeds
Oilseed products
Live animals
Meat
Other animal products
Dairy products
Poultry and Eggs
Fruits and Nuts
Vegetables
Potatoes
Seed for sowing
Maple products
Honey
Sugar
Tobacco
Vegetable fibres
Plantation crops
Other agricultural crops

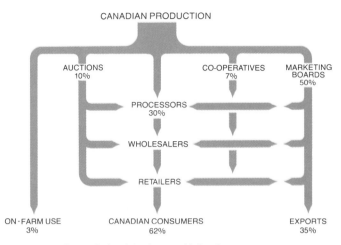

Industry

Percent
0 10 20 30 40 50 60 70 80 90 100

cco
er products
eum and coal
cts
portation equipment
rical products
l fuels
and allied products
mining

ture
ing
truction
ulture, Forestry and
ng
c utilities

FOREIGN-OWNED ASSETS
AS A PERCENT OF
TOTAL ASSETS IN CANADA

Statistics about agriculture can be deceiving. Here are some examples. Only one worker in 20 earns a living in agriculture. In the past 30 years, one out of every two farms has ceased to exist. Over 10 000 ha (hectares) of prime land are lost every year to urban use.

These statistics may create the impression that agriculture in Canada is small-scale and declining. However, this primary industry is big business, and has a major impact on Canada's economy. Largely Canadian owned and operated, agriculture creates many associated jobs in processing, transporting, regulating, and retailing. Farm sizes and land values are increasing rapidly. New technology brings to the industry new products, equipment, and methods every year.

THE AGRICULTURAL MARKETING SYSTEM

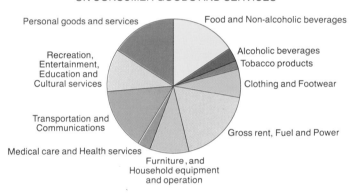

CANADIAN PRODUCTION

AUCTIONS 10%   CO-OPERATIVES 7%   MARKETING BOARDS 50%

PROCESSORS 30%

WHOLESALERS

RETAILERS

ON-FARM USE 3%   CANADIAN CONSUMERS 62%   EXPORTS 35%

Few agricultural goods are sold directly to consumers. A complex network takes farm products to their ultimate destination. Marketing boards and co-operatives have been developed to help stabilize the production and pricing of these products.

AGRICULTURAL WAGES

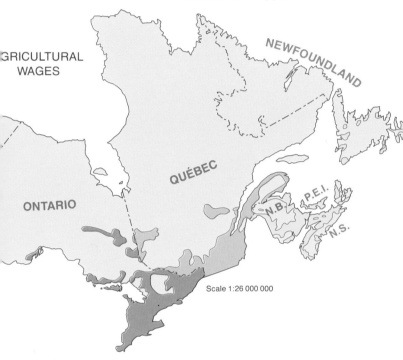

NEWFOUNDLAND

QUÉBEC

ONTARIO

N.B. P.E.I.

N.S.

Scale 1:26 000 000

TOTAL PERSONAL EXPENDITURE ON CONSUMER GOODS AND SERVICES

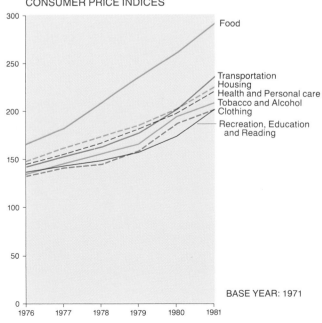

Personal goods and services

Food and Non-alcoholic beverages

Recreation, Entertainment, Education and Cultural services

Alcoholic beverages
Tobacco products

Clothing and Footwear

Transportation and Communications

Gross rent, Fuel and Power

Medical care and Health services

Furniture, and Household equipment and operation

The Consumer Price Index is a general indicator of the rate of price change for consumer goods and services. Using 100 as a base figure, the C.P.I. measures price changes, not actual price levels. If the price of a product has risen 5%, the index will stand at 105.

CONSUMER PRICE INDICES

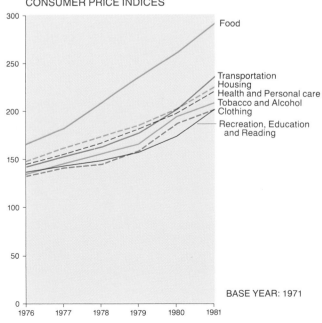

Food

Transportation
Housing
Health and Personal care
Tobacco and Alcohol
Clothing
Recreation, Education and Reading

BASE YEAR: 1971

1976 1977 1978 1979 1980 1981

IMPORTS OF AGRICULTURAL PRODUCTS

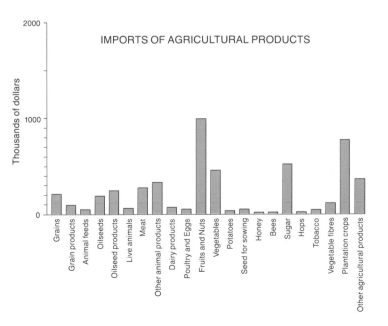

Thousands of dollars

2000

1000

0

Grains
Grain products
Animal feeds
Oilseeds
Oilseed products
Live animals
Meat
Other animal products
Dairy products
Poultry and Eggs
Fruits and Nuts
Vegetables
Potatoes
Seed for sowing
Honey
Bees
Sugar
Hops
Tobacco
Vegetable fibres
Plantation crops
Other agricultural products

For explanation of terms, see glossary. **50**

CANADA

Most of Canada is covered by forest, tundra, or grassland. These broad areas can be further divided into the vegetation regions shown on the central map. The different regions reflect the influence of climate, particularly temperature and precipitation. Within each region, differences in the type and extent of vegetative cover are caused by factors such as rock type, soil type, slope, and drainage conditions. People have often changed the state of the vegetation in many areas. For example, in grassland, parkland, and broadleaf forest regions, agricultural and urban land uses have been introduced, and the original natural vegetation has disappeared.

SURFACE COMPOSITION
OF CANADA

Tundra and exposed rock 30.9%

Forest 44.0%

Glaciers 2.3%

Wetland 8.2%

Fresh water 7.9%

Grassland and cropland 6.7%

YUKON TERRITORY

NORTHWEST TERRITORIES

BRITISH COLUMBIA

ALBERTA

SASKATCHEWAN

MANITOBA

Wildland fire occurrence

Frequent

Occasional

Rare

Very rare

Scale 1:50 000 000

Satellite image of a forest fire in the Northwest Territories

VEGETATION REGIONS AND CHARACTERISTIC FLORA

TUNDRA
- Lichen / heath
- Dwarf shrubs / sedges / lichen / heath
- Alpine sedges / grasses and shrubs

OPEN WOODLAND — Scattered needleleaf trees / broadleaf shrubs / heath / grass

BOGS — Moss / sedges / strings of needleleaf trees

BOREAL FOREST (TAIGA)
- Needleleaf trees
- Mostly needleleaf trees with some broadleaf trees

COASTAL FOREST — Large needleleaf trees

SUB-ALPINE FOREST — Needleleaf trees

HIGH PLATEAU / ALPINE FOREST — Mostly needleleaf trees with some broadleaf trees and grassland

SOUTHEASTERN MIXED FOREST — Mixture of broadleaf and needleleaf trees

SOUTHERN BROADLEAF FOREST — Broadleaf trees

PARKLAND — Broadleaf or needleleaf trees with patches of grassland

GRASSLAND — Low, medium, and tall grasses

Glaciers and permanent snow (no vegetation)

NEWFOUNDLAND

QUÉBEC

ONTARIO

P.E.I.

NEW BRUNSWICK

NOVA SCOTIA

Area near Wawa, Ontario

This satellite photograph shows the effect of pollutants from a smelter on nearby forests. The photograph was used in a court case involving the owners of the smelter who were charged with damage to the environment.

ch year, fires destroy over 00 000 ha (hectares) of est in Canada. Lightning s off some fires; others are used by people. The risk of depends on precipitation, d, humidity, and temperature.

1 cm represents 140 km

0   200   400   600

kilometres

Scale 1 : 14 000 000

For explanation of terms, see glossary. **52**

CANADA

Western Red Cedar

Douglas Fir

Lodgepole Pine

Western Hemlock

Trembling Aspen

Note: Trees are not drawn to a common scale.

Black Spruce

Engelmann Spruce

Sugar Maple

Balsam Fir

Most coniferous trees (spruce, pine, fir) are called softwoods; many deciduous trees (maple, oak, cherry, hickory) are called hardwoods. Many areas of deciduous forest have been largely cleared of trees. Because of this scarcity of hardwoods, the furniture industry uses veneers (thin hardwood layers over softwood structures) more frequently.

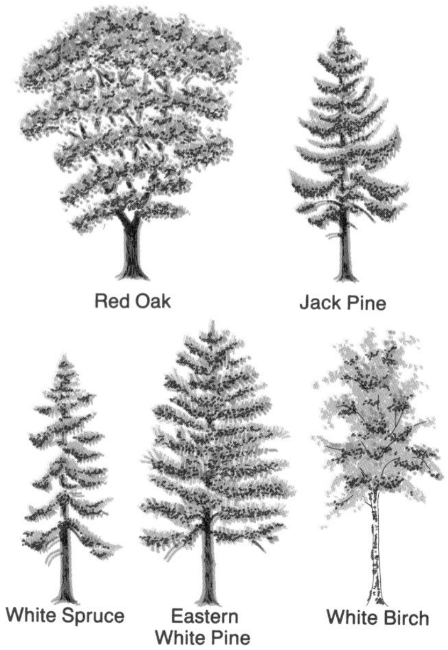

Red Oak

Jack Pine

White Spruce

Eastern White Pine

White Birch

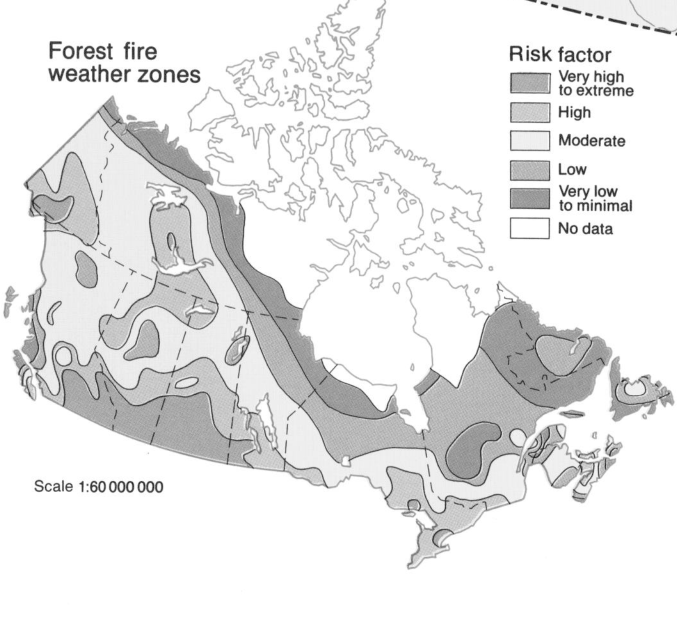

YUKON TERRITORY

NORTHWEST TERRITORIES

BRITISH COLUMBIA

ALBERTA

SASKATCHEWAN

MANITOBA

Millions of cubic metres

8000	7000	6000	5000	4000	3000	2000	1000

BRITISH COLUMBIA
ONTARIO
QUÉBEC
ALBERTA
NEW BRUNSWICK
NEWFOUNDLAND
MANITOBA
SASKATCHEWAN
YUKON TERRITORY
NOVA SCOTIA
NORTHWEST TERRITORIES

VOLUME OF STANDING TIMBER

Softwood
Hardwood

CANADA 19 281 000 000 m³

Forest fire weather zones

Risk factor
Very high to extreme
High
Moderate
Low
Very low to minimal
No data

Scale 1:60 000 000

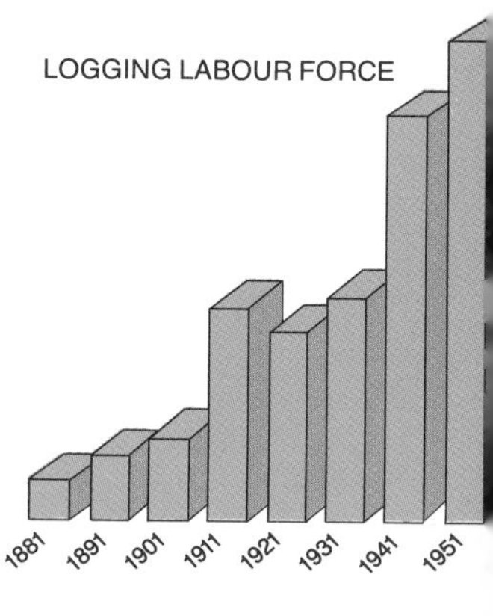

LOGGING LABOUR FORCE

1881 1891 1901 1911 1921 1931 1941 1951

FORESTRY

Canada's forests, which cover more than a third of the land area, are an important resource. When harvested, they create many export dollars, provide thousands of Canadians with jobs, and supply raw materials for many products such as lumber, paper, plywood, cellophane, cartons, and furniture. When left to grow, forests shelter wildlife, prevent erosion, and provide the opportunity for a variety of leisure activities. Harvesting, fire, insects, and diseases all consume this natural resource, but new trees can be planted to restore the supply of timber.

Saw mills are usually much smaller than pulp and paper mills, but more numerous. Pulp and paper mills are often large, integrated plants producing raw pulp for export, specialty papers, paperboard, and newsprint.

FOREST REGIONS AND PRINCIPAL TREE SPECIES

Region		Principal Tree Species
BOREAL	PREDOMINANTLY FOREST	Black Spruce, White Spruce, Balsam Fir, Jack Pine, White Birch, Trembling Aspen
	FOREST AND BARREN GROUND	Black Spruce, White Spruce, Tamarack
	FOREST AND GRASSLAND	Trembling Aspen, Willow
SUBALPINE		Alpine Fir, Engelmann Spruce, Lodgepole Pine
MONTANE		Douglas Fir, Lodgepole Pine, Ponderosa Pine, Trembling Aspen
COAST		Western Red Cedar, Western Hemlock, Douglas Fir, Sitka Spruce
COLUMBIA		Western Red Cedar, Western Hemlock, Douglas Fir
DECIDUOUS		Beech, Maple, Black Walnut, Hickory, Oak
GREAT LAKES- ST. LAWRENCE		Eastern White Pine, Eastern Hemlock, Red Pine, Yellow Birch, Maple, Oak
ACADIAN		Red Spruce, Balsam Fir, Maple, Yellow Birch
GRASSLAND		Trembling Aspen, Willow, Bur Oak
		No major tree species

∴∵∷ Each dot represents one saw mill

▲▲▲ Each symbol represents one pulp and paper mill with a production capacity of 300 t (tonnes) or more per day

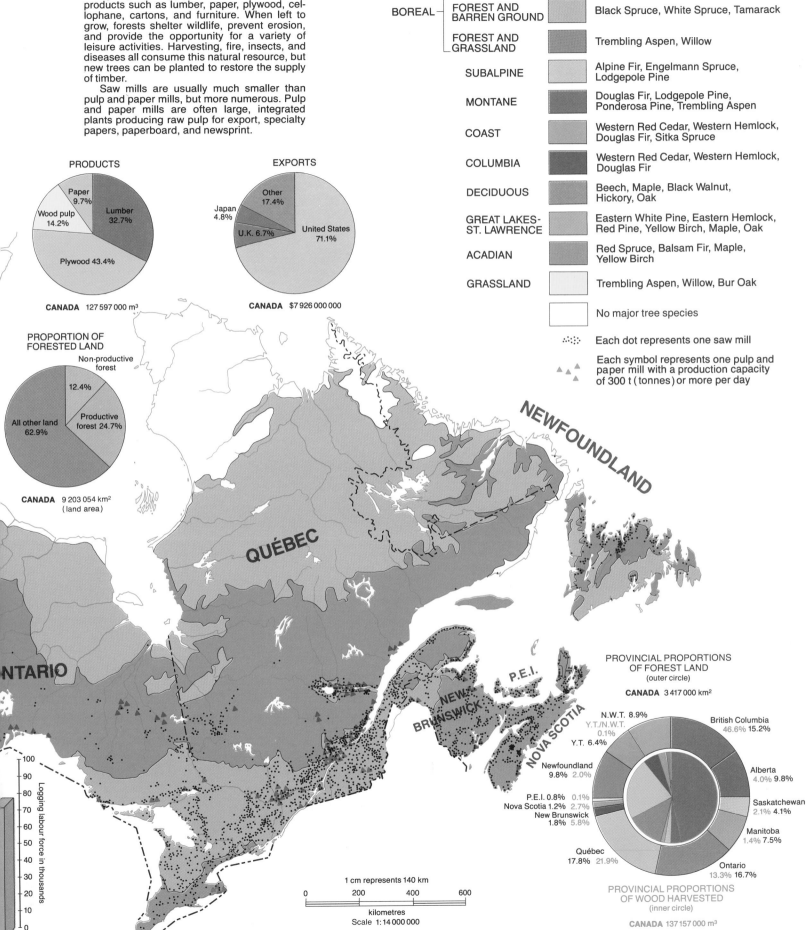

PRODUCTS
Paper 9.7%
Wood pulp 14.2%
Lumber 32.7%
Plywood 43.4%

CANADA 127 597 000 m³

EXPORTS
Other 17.4%
Japan 4.8%
U.K. 6.7%
United States 71.1%

CANADA $7 926 000 000

PROPORTION OF FORESTED LAND
Non-productive forest 12.4%
Productive forest 24.7%
All other land 62.9%

CANADA 9 203 054 km² (land area)

PROVINCIAL PROPORTIONS OF FOREST LAND
(outer circle)

CANADA 3 417 000 km²

N.W.T. 8.9%
Y.T./N.W.T. 0.1%
Y.T. 6.4%
British Columbia 46.6% 15.2%
Newfoundland 9.8% 2.0%
Alberta 4.0% 9.8%
P.E.I. 0.8% 0.1%
Nova Scotia 1.2% 2.7%
New Brunswick 1.8% 5.8%
Saskatchewan 2.1% 4.1%
Manitoba 1.4% 7.5%
Québec 17.8% 21.9%
Ontario 13.3% 16.7%

PROVINCIAL PROPORTIONS OF WOOD HARVESTED
(inner circle)

CANADA 137 157 000 m³

NEWFOUNDLAND

QUÉBEC

NTARIO

P.E.I.

NEW BRUNSWICK

NOVA SCOTIA

Logging labour force in thousands
100
90
80
70
60
50
40
30
20
10
0

1 cm represents 140 km
0   200   400   600
kilometres
Scale 1:14 000 000

CANADA

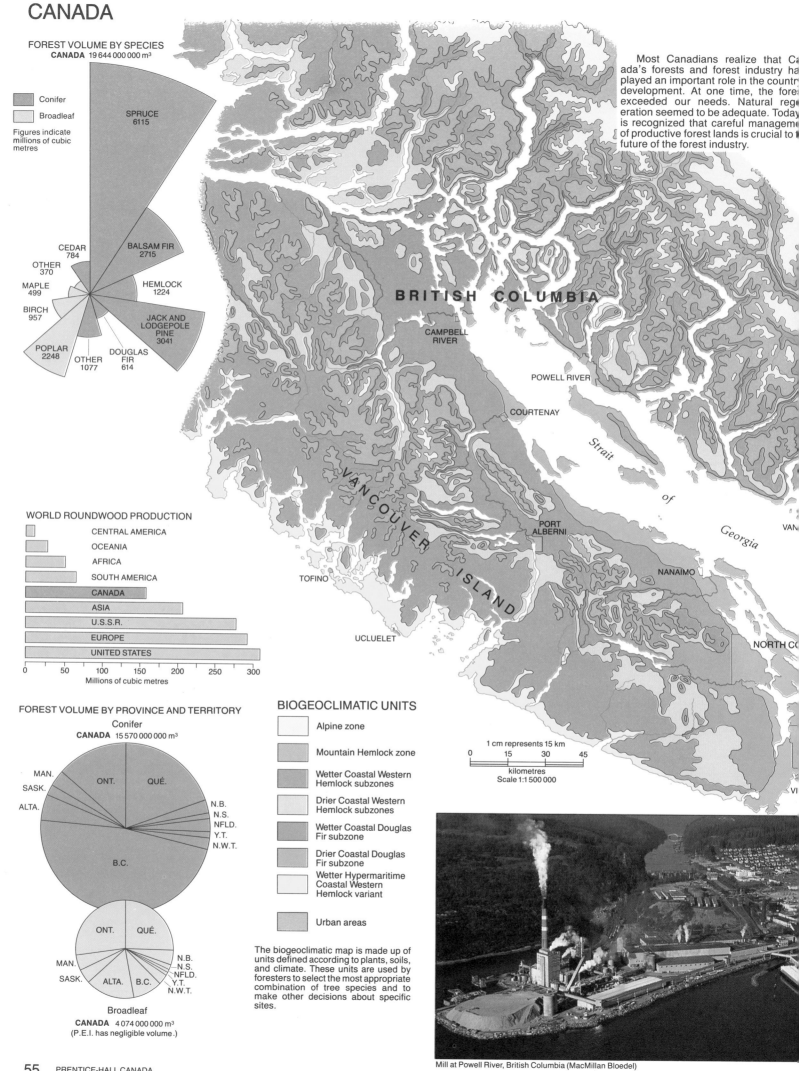

FOREST VOLUME BY SPECIES
CANADA 19 644 000 000 m³

- Conifer
- Broadleaf

Figures indicate millions of cubic metres

- SPRUCE 6115
- BALSAM FIR 2715
- CEDAR 784
- OTHER 370
- MAPLE 499
- BIRCH 957
- POPLAR 2248
- OTHER 1077
- DOUGLAS FIR 614
- JACK AND LODGEPOLE PINE 3041
- HEMLOCK 1224

WORLD ROUNDWOOD PRODUCTION

- CENTRAL AMERICA
- OCEANIA
- AFRICA
- SOUTH AMERICA
- CANADA
- ASIA
- U.S.S.R.
- EUROPE
- UNITED STATES

0 50 100 150 200 250 300
Millions of cubic metres

FOREST VOLUME BY PROVINCE AND TERRITORY

Conifer
CANADA 15 570 000 000 m³

ONT. QUÉ. MAN. SASK. ALTA. B.C. N.B. N.S. NFLD. Y.T. N.W.T.

Broadleaf
CANADA 4 074 000 000 m³
(P.E.I. has negligible volume.)

ONT. QUÉ. MAN. SASK. ALTA. B.C. N.B. N.S. NFLD. Y.T. N.W.T.

BIOGEOCLIMATIC UNITS

- Alpine zone
- Mountain Hemlock zone
- Wetter Coastal Western Hemlock subzones
- Drier Coastal Western Hemlock subzones
- Wetter Coastal Douglas Fir subzone
- Drier Coastal Douglas Fir subzone
- Wetter Hypermaritime Coastal Western Hemlock variant
- Urban areas

The biogeoclimatic map is made up of units defined according to plants, soils, and climate. These units are used by foresters to select the most appropriate combination of tree species and to make other decisions about specific sites.

Most Canadians realize that Canada's forests and forest industry have played an important role in the country's development. At one time, the forest exceeded our needs. Natural regeneration seemed to be adequate. Today is recognized that careful management of productive forest lands is crucial to the future of the forest industry.

BRITISH COLUMBIA

CAMPBELL RIVER
POWELL RIVER
COURTENAY
PORT ALBERNI
NANAIMO
TOFINO
UCLUELET
VANCOUVER ISLAND
Strait of Georgia
NORTH CO
VI

1 cm represents 15 km
0 15 30 45
kilometres
Scale 1:1 500 000

Mill at Powell River, British Columbia (MacMillan Bloedel)

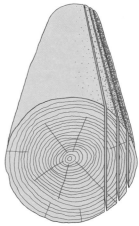

FROM LOG TO LUMBER

Logs are floated by water or hauled by land to mills. They are sorted by species, grade, and size. Large Douglas Fir logs with few knots are peeled into veneers at plywood mills. Medium-size and poorer grade logs go to sawmills. Here they are cut into lumber suitable for use in construction. Logs that are small, broken, and the poorest grades are cut into lumber or ground into pulp. The pulp may be converted into paper or exported.

First cutting

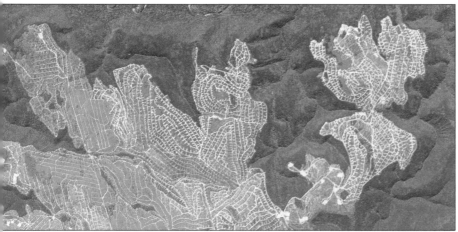

Infrared aerial photograph of forestry practices near Cranbrook, British Columbia

THE ANATOMY OF A TREE

BARK
The bark insulates the tree from extreme heat and cold, helps keep out moisture, and protects the tree against insect enemies.

INNER BARK OR PHLOEM
The phloem conducts food from the leaves to the rest of the tree. Eventually, it becomes part of the bark.

Second cutting

VASCULAR CAMBIUM LAYER
The cambium layer is one cell thick. It produces new bark and new wood annually in response to hormones that stimulate cell growth.

SAPWOOD
The sapwood is the pipeline for water moving from the roots to the leaves. When the inner cells of the sapwood lose their vitality, they turn into heartwood.

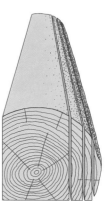

Third cutting

HEARTWOOD
The heartwood is the central supporting column for the tree. Although the heartwood is dead, it will not decay as long as the tree's outer layers remain intact.

THE STORY IN THE RINGS

- 1913: The pine tree is germinated.
- 1920: Undisturbed, the tree grows rapidly. Abundant moisture and light produce broad, evenly-spaced growth rings.
- 1936: A period of slow growth begins, possibly caused by a continued dry spell.
- 1942: A forest fire scars the tree, but in successive years the growth of new wood eventually covers the wound.
- 1955: Dry spells, competition from neighbouring trees, and insect attacks may be the cause of steady but slow growth.
- 1972: Surrounding trees are harvested, making available more nourishment and light. The tree grows quickly.
- 1984: The tree is harvested.

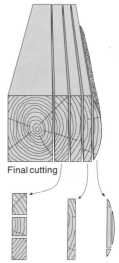

Final cutting

Milled lumber

Trees did not exist until the Carboniferous and Devonian periods about 300 000 000 a (years) ago. During these periods, the vascular cambium developed. The existing plants, which were weak and small, were gradually replaced by a different type of plant with strong woody stalks and branches.

Trees can be divided into two broad classes. Coniferous trees — for example, pine, spruce, and fir — have needle-like leaves. Their relatively soft wood is used for lumber and pulp and paper. Deciduous trees — for example, oak, maple, and ash — are broad-leafed trees. They provide hardwood for the lumber industry.

CANADA

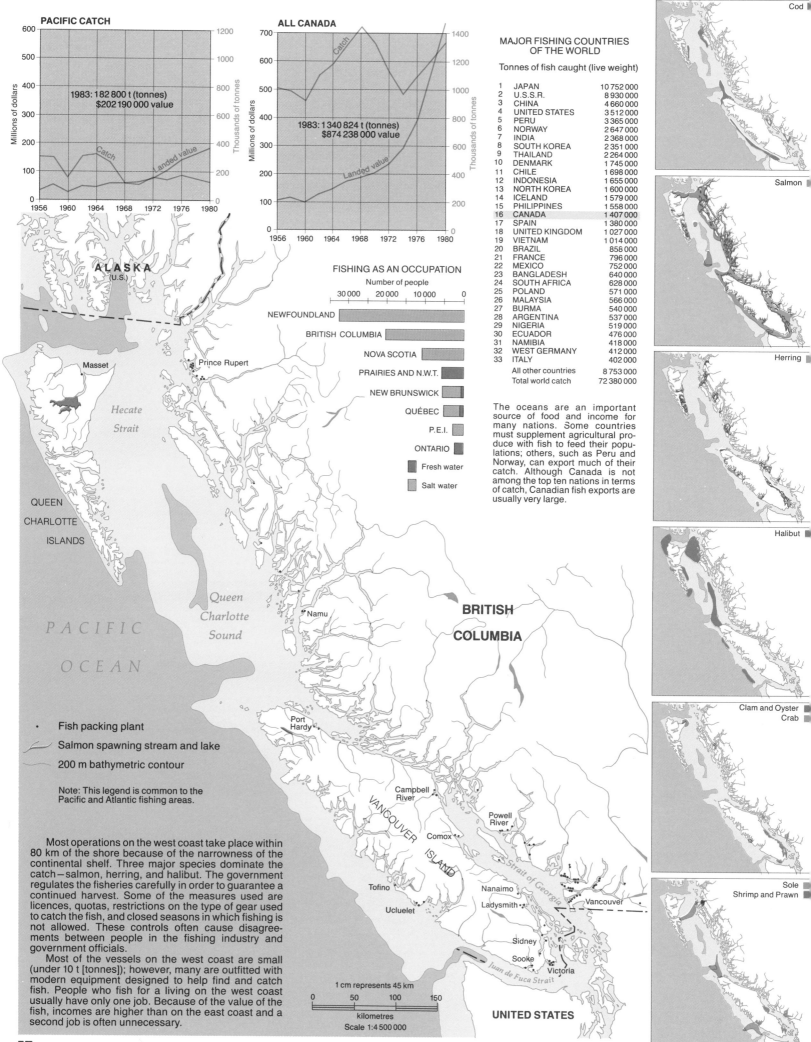

PACIFIC CATCH

1983: 182 800 t (tonnes)
$202 190 000 value

Catch
Landed value

1956 1960 1964 1968 1972 1976 1980

Millions of dollars
Thousands of tonnes

ALL CANADA

Catch

1983: 1 340 824 t (tonnes)
$874 238 000 value

Landed value

1956 1960 1964 1968 1972 1976 1980

Millions of dollars
Thousands of tonnes

MAJOR FISHING COUNTRIES OF THE WORLD

Tonnes of fish caught (live weight)

1	JAPAN	10 752 000
2	U.S.S.R.	8 930 000
3	CHINA	4 660 000
4	UNITED STATES	3 512 000
5	PERU	3 365 000
6	NORWAY	2 647 000
7	INDIA	2 368 000
8	SOUTH KOREA	2 351 000
9	THAILAND	2 264 000
10	DENMARK	1 745 000
11	CHILE	1 698 000
12	INDONESIA	1 655 000
13	NORTH KOREA	1 600 000
14	ICELAND	1 579 000
15	PHILIPPINES	1 558 000
16	CANADA	1 407 000
17	SPAIN	1 380 000
18	UNITED KINGDOM	1 027 000
19	VIETNAM	1 014 000
20	BRAZIL	858 000
21	FRANCE	796 000
22	MEXICO	752 000
23	BANGLADESH	640 000
24	SOUTH AFRICA	628 000
25	POLAND	571 000
26	MALAYSIA	566 000
27	BURMA	540 000
28	ARGENTINA	537 000
29	NIGERIA	519 000
30	ECUADOR	476 000
31	NAMIBIA	418 000
32	WEST GERMANY	412 000
33	ITALY	402 000
	All other countries	8 753 000
	Total world catch	72 380 000

The oceans are an important source of food and income for many nations. Some countries must supplement agricultural produce with fish to feed their populations; others, such as Peru and Norway, can export much of their catch. Although Canada is not among the top ten nations in terms of catch, Canadian fish exports are usually very large.

FISHING AS AN OCCUPATION

Number of people

30 000 20 000 10 000 0

NEWFOUNDLAND
BRITISH COLUMBIA
NOVA SCOTIA
PRAIRIES AND N.W.T.
NEW BRUNSWICK
QUÉBEC
P.E.I.
ONTARIO

Fresh water
Salt water

Cod
Salmon
Herring
Halibut
Clam and Oyster
Crab
Sole
Shrimp and Prawn

ALASKA
(U.S.)

Masset
Prince Rupert

Hecate
Strait

QUEEN
CHARLOTTE
ISLANDS

PACIFIC

OCEAN

Queen
Charlotte
Sound

Namu

BRITISH
COLUMBIA

Port
Hardy

Campbell
River

Powell
River

VANCOUVER

Comox

ISLAND

Tofino

Nanaimo
Ladysmith

Strait of Georgia

Vancouver

Ucluelet

Sidney

Sooke
Victoria

Juan de Fuca Strait

UNITED STATES

- Fish packing plant
- Salmon spawning stream and lake
- 200 m bathymetric contour

Note: This legend is common to the Pacific and Atlantic fishing areas.

Most operations on the west coast take place within 80 km of the shore because of the narrowness of the continental shelf. Three major species dominate the catch—salmon, herring, and halibut. The government regulates the fisheries carefully in order to guarantee a continued harvest. Some of the measures used are licences, quotas, restrictions on the type of gear used to catch the fish, and closed seasons in which fishing is not allowed. These controls often cause disagreements between people in the fishing industry and government officials.

Most of the vessels on the west coast are small (under 10 t [tonnes]); however, many are outfitted with modern equipment designed to help find and catch fish. People who fish for a living on the west coast usually have only one job. Because of the value of the fish, incomes are higher than on the east coast and a second job is often unnecessary.

1 cm represents 45 km

0   50   100   150
kilometres
Scale 1:4 500 000

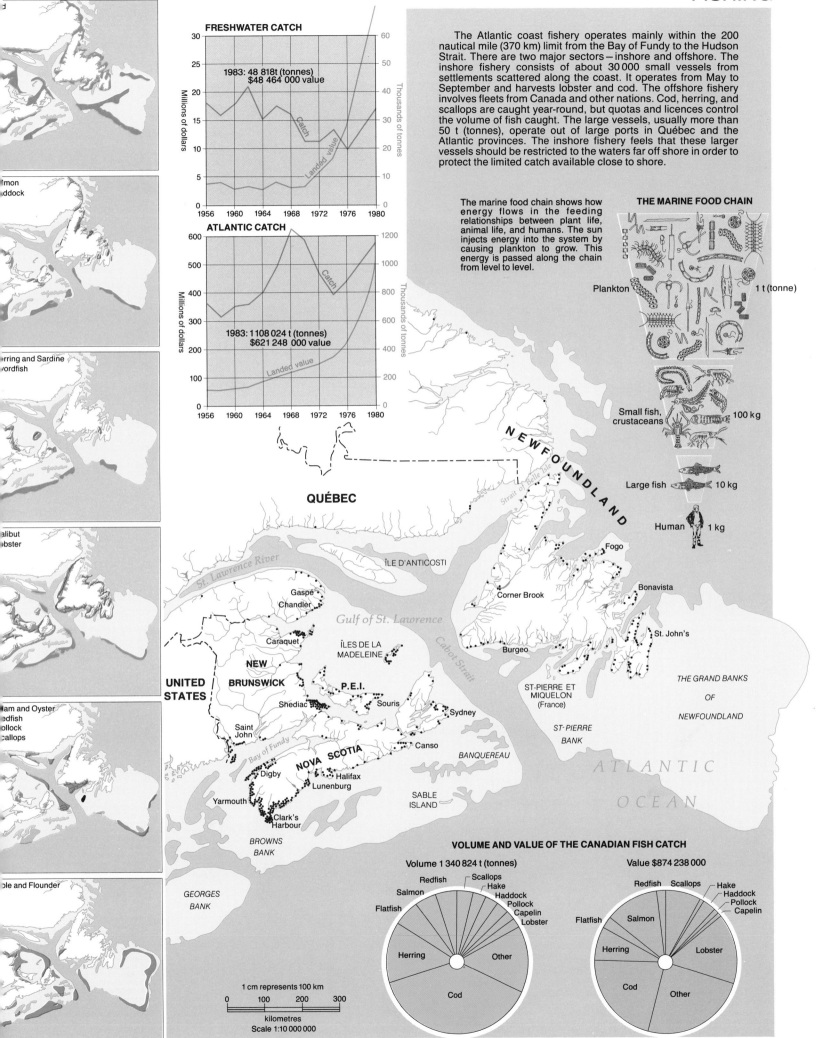

The Atlantic coast fishery operates mainly within the 200 nautical mile (370 km) limit from the Bay of Fundy to the Hudson Strait. There are two major sectors—inshore and offshore. The inshore fishery consists of about 30 000 small vessels from settlements scattered along the coast. It operates from May to September and harvests lobster and cod. The offshore fishery involves fleets from Canada and other nations. Cod, herring, and scallops are caught year-round, but quotas and licences control the volume of fish caught. The large vessels, usually more than 50 t (tonnes), operate out of large ports in Québec and the Atlantic provinces. The inshore fishery feels that these larger vessels should be restricted to the waters far off shore in order to protect the limited catch available close to shore.

FRESHWATER CATCH

1983: 48 818t (tonnes)
$48 464 000 value

Catch

Landed value

Millions of dollars

Thousands of tonnes

ATLANTIC CATCH

1983: 1 108 024 t (tonnes)
$621 248 000 value

Catch

Landed value

Millions of dollars

Thousands of tonnes

The marine food chain shows how energy flows in the feeding relationships between plant life, animal life, and humans. The sun injects energy into the system by causing plankton to grow. This energy is passed along the chain from level to level.

THE MARINE FOOD CHAIN

Plankton — 1 t (tonne)

Small fish, crustaceans — 100 kg

Large fish — 10 kg

Human — 1 kg

QUÉBEC

NEWFOUNDLAND

St. Lawrence River

ÎLE D'ANTICOSTI

Strait of Belle Isle

Gulf of St. Lawrence

Gaspé

Chandler

Caraquet

ÎLES DE LA MADELEINE

Fogo

Corner Brook

Bonavista

St. John's

NEW BRUNSWICK

P.E.I.

Souris

Burgeo

ST-PIERRE ET MIQUELON (France)

THE GRAND BANKS OF NEWFOUNDLAND

UNITED STATES

Shediac

Sydney

Cabot Strait

Saint John

Canso

ST-PIERRE BANK

Bay of Fundy

NOVA SCOTIA

BANQUEREAU

ATLANTIC

Digby

Halifax

Lunenburg

SABLE ISLAND

OCEAN

Yarmouth

Clark's Harbour

BROWNS BANK

GEORGES BANK

1 cm represents 100 km

0   100   200   300

kilometres

Scale 1:10 000 000

VOLUME AND VALUE OF THE CANADIAN FISH CATCH

Volume 1 340 824 t (tonnes)

Redfish
Salmon
Flatfish
Scallops
Hake
Haddock
Pollock
Capelin
Lobster
Herring
Other
Cod

Value $874 238 000

Redfish
Scallops
Hake
Haddock
Pollock
Capelin
Flatfish
Salmon
Herring
Lobster
Cod
Other

CANADA

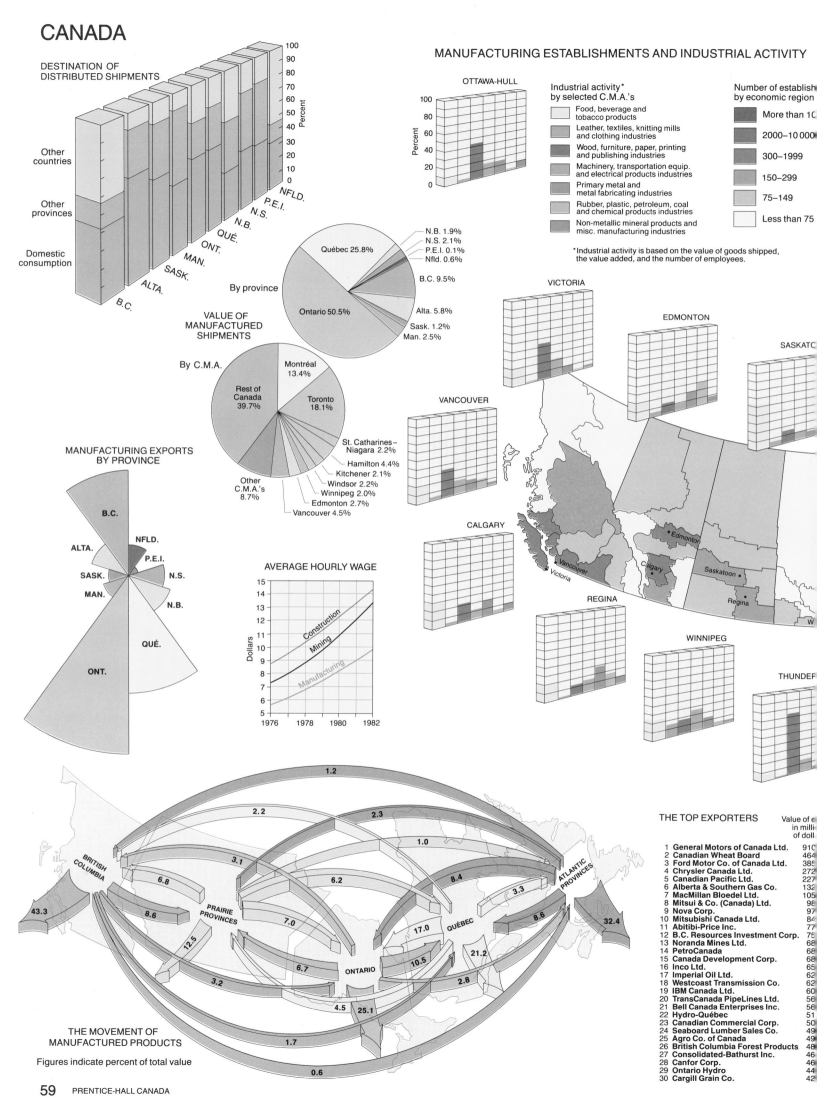

DESTINATION OF DISTRIBUTED SHIPMENTS

Other countries

Other provinces

Domestic consumption

B.C.
ALTA.
SASK.
MAN.
ONT.
QUÉ.
N.B.
N.S.
P.E.I.
NFLD.

Percent

VALUE OF MANUFACTURED SHIPMENTS

By province

Québec 25.8%
N.B. 1.9%
N.S. 2.1%
P.E.I. 0.1%
Nfld. 0.6%
B.C. 9.5%
Alta. 5.8%
Sask. 1.2%
Man. 2.5%
Ontario 50.5%

By C.M.A.

Montréal 13.4%
Rest of Canada 39.7%
Toronto 18.1%
St. Catharines–Niagara 2.2%
Hamilton 4.4%
Kitchener 2.1%
Windsor 2.2%
Winnipeg 2.0%
Edmonton 2.7%
Vancouver 4.5%
Other C.M.A.'s 8.7%

MANUFACTURING EXPORTS BY PROVINCE

B.C.
ALTA.
SASK.
MAN.
NFLD.
P.E.I.
N.S.
N.B.
QUÉ.
ONT.

AVERAGE HOURLY WAGE

Dollars

Construction
Mining
Manufacturing

1976 1978 1980 1982

MANUFACTURING ESTABLISHMENTS AND INDUSTRIAL ACTIVITY

OTTAWA-HULL

Percent

Industrial activity* by selected C.M.A.'s

- Food, beverage and tobacco products
- Leather, textiles, knitting mills and clothing industries
- Wood, furniture, paper, printing and publishing industries
- Machinery, transportation equip. and electrical products industries
- Primary metal and metal fabricating industries
- Rubber, plastic, petroleum, coal and chemical products industries
- Non-metallic mineral products and misc. manufacturing industries

Number of establish by economic region

- More than 10
- 2000–10 000
- 300–1999
- 150–299
- 75–149
- Less than 75

*Industrial activity is based on the value of goods shipped, the value added, and the number of employees.

VICTORIA
EDMONTON
SASKATC
VANCOUVER
CALGARY
REGINA
WINNIPEG
THUNDER
W

Edmonton
Vancouver
Calgary
Victoria
Saskatoon
Regina

THE MOVEMENT OF MANUFACTURED PRODUCTS

Figures indicate percent of total value

1.2
2.2
2.3
1.0
3.1
6.8
6.2
8.4
3.3
43.3
8.6
7.0
17.0
10.5
21.2
8.6
32.4
12.5
6.7
2.8
3.2
4.5
25.1
1.7
0.6

BRITISH COLUMBIA
PRAIRIE PROVINCES
ONTARIO
QUÉBEC
ATLANTIC PROVINCES

THE TOP EXPORTERS

Value of e in milli of doll

1	General Motors of Canada Ltd.	910
2	Canadian Wheat Board	464
3	Ford Motor Co. of Canada Ltd.	385
4	Chrysler Canada Ltd.	272
5	Canadian Pacific Ltd.	227
6	Alberta & Southern Gas Co.	132
7	MacMillan Bloedel Ltd.	105
8	Mitsui & Co. (Canada) Ltd.	98
9	Nova Corp.	97
10	Mitsubishi Canada Ltd.	84
11	Abitibi-Price Inc.	77
12	B.C. Resources Investment Corp.	75
13	Noranda Mines Ltd.	68
14	PetroCanada	68
15	Canada Development Corp.	68
16	Inco Ltd.	65
17	Imperial Oil Ltd.	62
18	Westcoast Transmission Co.	62
19	IBM Canada Ltd.	60
20	TransCanada PipeLines Ltd.	56
21	Bell Canada Enterprises Inc.	56
22	Hydro-Québec	51
23	Canadian Commercial Corp.	50
24	Seaboard Lumber Sales Co.	49
25	Agro Co. of Canada	49
26	British Columbia Forest Products	48
27	Consolidated-Bathurst Inc.	46
28	Canfor Corp.	46
29	Ontario Hydro	44
30	Cargill Grain Co.	42

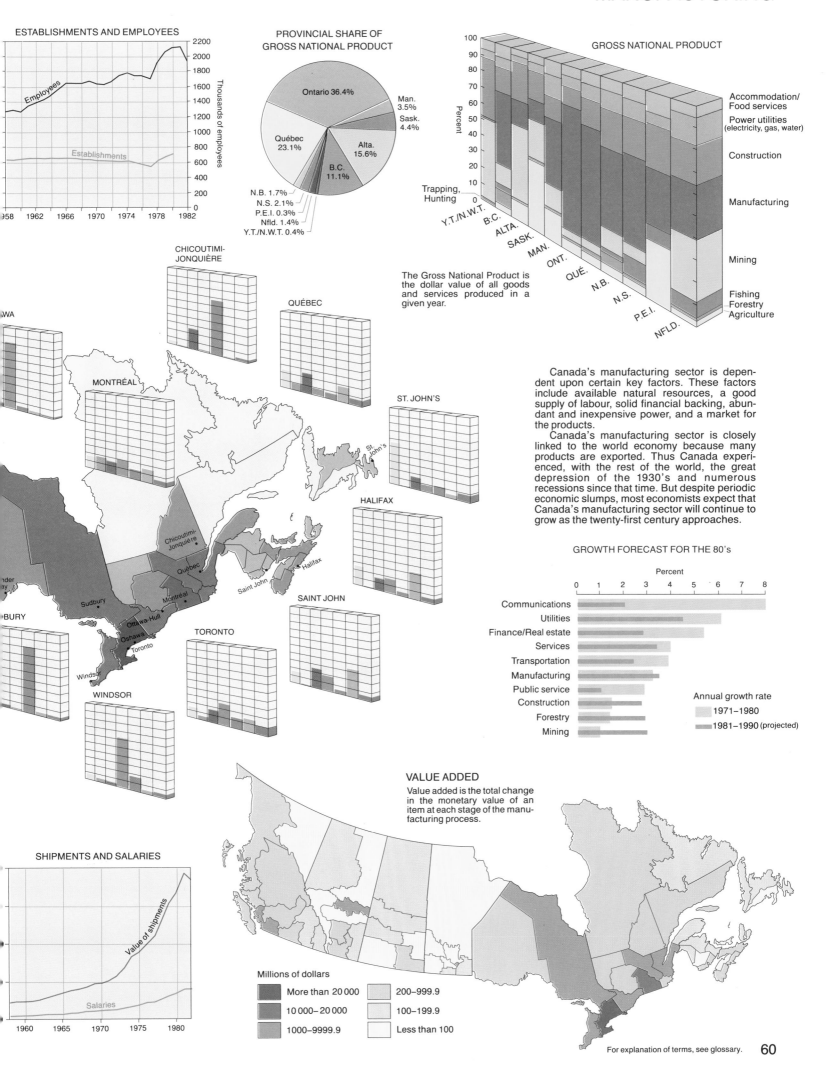

ESTABLISHMENTS AND EMPLOYEES

Thousands of employees

Employees

Establishments

958 1962 1966 1970 1974 1978 1982

PROVINCIAL SHARE OF GROSS NATIONAL PRODUCT

Ontario 36.4%

Man. 3.5%

Sask. 4.4%

Québec 23.1%

Alta. 15.6%

B.C. 11.1%

N.B. 1.7%
N.S. 2.1%
P.E.I. 0.3%
Nfld. 1.4%
Y.T./N.W.T. 0.4%

GROSS NATIONAL PRODUCT

Percent

Accommodation/Food services

Power utilities (electricity, gas, water)

Construction

Manufacturing

Trapping, Hunting

Y.T./N.W.T.
B.C.
ALTA.
SASK.
MAN.
ONT.
QUÉ.
N.B.
N.S.
P.E.I.
NFLD.

Mining

Fishing
Forestry
Agriculture

The Gross National Product is the dollar value of all goods and services produced in a given year.

Canada's manufacturing sector is dependent upon certain key factors. These factors include available natural resources, a good supply of labour, solid financial backing, abundant and inexpensive power, and a market for the products.

Canada's manufacturing sector is closely linked to the world economy because many products are exported. Thus Canada experienced, with the rest of the world, the great depression of the 1930's and numerous recessions since that time. But despite periodic economic slumps, most economists expect that Canada's manufacturing sector will continue to grow as the twenty-first century approaches.

GROWTH FORECAST FOR THE 80's

Percent

0 1 2 3 4 5 6 7 8

Communications
Utilities
Finance/Real estate
Services
Transportation
Manufacturing
Public service
Construction
Forestry
Mining

Annual growth rate

1971–1980
1981–1990 (projected)

CHICOUTIMI-JONQUIÈRE

QUÉBEC

WA

MONTRÉAL

ST. JOHN'S

St. John's

HALIFAX

Thunder Bay

Sudbury

Chicoutimi-Jonquière

Québec

Halifax

Saint John

Montréal

BURY

Ottawa-Hull

Oshawa

Toronto

Windsor

SAINT JOHN

TORONTO

WINDSOR

VALUE ADDED

Value added is the total change in the monetary value of an item at each stage of the manufacturing process.

SHIPMENTS AND SALARIES

Value of shipments

Salaries

1960 1965 1970 1975 1980

Millions of dollars

More than 20 000

10 000–20 000

1000–9999.9

200–999.9

100–199.9

Less than 100

CANADA

TWO-INCOME HOUSEHOLDS

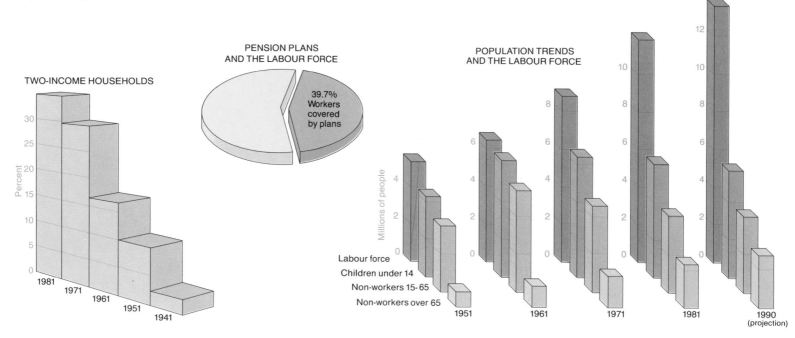

Percent

30
25
20
15
10
5
0

1981 1971 1961 1951 1941

PENSION PLANS AND THE LABOUR FORCE

39.7% Workers covered by plans

POPULATION TRENDS AND THE LABOUR FORCE

Millions of people

Labour force
Children under 14
Non-workers 15-65
Non-workers over 65

1951   1961   1971   1981   1990 (projection)

AVERAGE WEEKLY EARNINGS BY INDUSTRY

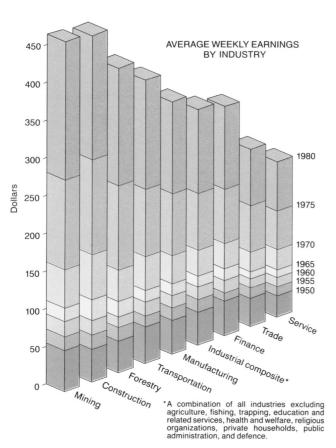

Dollars

450
400
350
300
250
200
150
100
50
0

1980
1975
1970
1965
1960
1955
1950

Mining
Construction
Forestry
Transportation
Manufacturing
Industrial composite*
Finance
Trade
Service

*A combination of all industries excluding agriculture, fishing, trapping, education and related services, health and welfare, religious organizations, private households, public administration, and defence.

PERCENT OF TOTAL LABOUR FORCE BY PROVINCE

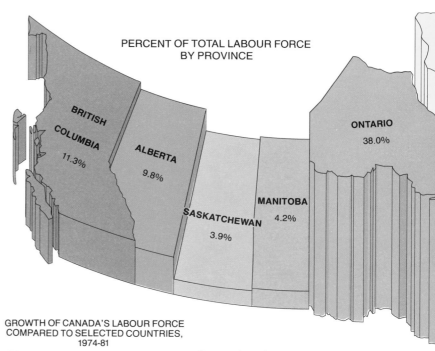

BRITISH COLUMBIA 11.3%
ALBERTA 9.8%
SASKATCHEWAN 3.9%
MANITOBA 4.2%
ONTARIO 38.0%

GROWTH OF CANADA'S LABOUR FORCE COMPARED TO SELECTED COUNTRIES, 1974-81

WEST GERMANY
UNITED KINGDOM
ITALY
JAPAN
UNITED STATES
CANADA

0   5   10   15   20
Percent

Compared to other countries, Canada's total labour force has grown substantially in recent years. Employment patterns vary according to type of employment, geographic location, and the worker's age and sex. Unemployment tends to be high among the youth of the country and in specific regions such as the Maritimes.

MEN AND WOMEN AS PERCENT OF ADULT* POPULATION IN THE LABOUR FORCE

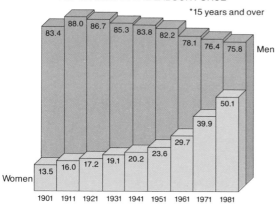

*15 years and over

Men: 83.4 88.0 86.7 85.3 83.8 82.2 78.1 76.4 75.8

Women: 13.5 16.0 17.2 19.1 20.2 23.6 29.7 39.9 50.1

1901 1911 1921 1931 1941 1951 1961 1971 1981

MEN AND WOMEN AS PERCENT OF THE LABOUR FORCE

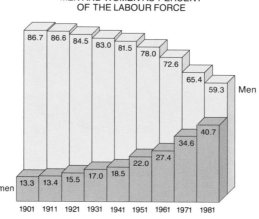

Men: 86.7 86.6 84.5 83.0 81.5 78.0 72.6 65.4 59.3

Women: 13.3 13.4 15.5 17.0 18.5 22.0 27.4 34.6 40.7

1901 1911 1921 1931 1941 1951 1961 1971 1981

THE GROWTH OF THE LABOUR FORCE

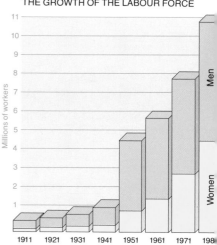

Millions of workers

11
10
9
8
7
6
5
4
3
2
1

Men
Women

1911 1921 1931 1941 1951 1961 1971 198

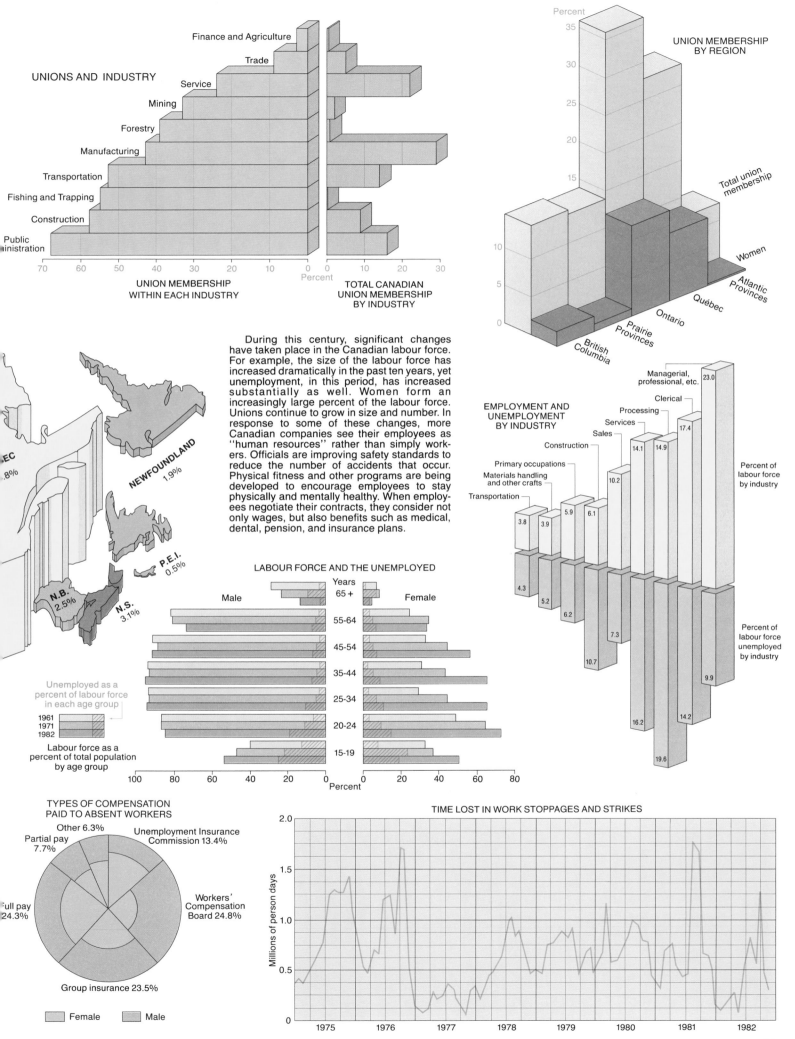

UNIONS AND INDUSTRY

Finance and Agriculture
Trade
Service
Mining
Forestry
Manufacturing
Transportation
Fishing and Trapping
Construction
Public Administration

UNION MEMBERSHIP
WITHIN EACH INDUSTRY

TOTAL CANADIAN
UNION MEMBERSHIP
BY INDUSTRY

Percent

UNION MEMBERSHIP
BY REGION

Total union membership
Women

British Columbia
Prairie Provinces
Ontario
Québec
Atlantic Provinces

During this century, significant changes have taken place in the Canadian labour force. For example, the size of the labour force has increased dramatically in the past ten years, yet unemployment, in this period, has increased substantially as well. Women form an increasingly large percent of the labour force. Unions continue to grow in size and number. In response to some of these changes, more Canadian companies see their employees as ''human resources'' rather than simply workers. Officials are improving safety standards to reduce the number of accidents that occur. Physical fitness and other programs are being developed to encourage employees to stay physically and mentally healthy. When employees negotiate their contracts, they consider not only wages, but also benefits such as medical, dental, pension, and insurance plans.

EMPLOYMENT AND
UNEMPLOYMENT
BY INDUSTRY

Managerial, professional, etc. 23.0
Clerical 17.4
Processing 14.9
Services 14.1
Sales 10.2
Construction 6.1
Primary occupations 5.9
Materials handling and other crafts 3.9
Transportation 3.8

Percent of labour force by industry

4.3
5.2
6.2
7.3
10.7
9.9
16.2
14.2
19.6

Percent of labour force unemployed by industry

NEWFOUNDLAND 1.9%
P.E.I. 0.5%
N.B. 2.5%
N.S. 3.1%
EC .8%

LABOUR FORCE AND THE UNEMPLOYED

Years
Male
65 +
55-64
45-54
35-44
25-34
20-24
15-19
Female

Unemployed as a percent of labour force in each age group

1961
1971
1982

Labour force as a percent of total population by age group

Percent

TYPES OF COMPENSATION PAID TO ABSENT WORKERS

Other 6.3%
Partial pay 7.7%
Unemployment Insurance Commission 13.4%
Full pay 24.3%
Workers' Compensation Board 24.8%
Group insurance 23.5%

Female   Male

TIME LOST IN WORK STOPPAGES AND STRIKES

Millions of person days

2.0
1.5
1.0
0.5
0

1975   1976   1977   1978   1979   1980   1981   1982

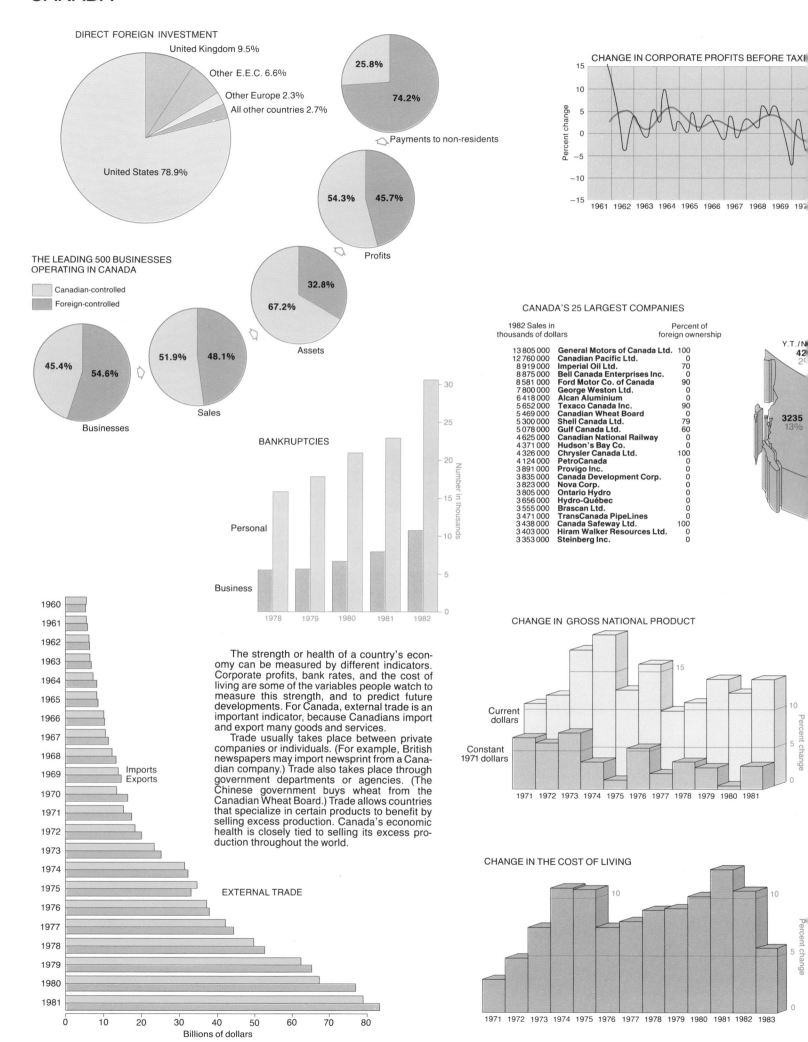

DIRECT FOREIGN INVESTMENT

United Kingdom 9.5%

Other E.E.C. 6.6%

Other Europe 2.3%

All other countries 2.7%

United States 78.9%

25.8%

74.2%

⟵ Payments to non-residents

54.3% 45.7%

⟵ Profits

THE LEADING 500 BUSINESSES OPERATING IN CANADA

- Canadian-controlled
- Foreign-controlled

45.4% 54.6%

Businesses

51.9% 48.1%

Sales

32.8%

67.2%

Assets

CHANGE IN CORPORATE PROFITS BEFORE TAXES

Percent change

15 10 5 0 −5 −10 −15

1961 1962 1963 1964 1965 1966 1967 1968 1969 197

BANKRUPTCIES

Number in thousands

30 25 20 15 10 5 0

Personal

Business

1978 1979 1980 1981 1982

CANADA'S 25 LARGEST COMPANIES

1982 Sales in thousands of dollars		Percent of foreign ownership
13 805 000	General Motors of Canada Ltd.	100
12 760 000	Canadian Pacific Ltd.	0
8 919 000	Imperial Oil Ltd.	70
8 875 000	Bell Canada Enterprises Inc.	0
8 581 000	Ford Motor Co. of Canada	90
7 800 000	George Weston Ltd.	0
6 418 000	Alcan Aluminium	0
5 652 000	Texaco Canada Inc.	90
5 469 000	Canadian Wheat Board	0
5 300 000	Shell Canada Ltd.	79
5 078 000	Gulf Canada Ltd.	60
4 625 000	Canadian National Railway	0
4 371 000	Hudson's Bay Co.	0
4 326 000	Chrysler Canada Ltd.	100
4 124 000	PetroCanada	0
3 891 000	Provigo Inc.	0
3 835 000	Canada Development Corp.	0
3 823 000	Nova Corp.	0
3 805 000	Ontario Hydro	0
3 656 000	Hydro-Québec	0
3 555 000	Brascan Ltd.	0
3 471 000	TransCanada PipeLines	0
3 438 000	Canada Safeway Ltd.	100
3 403 000	Hiram Walker Resources Ltd.	0
3 353 000	Steinberg Inc.	0

Y.T./N

42

3235

13%

The strength or health of a country's economy can be measured by different indicators. Corporate profits, bank rates, and the cost of living are some of the variables people watch to measure this strength, and to predict future developments. For Canada, external trade is an important indicator, because Canadians import and export many goods and services.

Trade usually takes place between private companies or individuals. (For example, British newspapers may import newsprint from a Canadian company.) Trade also takes place through government departments or agencies. (The Chinese government buys wheat from the Canadian Wheat Board.) Trade allows countries that specialize in certain products to benefit by selling excess production. Canada's economic health is closely tied to selling its excess production throughout the world.

EXTERNAL TRADE

1960
1961
1962
1963
1964
1965
1966
1967
1968
1969
1970
1971
1972
1973
1974
1975
1976
1977
1978
1979
1980
1981

Imports
Exports

0 10 20 30 40 50 60 70 80

Billions of dollars

CHANGE IN GROSS NATIONAL PRODUCT

Current dollars

Constant 1971 dollars

Percent change

15 10 5 0

1971 1972 1973 1974 1975 1976 1977 1978 1979 1980 1981

CHANGE IN THE COST OF LIVING

Percent change

10 5 0

1971 1972 1973 1974 1975 1976 1977 1978 1979 1980 1981 1982 1983

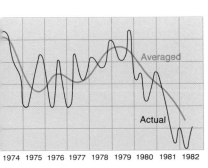

1974 1975 1976 1977 1978 1979 1980 1981 1982

Averaged

Actual

HOUSING STARTS AND MORTGAGE RATES

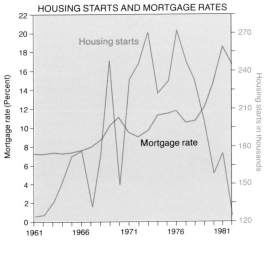

Housing starts

Mortgage rate

New housing starts and mortgage rates are closely related. In the early 1980's, for example, rates climbed to record highs. Consumers could not afford to buy houses, so new house construction dropped dramatically.

ABLE INCOME DECLARED BY CORPORATIONS
(Millions of dollars)

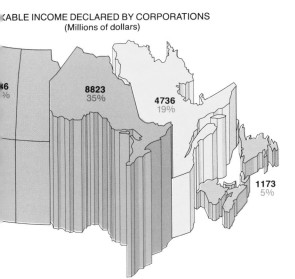

ESTIMATED RESIDENTIAL MORTGAGES OUTSTANDING

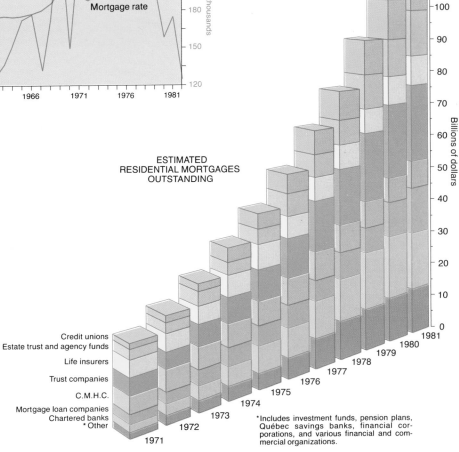

Credit unions
Estate trust and agency funds
Life insurers
Trust companies
C.M.H.C.
Mortgage loan companies
Chartered banks
* Other

*Includes investment funds, pension plans, Québec savings banks, financial corporations, and various financial and commercial organizations.

BANK OF CANADA RATE

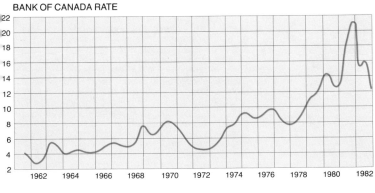

VALUE OF CANADIAN DOLLAR IN U.S. DOLLARS

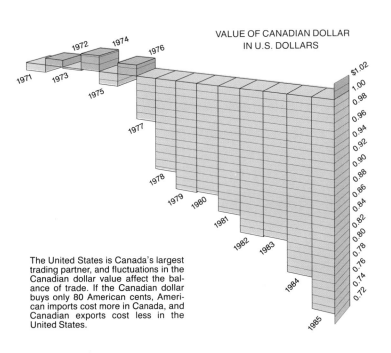

INDEX OF STOCK PRICES

The United States is Canada's largest trading partner, and fluctuations in the Canadian dollar value affect the balance of trade. If the Canadian dollar buys only 80 American cents, American imports cost more in Canada, and Canadian exports cost less in the United States.

CANADA

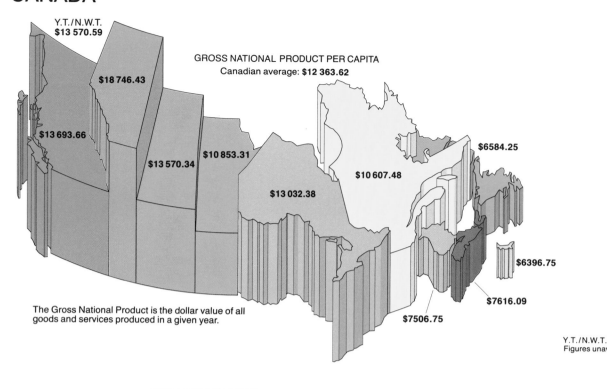

GROSS NATIONAL PRODUCT PER CAPITA
Canadian average: $12 363.62

Y.T./N.W.T. $13 570.59

$18 746.43

$13 693.66

$13 570.34

$10 853.31

$13 032.38

$10 607.48

$6584.25

$6396.75

$7616.09

$7506.75

The Gross National Product is the dollar value of all goods and services produced in a given year.

AVERAGE YEARLY INCOME PER CAPITA

Top 10 centres:

Markham, Ont. 1	$16 461
Oakville, Ont. 1	15 781
Calgary, Alta.	15 030
Burlington, Ont.	14 751
Edmonton, Alta.	14 192
Mississauga, Ont. 1	14 080
Vancouver, B.C.	14 009
Ottawa, Ont.	13 887
Prince George, B.C.	13 658
Brossard, Qué. 2	13 653

Bottom 10 centres:

Jonquière, Qué.	$10 364
St-Jérôme, Qué.	10 335
Timmins, Ont.	10 184
Drummondville, Qué.	10 100
Owen Sound, Ont.	10 087
Valley East, Ont.	9879
Orillia, Ont.	9860
Brandon, Man.	9736
Cornwall, Ont.	9649
Sydney, N.S.	9431

1 Toronto C.M.A.
2 Montréal C.M.A.

AVERAGE WEEKLY EARNI PER CAPITA

Y.T./N.W.T. Figures unavailable

Canadian average: $39

B.C. $450

ALTA. $440

SAS $37

AVERAGE FAMILY EXPENDITURE

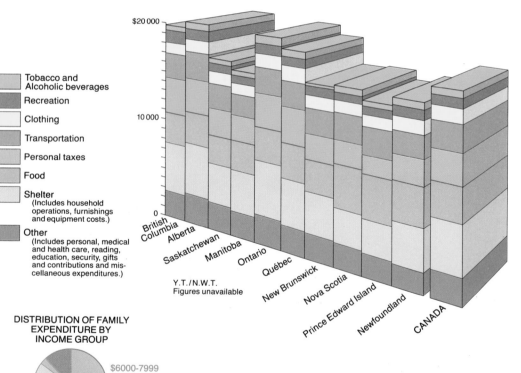

Legend:
- Tobacco and Alcoholic beverages
- Recreation
- Clothing
- Transportation
- Personal taxes
- Food
- Shelter (Includes household operations, furnishings and equipment costs.)
- Other (Includes personal, medical and health care, reading, education, security, gifts and contributions and miscellaneous expenditures.)

$20 000

10 000

0

British Columbia, Alberta, Saskatchewan, Manitoba, Ontario, Québec, New Brunswick, Nova Scotia, Prince Edward Island, Newfoundland, CANADA

Y.T./N.W.T. Figures unavailable

The average Canadian income is one of the highe in the world. Within the country, however, there a great differences in income. These differences are th result of many factors, including job opportunitie training, and the influence of unions in the area. Wi such differences in earning power, the habits Canadian consumers also vary. Families in high income groups can often spend their earnings in mar categories. Lower income groups may need to spend higher proportion of their wages on food and shelte Most producers of consumer goods look at the averag income level of their target consumers. Then they ca market their product more effectively.

DISTRIBUTION OF FAMILY EXPENDITURE BY INCOME GROUP

$6000-7999

$16 000-19 999

$35 000 +

BUYING POWER OF THE PROVINCES
Total real disposable income—$93 200 000 000

BRITISH COLUMBIA 12.3%

ALBERTA 9.7%

SASKATCHEWAN 3.8%

MANITOBA 4.1%

ONTARIO 38.6%

NEW BRUNSWICK 2.2%

NOVA SCOTIA 2.9%

NEWFOUNDLAN 1.6%

QUÉ 24.

PRIN EDWA ISLA 0.

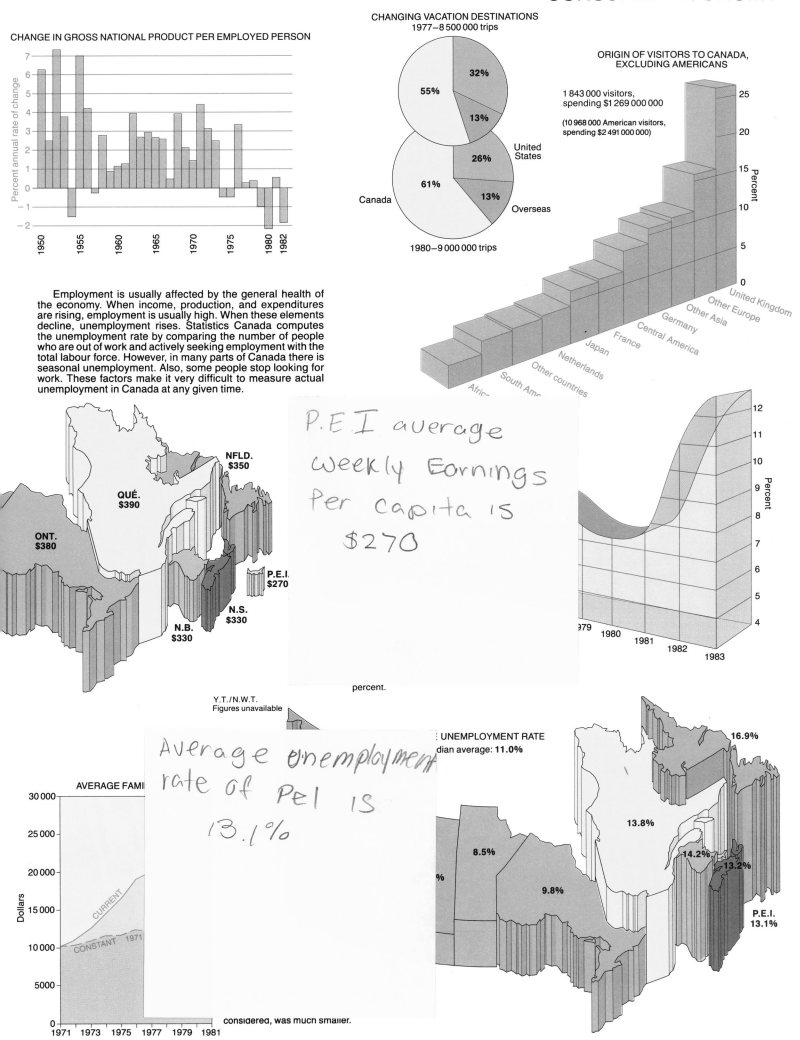

CHANGE IN GROSS NATIONAL PRODUCT PER EMPLOYED PERSON

Percent annual rate of change
7
6
5
4
3
2
1
0
−1
−2
1950 1955 1960 1965 1970 1975 1980 1982

CHANGING VACATION DESTINATIONS
1977–8 500 000 trips

55%
32%
13%

United States
26%
61%
13%
Canada
Overseas

1980–9 000 000 trips

ORIGIN OF VISITORS TO CANADA, EXCLUDING AMERICANS

1 843 000 visitors, spending $1 269 000 000

(10 968 000 American visitors, spending $2 491 000 000)

Percent
25
20
15
10
5
0

United Kingdom
Other Europe
Other Asia
Germany
Central America
France
Japan
Netherlands
Other countries
South Ame...
Africa

Employment is usually affected by the general health of the economy. When income, production, and expenditures are rising, employment is usually high. When these elements decline, unemployment rises. Statistics Canada computes the unemployment rate by comparing the number of people who are out of work and actively seeking employment with the total labour force. However, in many parts of Canada there is seasonal unemployment. Also, some people stop looking for work. These factors make it very difficult to measure actual unemployment in Canada at any given time.

NFLD. $350
QUÉ. $390
ONT. $380
P.E.I. $270
N.S. $330
N.B. $330

P.E.I average weekly Earnings Per capita is $270 (handwritten)

Percent
12
11
10
9
8
7
6
5
4

1979 1980 1981 1982 1983

percent.

Y.T./N.W.T. Figures unavailable

Average unemployment rate of PEI is 13.1% (handwritten)

UNEMPLOYMENT RATE
...dian average: 11.0%

16.9%
13.8%
8.5%
14.2%
13.2%
9.8%
P.E.I. 13.1%

AVERAGE FAMI...

Dollars
30 000
25 000
20 000
15 000
10 000
5000
0
1971 1973 1975 1977 1979 1981

CURRENT
CONSTANT 1971

considered, was much smaller.

CANADA

EDUCATIONAL ATTAINMENT BY PROVINCE

University graduate
Post-secondary*
High school
0-8 years

British Columbia, Alberta, Saskatchewan, Manitoba, Ontario, Québec, New Brunswick, Nova Scotia, Prince Edward Island, Newfoundland

Percent of provincial population age 15 and over
100 90 80 70 60 50 40 30 20 10 0

*Includes persons who have either completed a certificate or diploma, or have some post-secondary education.

NATIONAL DAY CARE

1971 — 17 391 spaces
1982 — 109 595 spaces*

Spaces in registered day care centres
*600% increase in a decade

TYPE OF SMOKER AND DAILY NUMBER OF CIGARETTES

Occasional smoker
Former smoker
Never smoked
Type of smoker unknown
1-12
13-22
23-32
33 +

TYPE OF DRINKER AND WEEKLY INTAKE OF ALC...

Occasional drinker
Former drinker
Never drank
Type of drinker unknown
Consumption unknown
<1
1-6 drink...
7-13
14 +

SCHOOL ENROLMENT

Thousands of students
4000 3800 3600 3400 3200 3000 2800
Grade 9 and higher
Grades 1-8

Thousands of students
2000 1800 1600 1400 1200 1000 800

1968-69 71-72 74-75 77-78 80-81 83-84

PEOPLE, HOUSING, AND EARNING...
Percent by province

British Columbia
Alberta
Saskatchewan

HOUSEHOLDS

Primary family 85.6%
Non-family female head
Non-family 14.4%
Non-family male head
Lone parent female head
Lone parent male head
Husband-wife families

1961
1976 — 78.2% / 21.8%
1991 (estimated) — 74.6% / 25.4%

SUICIDE BY AGE GROUP

Years
1961
1971
1981

80 +
75-79
70-74
65-69
60-64
55-59
50-54
45-49
40-44
35-39
30-34
25-29
20-24
15-19

Male
Female

15 10 5 0   0 5 10 15
Percent

Infant mortality

Rate per 100 000
30 25 20 15 10 5 0

1961 1966 1971 1976 1981

POPUL...
DWEL...
PERS... INCO...

SUICIDE

Percent
25 20 15 10 5 0

Suicide as a percent of all deaths by accident, poisoning, or violence

Suicide rate

Rate per 100 000

1921 26 31 36 41 46 51 56 61 66 71 76 81

Births
Deaths
Natural increase

Rate per 1000
30 25 20 15 10 5 0

1961 1966 1971 1976 1981

VITAL STATISTICS

Marri...
Divor...

Rate per 1000
10 9 8 7 6 5 4 3 2 1 0

1961 1966 1971 1976 19...

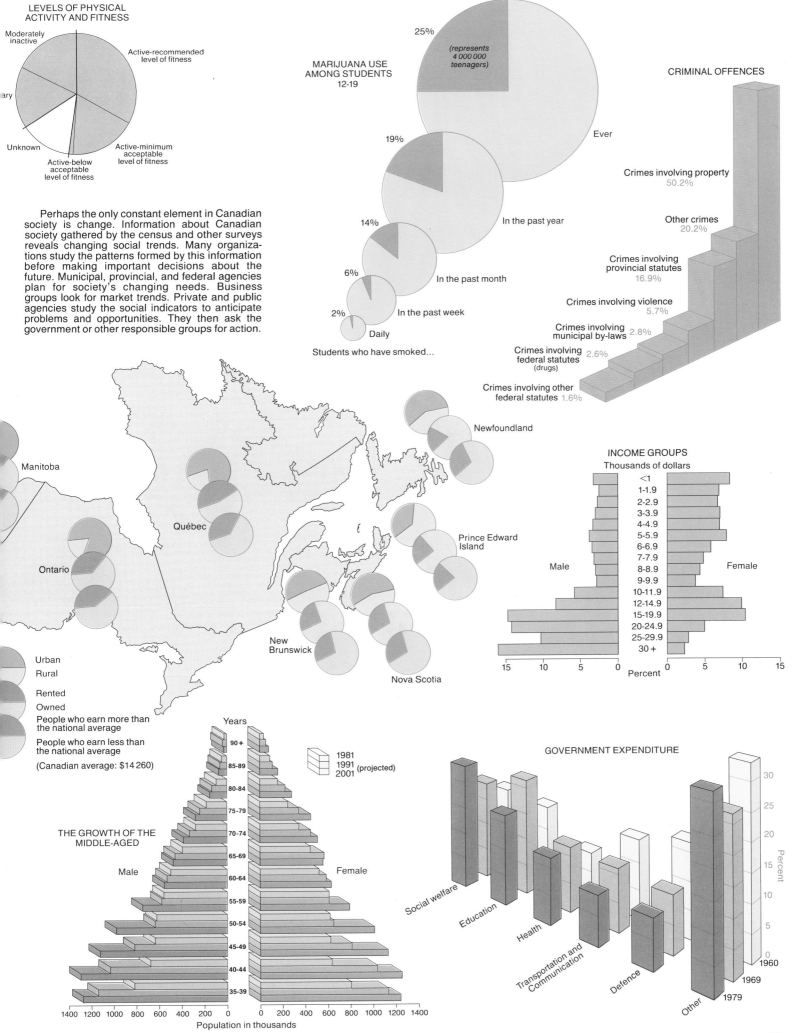

LEVELS OF PHYSICAL ACTIVITY AND FITNESS

Moderately inactive

Active-recommended level of fitness

...ary

Unknown

Active-below acceptable level of fitness

Active-minimum acceptable level of fitness

Perhaps the only constant element in Canadian society is change. Information about Canadian society gathered by the census and other surveys reveals changing social trends. Many organizations study the patterns formed by this information before making important decisions about the future. Municipal, provincial, and federal agencies plan for society's changing needs. Business groups look for market trends. Private and public agencies study the social indicators to anticipate problems and opportunities. They then ask the government or other responsible groups for action.

MARIJUANA USE AMONG STUDENTS 12-19

25% (represents 4 000 000 teenagers)

Ever

19%

In the past year

14%

In the past month

6%

In the past week

2%

Daily

Students who have smoked...

CRIMINAL OFFENCES

Crimes involving property 50.2%

Other crimes 20.2%

Crimes involving provincial statutes 16.9%

Crimes involving violence 5.7%

Crimes involving municipal by-laws 2.8%

Crimes involving federal statutes (drugs) 2.6%

Crimes involving other federal statutes 1.6%

Manitoba

Newfoundland

Québec

Prince Edward Island

Ontario

New Brunswick

Nova Scotia

Urban
Rural

Rented
Owned

People who earn more than the national average

People who earn less than the national average

(Canadian average: $14 260)

INCOME GROUPS
Thousands of dollars

	<1	
	1-1.9	
	2-2.9	
	3-3.9	
	4-4.9	
	5-5.9	
	6-6.9	
Male	7-7.9	Female
	8-8.9	
	9-9.9	
	10-11.9	
	12-14.9	
	15-19.9	
	20-24.9	
	25-29.9	
	30 +	

15 10 5 0   0 5 10 15
Percent

THE GROWTH OF THE MIDDLE-AGED

Years

90 +
85-89
80-84
75-79
70-74
65-69
60-64
55-59
50-54
45-49
40-44
35-39

Male

Female

1981
1991 (projected)
2001

1400 1200 1000 800 600 400 200 0   0 200 400 600 800 1000 1200 1400
Population in thousands

GOVERNMENT EXPENDITURE

Social welfare

Education

Health

Transportation and Communication

Defence

Other

1960
1969
1979

Percent
30
25
20
15
10
5
0

CANADA

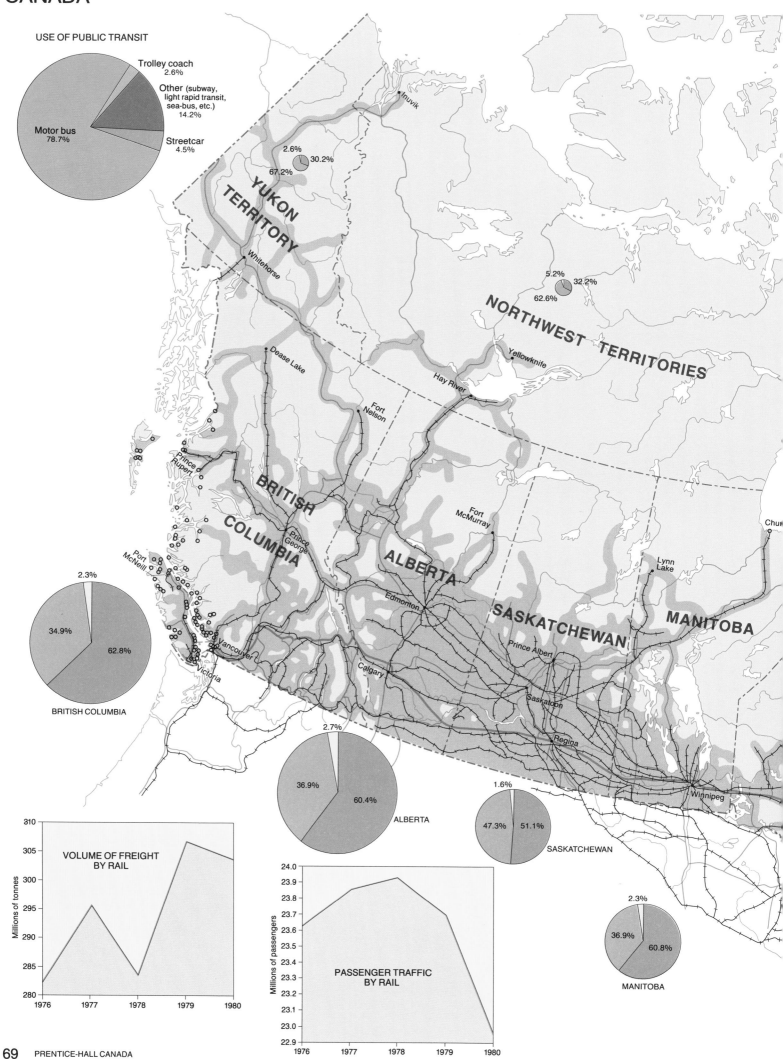

USE OF PUBLIC TRANSIT

Trolley coach
2.6%

Other (subway,
light rapid transit,
sea-bus, etc.)
14.2%

Motor bus
78.7%

Streetcar
4.5%

2.6%
67.2%   30.2%

5.2%
62.6%   32.2%

YUKON TERRITORY

NORTHWEST TERRITORIES

Inuvik

Whitehorse

Dease Lake

Hay River

Yellowknife

Fort Nelson

BRITISH COLUMBIA

Prince Rupert

Port McNeill

Prince George

Fort McMurray

ALBERTA

SASKATCHEWAN

MANITOBA

Churchill

Lynn Lake

Edmonton

Vancouver

Victoria

2.3%
34.9%   62.8%

BRITISH COLUMBIA

Calgary

Prince Albert

Saskatoon

Regina

Winnipeg

2.7%
36.9%   60.4%

ALBERTA

1.6%
47.3%   51.1%

SASKATCHEWAN

2.3%
36.9%   60.8%

MANITOBA

VOLUME OF FREIGHT BY RAIL

Millions of tonnes

310
305
300
295
290
285
280

1976   1977   1978   1979   1980

PASSENGER TRAFFIC BY RAIL

Millions of passengers

24.0
23.9
23.8
23.7
23.6
23.5
23.4
23.3
23.2
23.1
23.0
22.9

1976   1977   1978   1979   1980

VEHICLE OWNERSHIP

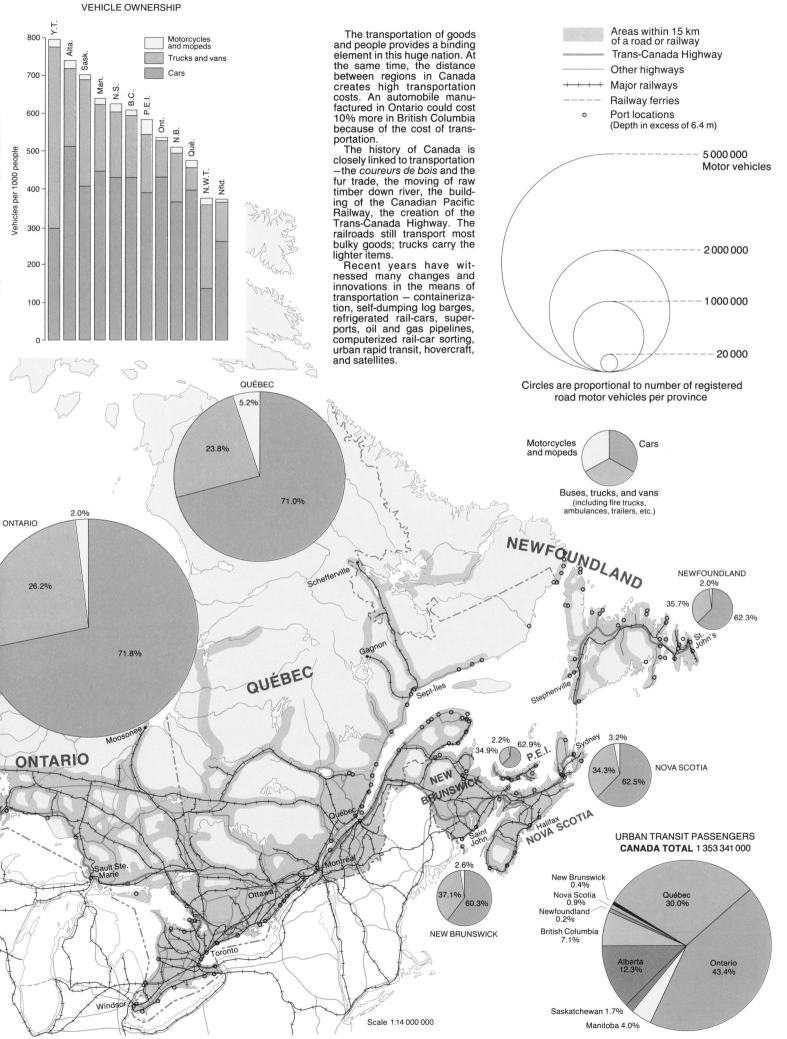

Vehicles per 1000 people

Y.T. Alta. Sask. Man. N.S. B.C. P.E.I. Ont. N.B. Qué. N.W.T. Nfld.

- Motorcycles and mopeds
- Trucks and vans
- Cars

The transportation of goods and people provides a binding element in this huge nation. At the same time, the distance between regions in Canada creates high transportation costs. An automobile manufactured in Ontario could cost 10% more in British Columbia because of the cost of transportation.

The history of Canada is closely linked to transportation — the *coureurs de bois* and the fur trade, the moving of raw timber down river, the building of the Canadian Pacific Railway, the creation of the Trans-Canada Highway. The railroads still transport most bulky goods; trucks carry the lighter items.

Recent years have witnessed many changes and innovations in the means of transportation — containerization, self-dumping log barges, refrigerated rail-cars, superports, oil and gas pipelines, computerized rail-car sorting, urban rapid transit, hovercraft, and satellites.

- Areas within 15 km of a road or railway
- Trans-Canada Highway
- Other highways
- Major railways
- Railway ferries
- ○ Port locations (Depth in excess of 6.4 m)

5 000 000 Motor vehicles

2 000 000

1 000 000

20 000

Circles are proportional to number of registered road motor vehicles per province

Motorcycles and mopeds — Cars

Buses, trucks, and vans (including fire trucks, ambulances, trailers, etc.)

QUÉBEC
5.2%
23.8%
71.0%

ONTARIO
2.0%
26.2%
71.8%

NEWFOUNDLAND
2.0%
35.7%
62.3%

QUÉBEC

NEWFOUNDLAND

Schefferville

Gagnon

Sept-Îles

Stephenville

St. John's

ONTARIO

Moosonee

Sault Ste. Marie

Ottawa

Québec

Montréal

Toronto

Windsor

P.E.I.
2.2%
34.9%
62.9%

Sydney

NOVA SCOTIA
3.2%
34.3%
62.5%

NEW BRUNSWICK

Saint John

Halifax

NOVA SCOTIA

NEW BRUNSWICK
2.6%
37.1%
60.3%

Scale 1:14 000 000

URBAN TRANSIT PASSENGERS
CANADA TOTAL 1 353 341 000

New Brunswick 0.4%
Nova Scotia 0.9%
Newfoundland 0.2%
British Columbia 7.1%

Québec 30.0%

Ontario 43.4%

Alberta 12.3%

Saskatchewan 1.7%

Manitoba 4.0%

CANADA

Technology has greatly changed Canadian transportation. At Confederation, there were no road or rail connections across Canada. A trip from Halifax to Vancouver involved ship, rail, and ground travel and could take weeks—even months. Today, the same distance can be travelled in five hours.

Air transportation allows fast — although relatively expensive — movement of goods and people. In the Far North, transportation by air is essential to link individual communities, mining exploration sites, and weather stations with southern Canada. Food, mail, personal goods, mining equipment, and construction materials are shipped by air. Air ambulances provide people living in isolated communities with emergency transportation to urban hospitals.

Canadians are seasoned air travellers. In the early 1980's, however, air travel decreased because of the economic recession. In an effort to encourage air travel, the Canadian government passed a bill that allows airlines to lower fares and to compete more actively for passengers.

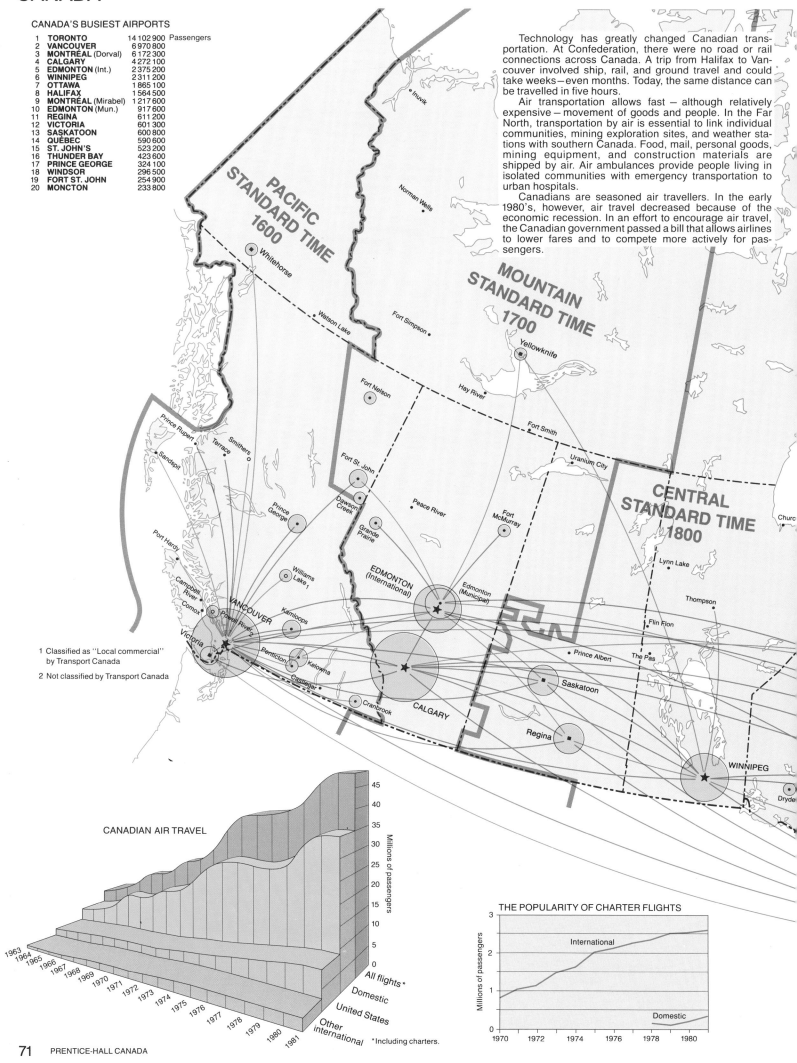

1 Classified as "Local commercial" by Transport Canada

2 Not classified by Transport Canada

CANADIAN AIR TRAVEL

THE POPULARITY OF CHARTER FLIGHTS

*Including charters.

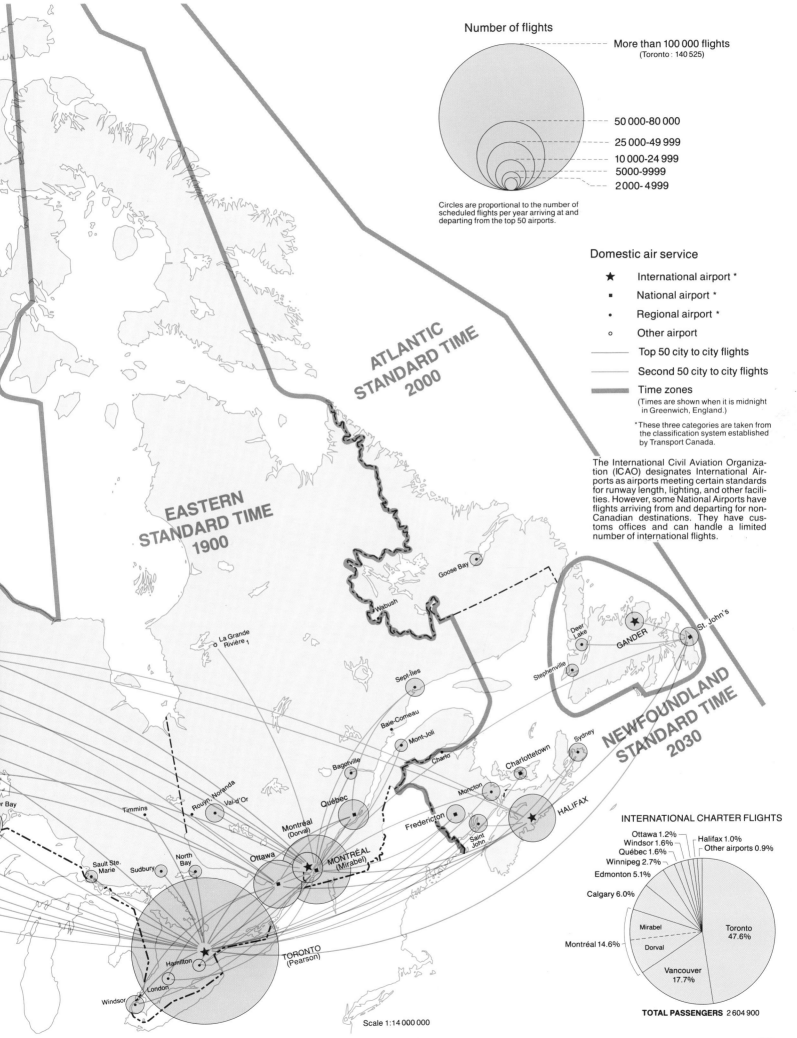

AIR TRANSPORTATION

Number of flights

More than 100 000 flights
(Toronto : 140 525)

50 000-80 000

25 000-49 999

10 000-24 999

5000-9999

2000- 4999

Circles are proportional to the number of
scheduled flights per year arriving at and
departing from the top 50 airports.

Domestic air service

★ International airport *

▪ National airport *

• Regional airport *

○ Other airport

—— Top 50 city to city flights

—— Second 50 city to city flights

━━ Time zones
(Times are shown when it is midnight
in Greenwich, England.)

* These three categories are taken from
the classification system established
by Transport Canada.

The International Civil Aviation Organization (ICAO) designates International Airports as airports meeting certain standards
for runway length, lighting, and other facilities. However, some National Airports have
flights arriving from and departing for non-
Canadian destinations. They have customs offices and can handle a limited
number of international flights.

ATLANTIC
STANDARD TIME
2000

EASTERN
STANDARD TIME
1900

NEWFOUNDLAND
STANDARD TIME
2030

Goose Bay

Wabush

La Grande
Rivière

Deer
Lake

GANDER

St. John's

Stephenville

Sept-Îles

Baie-Comeau

Mont-Joli

Charlottetown

Sydney

Bagotville

Charlo

Moncton

Québec

Fredericton

HALIFAX

Rouyn, Noranda

Val-d'Or

Saint
John

Timmins

Montréal
(Dorval)

MONTRÉAL
(Mirabel)

er Bay

Sault Ste.
Marie

Sudbury

North
Bay

Ottawa

Hamilton

London

Windsor

TORONTO
(Pearson)

Scale 1:14 000 000

INTERNATIONAL CHARTER FLIGHTS

Ottawa 1.2%
Windsor 1.6%
Québec 1.6%
Winnipeg 2.7%
Edmonton 5.1%
Calgary 6.0%
Mirabel
Montréal 14.6%
Dorval
Halifax 1.0%
Other airports 0.9%
Toronto
47.6%
Vancouver
17.7%

TOTAL PASSENGERS 2 604 900

CANADA

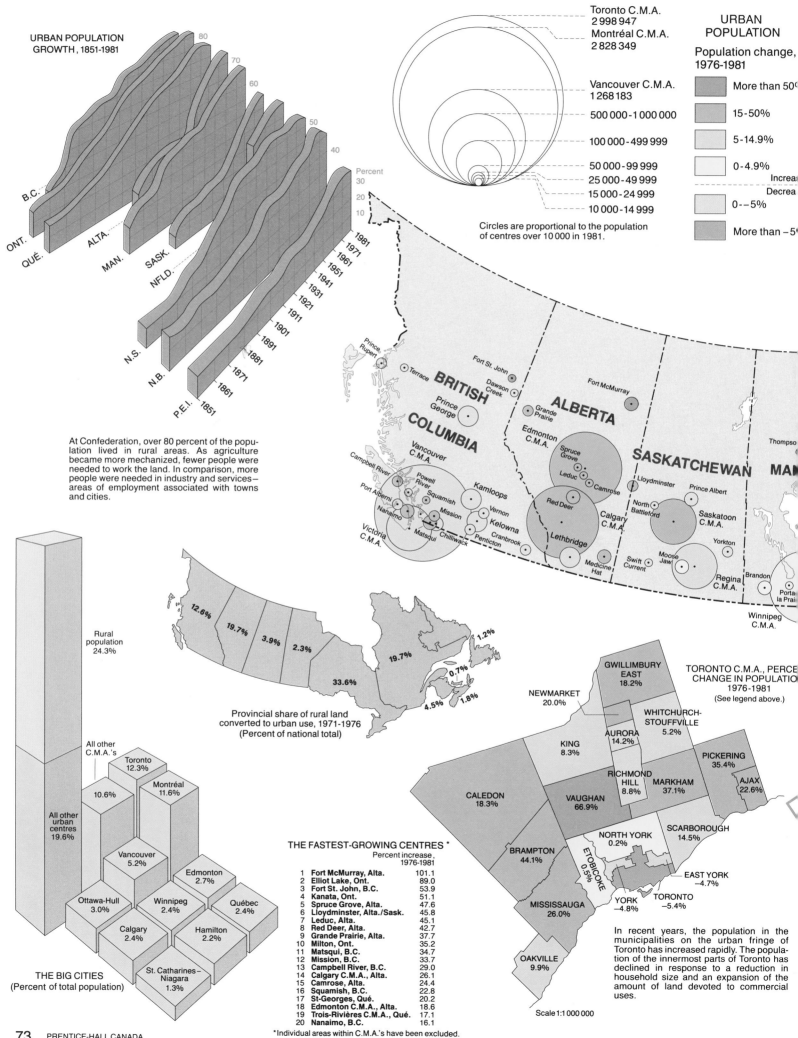

URBAN POPULATION GROWTH, 1851-1981

Percent
80
70
60
50
40
30
20
10

B.C.
ONT.
QUÉ.
ALTA.
MAN.
SASK.
NFLD.
N.S.
N.B.
P.E.I.

1981
1971
1961
1951
1941
1931
1921
1911
1901
1891
1881
1871
1861
1851

At Confederation, over 80 percent of the population lived in rural areas. As agriculture became more mechanized, fewer people were needed to work the land. In comparison, more people were needed in industry and services—areas of employment associated with towns and cities.

URBAN POPULATION

Toronto C.M.A. 2 998 947
Montréal C.M.A. 2 828 349
Vancouver C.M.A. 1 268 183
500 000 - 1 000 000
100 000 - 499 999
50 000 - 99 999
25 000 - 49 999
15 000 - 24 999
10 000 - 14 999

Circles are proportional to the population of centres over 10 000 in 1981.

URBAN POPULATION

Population change, 1976-1981

More than 50%
15 - 50%
5 - 14.9%
0 - 4.9%

Increase

Decrease

0 - -5%
More than -5%

BRITISH COLUMBIA
Prince Rupert
Terrace
Fort St. John
Dawson Creek
Prince George
Campbell River
Vancouver C.M.A.
Powell River
Squamish
Port Alberni
Nanaimo
Mission
Matsqui
Chilliwack
Victoria C.M.A.
Kamloops
Vernon
Kelowna
Penticton
Cranbrook

ALBERTA
Fort McMurray
Grande Prairie
Edmonton C.M.A.
Spruce Grove
Leduc
Camrose
Red Deer
Calgary C.M.A.
Lethbridge
Medicine Hat

SASKATCHEWAN
Lloydminster
Prince Albert
North Battleford
Saskatoon C.M.A.
Yorkton
Moose Jaw
Swift Current
Regina C.M.A.

Thompso
MA
Brandon
Porta la Prai
Winnipeg C.M.A.

Provincial share of rural land converted to urban use, 1971-1976 (Percent of national total)

12.6%
19.7%
3.9%
2.3%
33.6%
19.7%
0.7%
0.5%
1.2%
4.5%
1.8%

Rural population 24.3%

All other urban centres 19.6%

All other C.M.A.'s
Toronto 12.3%
Montréal 11.6%
10.6%
Vancouver 5.2%
Ottawa-Hull 3.0%
Winnipeg 2.4%
Edmonton 2.7%
Calgary 2.4%
Hamilton 2.2%
Québec 2.4%
St. Catharines-Niagara 1.3%

THE BIG CITIES
(Percent of total population)

THE FASTEST-GROWING CENTRES *

Percent increase, 1976-1981

1	Fort McMurray, Alta.	101.1
2	Elliot Lake, Ont.	89.0
3	Fort St. John, B.C.	53.9
4	Kanata, Ont.	51.1
5	Spruce Grove, Alta.	47.6
6	Lloydminster, Alta./Sask.	45.8
7	Leduc, Alta.	45.1
8	Red Deer, Alta.	42.7
9	Grande Prairie, Alta.	37.7
10	Milton, Ont.	35.2
11	Matsqui, B.C.	34.7
12	Mission, B.C.	33.7
13	Campbell River, B.C.	29.0
14	Calgary C.M.A., Alta.	26.1
15	Camrose, Alta.	24.4
16	Squamish, B.C.	22.8
17	St-Georges, Qué.	20.2
18	Edmonton C.M.A., Alta.	18.6
19	Trois-Rivières C.M.A., Qué.	17.1
20	Nanaimo, B.C.	16.1

*Individual areas within C.M.A.'s have been excluded.

TORONTO C.M.A., PERCE CHANGE IN POPULATION 1976-1981
(See legend above.)

GWILLIMBURY EAST 18.2%
NEWMARKET 20.0%
WHITCHURCH-STOUFFVILLE 5.2%
AURORA 14.2%
KING 8.3%
PICKERING 35.4%
RICHMOND HILL 8.8%
MARKHAM 37.1%
AJAX 22.6%
CALEDON 18.3%
VAUGHAN 66.9%
NORTH YORK 0.2%
SCARBOROUGH 14.5%
BRAMPTON 44.1%
ETOBICOKE 0.5%
EAST YORK -4.7%
MISSISSAUGA 26.0%
YORK -4.8%
TORONTO -5.4%
OAKVILLE 9.9%

In recent years, the population in the municipalities on the urban fringe of Toronto has increased rapidly. The population of the innermost parts of Toronto has declined in response to a reduction in household size and an expansion of the amount of land devoted to commercial uses.

Scale 1:1 000 000

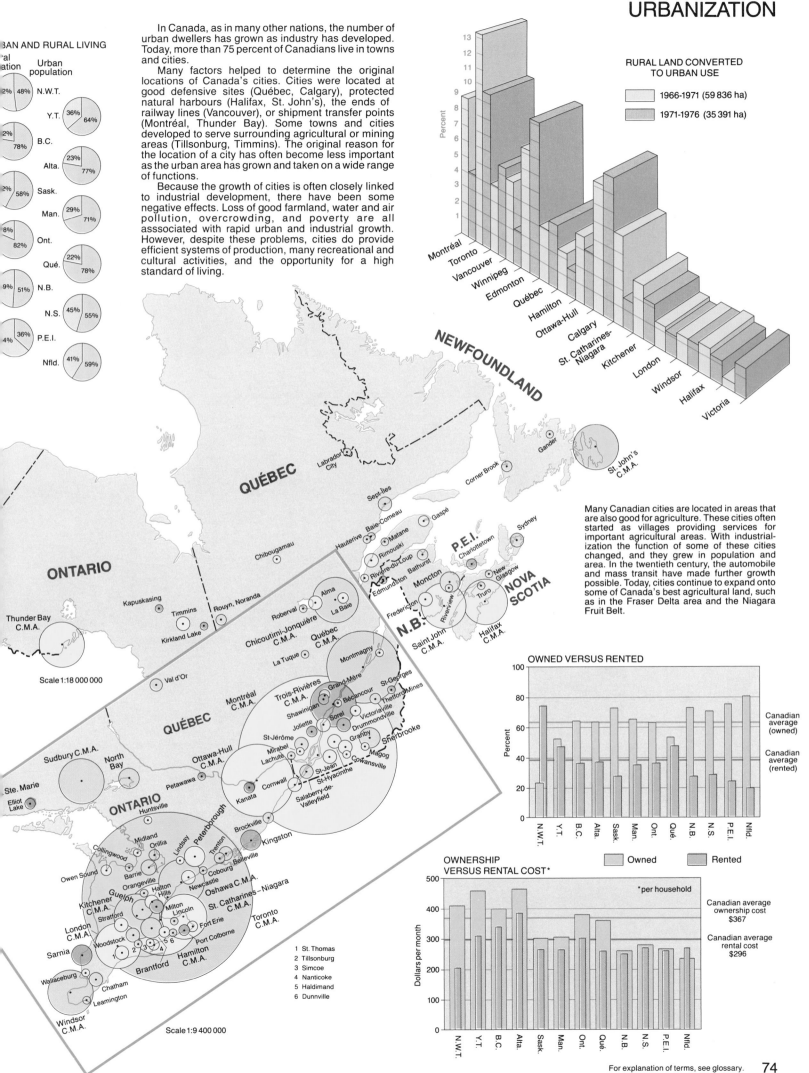

In Canada, as in many other nations, the number of urban dwellers has grown as industry has developed. Today, more than 75 percent of Canadians live in towns and cities.

Many factors helped to determine the original locations of Canada's cities. Cities were located at good defensive sites (Québec, Calgary), protected natural harbours (Halifax, St. John's), the ends of railway lines (Vancouver), or shipment transfer points (Montréal, Thunder Bay). Some towns and cities developed to serve surrounding agricultural or mining areas (Tillsonburg, Timmins). The original reason for the location of a city has often become less important as the urban area has grown and taken on a wide range of functions.

Because the growth of cities is often closely linked to industrial development, there have been some negative effects. Loss of good farmland, water and air pollution, overcrowding, and poverty are all asssociated with rapid urban and industrial growth. However, despite these problems, cities do provide efficient systems of production, many recreational and cultural activities, and the opportunity for a high standard of living.

BAN AND RURAL LIVING

al ation / Urban population

- 2% 48% N.W.T.
- Y.T. 36% 64%
- 2% B.C. 78%
- Alta. 23% 77%
- 2% Sask. 58%
- Man. 29% 71%
- 8% Ont. 82%
- Qué. 22% 78%
- 9% N.B. 51%
- N.S. 45% 55%
- 4% P.E.I. 36%
- Nfld. 41% 59%

RURAL LAND CONVERTED TO URBAN USE

- 1966-1971 (59 836 ha)
- 1971-1976 (35 391 ha)

Montréal, Toronto, Vancouver, Winnipeg, Edmonton, Québec, Hamilton, Ottawa-Hull, Calgary, St. Catharines-Niagara, Kitchener, London, Windsor, Halifax, Victoria

Many Canadian cities are located in areas that are also good for agriculture. These cities often started as villages providing services for important agricultural areas. With industrialization the function of some of these cities changed, and they grew in population and area. In the twentieth century, the automobile and mass transit have made further growth possible. Today, cities continue to expand onto some of Canada's best agricultural land, such as in the Fraser Delta area and the Niagara Fruit Belt.

NEWFOUNDLAND

QUÉBEC

ONTARIO

P.E.I.

NOVA SCOTIA

N.B.

Gander
St. John's C.M.A.
Labrador City
Corner Brook
Sept-Îles
Gaspé
Baie-Comeau
Hauterive
Matane
Rimouski
Chibougamau
Rivière-du-Loup
Bathurst
Sydney
Charlottetown
New Glasgow
Edmundston
Moncton
Truro
Fredericton
Riverview
Halifax C.M.A.
Saint John C.M.A.

Thunder Bay C.M.A.
Kapuskasing
Timmins
Rouyn, Noranda
Roberval
Alma
La Baie
Chicoutimi-Jonquière C.M.A.
Kirkland Lake
Québec C.M.A.
La Tuque
Val d'Or
Montmagny
Grand-Mère
St-Georges
Trois-Rivières C.M.A.
Bécancour
Thetford Mines
Shawinigan
Victoriaville
Montréal C.M.A.
Joliette
Sorel
Drummondville
St-Jérôme
Granby
Sherbrooke
Mirabel
Magog
Lachute
Cowansville
Ottawa-Hull C.M.A.
St-Jean
Cornwall
St-Hyacinthe
Kanata
Salaberry-de-Valleyfield

Scale 1:18 000 000

Sudbury C.M.A.
North Bay
Ste. Marie
Elliot Lake
Petawawa
Brockville
Kingston
Huntsville
Midland
Orillia
Collingwood
Lindsay
Peterborough
Owen Sound
Barrie
Trenton
Belleville
Orangeville
Cobourg
Newcastle
Kitchener C.M.A.
Guelph
Halton Hills
Oshawa C.M.A.
St. Catharines-Niagara
Milton
Lincoln
London C.M.A.
Stratford
Fort Erie
Toronto C.M.A.
Sarnia
Woodstock
Port Colborne
Wallaceburg
Hamilton C.M.A.
Brantford
Chatham
Leamington
Windsor C.M.A.

1 St. Thomas
2 Tillsonburg
3 Simcoe
4 Nanticoke
5 Haldimand
6 Dunnville

Scale 1:9 400 000

OWNED VERSUS RENTED

Canadian average (owned)
Canadian average (rented)

N.W.T., Y.T., B.C., Alta., Sask., Man., Ont., Qué., N.B., N.S., P.E.I., Nfld.

Owned   Rented

OWNERSHIP VERSUS RENTAL COST*

*per household

Canadian average ownership cost $367
Canadian average rental cost $296

N.W.T., Y.T., B.C., Alta., Sask., Man., Ont., Qué., N.B., N.S., P.E.I., Nfld.

CANADA

THE POPULATION BOOM

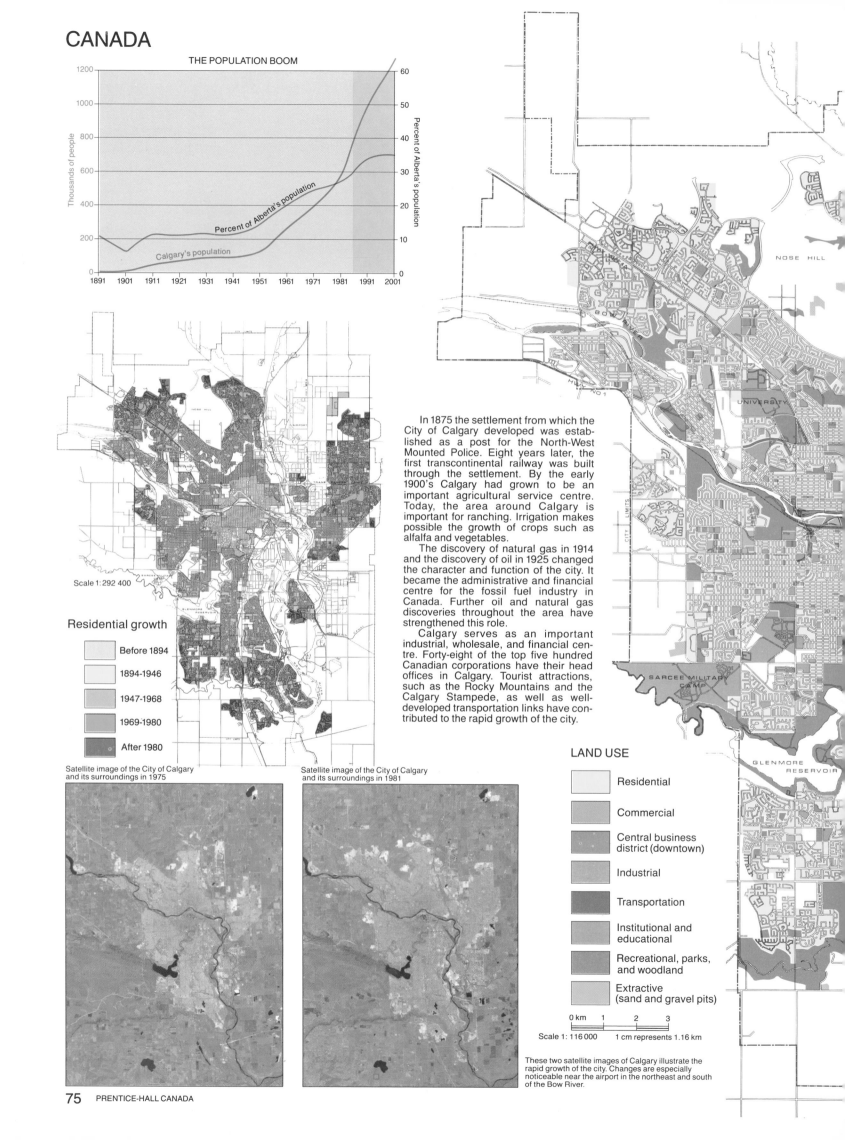

Percent of Alberta's population

Calgary's population

Thousands of people

1891 1901 1911 1921 1931 1941 1951 1961 1971 1981 1991 2001

Scale 1: 292 400

Residential growth

- Before 1894
- 1894-1946
- 1947-1968
- 1969-1980
- After 1980

In 1875 the settlement from which the City of Calgary developed was established as a post for the North-West Mounted Police. Eight years later, the first transcontinental railway was built through the settlement. By the early 1900's Calgary had grown to be an important agricultural service centre. Today, the area around Calgary is important for ranching. Irrigation makes possible the growth of crops such as alfalfa and vegetables.

The discovery of natural gas in 1914 and the discovery of oil in 1925 changed the character and function of the city. It became the administrative and financial centre for the fossil fuel industry in Canada. Further oil and natural gas discoveries throughout the area have strengthened this role.

Calgary serves as an important industrial, wholesale, and financial centre. Forty-eight of the top five hundred Canadian corporations have their head offices in Calgary. Tourist attractions, such as the Rocky Mountains and the Calgary Stampede, as well as well-developed transportation links have contributed to the rapid growth of the city.

Satellite image of the City of Calgary and its surroundings in 1975

Satellite image of the City of Calgary and its surroundings in 1981

LAND USE

- Residential
- Commercial
- Central business district (downtown)
- Industrial
- Transportation
- Institutional and educational
- Recreational, parks, and woodland
- Extractive (sand and gravel pits)

0 km 1 2 3

Scale 1: 116 000   1 cm represents 1.16 km

These two satellite images of Calgary illustrate the rapid growth of the city. Changes are especially noticeable near the airport in the northeast and south of the Bow River.

NOSE HILL

UNIVERSITY

SARCEE MILITARY CAMP

GLENMORE RESERVOIR

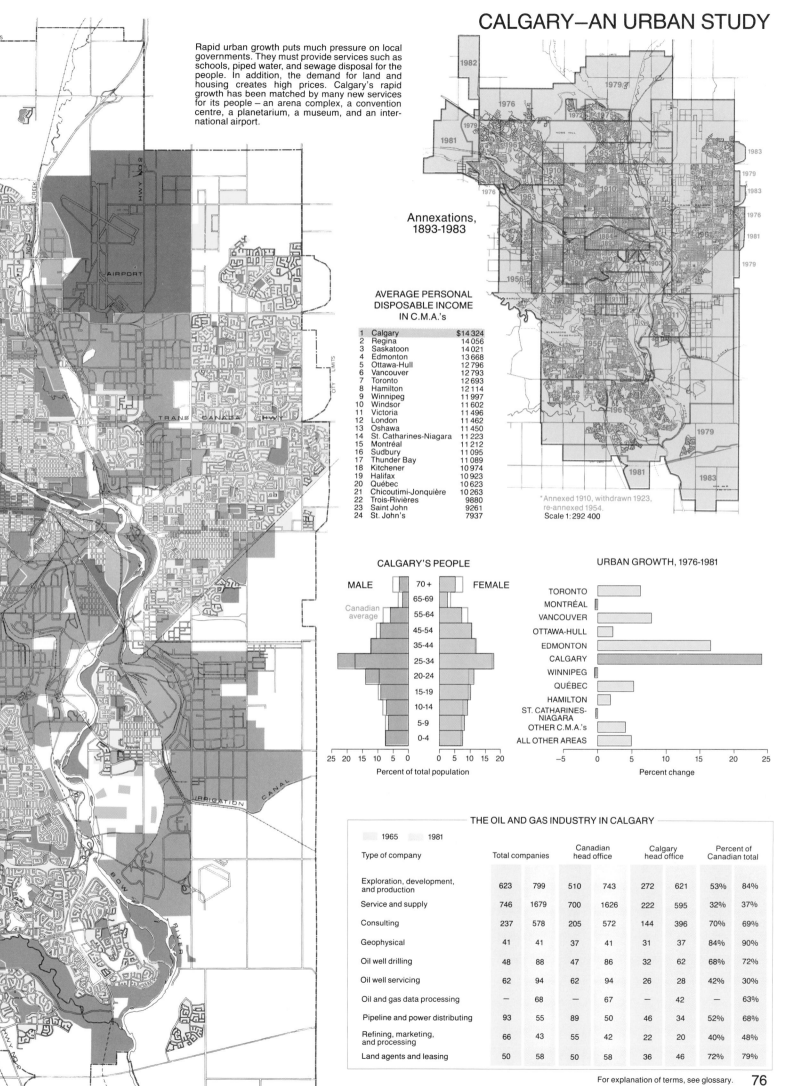

Rapid urban growth puts much pressure on local governments. They must provide services such as schools, piped water, and sewage disposal for the people. In addition, the demand for land and housing creates high prices. Calgary's rapid growth has been matched by many new services for its people – an arena complex, a convention centre, a planetarium, a museum, and an international airport.

Annexations, 1893-1983

*Annexed 1910, withdrawn 1923, re-annexed 1954.
Scale 1: 292 400

AVERAGE PERSONAL DISPOSABLE INCOME IN C.M.A.'s

1	Calgary	$14 324
2	Regina	14 056
3	Saskatoon	14 021
4	Edmonton	13 668
5	Ottawa-Hull	12 796
6	Vancouver	12 793
7	Toronto	12 693
8	Hamilton	12 114
9	Winnipeg	11 997
10	Windsor	11 602
11	Victoria	11 496
12	London	11 462
13	Oshawa	11 450
14	St. Catharines-Niagara	11 223
15	Montréal	11 212
16	Sudbury	11 095
17	Thunder Bay	11 089
18	Kitchener	10 974
19	Halifax	10 923
20	Québec	10 623
21	Chicoutimi-Jonquière	10 263
22	Trois-Rivières	9880
23	Saint John	9261
24	St. John's	7937

CALGARY'S PEOPLE

MALE — Canadian average — FEMALE

70 +, 65-69, 55-64, 45-54, 35-44, 25-34, 20-24, 15-19, 10-14, 5-9, 0-4

Percent of total population

URBAN GROWTH, 1976-1981

TORONTO
MONTRÉAL
VANCOUVER
OTTAWA-HULL
EDMONTON
CALGARY
WINNIPEG
QUÉBEC
HAMILTON
ST. CATHARINES-NIAGARA
OTHER C.M.A.'s
ALL OTHER AREAS

Percent change

THE OIL AND GAS INDUSTRY IN CALGARY

1965   1981

Type of company	Total companies		Canadian head office		Calgary head office		Percent of Canadian total	
Exploration, development, and production	623	799	510	743	272	621	53%	84%
Service and supply	746	1679	700	1626	222	595	32%	37%
Consulting	237	578	205	572	144	396	70%	69%
Geophysical	41	41	37	41	31	37	84%	90%
Oil well drilling	48	88	47	86	32	62	68%	72%
Oil well servicing	62	94	62	94	26	28	42%	30%
Oil and gas data processing	—	68	—	67	—	42	—	63%
Pipeline and power distributing	93	55	89	50	46	34	52%	68%
Refining, marketing, and processing	66	43	55	42	22	20	40%	48%
Land agents and leasing	50	58	50	58	36	46	72%	79%

For explanation of terms, see glossary.

CANADA

FAR NORTH

ARCTIC OCEAN

QUEEN ELIZABETH ISLANDS

AXEL HEIBERG ISLAND

SVERDRUP ISLANDS

PRINCE PATRICK ISLAND

Isachsen

MACKENZIE KING I.

North • magnetic pole

BATHURST ISLAND

MELVILLE ISLAND

CORNWALLIS ISLAND

Kaujuitoq

BEAUFORT SEA

Viscount Melville Sound

DISTRICT OF FRANKLIN

SOMERSET ISLAND

BANKS ISLAND

Sachs Harbour

ALASKA

Tuktoyaktuk

Cape Bathurst

Amundsen Gulf

Cape Parry

Holman

VICTORIA ISLAND

PRINCE OF WALES I.

Aklavik

Old Crow

Inuvik

Paulatuk

NORTHWEST TERRITORIES

BOOTHIA PENINSULA

Fort McPherson

YUKON TERRITORY

Peel

Mackenzie

Fort Good Hope

DISTRICT OF MACKENZIE

Coppermine

Cambridge Bay

Spence Bay

Dawson

Mayo

Stewart

Yukon

Norman Wells

Gjoa Haven

KLUANE

Carmacks

Fort Norman

Great Bear Lake

Queen Maud Gulf

Coppermine

Whitehorse

Faro

Fort Franklin

Arctic Circle

DISTRICT OF KEEWA

Pelly

Testin

Wrigley

Back

Tungsten

Baker Lake

NAHANNI

Thelon

Liard

Watson Lake

Dubawnt Lake

Rankin Inlet

B.C.

Dubawnt

MANITOBA

Tadoule Lake

Chur

SASK.

Satellite image of Melville Island, Northwest Territories

The physical environment, recent economic developments, and a variety of cultures contribute to the unique character of the Far North, Canada's largest region.

Before the European settlers, various Indian cultural groups lived in the south, and various Inuit groups in the north. The entire region has a harsh climate, but the area occupied by the Inuit was most severe. With ingenuity, adaptability, and physical toughness, they survived long, cold winters, long periods of darkness, a lack of vegetation, and permanently frozen ground.

The search for the Northwest Passage, and then whales, white fox, and seals attracted Europeans to the Far North. With exploration and settlement came change. Today, the quest for minerals, gas, and oil has affected the landscape and the lives of the 20 000 Inuit. Government assistance and modern technology conflict with traditional nomadic lifestyles, and in less than eighty years, the Inuit have adapted to many changes brought about by contemporary consumer society. Some of these changes may be beneficial—education, medical services, and employment opportunities. Others are less welcome—pollution, alcoholism, tuberculosis, and potential loss of cultural identity.

For non-Natives, life in the Far North can be isolated, costly, and dangerous, so to encourage workers to migrate from the south, employers pay well. Many people enjoy the rugged beauty of the landscape and the challenge of working in a frontier community.

Satellite image of the west coast of Baffin Island, Northwest Territories

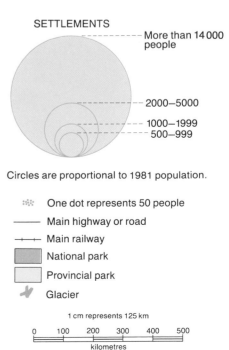

SETTLEMENTS

More than 14 000 people

2000–5000

1000–1999
500–999

Circles are proportional to 1981 population.

∴ One dot represents 50 people

—— Main highway or road

+++ Main railway

National park

Provincial park

Glacier

1 cm represents 125 km

0   100   200   300   400   500
kilometres
Scale 1: 12 500 000

CANADA

In the Far North, the climate has limited development of the land. Many areas are like cold deserts, with average temperatures below zero and with less than 250 mm/a (per year) of precipitation. The permafrost, which can be 400 m deep, prevents moisture from draining, and in the summer, the top layer of permafrost melts, creating bogs. When people remove the vegetation that insulates the permafrost, the balance of nature in the fragile north is upset. Therefore, the construction of buildings, pipelines, oil drilling sites, and airstrips must be carefully planned to avoid environmental damage.

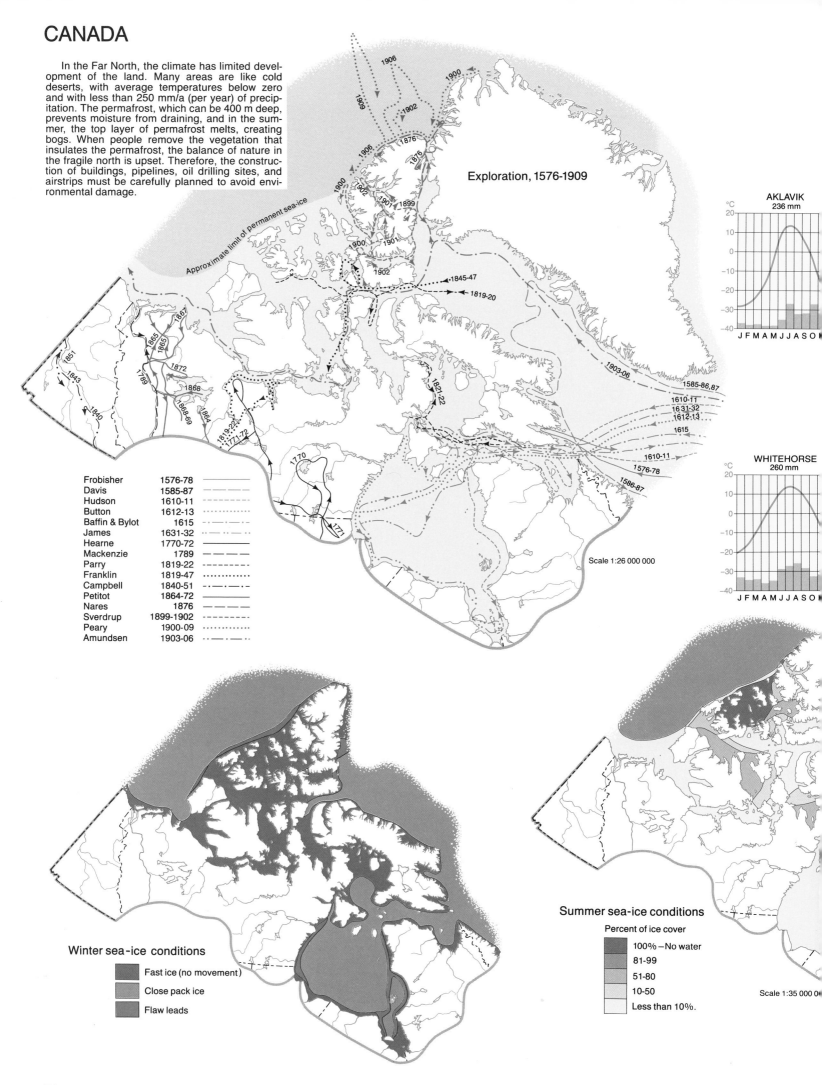

Exploration, 1576-1909

Frobisher	1576-78
Davis	1585-87
Hudson	1610-11
Button	1612-13
Baffin & Bylot	1615
James	1631-32
Hearne	1770-72
Mackenzie	1789
Parry	1819-22
Franklin	1819-47
Campbell	1840-51
Petitot	1864-72
Nares	1876
Sverdrup	1899-1902
Peary	1900-09
Amundsen	1903-06

Scale 1:26 000 000

AKLAVIK
236 mm

WHITEHORSE
260 mm

Winter sea-ice conditions

Fast ice (no movement)
Close pack ice
Flaw leads

Summer sea-ice conditions

Percent of ice cover

100% – No water
81-99
51-80
10-50
Less than 10%.

Scale 1:35 000 00

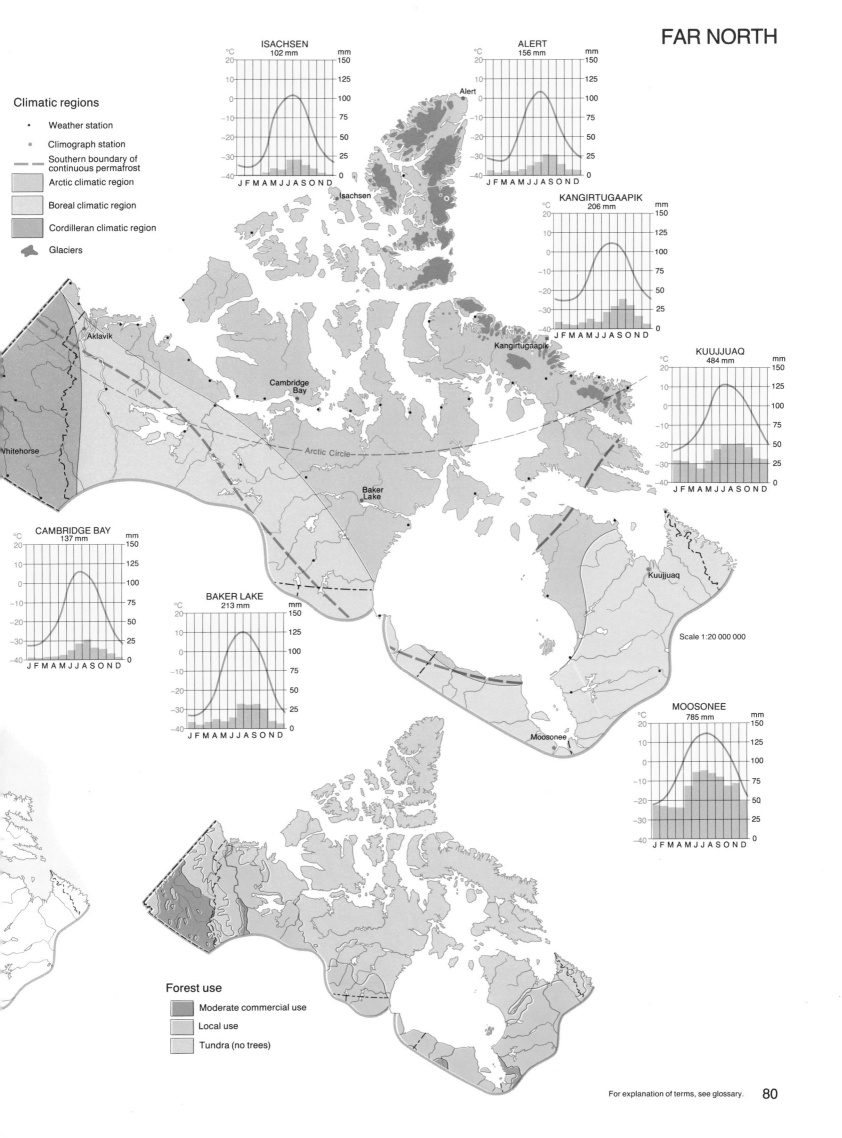

Climatic regions

- • Weather station
- ○ Climograph station
- –– Southern boundary of continuous permafrost
- Arctic climatic region
- Boreal climatic region
- Cordilleran climatic region
- Glaciers

ISACHSEN 102 mm

ALERT 156 mm

KANGIRTUGAAPIK 206 mm

KUUJJUAQ 484 mm

CAMBRIDGE BAY 137 mm

BAKER LAKE 213 mm

MOOSONEE 785 mm

Scale 1:20 000 000

Forest use

- Moderate commercial use
- Local use
- Tundra (no trees)

For explanation of terms, see glossary. **80**

Delta area of the Mackenzie River near Inuvik, Northwest Territories

FORT McPHERSON, N.W.T.

0 km   5   10   15

Scale 1:250 000   Contour values in feet

The contact of the Canadian Shield with the Great Lakes–
St. Lawrence Lowlands near Ottawa, Ontario

CANTON DE PONTEFRACT
CANTON DE MANSFIELD

Lac
de
Traverse

COULONGE

Lac
Bertrand

Lac
La Frontière

Davidson

Cour à bois

Poste de transformateurs

Coreille
Island

Bruyère

Scierie

Cheminée

Pont Couvert

NORTH
FRONT
D

RIVIÈRE

Foyer de l'âge d'or

Grande Chute

Dump

Pointe
à l'Achigan

EAST

Cour à bois

FORT COULONGE, QUÉBEC

0 m	1000	2000	3000

Scale 1:50 000   Contour values in feet

Fort-
Coulonge

CANADA

Satellite image of part of the Canadian Shield near Yellowknife, Northwest Territories

Where there is a distinct difference in elevation at the edge of the Shield, rivers such as this one in Québec are often used for hydro-electric power.

The Clay Belts of northern Ontario and Québec are used for agriculture in the Near North.

Map labels

NORTHWEST TERRITORIES

NAHANNI

Great Bear Lake

Y.T.

Liard

Fort Simpson

Rae-Edzo

Yellowknife

Fort Liard

Fort Providence

Mackenzie

Hay River

Pine Point

Great Slave Lake

Fort Resolution

B.C.

WOOD BUFFALO

Fort Smith

ALBERTA

Slave

Uranium City

Fond-du-Lac

Lake Athabasca

SASKATCHEWAN

Cree Lake

Wollaston Lake

Brochet

Reindeer Lake

Southern Indian Lake

Churchill

HUDSON BAY

Lynn Lake

Leaf Rapids

Split Lake

Nelson

Gillam

Thompson

Hayes

MANITOBA

Oxford House

Gods River

GRASS RIVER

Cross Lake

Big Trout Lake

Norway House

Garden Hill

St. Theresa Point

Sandy Lake

Severn

Lake Winnipeg

Negginan

Berens River

Bloodvein River

New Osnaburgh

NOPIMING

Red Lake

Ear Falls

Sioux Lookout

Lac Seul

Lake Nipigon

WHITESHELL

Dryden

Thunder Bay C.M.A.

Winnipeg

Kenora

Ignace

U.S.

Lake of the Woods

Fort Frances

QUETICO

NEAR NORTH

NEAR NORTH

The Near North, as its name suggests, is a transitional area between the industrialized south and the more isolated Far North. It stretches across Canada in an arc which includes much of the Canadian Shield. A great variety of wildlife lives here: beaver, mink, wolf, moose, deer, caribou, and more than 60 species of black flies.

Originally Indian groups, primarily Algonquian and Athapascan, lived nomadically by hunting and fishing. The important methods of transportation that they developed—such as the canoe, toboggan, and snowshoe—were also used by the Europeans, who were attracted to the region by its rich natural resources. The Indians and the Europeans often worked together, trapping and trading furs. Conflicts later arose between the two groups when the Europeans tapped lumber, mineral, and water resources.

Today, the population and the economy are still closely tied to the natural resources. Many cities such as Thompson, Chibougamau, and Sudbury have developed because of nearby mineral resources. Forests, particularly in the southern and eastern parts, are harvested for pulp and paper. Agriculture is practiced in a few areas. National and provincial parks preserve the scenic beauty of many areas in the Near North.

...es and ridges reveal folded Shield rocks.

LABRADOR SEA

NEWFOUNDLAND

Hopedale
North West River
Lake Melville
Cartwright
Happy Valley–Goose Bay
Smallwood Res.
Churchill
Schefferville
Churchill Falls
Labrador City
Gagnon
Reservoir Manicouagan
SEPT-ÎLES-PORT-CARTIER
Sept-Îles
Havre-St-Pierre
Natashquan
Port-Cartier
Baie-Comeau
Hauterive
GULF OF ST. LAWRENCE
St. Lawrence

POLAR BEAR

JAMES BAY

MISTASSINI
Lac Mistassini

Eastmain

QUÉBEC

Chibougamau
Chicoutimi-Jonquière C.M.A.
Mistassini
Alma
Dolbeau
CHIBOUGAMAU
Réservoir Gouin
St-Félicien
Roberval
La Baie
LAURENTIDES
Matagami
Rouyn, Noranda
Amos
La Tuque
ST-MAURICE
PORTNEUF
Hearst
Iroquois Falls
La Sarre
Val-d'Or
LA VÉRENDRYE
MONT-TREMBLANT
LA MAURICE
MASTIGOUCHE
Kapuskasing
Timmins
Kirkland Lake
New Liskeard
Mont-Laurier
Maniwaki
PAPINEAU-LABELLE
White River
MISSINAIBI LAKE
Sudbury C.M.A.
North Bay
Deep River
Pembroke
Petawawa
Elliot Lake
Sturgeon Falls
Ottawa
Arnprior
Carleton Place
Montréal
Sault Ste. Marie
Espanola
KILLARNEY
ALGONQUIN
Renfrew
Perth
Parry Sound
Huntsville
Bracebridge
Boston
Toronto
Lake Ontario
New York
Lake Erie

P.E.I.
N.B.
N.S.

UNITED STATES

Missinaibi
Albany
Mattagami
Abitibi
Ottawa
Lake Superior
Lake Huron
Lake Michigan

URBAN CENTRES

More than 100 000 people

50 000–100 000

25 000–49 999

10 000–24 999

5000–9999

Circles are proportional to the 1981 population. Census Metropolitan Areas (C.M.A.'s) are plotted for urban areas greater than 100 000 population.

One dot represents 50 people

Main highway and road

Main railway

National park

Provincial park or reserve

1 cm represents 100 km

0   100   200   300   400   500
kilometres

Scale 1: 10 000 000

For explanation of terms, see glossary.   84

CANADA

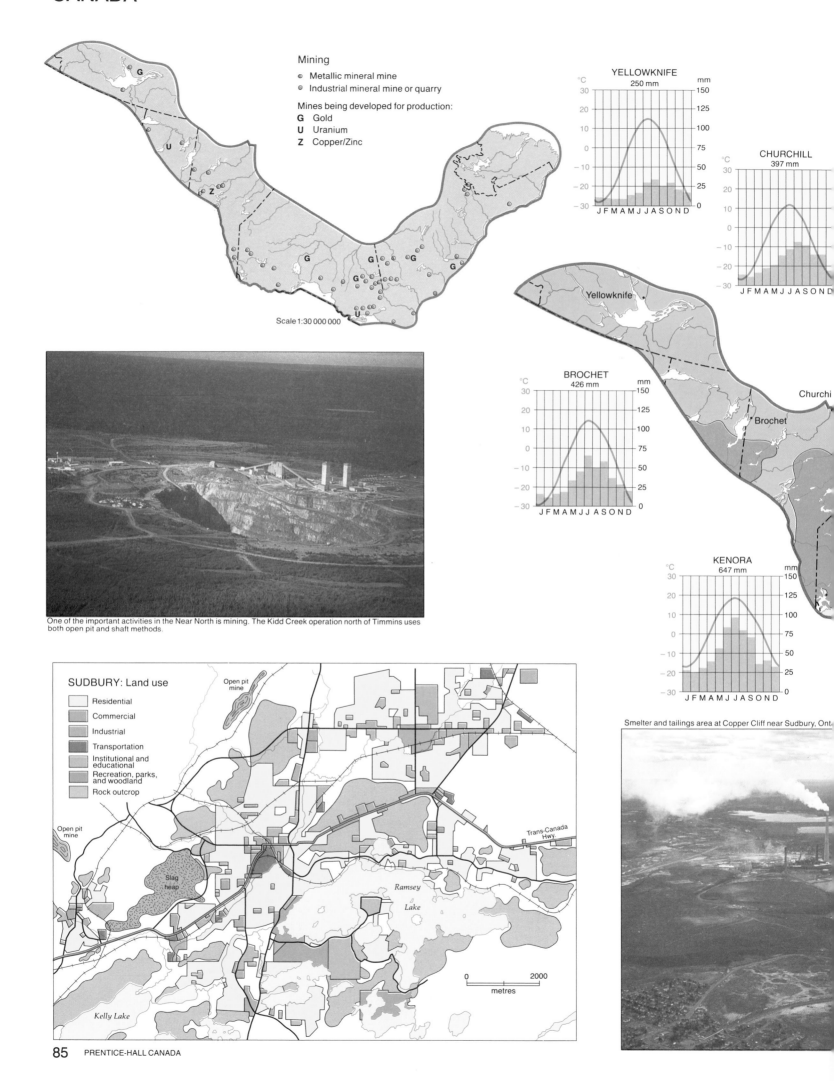

Mining

- ● Metallic mineral mine
- ● Industrial mineral mine or quarry

Mines being developed for production:
- **G** Gold
- **U** Uranium
- **Z** Copper/Zinc

Scale 1:30 000 000

YELLOWKNIFE
250 mm

CHURCHILL
397 mm

BROCHET
426 mm

KENORA
647 mm

One of the important activities in the Near North is mining. The Kidd Creek operation north of Timmins uses both open pit and shaft methods.

SUDBURY: Land use

- Residential
- Commercial
- Industrial
- Transportation
- Institutional and educational
- Recreation, parks, and woodland
- Rock outcrop

Open pit mine

Open pit mine

Trans-Canada Hwy.

Slag heap

Ramsey Lake

Kelly Lake

0   2000
metres

Smelter and tailings area at Copper Cliff near Sudbury, Ont.

The Near North is rich in natural resources — metallic mineral deposits, forests, and flowing water. These resources have brought prosperity to the region, but they have also made it vulnerable. Changes in the market demand and reductions in the supply of resources can affect the economy.

The effect of resource development on the environment is also a concern. Air and water pollution often occur near smelters and pulp and paper plants. Large power developments may require extensive flooding and changes in natural drainage patterns.

The potential of the Near North is great. With careful and orderly management, its resources will benefit both the region and Canada as a whole.

EXTENT OF THE NEAR NORTH

The inner segments, along with the given values, represent that percent of each province or territory which falls within the Near North.

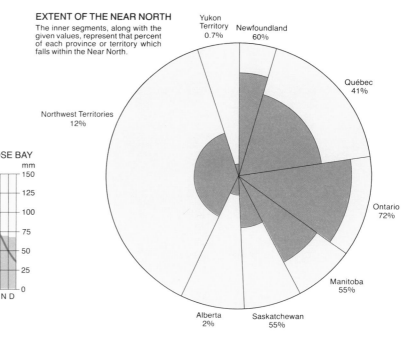

Yukon Territory 0.7%
Newfoundland 60%
Québec 41%
Northwest Territories 12%
Ontario 72%
Manitoba 55%
Alberta 2%
Saskatchewan 55%

HAPPY VALLEY-GOOSE BAY
877 mm

KAPUSKASING
871 mm

PREDOMINANT LAND CLASSES

- Productive forest
- Improved land
- Wild land
- Climograph station

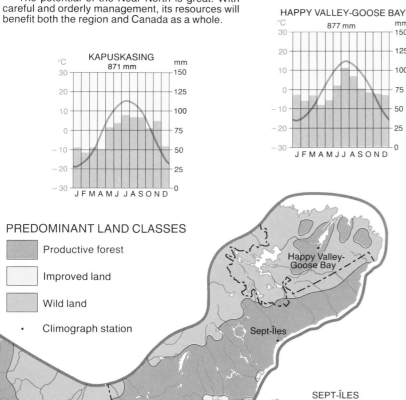

Happy Valley-Goose Bay
Sept-Îles
Kapuskasing
Sudbury

Scale 1:20 000 000

SEPT-ÎLES
1090 mm

SUDBURY
835 mm

A view of Sept-Îles and Baie des Sept-Îles

LAND CLASSES IN CANADA
Thousands of square kilometres

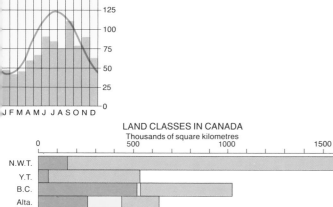

N.W.T.
Y.T.
B.C.
Alta.
Sask.
Man.
Ont.
Qué.
N.B.
N.S.
P.E.I.
Nfld.

- Productive forest
- Improved land
- Wild land

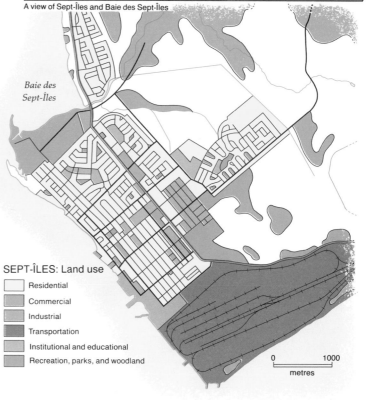

Baie des Sept-Îles

SEPT-ÎLES: Land use

- Residential
- Commercial
- Industrial
- Transportation
- Institutional and educational
- Recreation, parks, and woodland

0 1000 metres

CANADA

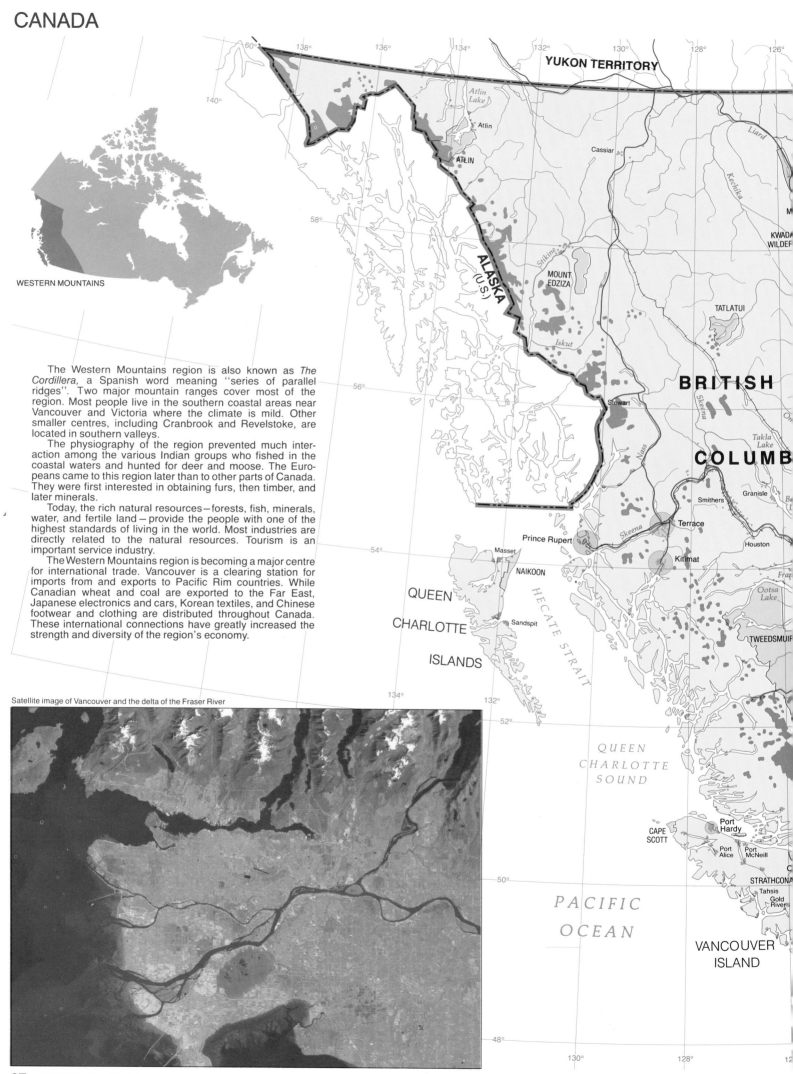

WESTERN MOUNTAINS

The Western Mountains region is also known as *The Cordillera,* a Spanish word meaning "series of parallel ridges". Two major mountain ranges cover most of the region. Most people live in the southern coastal areas near Vancouver and Victoria where the climate is mild. Other smaller centres, including Cranbrook and Revelstoke, are located in southern valleys.

The physiography of the region prevented much interaction among the various Indian groups who fished in the coastal waters and hunted for deer and moose. The Europeans came to this region later than to other parts of Canada. They were first interested in obtaining furs, then timber, and later minerals.

Today, the rich natural resources—forests, fish, minerals, water, and fertile land—provide the people with one of the highest standards of living in the world. Most industries are directly related to the natural resources. Tourism is an important service industry.

The Western Mountains region is becoming a major centre for international trade. Vancouver is a clearing station for imports from and exports to Pacific Rim countries. While Canadian wheat and coal are exported to the Far East, Japanese electronics and cars, Korean textiles, and Chinese footwear and clothing are distributed throughout Canada. These international connections have greatly increased the strength and diversity of the region's economy.

Satellite image of Vancouver and the delta of the Fraser River

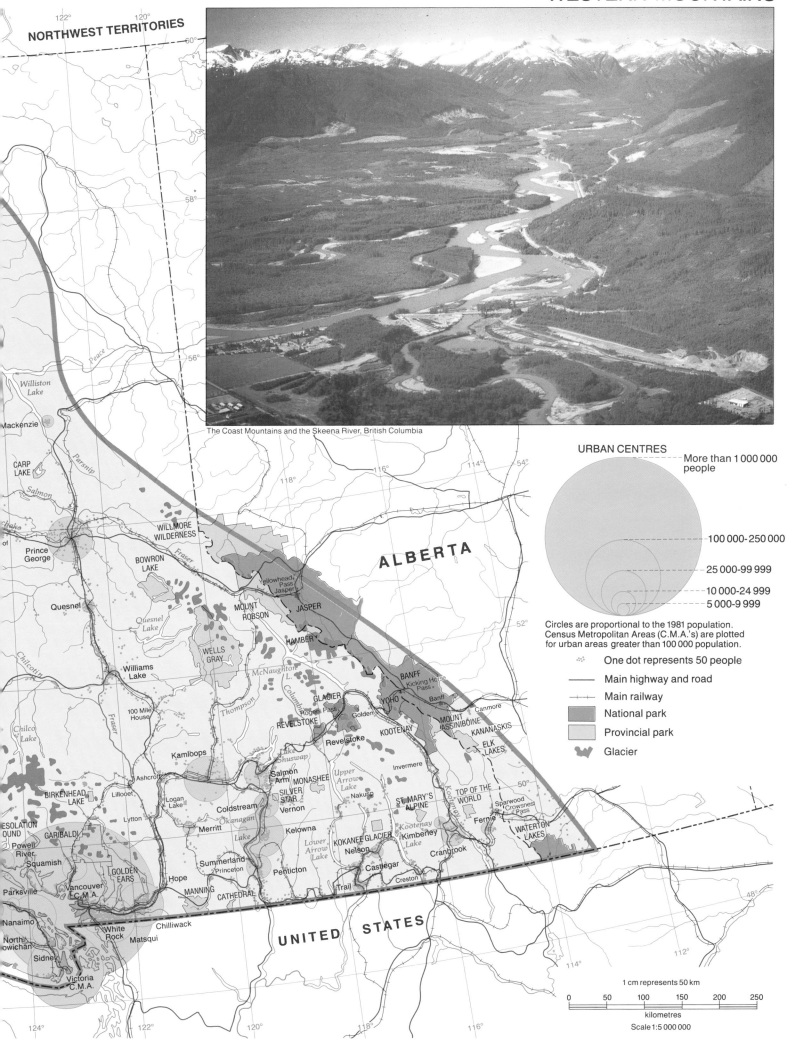

NORTHWEST TERRITORIES

The Coast Mountains and the Skeena River, British Columbia

ALBERTA

UNITED STATES

URBAN CENTRES

More than 1 000 000 people

100 000-250 000

25 000-99 999

10 000-24 999

5 000-9 999

Circles are proportional to the 1981 population. Census Metropolitan Areas (C.M.A.'s) are plotted for urban areas greater than 100 000 population.

One dot represents 50 people

Main highway and road

Main railway

National park

Provincial park

Glacier

1 cm represents 50 km

0   50   100   150   200   250

kilometres

Scale 1:5 000 000

For explanation of terms, see glossary.   **88**

CANADA

The Western Mountains area extends more than 1600 km from north to south, and from 118°W to 141°W. In an area of this size, variations in the climate are large. The north-south mountain ranges make the weather patterns even more complex. Certain locations within the Western Mountains have conditions similar to those in Norway, Chile, central U.S.S.R., and southern Australia.

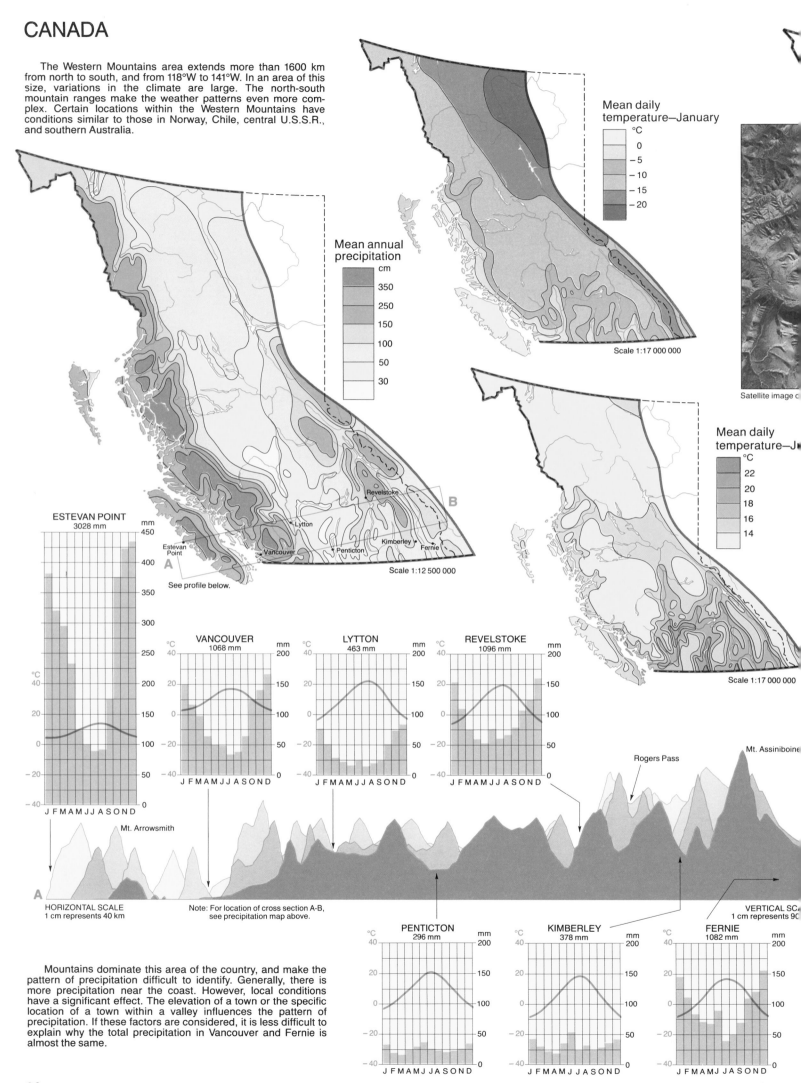

Mean daily temperature–January

°C
0
−5
−10
−15
−20

Scale 1:17 000 000

Satellite image

Mean annual precipitation

cm
350
250
150
100
50
30

Mean daily temperature–J

°C
22
20
18
16
14

Scale 1:17 000 000

Scale 1:12 500 000

See profile below.

ESTEVAN POINT
3028 mm

VANCOUVER
1068 mm

LYTTON
463 mm

REVELSTOKE
1096 mm

HORIZONTAL SCALE
1 cm represents 40 km

Note: For location of cross section A-B, see precipitation map above.

VERTICAL SCALE
1 cm represents 90

PENTICTON
296 mm

KIMBERLEY
378 mm

FERNIE
1082 mm

Mountains dominate this area of the country, and make the pattern of precipitation difficult to identify. Generally, there is more precipitation near the coast. However, local conditions have a significant effect. The elevation of a town or the specific location of a town within a valley influences the pattern of precipitation. If these factors are considered, it is less difficult to explain why the total precipitation in Vancouver and Fernie is almost the same.

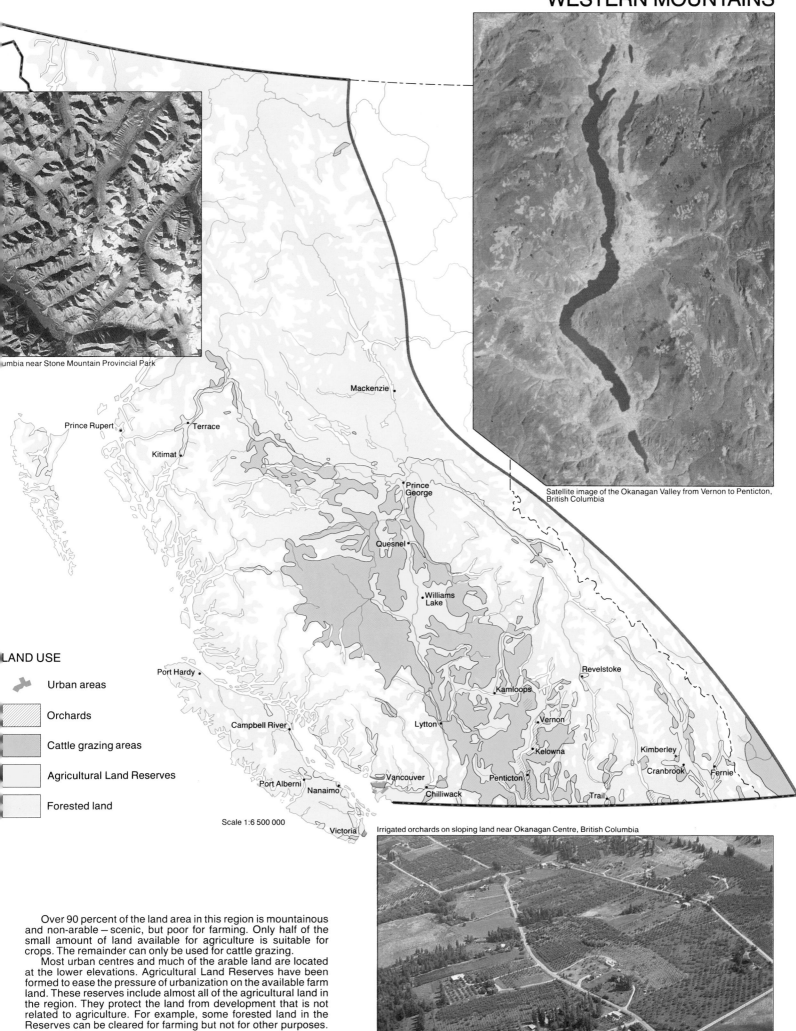

...umbia near Stone Mountain Provincial Park

Satellite image of the Okanagan Valley from Vernon to Penticton, British Columbia

LAND USE

- Urban areas
- Orchards
- Cattle grazing areas
- Agricultural Land Reserves
- Forested land

Scale 1:6 500 000

Mackenzie

Prince Rupert • Terrace

Kitimat

Prince George

Quesnel

Williams Lake

Port Hardy

Revelstoke

Kamloops

Campbell River

Lytton

Vernon

Kelowna

Kimberley

Cranbrook

Fernie

Port Alberni

Nanaimo

Vancouver

Chilliwack

Penticton

Trail

Victoria

Irrigated orchards on sloping land near Okanagan Centre, British Columbia

Over 90 percent of the land area in this region is mountainous and non-arable — scenic, but poor for farming. Only half of the small amount of land available for agriculture is suitable for crops. The remainder can only be used for cattle grazing.

Most urban centres and much of the arable land are located at the lower elevations. Agricultural Land Reserves have been formed to ease the pressure of urbanization on the available farm land. These reserves include almost all of the agricultural land in the region. They protect the land from development that is not related to agriculture. For example, some forested land in the Reserves can be cleared for farming but not for other purposes.

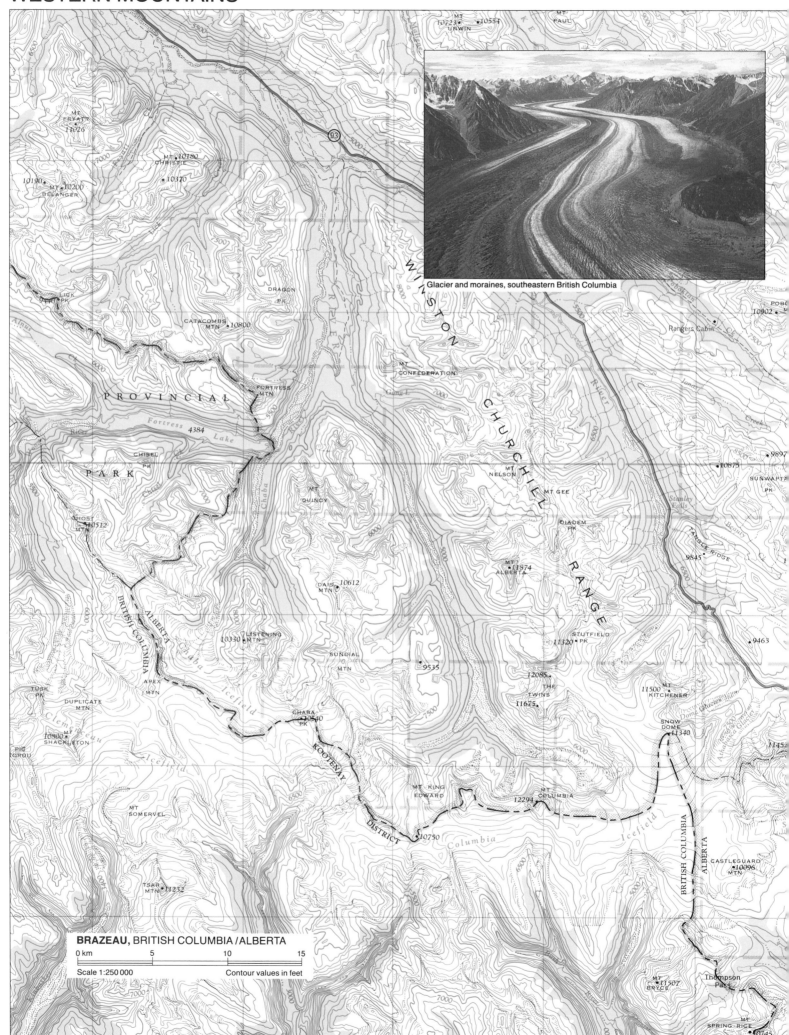

Glacier and moraines, southeastern British Columbia

BRAZEAU, BRITISH COLUMBIA / ALBERTA

0 km   5   10   15

Scale 1:250 000   Contour values in feet

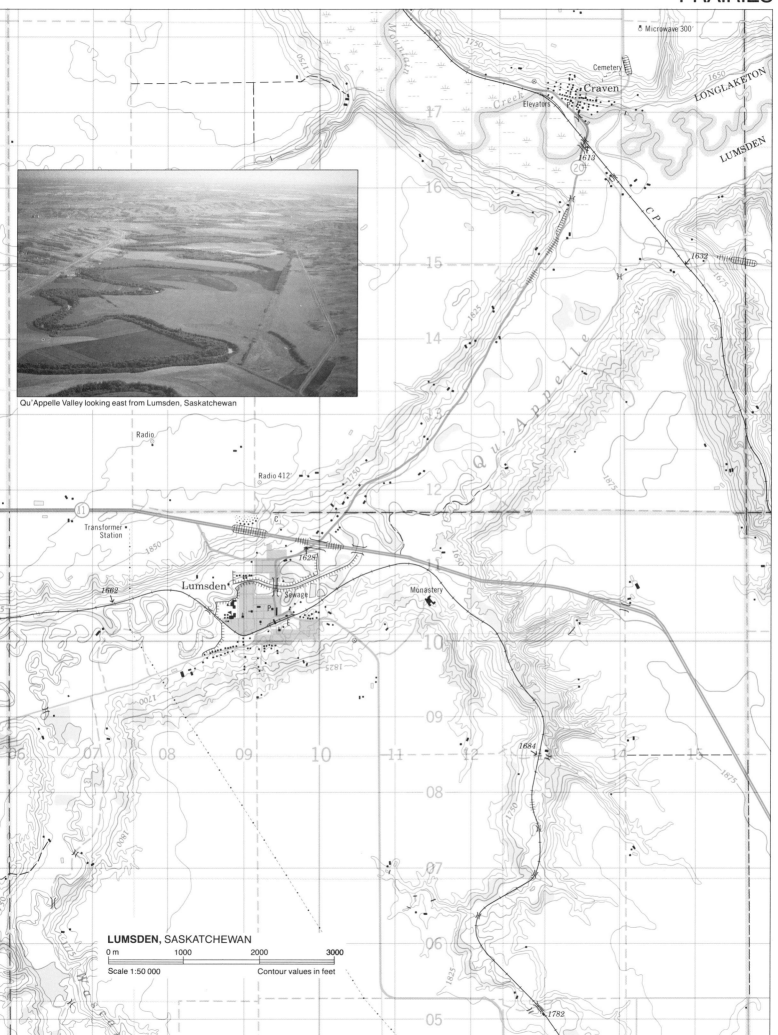

Qu'Appelle Valley looking east from Lumsden, Saskatchewan

Craven

Cemetery

δ Microwave 300'

LONGLAKETON

LUMSDEN

Elevators

Creek

Mountain

C P

1613

1632

1750

1650

1675

1825

1775

1875

Qu'Appelle

Radio

Radio 412

1750

Transformer
Station

1850

1628

C

Lumsden

Sewage

1662

P

Monastery

1650

1825

1700

1684

1875

1750

1782

LUMSDEN, SASKATCHEWAN

0 m	1000	2000	3000

Scale 1:50 000   Contour values in feet

CANADA

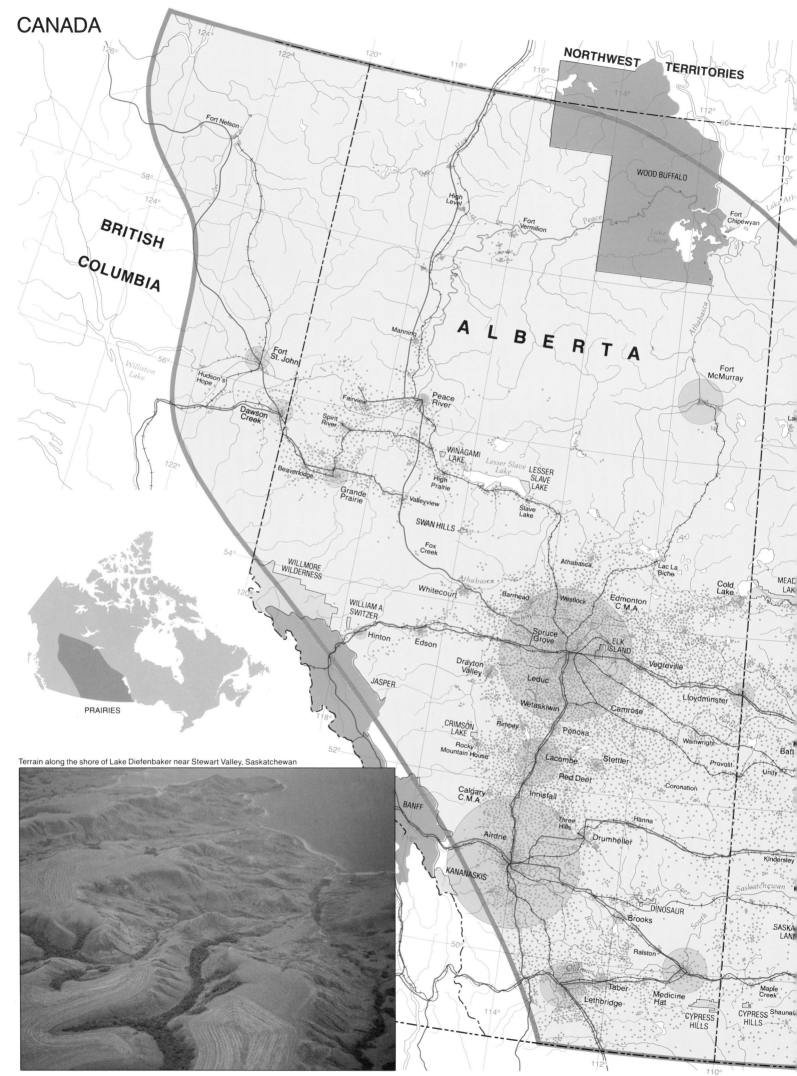

BRITISH COLUMBIA

NORTHWEST TERRITORIES

WOOD BUFFALO

A L B E R T A

PRAIRIES

Terrain along the shore of Lake Diefenbaker near Stewart Valley, Saskatchewan

The Prairies are often known as Canada's breadbasket and agricultural heartland. No other region in Canada has as much uniformity in its physical character. Ethnically, however, the region is diverse. Although people of British ancestry are in the majority, there are many small communities of immigrants from countries such as the Soviet Union, the Ukraine, Finland, and Germany, and their descendants. Native people represent 3 percent of the population.

Economically, the region has changed. The original inhabitants, the nomadic Cree, Blackfoot, Blood, and Pigeon Indians hunted buffalo for food, clothing, tools, and shelter. When the Europeans came to the area in search of furs, the Indians traded furs and pemmican (dried buffalo meat) for many European goods.

Tcday, the land is used mostly for agriculture. Wheat is the main crop in Saskatchewan, while ranching dominates most of Alberta. Irrigation has been introduced to make drier areas more fertiie. The discovery of oil, natural gas, and potash deposits has also stimulated the economic growth of the region.

In just over 100 a (years) the Prairies have changed from a nomadic, hunting economy to a modern, complex society based on a variety of resources.

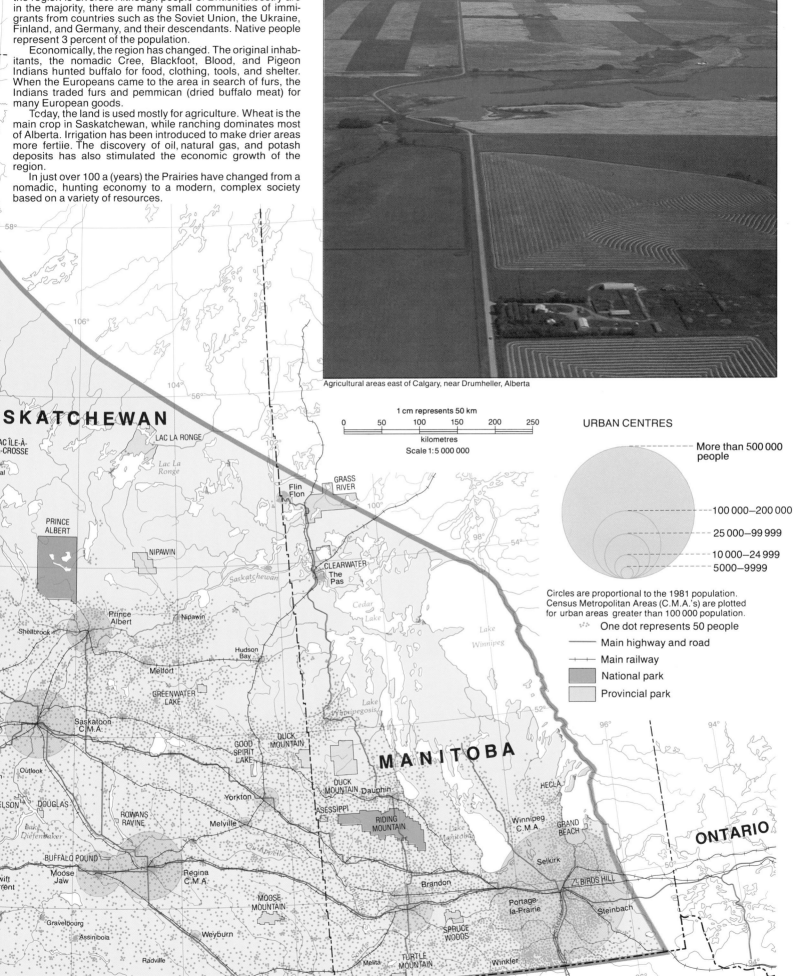

Agricultural areas east of Calgary, near Drumheller, Alberta

1 cm represents 50 km

0   50   100   150   200   250
kilometres
Scale 1:5 000 000

URBAN CENTRES

More than 500 000 people

100 000–200 000

25 000–99 999

10 000–24 999

5000–9999

Circles are proportional to the 1981 population. Census Metropolitan Areas (C.M.A.'s) are plotted for urban areas greater than 100 000 population.

One dot represents 50 people

Main highway and road

Main railway

National park

Provincial park

CANADA

At Confederation the Prairies were considered an agricultural frontier. By the 1920's the area had become the home of hundreds of thousands of new immigrants. Settlement created markets for agricultural machinery. New rail lines were built. The Prairies provided Canada with its most important single export—grain.

In recent years, the agriculture of the Prairies has greatly changed. Larger farms and expensive equipment have made heavy financial investment necessary. Irrigation, needed because of the low precipitation in the region, has become more widespread.

Although the economy of the Prairies is more diversified today than in the past, agriculture is still an important sector.

Mean annual moisture deficiency
(in millimetres)

250
200
150
100
50
0

Scale 1:22 000 000

Soil moisture deficiency measures the difference between the amount of moisture needed for plant growth and the amount of moisture needed that can be obtained from the soil. The mean annual soil moisture deficiency figure can be used to estimate irrigation requirements.

FORT McMURRAY
435 mm

Gross annual farm sales per farm

More than $90 000
50 000-90 000
30 000-49 999
10 000-29 999

Scale 1:20 000 000

FORT NELSON
446 mm

WORLD WHEAT EXPORTS

United States 42%
Canada 19%
Australia 13%
France 11%
Other 10%
Argentina 5%

Fort Nelson
Fort Vermilion
B.C.
Peace River
Fort McMurray
Grande Prairie
ALBERTA
Edmonton
Red Deer
Calgary
Medicine Hat
Lethbridge

Average farm size
(hectares)

More than 500 ha
400-500
300-399
200-299
100-199

Scale 1:20 000 000

Boundaries shown are census divisions.

TRENDS IN FARMING

Number of farms
Occupied hectares
Improved hectares
Hectares of crops

Millions of hectares
Thousands of farms

1901 1911 1921 1931 1941 1951 1961 1971 1981

RED DEER
449 mm

Satellite image showing irrigation patterns in southwestern Alberta

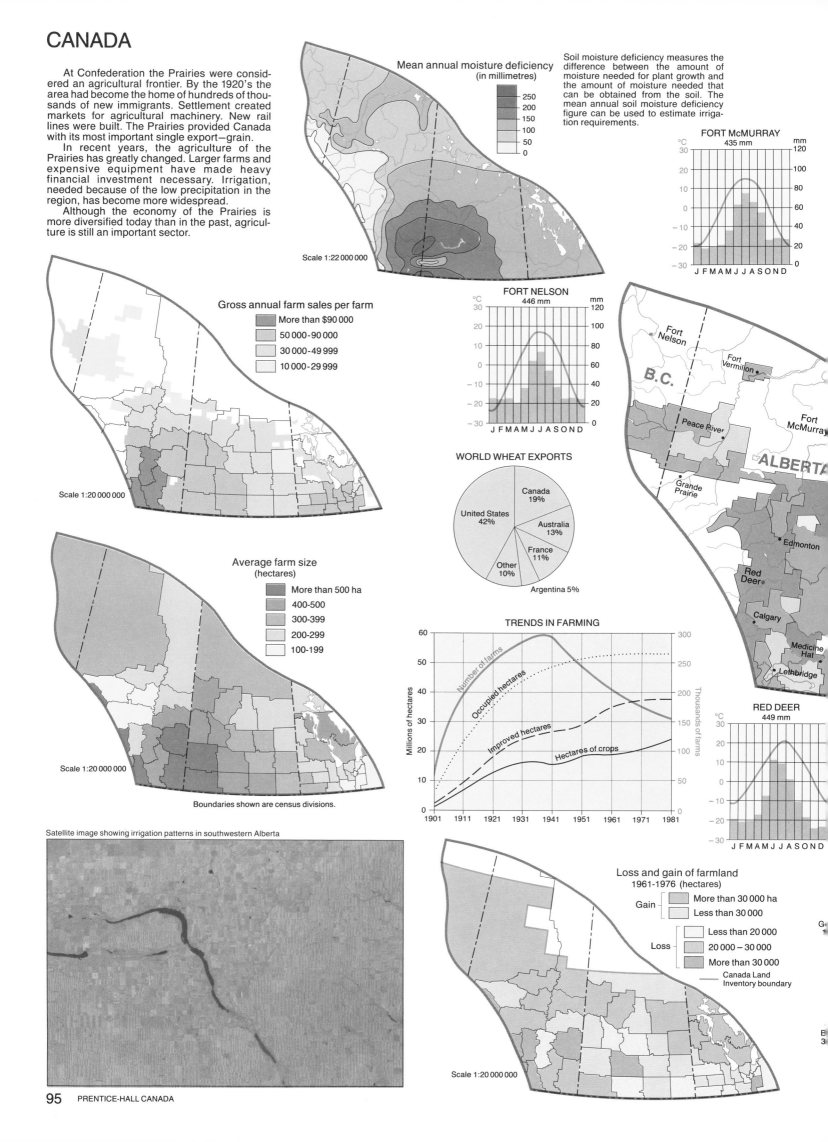

Loss and gain of farmland
1961-1976 (hectares)

Gain
More than 30 000 ha
Less than 30 000

Loss
Less than 20 000
20 000 – 30 000
More than 30 000

Canada Land Inventory boundary

Scale 1:20 000 000

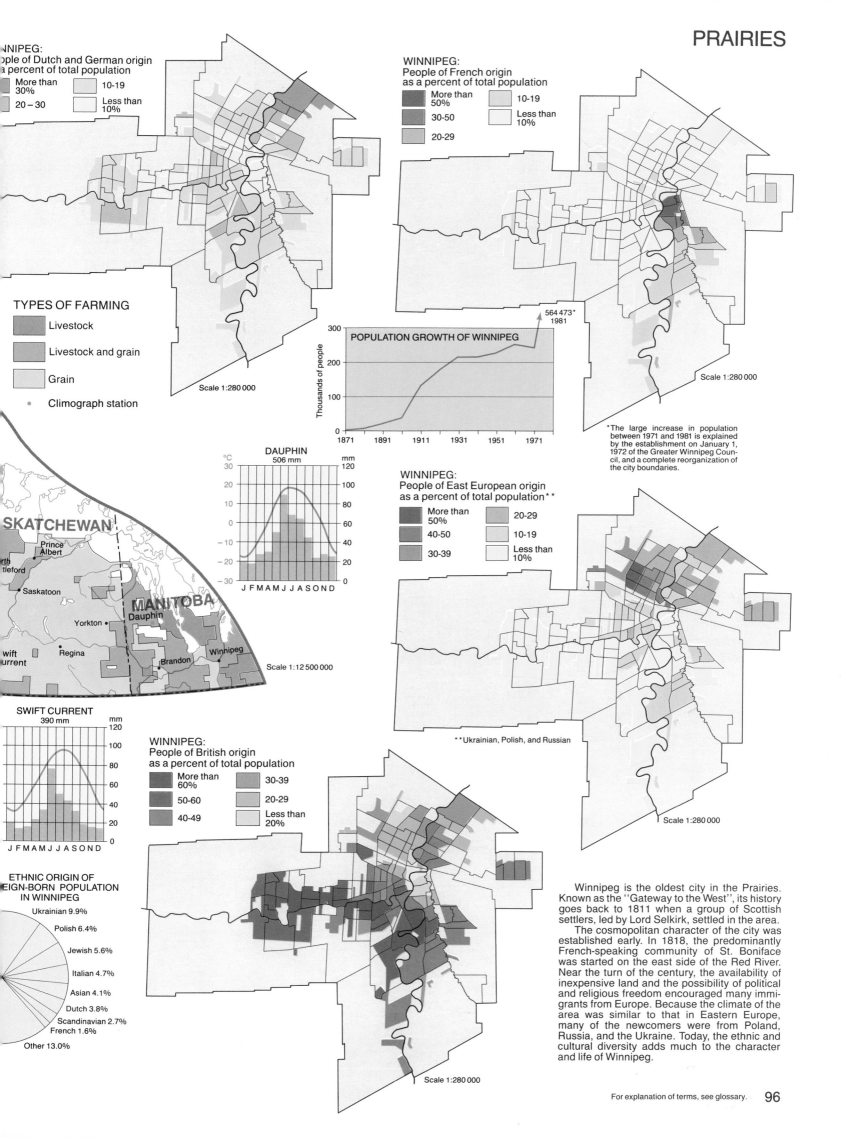

WINNIPEG:
People of Dutch and German origin
as a percent of total population

- More than 30%
- 20 – 30
- 10-19
- Less than 10%

WINNIPEG:
People of French origin
as a percent of total population

- More than 50%
- 30-50
- 20-29
- 10-19
- Less than 10%

TYPES OF FARMING

- Livestock
- Livestock and grain
- Grain

- Climograph station

Scale 1:280 000

POPULATION GROWTH OF WINNIPEG

564 473*
1981

Thousands of people

300

200

100

0

1871   1891   1911   1931   1951   1971

Scale 1:280 000

*The large increase in population between 1971 and 1981 is explained by the establishment on January 1, 1972 of the Greater Winnipeg Council, and a complete reorganization of the city boundaries.

DAUPHIN
506 mm

°C   mm
30   120
20   100
10   80
0   60
-10 40
-20 20
-30 0

J F M A M J J A S O N D

SASKATCHEWAN

North Battleford
Prince Albert

Saskatoon

MANITOBA

Yorkton

Dauphin

Swift Current

Regina

Brandon

Winnipeg

Scale 1:12 500 000

WINNIPEG:
People of East European origin
as a percent of total population**

- More than 50%
- 40-50
- 30-39
- 20-29
- 10-19
- Less than 10%

**Ukrainian, Polish, and Russian

SWIFT CURRENT
390 mm

mm
120
100
80
60
40
20
0

J F M A M J J A S O N D

WINNIPEG:
People of British origin
as a percent of total population

- More than 60%
- 50-60
- 40-49
- 30-39
- 20-29
- Less than 20%

Scale 1:280 000

ETHNIC ORIGIN OF FOREIGN-BORN POPULATION IN WINNIPEG

- Ukrainian 9.9%
- Polish 6.4%
- Jewish 5.6%
- Italian 4.7%
- Asian 4.1%
- Dutch 3.8%
- Scandinavian 2.7%
- French 1.6%
- Other 13.0%

Winnipeg is the oldest city in the Prairies. Known as the "Gateway to the West", its history goes back to 1811 when a group of Scottish settlers, led by Lord Selkirk, settled in the area.

The cosmopolitan character of the city was established early. In 1818, the predominantly French-speaking community of St. Boniface was started on the east side of the Red River. Near the turn of the century, the availability of inexpensive land and the possibility of political and religious freedom encouraged many immigrants from Europe. Because the climate of the area was similar to that in Eastern Europe, many of the newcomers were from Poland, Russia, and the Ukraine. Today, the ethnic and cultural diversity adds much to the character and life of Winnipeg.

Scale 1:280 000

CANADA

The Great Lakes-St. Lawrence region has been described as Canada's main street, its heartland. Approximately 50 percent of Canada's population and 11 of the 24 Canadian cities with over 100 000 people are found in this small region in southern Québec and Ontario. Many internal differences exist — in historical and economic development, language, and culture. However, the region is unified by its physical base and its advantages for industrial development.

The earliest inhabitants of the region, the Algonquian and Iroquois Indians, lived by hunting, trapping, and farming. When the French arrived, these Indians guided them into the interior and helped them build a vast fur-trading empire.

Over the years, many factors have contributed to make the Great Lakes-St. Lawrence a wealthy region with a significant economic and political influence on the rest of Canada. Agriculture was developed early and has become a major source of wealth because of the fertile soils and relatively mild climate. Other factors—such as superior water transportation routes and proximity to the industrial heartland of the United States — have encouraged the growth of industry. Today, 70 percent of Canada's manufactured goods are produced in the Great Lakes-St. Lawrence region.

Satellite image of the area including Toronto, Kitchener-Waterloo, and Niagara Falls

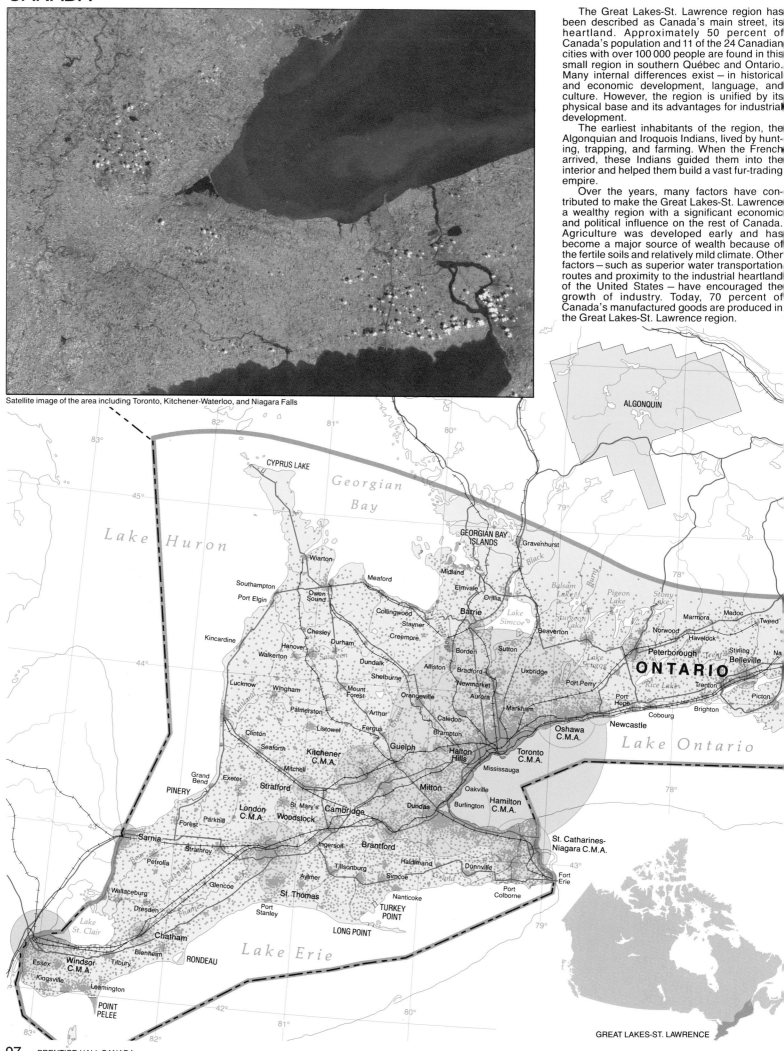

GREAT LAKES-ST. LAWRENCE

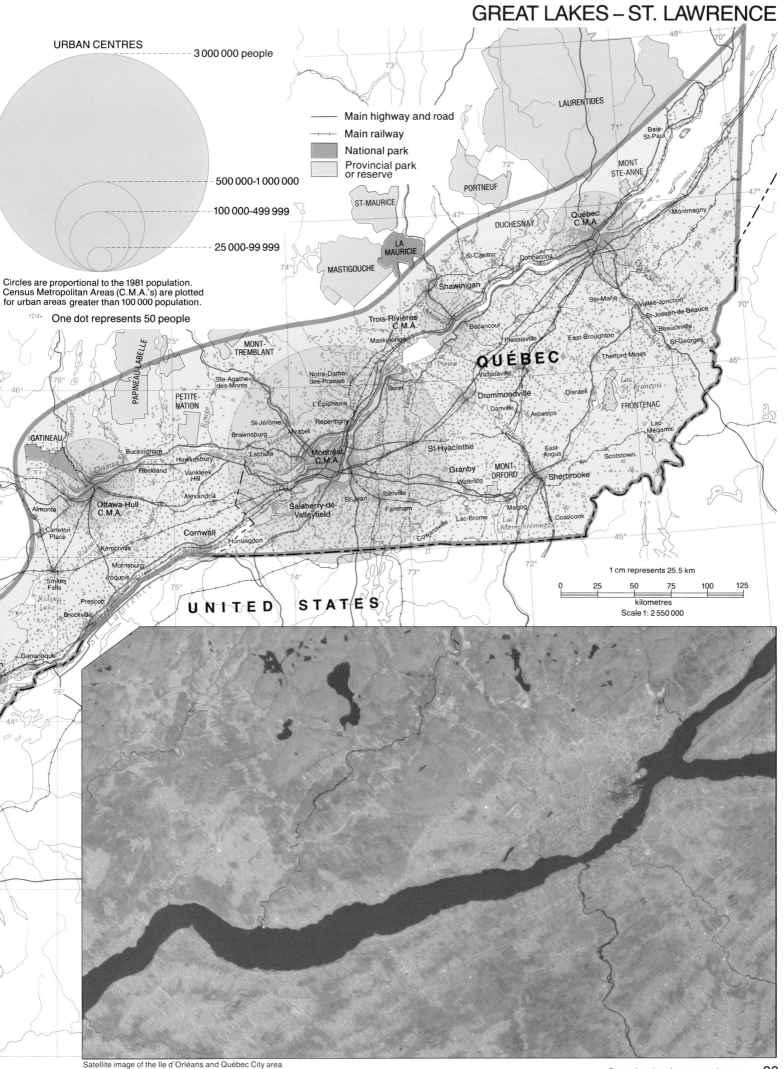

URBAN CENTRES

—— 3 000 000 people

—— 500 000-1 000 000

—— 100 000-499 999

—— 25 000-99 999

Circles are proportional to the 1981 population.
Census Metropolitan Areas (C.M.A.'s) are plotted
for urban areas greater than 100 000 population.

·:· One dot represents 50 people

—————— Main highway and road

—+—+—+— Main railway

National park

Provincial park
or reserve

LAURENTIDES

Baie-St-Paul

MONT STE-ANNE

PORTNEUF

Montmagny

ST-MAURICE

DUCHESNAY

Québec C.M.A.

LA MAURICIE

St-Casimir

Donnacona

MASTIGOUCHE

Shawinigan

Ste-Marie

Vallée-Jonction
St-Joseph-de-Beauce
Beauceville

Trois-Rivières C.M.A.

Bécancour

St-Georges

MONT-TREMBLANT

Maskinongé

Plessisville

East-Broughton

QUÉBEC

Thetford Mines

Notre-Dame-des-Prairies

Victoriaville

Lac St-François

Ste-Agathe-des-Monts

Sorel

Drummondville

Disraeli

FRONTENAC

PETITE-NATION

St-Jérôme

L'Épiphanie

Repentigny

Danville

Asbestos

Lac Mégantic

PAPINEAU-LABELLE

Brownsburg
Mirabel

St-Hyacinthe

East-Angus

Scotstown

GATINEAU

Buckingham
Hawkesbury
Lachute

Montréal C.M.A.

Granby

Waterloo

MONT-ORFORD

Sherbrooke

Rockland
Vankleek Hill

Iberville

Magog

Ottawa-Hull C.M.A.

Alexandria

Salaberry-de-Valleyfield

St-Jean

Farnham

Lac-Brome

Coaticook

Almonte

Carleton Place

Cornwall

Huntingdon

Cowansville

Lac Memphrémagog

Kemptville

Morrisburg
Iroquois

Smiths Falls

Prescott

Rideau Lake

Brockville

UNITED STATES

Gananoque

Satellite image of the Ile d'Orléans and Québec City area

1 cm represents 25.5 km

0   25   50   75   100   125

kilometres

Scale 1: 2 550 000

CANADA

Few cities in North America have changed as quickly and dramatically as Toronto has in the past 25 a (years). Like most cities, Toronto's physical appearance has changed. But in addition, its character and ethnic structure have undergone a transformation. Population growth has been caused mainly by an influx of people needed to fill available jobs. Almost 70 percent of immigrants to Ontario come to the Toronto area.

Following World War II immigration increased, particularly from Italy, the Ukraine, and Eastern Europe. In recent years, much of the immigration has been from the Far East and Portugal. Many immigrants from Africa and the Caribbean have also come to Toronto. They are not shown on the maps because their first language is often English.

Individual ethnic groups often settle in one or more specific areas. Toronto has five different areas with a distinct Chinese character. Over several years, groups also move within the city. Kensington Market, for example, once had a high Jewish population, but is now more Caribbean and Portuguese. Second and third generation Canadian families are tending to move to suburban areas.

The ethnic variety of the city is indicated by the media associated with individual cultural groups and the many cultural festivals held each year. Toronto has become a vivid example in a concentrated setting of the multicultural nature of Canada.

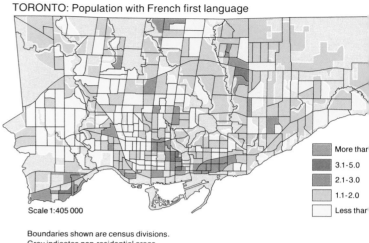

TORONTO: Population with French first language

Scale 1:405 000

More than
3.1-5.0
2.1-3.0
1.1-2.0
Less than

Boundaries shown are census divisions.
Grey indicates non-residential areas.

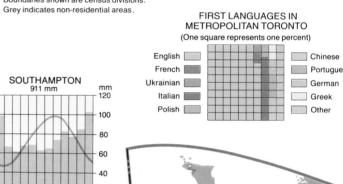

FIRST LANGUAGES IN
METROPOLITAN TORONTO
(One square represents one percent)

English
French
Ukrainian
Italian
Polish

Chinese
Portugue
German
Greek
Other

TORONTO: Population with Italian first language

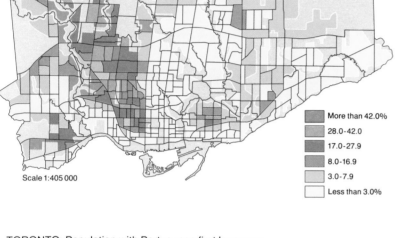

More than 42.0%
28.0-42.0
17.0-27.9
8.0-16.9
3.0-7.9
Less than 3.0%

Scale 1:405 000

SOUTHAMPTON
911 mm

LONDON
925 mm

TORONTO: Population with Portuguese first language

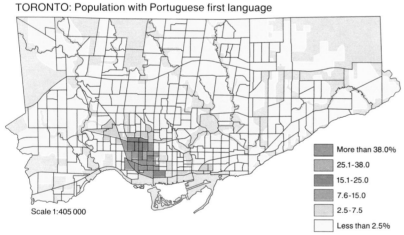

More than 38.0%
25.1-38.0
15.1-25.0
7.6-15.0
2.5-7.5
Less than 2.5%

Scale 1:405 000

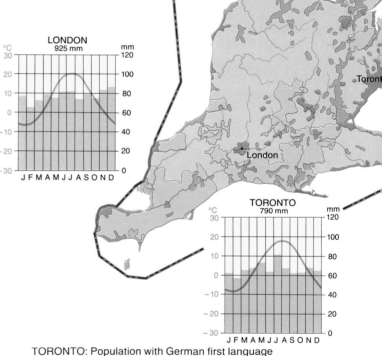

Southampton

London

Toron

TORONTO
790 mm

TORONTO: Population with Greek first language

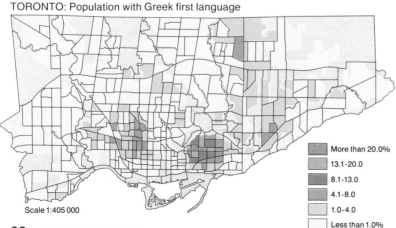

More than 20.0%
13.1-20.0
8.1-13.0
4.1-8.0
1.0-4.0
Less than 1.0%

Scale 1:405 000

TORONTO: Population with German first language

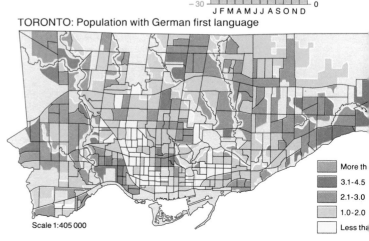

More th
3.1-4.5
2.1-3.0
1.0-2.0
Less tha

Scale 1:405 000

RONTO: Population with Chinese or Japanese first language

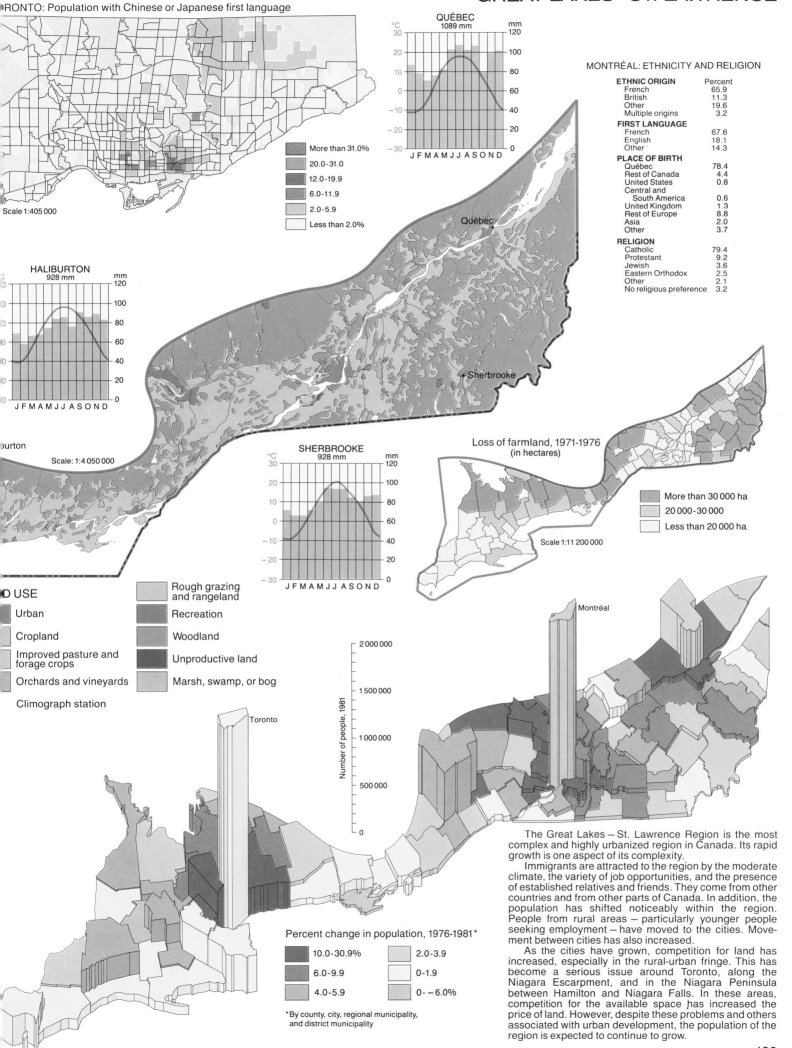

Scale 1:405 000

More than 31.0%
20.0–31.0
12.0–19.9
6.0–11.9
2.0–5.9
Less than 2.0%

QUÉBEC
1089 mm

HALIBURTON
928 mm

urton

Scale: 1:4 050 000

SHERBROOKE
928 mm

MONTRÉAL: ETHNICITY AND RELIGION

ETHNIC ORIGIN	Percent
French	65.9
British	11.3
Other	19.6
Multiple origins	3.2
FIRST LANGUAGE	
French	67.6
English	18.1
Other	14.3
PLACE OF BIRTH	
Québec	78.4
Rest of Canada	4.4
United States	0.8
Central and South America	0.6
United Kingdom	1.3
Rest of Europe	8.8
Asia	2.0
Other	3.7
RELIGION	
Catholic	79.4
Protestant	9.2
Jewish	3.6
Eastern Orthodox	2.5
Other	2.1
No religious preference	3.2

Québec

Sherbrooke

Loss of farmland, 1971-1976
(in hectares)

More than 30 000 ha
20 000 - 30 000
Less than 20 000 ha.

Scale 1:11 200 000

D USE

Urban

Cropland

Improved pasture and forage crops

Orchards and vineyards

Climograph station

Rough grazing and rangeland

Recreation

Woodland

Unproductive land

Marsh, swamp, or bog

Montréal

Toronto

Number of people, 1981

2 000 000

1 500 000

1 000 000

500 000

0

Percent change in population, 1976-1981*

10.0–30.9%
6.0–9.9
4.0–5.9

2.0–3.9
0–1.9
0– –6.0%

*By county, city, regional municipality, and district municipality

The Great Lakes – St. Lawrence Region is the most complex and highly urbanized region in Canada. Its rapid growth is one aspect of its complexity.

Immigrants are attracted to the region by the moderate climate, the variety of job opportunities, and the presence of established relatives and friends. They come from other countries and from other parts of Canada. In addition, the population has shifted noticeably within the region. People from rural areas — particularly younger people seeking employment — have moved to the cities. Movement between cities has also increased.

As the cities have grown, competition for land has increased, especially in the rural-urban fringe. This has become a serious issue around Toronto, along the Niagara Escarpment, and in the Niagara Peninsula between Hamilton and Niagara Falls. In these areas, competition for the available space has increased the price of land. However, despite these problems and others associated with urban development, the population of the region is expected to continue to grow.

For explanation of terms, see glossary. **100**

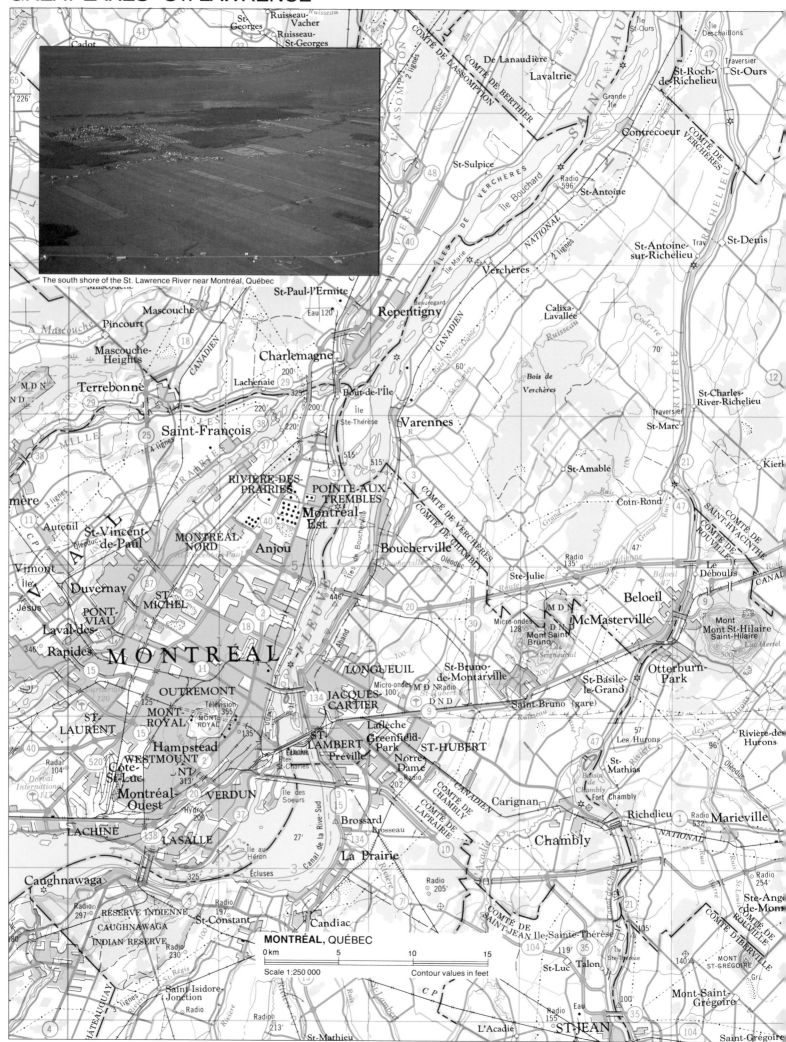

The south shore of the St. Lawrence River near Montréal, Québec

MONTRÉAL, QUÉBEC

0 km 5 10 15

Scale 1:250 000   Contour values in feet

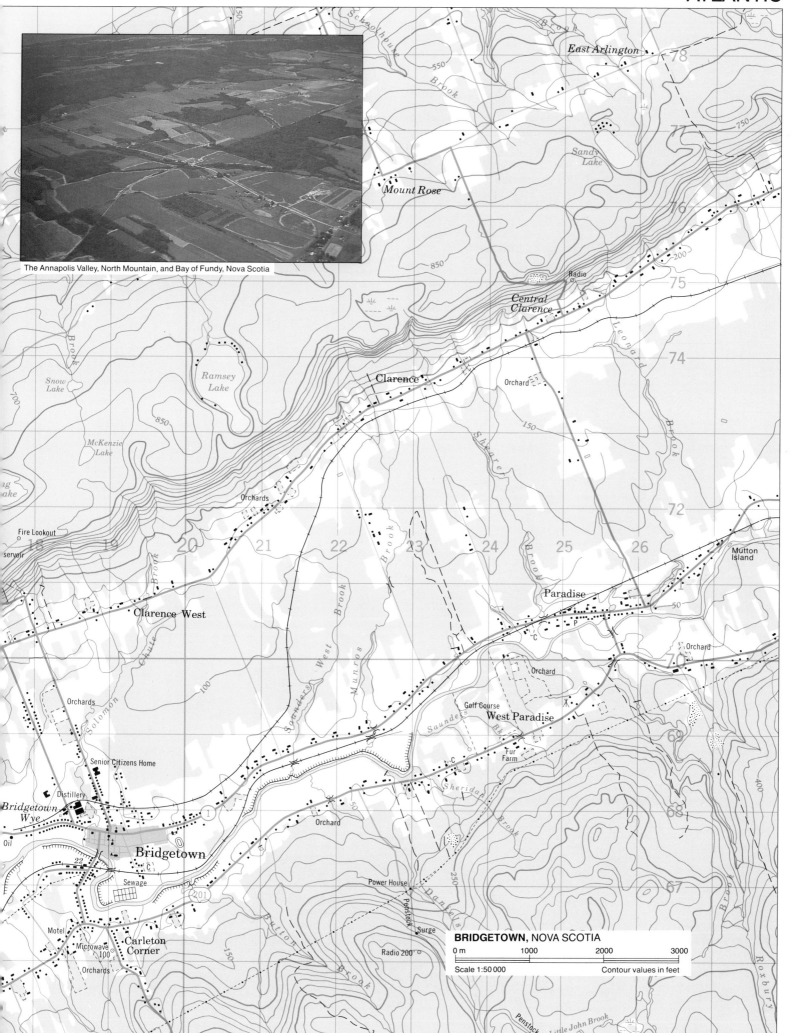

The Annapolis Valley, North Mountain, and Bay of Fundy, Nova Scotia

East Arlington

Mount Rose

Central Clarence

Radio

Clarence

Orchard

Snow Lake

Ramsey Lake

McKenzie Lake

Orchards

Fire Lookout

Reservoir

18   19   20   21   22   23   24   25   26

Mutton Island

Paradise

Clarence West

Orchards

West Paradise

Golf Course

Orchard

Orchard

Fur Farm

Senior Citizens Home

Sheridan

Distillery

Bridgetown Wye

Oil

Orchard

Bridgetown

Power House

Penstock

Surge

Sewage

201

Motel

Carleton Corner

Microwave

Orchards

Radio 200

BRIDGETOWN, NOVA SCOTIA

0 m	1000	2000	3000

Scale 1:50 000   Contour values in feet

Little John Brook

Penstock

CANADA

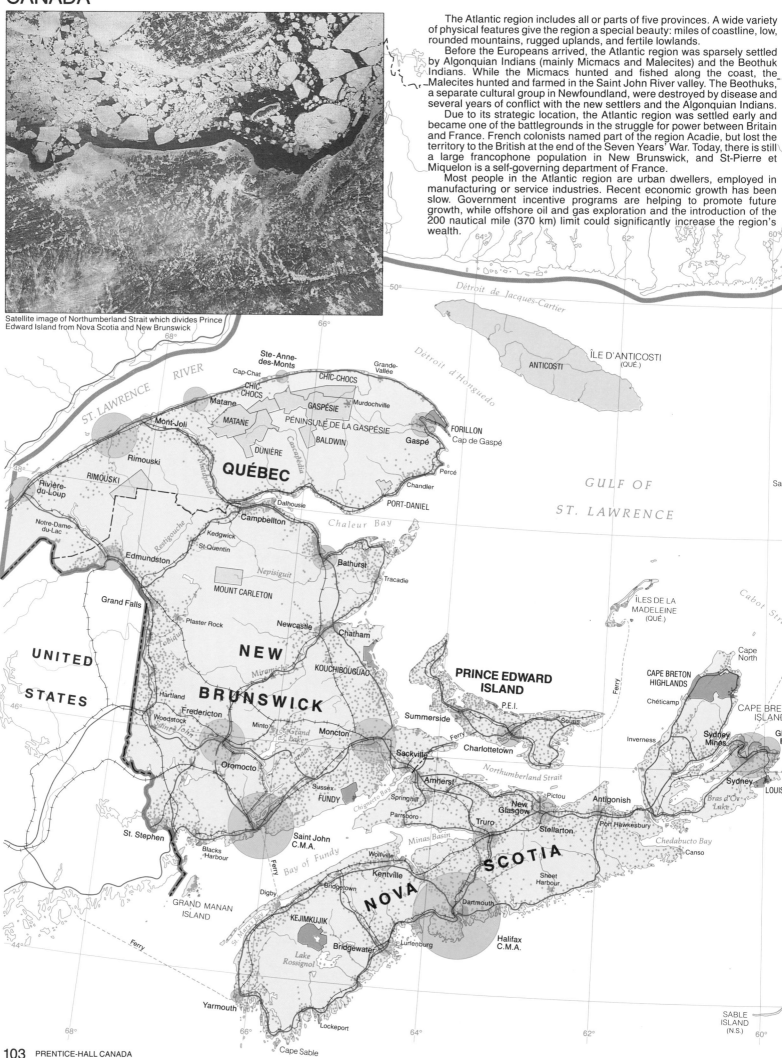

The Atlantic region includes all or parts of five provinces. A wide variety of physical features give the region a special beauty: miles of coastline, low, rounded mountains, rugged uplands, and fertile lowlands.

Before the Europeans arrived, the Atlantic region was sparsely settled by Algonquian Indians (mainly Micmacs and Malecites) and the Beothuk Indians. While the Micmacs hunted and fished along the coast, the Malecites hunted and farmed in the Saint John River valley. The Beothuks, a separate cultural group in Newfoundland, were destroyed by disease and several years of conflict with the new settlers and the Algonquian Indians.

Due to its strategic location, the Atlantic region was settled early and became one of the battlegrounds in the struggle for power between Britain and France. French colonists named part of the region Acadie, but lost the territory to the British at the end of the Seven Years' War. Today, there is still a large francophone population in New Brunswick, and St-Pierre et Miquelon is a self-governing department of France.

Most people in the Atlantic region are urban dwellers, employed in manufacturing or service industries. Recent economic growth has been slow. Government incentive programs are helping to promote future growth, while offshore oil and gas exploration and the introduction of the 200 nautical mile (370 km) limit could significantly increase the region's wealth.

Satellite image of Northumberland Strait which divides Prince Edward Island from Nova Scotia and New Brunswick

QUÉBEC

Mary's Harbour

BELLE
ISLE

Red
Bay

L'ANSE AUX MEADOWS
(National park)

St. Anthony

Strait of Belle Isle

Roddickton

GREY
ISLANDS

Port au Choix

HORSE
ISLANDS

White Bay

La Scie

GROS
MORNE

Baie Verte

Notre Dame
Bay

FOGO
ISLAND

Norris Point

SIR RICHARD
SQUIRES

Cox's Cove

Deer Lake

Windsor

Wesleyville

Bonavista
Bay

Corner
Brook

Grand
Lake

Red Indian
Lake

Gander
Lake

Gander

Bonavista Cape Bonavista

ATLANTIC

Stephenville

Buchans

Grand
Falls

Exploits

Catalina

OCEAN

St. George's

BARACHOIS
POND

NEWFOUNDLAND

TERRA
NOVA

Meelpaeg
Lake

Round
Pond

Trinity Bay

St. Alban's

St. John's
C.M.A.

Grey

Burgeo

Arnold's Cove

Carbonear

Conception Bay

Channel-
Port aux Basques

Harbour Breton

AVALON

BUTTER
POT

Grand Bank

Marystown

Placentia

Fortune

Burin

Placentia
Bay

PENINSULA

MIQUELON
(France)
ST-PIERRE

Fortune
Bay

Trepassey

Ferry

Cape Race

58°   56°   54°   52°   50°   50°   48°   46°   52°   54°   56°   58°

ATLANTIC

URBAN CENTRES

More than 200 000 people

60 000–160 000

25 000–59 999

10 000–24 999

5000–9999

Circles are proportional to the 1981 population.
Census Metropolitan Areas (C.M.A.'s) are plotted
for urban areas greater than 100 000 population.

One dot represents 50 people

Main highway and road

Main railway

National park

Provincial park or reserve

1 cm represents 35 km

0   50   100   150

kilometres

Scale 1:3 500 000

Sea stacks and cliffs along the shore of Conception Bay, Newfoundland

CANADA

Certain specialty products, such as potatoes, are associated with the Atlantic region. However, most agricultural income comes from the sale of general agricultural goods—dairy products, poultry and eggs, beef cattle and hogs—within the region. In recent years, the amount of land farmed, the number of active farms, and the number of young people working in agriculture have all declined. Various government incentive programs are trying to reverse these trends, and to modernize farming methods.

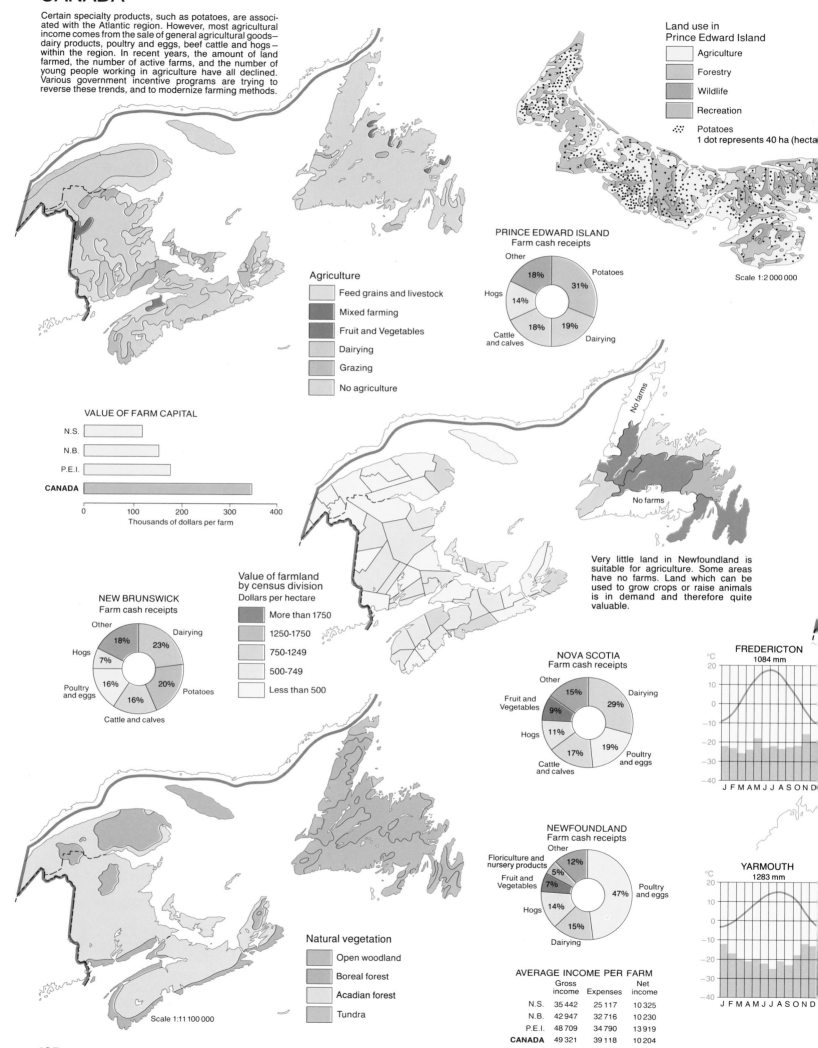

Land use in Prince Edward Island

- Agriculture
- Forestry
- Wildlife
- Recreation
- Potatoes
  1 dot represents 40 ha (hecta

Scale 1:2 000 000

Agriculture

- Feed grains and livestock
- Mixed farming
- Fruit and Vegetables
- Dairying
- Grazing
- No agriculture

PRINCE EDWARD ISLAND
Farm cash receipts

- Other 18%
- Potatoes 31%
- Dairying 19%
- Cattle and calves 18%
- Hogs 14%

VALUE OF FARM CAPITAL

- N.S.
- N.B.
- P.E.I.
- **CANADA**

0   100   200   300   400
Thousands of dollars per farm

No farms

Very little land in Newfoundland is suitable for agriculture. Some areas have no farms. Land which can be used to grow crops or raise animals is in demand and therefore quite valuable.

NEW BRUNSWICK
Farm cash receipts

- Other 18%
- Dairying 23%
- Hogs 7%
- Poultry and eggs 16%
- Potatoes 20%
- Cattle and calves 16%

Value of farmland by census division
Dollars per hectare

- More than 1750
- 1250-1750
- 750-1249
- 500-749
- Less than 500

NOVA SCOTIA
Farm cash receipts

- Other 15%
- Dairying 29%
- Fruit and Vegetables 9%
- Poultry and eggs 19%
- Hogs 11%
- Cattle and calves 17%

FREDERICTON
1084 mm
°C
20
10
0
-10
-20
-30
-40
J F M A M J J A S O N D

NEWFOUNDLAND
Farm cash receipts

- Other 12%
- Floriculture and nursery products 5%
- Fruit and Vegetables 7%
- Poultry and eggs 47%
- Hogs 14%
- Dairying 15%

Natural vegetation

- Open woodland
- Boreal forest
- Acadian forest
- Tundra

Scale 1:11 100 000

YARMOUTH
1283 mm
°C
20
10
0
-10
-20
-30
-40
J F M A M J J A S O N D

AVERAGE INCOME PER FARM

	Gross income	Expenses	Net income
N.S.	35 442	25 117	10 325
N.B.	42 947	32 716	10 230
P.E.I.	48 709	34 790	13 919
CANADA	49 321	39 118	10 204

The climate of the Atlantic region is characterized by two distinct seasons, summer and winter. In summer, warm air masses move in from the south. The ocean and the Gulf of St. Lawrence moderate the temperature and provide the moisture for precipitation. Some stations may experience precipitation, often in the form of light drizzle, 180 d (days) a year. Fog is common along the coast.

In winter, cold air masses from the north dominate the weather. The Labrador current carries icebergs south, making shipping dangerous. Pack ice as far south as Cape Breton Island limits the use of the Gulf of St. Lawrence. Saint John and Halifax are important ice-free ports for importing and exporting goods.

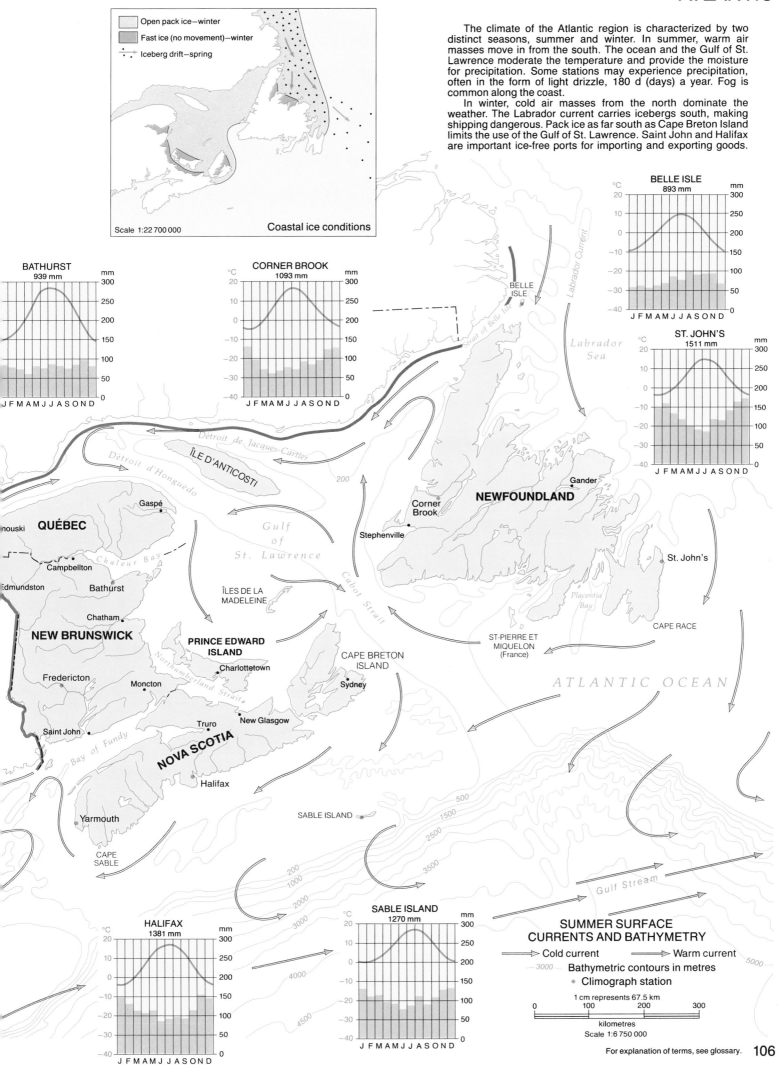

Coastal ice conditions

- Open pack ice—winter
- Fast ice (no movement)—winter
- ·····► Iceberg drift—spring

Scale 1:22 700 000

BATHURST 939 mm

CORNER BROOK 1093 mm

BELLE ISLE 893 mm

ST. JOHN'S 1511 mm

HALIFAX 1381 mm

SABLE ISLAND 1270 mm

QUÉBEC
Gaspé
ÎLE D'ANTICOSTI
Détroit de Jacques-Cartier
Détroit d'Honguedo
Gulf of St. Lawrence
Chaleur Bay
Campbellton
Edmundston
Bathurst
Chatham
NEW BRUNSWICK
Fredericton
Moncton
Saint John
Bay of Fundy
NOVA SCOTIA
Yarmouth
CAPE SABLE
Halifax
Truro
New Glasgow
Northumberland Strait
PRINCE EDWARD ISLAND
Charlottetown
ÎLES DE LA MADELEINE
CAPE BRETON ISLAND
Sydney
Cabot Strait
NEWFOUNDLAND
Corner Brook
Stephenville
Gander
St. John's
Placentia Bay
CAPE RACE
BELLE ISLE
Strait of Belle Isle
Labrador Current
Labrador Sea
ST-PIERRE ET MIQUELON (France)
ATLANTIC OCEAN
SABLE ISLAND
Gulf Stream

SUMMER SURFACE CURRENTS AND BATHYMETRY

⇒ Cold current   ⇒ Warm current

3000 Bathymetric contours in metres

• Climograph station

1 cm represents 67.5 km

0   100   200   300
kilometres
Scale 1:6 750 000

CANADA

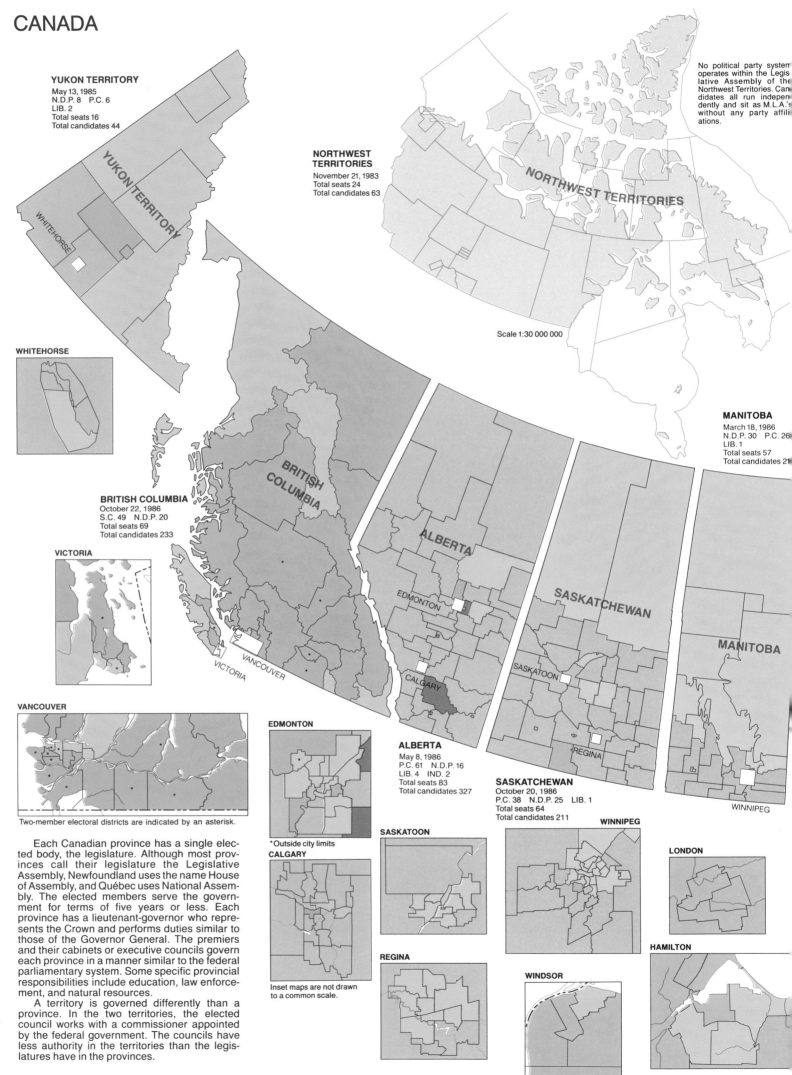

YUKON TERRITORY
May 13, 1985
N.D.P. 8   P.C. 6
LIB. 2
Total seats 16
Total candidates 44

WHITEHORSE

WHITEHORSE

NORTHWEST TERRITORIES
November 21, 1983
Total seats 24
Total candidates 63

No political party system operates within the Legislative Assembly of the Northwest Territories. Candidates all run independently and sit as M.L.A.'s without any party affiliations.

NORTHWEST TERRITORIES

Scale 1:30 000 000

BRITISH COLUMBIA
October 22, 1986
S.C. 49   N.D.P. 20
Total seats 69
Total candidates 233

BRITISH COLUMBIA

VICTORIA

VICTORIA   VANCOUVER

VANCOUVER

Two-member electoral districts are indicated by an asterisk.

MANITOBA
March 18, 1986
N.D.P. 30   P.C. 26
LIB. 1
Total seats 57
Total candidates 21

ALBERTA
EDMONTON
CALGARY

SASKATCHEWAN
SASKATOON
REGINA

MANITOBA

EDMONTON

*Outside city limits

CALGARY

Inset maps are not drawn to a common scale.

ALBERTA
May 8, 1986
P.C. 61   N.D.P. 16
LIB. 4   IND. 2
Total seats 83
Total candidates 327

SASKATCHEWAN
October 20, 1986
P.C. 38   N.D.P. 25   LIB. 1
Total seats 64
Total candidates 211

SASKATOON

REGINA

WINNIPEG

WINNIPEG

WINDSOR

LONDON

HAMILTON

Each Canadian province has a single elected body, the legislature. Although most provinces call their legislature the Legislative Assembly, Newfoundland uses the name House of Assembly, and Québec uses National Assembly. The elected members serve the government for terms of five years or less. Each province has a lieutenant-governor who represents the Crown and performs duties similar to those of the Governor General. The premiers and their cabinets or executive councils govern each province in a manner similar to the federal parliamentary system. Some specific provincial responsibilities include education, law enforcement, and natural resources.

A territory is governed differently than a province. In the two territories, the elected council works with a commissioner appointed by the federal government. The councils have less authority in the territories than the legislatures have in the provinces.

VOTER TURNOUT

Colours indicate the party with the largest number of seats.

Percent of electorate that voted in the elections shown

100
90
80
70
60
50
40
30
20
10
0

Northwest Territories
Yukon Territory
British Columbia
Alberta
Saskatchewan
Manitoba
Ontario
Québec
New Brunswick
Prince Edward Island
Nova Scotia
Newfoundland

Progressive Conservative (P.C.)

Liberal (LIB.)

New Democratic Party (N.D.P.)

Social Credit (SOC. CR.)

Parti Québécois (P.Q.)

Independent (IND.)

No affiliation

MONTRÉAL

QUÉBEC

NEWFOUNDLAND
April 2, 1985
P.C. 36   LIB. 15
N.D.P. 1
Total seats 52
Total candidates 129

ST. JOHN'S

NEWFOUNDLAND

ST. JOHN'S

ONTARIO
September 10, 1987
LIB. 95   N.D.P. 19
P.C. 16
Total seats 130
Total candidates 495

QUÉBEC
December 2, 1985
LIB. 99   P.Q. 23
Total seats 122
Total candidates 663

ONTARIO

QUÉBEC

SYDNEY

PRINCE EDWARD ISLAND   (See below.)
April 21, 1986
LIB. 21   P.C. 11
Total seats 32
Total candidates 80

Scale 1:10 000 000

P.E.I.

SYDNEY

N.B.

MONCTON

SAINT JOHN

N.S.

HALIFAX/DARTMOUTH

QUÉBEC

NEW BRUNSWICK
October 13, 1987
LIB. 58   P.C. 0
N.D.P. 0
Total seats 58
Total candidates 184

SAINT JOHN

NOVA SCOTIA
November 6, 1984
P.C. 42   LIB. 6
N.D.P. 3   IND. 1
Total seats 52
Total candidates 175

MONCTON

HALIFAX/DARTMOUTH

OTTAWA

MONTRÉAL

OTTAWA

TORONTO

HAMILTON

LONDON

WINDSOR

Scale 1:14 000 000

TORONTO

Prince Edward Island has a provincial assembly whose members are elected in pairs—a relic from the past when there were two "houses" or levels of government in the province. In those districts which have elected members from the two opposing parties, the colour shown is that of the party with the greater number of votes.

For explanation of terms, see glossary.   **108**

CANADA

Canada's first election was actually a series of elections conducted in the four provinces. Unlike modern times, when elections take place in one day, the first election was spread over a six-week period. Open voting, rather than the use of secret ballots, was common. This method of voting allowed unusual and illegal ways of influencing voters (such as bribery) to take place.

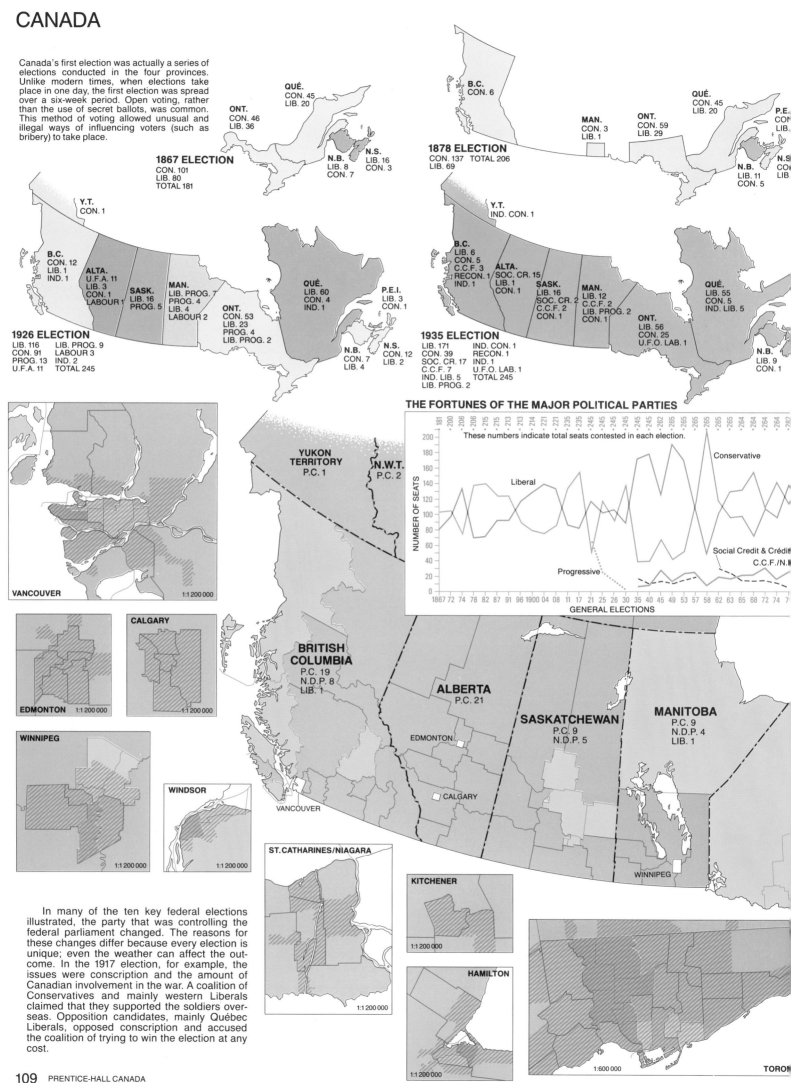

QUÉ.
CON. 45
LIB. 20

ONT.
CON. 46
LIB. 36

N.B.
LIB. 8
CON. 7

N.S.
LIB. 16
CON. 3

1867 ELECTION
CON. 101
LIB. 80
TOTAL 181

B.C.
CON. 6

MAN.
CON. 3
LIB. 1

ONT.
CON. 59
LIB. 29

QUÉ.
CON. 45
LIB. 20

P.E.
CO
LIB

N.B.
LIB. 11
CON. 5

N.S.
CO
LIB

1878 ELECTION
CON. 137   TOTAL 206
LIB. 69

Y.T.
CON. 1

B.C.
CON. 12
LIB. 1
IND. 1

ALTA.
U.F.A. 11
LIB. 3
CON. 1
LABOUR 1

SASK.
LIB. 16
PROG. 5

MAN.
LIB. PROG. 7
PROG. 4
LIB. 4
LABOUR 2

ONT.
CON. 53
LIB. 23
PROG. 4
LIB. PROG. 2

QUÉ.
LIB. 60
CON. 4
IND. 1

P.E.I.
LIB. 3
CON. 1

N.S.
CON. 7
LIB. 4

1926 ELECTION
LIB. 116   LIB. PROG. 9
CON. 91   LABOUR 3
PROG. 13   IND. 2
U.F.A. 11 TOTAL 245

Y.T.
IND. CON. 1

B.C.
LIB. 6
CON. 5
C.C.F. 3
RECON. 1
IND. 1

ALTA.
SOC. CR. 15
LIB. 1
CON. 1

SASK.
LIB. 16
SOC. CR. 2
C.C.F. 2
CON. 1

MAN.
LIB. 12
C.C.F. 2
LIB. PROG. 2
CON. 1

ONT.
LIB. 56
CON. 25
U.F.O. LAB. 1

QUÉ.
LIB. 55
CON. 5
IND. LIB. 5

N.B.
LIB. 9
CON. 1

1935 ELECTION
LIB. 171   IND. CON. 1
CON. 39   RECON. 1
SOC. CR. 17   IND. 1
C.C.F. 7   U.F.O. LAB. 1
IND. LIB. 5   TOTAL 245
LIB. PROG. 2

THE FORTUNES OF THE MAJOR POLITICAL PARTIES

These numbers indicate total seats contested in each election.

*181 *200 *206 *206 *215 *215 *213 *213 *214 *221 *221 *235 *235 *245 *245 *245 *245 *245 *262 *265 *265 *265 *265 *265 *264 *264 *264 *264 *282

NUMBER OF SEATS — 200, 180, 160, 140, 120, 100, 80, 60, 40, 20

Conservative

Liberal

Social Credit & Crédit

C.C.F./N.

Progressive

GENERAL ELECTIONS — 1867 72 74 78 82 87 91 96 1900 04 08 11 17 21 25 26 30 35 40 45 49 53 57 58 62 65 68 72 74 7

YUKON TERRITORY
P.C. 1

N.W.T.
P.C. 2

VANCOUVER 1:1 200 000

CALGARY 1:1 200 000

EDMONTON 1:1 200 000

WINNIPEG 1:1 200 000

WINDSOR 1:1 200 000

BRITISH COLUMBIA
P.C. 19
N.D.P. 8
LIB. 1

ALBERTA
P.C. 21

EDMONTON

SASKATCHEWAN
P.C. 9
N.D.P. 5

MANITOBA
P.C. 9
N.D.P. 4
LIB. 1

CALGARY

VANCOUVER

WINNIPEG

ST. CATHARINES/NIAGARA 1:1 200 000

KITCHENER 1:1 200 000

HAMILTON 1:1 200 000

1:600 000   TORO

In many of the ten key federal elections illustrated, the party that was controlling the federal parliament changed. The reasons for these changes differ because every election is unique; even the weather can affect the outcome. In the 1917 election, for example, the issues were conscription and the amount of Canadian involvement in the war. A coalition of Conservatives and mainly western Liberals claimed that they supported the soldiers overseas. Opposition candidates, mainly Québec Liberals, opposed conscription and accused the coalition of trying to win the election at any cost.

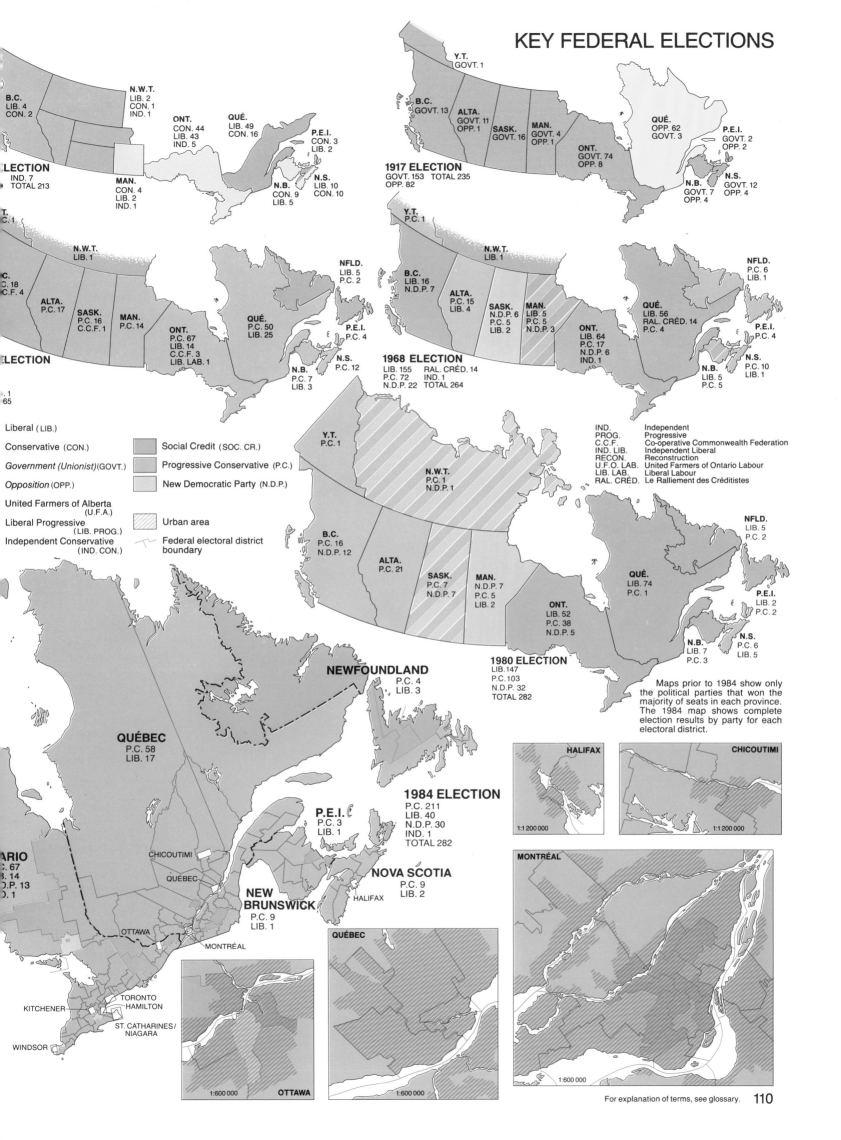

KEY FEDERAL ELECTIONS

1917 ELECTION
Y.T.
GOVT. 1

B.C.
GOVT. 13

ALTA.
GOVT. 11
OPP. 1

SASK.
GOVT. 16

MAN.
GOVT. 4
OPP. 1

ONT.
GOVT. 74
OPP. 8

QUÉ.
OPP. 62
GOVT. 3

P.E.I.
GOVT. 2
OPP. 2

N.B.
GOVT. 7
OPP. 4

N.S.
GOVT. 12
OPP. 4

1917 ELECTION
GOVT. 153   TOTAL 235
OPP. 82

(upper left partial map)
B.C.
LIB. 4
CON. 2

N.W.T.
LIB. 2
CON. 1
IND. 1

ONT.
CON. 44
LIB. 43
IND. 5

QUÉ.
LIB. 49
CON. 16

P.E.I.
CON. 3
LIB. 2

N.B.
CON. 9
LIB. 5

N.S.
LIB. 10
CON. 10

MAN.
CON. 4
LIB. 2
IND. 1

ELECTION
IND. 7
TOTAL 213

(middle left partial map)
N.W.T.
LIB. 1

ALTA.
P.C. 17

SASK.
P.C. 16
C.C.F. 1

MAN.
P.C. 14

ONT.
P.C. 67
LIB. 14
C.C.F. 3
LIB. LAB. 1

QUÉ.
P.C. 50
LIB. 25

NFLD.
LIB. 5
P.C. 2

P.E.I.
P.C. 4

N.B.
P.C. 7
LIB. 3

N.S.
P.C. 12

.C. 1

C. 18
C.F. 4

ELECTION
.1
65

1968 ELECTION
Y.T.
P.C. 1

B.C.
LIB. 16
N.D.P. 7

N.W.T.
LIB. 1

ALTA.
P.C. 15
LIB. 4

SASK.
N.D.P. 6
P.C. 5
LIB. 2

MAN.
LIB. 5
P.C. 5
N.D.P. 3

ONT.
LIB. 64
P.C. 17
N.D.P. 6
IND. 1

QUÉ.
LIB. 56
RAL. CRÉD. 14
P.C. 4

NFLD.
P.C. 6
LIB. 1

P.E.I.
P.C. 4

N.B.
LIB. 5
P.C. 5

N.S.
P.C. 10
LIB. 1

1968 ELECTION
LIB. 155   RAL. CRÉD. 14
P.C. 72   IND. 1
N.D.P. 22   TOTAL 264

Legend
Liberal (LIB.)

Conservative (CON.)

Government (Unionist) (GOVT.)

Opposition (OPP.)

United Farmers of Alberta (U.F.A.)

Liberal Progressive (LIB. PROG.)

Independent Conservative (IND. CON.)

Social Credit (SOC. CR.)

Progressive Conservative (P.C.)

New Democratic Party (N.D.P.)

Urban area

Federal electoral district boundary

IND.   Independent
PROG.   Progressive
C.C.F.   Co-operative Commonwealth Federation
IND. LIB.   Independent Liberal
RECON.   Reconstruction
U.F.O. LAB.   United Farmers of Ontario Labour
LIB. LAB.   Liberal Labour
RAL. CRÉD.   Le Ralliement des Créditistes

1980 ELECTION
Y.T.
P.C. 1

N.W.T.
P.C. 1
N.D.P. 1

B.C.
P.C. 16
N.D.P. 12

ALTA.
P.C. 21

SASK.
P.C. 7
N.D.P. 7

MAN.
N.D.P. 7
P.C. 5
LIB. 2

ONT.
LIB. 52
P.C. 38
N.D.P. 5

QUÉ.
LIB. 74
P.C. 1

NFLD.
LIB. 5
P.C. 2

P.E.I.
LIB. 2
P.C. 2

N.B.
LIB. 7
P.C. 3

N.S.
P.C. 6
LIB. 5

1980 ELECTION
LIB. 147
P.C. 103
N.D.P. 32
TOTAL 282

Maps prior to 1984 show only the political parties that won the majority of seats in each province. The 1984 map shows complete election results by party for each electoral district.

1984 ELECTION
QUÉBEC
P.C. 58
LIB. 17

NEWFOUNDLAND
P.C. 4
LIB. 3

ARIO
C. 67
. 14
.D.P. 13
. 1

P.E.I.
P.C. 3
LIB. 1

NEW BRUNSWICK
P.C. 9
LIB. 1

NOVA SCOTIA
P.C. 9
LIB. 2

1984 ELECTION
P.C. 211
LIB. 40
N.D.P. 30
IND. 1
TOTAL 282

HALIFAX   1:1 200 000

CHICOUTIMI   1:1 200 000

MONTRÉAL   1:600 000

QUÉBEC   1:600 000

OTTAWA   1:600 000

For explanation of terms, see glossary. 110

CANADA

EXPORTS

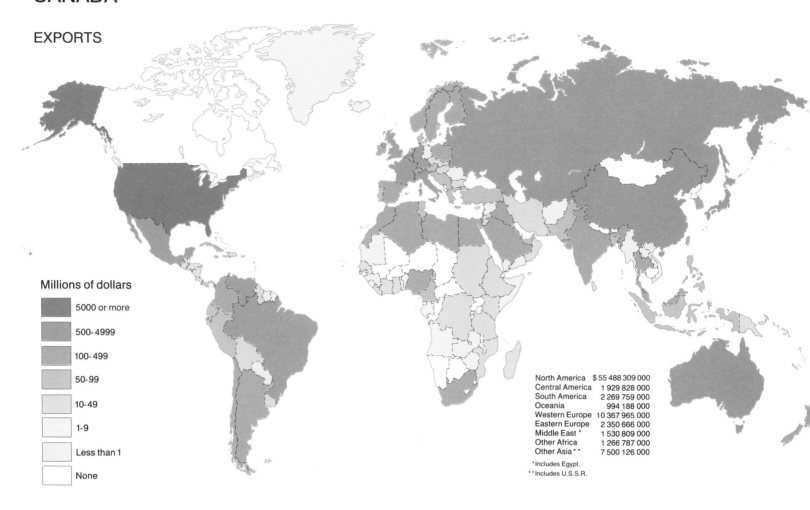

Millions of dollars

- 5000 or more
- 500-4999
- 100-499
- 50-99
- 10-49
- 1-9
- Less than 1
- None

North America	$55 488 309 000
Central America	1 929 828 000
South America	2 269 759 000
Oceania	994 188 000
Western Europe	10 367 965 000
Eastern Europe	2 350 666 000
Middle East *	1 530 809 000
Other Africa	1 266 787 000
Other Asia * *	7 500 126 000

*Includes Egypt.
* *Includes U.S.S.R.

IMPORTS

Millions of dollars

- 5000 or more
- 500-4999
- 100-499
- 50-99
- 10-49
- 1-9
- Less than 1
- None

North America	$54 311 502 000
Central America	1 821 063 000
South America	3 247 370 000
Oceania	658 368 000
Western Europe	7 831 546 000
Eastern Europe	349 457 000
Middle East *	2 728 167 000
Other Africa	1 047 059 000
Other Asia * *	6 881 330 000

*Includes Egypt.
* *Includes U.S.S.R.

NERGY FLOWS

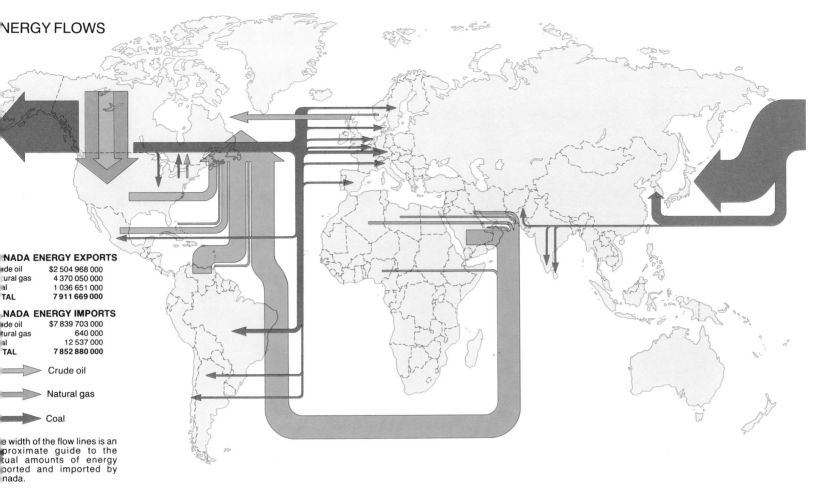

NADA ENERGY EXPORTS

de oil	$2 504 968 000
tural gas	4 370 050 000
al	1 036 651 000
TAL	**7 911 669 000**

NADA ENERGY IMPORTS

de oil	$7 839 703 000
tural gas	640 000
al	12 537 000
TAL	**7 852 880 000**

Crude oil

Natural gas

Coal

e width of the flow lines is an
proximate guide to the
tual amounts of energy
ported and imported by
nada.

XTERNAL AID
conomic and technical
ssistance and food aid
om CIDA)

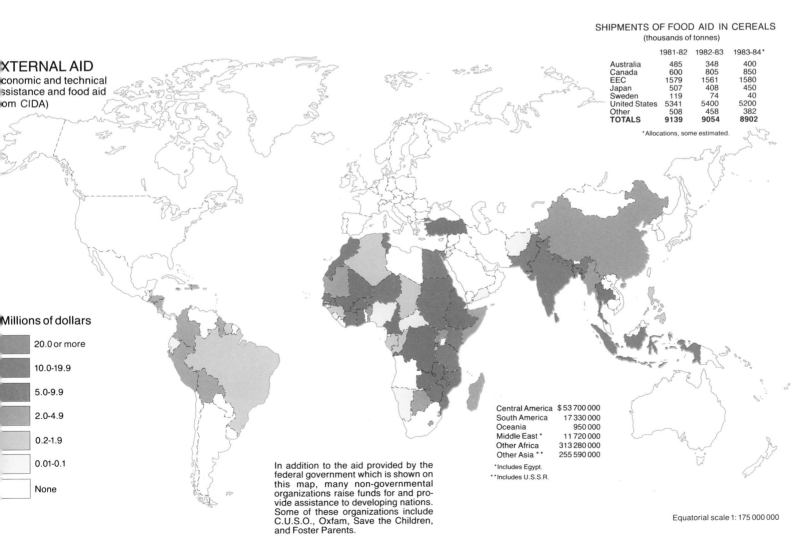

Millions of dollars

- 20.0 or more
- 10.0-19.9
- 5.0-9.9
- 2.0-4.9
- 0.2-1.9
- 0.01-0.1
- None

SHIPMENTS OF FOOD AID IN CEREALS
(thousands of tonnes)

	1981-82	1982-83	1983-84*
Australia	485	348	400
Canada	600	805	850
EEC	1579	1561	1580
Japan	507	408	450
Sweden	119	74	40
United States	5341	5400	5200
Other	508	458	382
TOTALS	**9139**	**9054**	**8902**

*Allocations, some estimated.

Central America	$53 700 000
South America	17 330 000
Oceania	950 000
Middle East *	11 720 000
Other Africa	313 280 000
Other Asia **	255 590 000

* Includes Egypt.
** Includes U.S.S.R.

In addition to the aid provided by the
federal government which is shown on
this map, many non-governmental
organizations raise funds for and provide assistance to developing nations.
Some of these organizations include
C.U.S.O., Oxfam, Save the Children,
and Foster Parents.

Equatorial scale 1: 175 000 000

For explanation of terms, see glossary.

CANADA

Millions of telephone calls

OVERSEAS TELEPHONE CALLS FROM CANADA
April 1981-March 1982

- United Kingdom
- West Germany
- Italy
- France
- Greece
- Hong Kong
- Holland
- Jamaica
- Switzerland
- Australia
- Israel
- Japan
- Philippines
- Bahamas
- Bermuda
- Ireland
- Belgium
- Trinidad and Tobago
- Sweden
- Venezuela
- Other countries

- ■ Canadian Embassy
- ● Canadian High Commission
- ▲ Canadian Consulate
- ◎ Permanent Mission of Canada to the Office of the United Nations (Geneva)
- · Airline destination *
- —— Air connection
- —— Submarine cable
- ▨ Developed country
- ▨ Developing country
- ▨ Least developed country

* Diplomatic symbols take precedence over airline destination symbols.

Equatorial scale 1:91 000 000

The countries of the world can be divided into two basic groups — developed and developing. These two groups are determined by examining factors such as economic development, G.N.P. per capita, income per capita, potential for development, energy use, literacy, and quantity and quality of food.

60°W 40°W 20°W 0° 20°E 40°E 60°E 80°E 100°E 120°E 140°E

BAFFIN
BAY

GREENLAND
SEA

BARENTS
SEA

Greenwich Meridian

KALAALLIT NUNAAT
(GREENLAND)
(Denmark)

Arctic Circle

NORWEGIAN SEA

ICELAND

NORWAY

SWEDEN

FINLAND

UNION OF SOVIET SOCIALIST REPUBLICS

MONGOLIA

DEN.

U.K.

IRELAND

NETH.
BEL.
LUX.

W. E.
GERM.

POLAND

CZECH

AUST. HUNG.

CASPIAN
SEA

ARAL
SEA

CHINA

FRANCE

SWITZ.

ITALY

YUGO.

ROM.

BULG.

BLACK SEA

ALB.

TURKEY

AZORES

PORT.

SPAIN

GREECE

CYPRUS

SYR.

IRAN

AFGHANISTAN

MALTA

LEB.

ISRAEL

IRAQ

JORDAN

KUWAIT

PAKISTAN

NEPAL

BHUTAN

TUNISIA

MEDITERRANEAN SEA

BERMUDA

BANG.

BAHAMAS

DOM. REP.

HAITI

P.R.

ANTIGUA AND
BARBUDA

BARBADOS

TRINIDAD AND TOBAGO

MOROCCO

ALGERIA

LIBYA

EGYPT

SAUDI
ARABIA

BAHRAIN

QATAR

U.A.E.

OMAN

INDIA

BAY
OF
BENGAL

ATLANTIC

OCEAN

RIBBEAN SEA

GUA

VENEZUELA

GUYANA

SURINAME

FR. GUIANA
(Fr.)

COLOMBIA

MAURITANIA

SENEGAL

GAMBIA

MALI

NIGER

CHAD

SUDAN

YEMEN

DEM.
YEMEN

DJIBOUTI

ARABIAN
SEA

SRI LANKA

GUINEA-BISSAU

GUINEA

SIERRA
LEONE

LIBERIA

IVORY
COAST

BURKINA
FASO

BENIN

NIGERIA

TOGO

GHANA

EQ.
GUINEA

CAMEROON

C.A.R.

ETHIOPIA

SOMALIA

PERU

GABON

CONGO

CABINDA
(Angola)

ZAIRE

UGANDA

RWANDA

BURUNDI

KENYA

TANZANIA

SEYCHELLES

INDIAN

OCEAN

0°

BRAZIL

BOLIVIA

PARAGUAY

ANGOLA

ZAMBIA

MALAWI

ZIMBABWE

MOZAMBIQUE

MADAGASCAR

NAMIBIA

BOTSWANA

Tropic of Capricorn

20°S

SWAZILAND

SOUTH
AFRICA

LESOTHO

ARGENTINA

URUGUAY

CHILE

FALKLAND
ISLANDS
(U.K.)

SOUTH
GEORGIA
(U.K.)

Antarctic Circle

ANTARCTICA

60°W 40°W 20° West of Greenwich 0° 20° East of Greenwich 40°E 60°E 80°E 100°E

MEMBER COUNTRIES
OF THE COMMONWEALTH

Antigua and	Nauru
Barbuda	New Zealand
Australia	Nigeria
Bahamas	Papua New Guinea
Bangladesh	Saint Christopher
Barbados	and Nevis
Belize	Saint Lucia
Botswana	Saint Vincent and
Canada	the Grenadines
Cyprus	Seychelles
Dominica	Sierra Leone
Fiji	Singapore
Gambia	Solomon Islands
Ghana	Sri Lanka
Grenada	Swaziland
Guyana	Tanzania
India	Tonga
Jamaica	Trinidad and Tobago
Kenya	Tuvalu
Kiribati	Uganda
Lesotho	United Kingdom
Malawi	Vanuatu
Malaysia	Western Samoa
Maldives	Zambia
Malta	Zimbabwe
Mauritius	

WORLD

ARCTIC OCEAN

BEAUFORT SEA

KALAALLIT NUNAAT (GREENLAND)
(Denmark)

ICELAND

ALASKA
(U.S.)

GULF OF ALASKA

C A N A D A

HUDSON BAY

NO

UNITED KINGDOM

DEN

IRELAND

NET

BE

LU

FRANC

ATLANTIC OCEAN

PACIFIC OCEAN

UNITED STATES

PORTUGAL

SPAIN

AZORES
(Portugal)

GIBRALTAR
(U.K.)

BERMUDA
(U.K.)

CANARY IS.
(Spain)

MOROCCO

ALGER

M E X I C O

GULF OF MEXICO

BAHAMAS

MAURITANIA

MALI

HAWAII
(U.S.)

CUBA

DOMINICAN REPUBLIC

PUERTO RICO
(U.S.)

CAPE VERDE

JAMAICA

HAITI

SENEGAL

GAMBIA

BELIZE

HONDURAS

DOMINICA

GUINEA-BISSAU

BURKINA FASO

GUATEMALA

CARIBBEAN SEA

GUINEA

BEN

EL SALVADOR

NICARAGUA

BARBADOS

SIERRA LEONE

IVORY COAST

GHANA

TOGO

COSTA RICA

TRINIDAD AND TOBAGO

LIBERIA

PANAMA

VENEZUELA

GUYANA

SURINAME

EQUA

G

COLOMBIA

FRENCH GUIANA
(France)

GALAPAGOS ISLANDS
(Ecuador)

ECUADOR

P E R U

B R A Z I L

ATLANTIC OCEAN

TYPE OF GOVERNMENT

BOLIVIA

Constitutional monarchy

Absolute monarchy

One party republic

PARAGUAY

Democratic republic

A R G E N T I N A

Democratic parliamentary system

Communist/Socialist republic

CHILE

Military regime

URUGUAY

Islamic republic

FALKLAND ISLANDS
(U.K.)

ARCTIC OCEAN

FINLAND

UNION OF SOVIET SOCIALIST REPUBLICS

BERING SEA

SEA OF OKHOTSK

...AND

...ING.

ROM.

...GO.

BULG.

...LB.

BLACK SEA

ARAL SEA

MONGOLIA

CASPIAN SEA

GREECE

TURKEY

...TA

CYPRUS

LEB.

SYRIA

...ERRANEAN SEA

ISRAEL

IRAQ

JORDAN

IRAN

AFGHANISTAN

5

NORTH KOREA

SOUTH KOREA

JAPAN

CHINA

YELLOW SEA

PACIFIC OCEAN

8

KUWAIT

PAKISTAN

NEPAL

BHUTAN

...YA

EGYPT

BAHRAIN

QATAR

3

4

U.A.E.

INDIA

BANGLADESH

BURMA

LAOS

HONG KONG (U.K.)

TAIWAN

PHILIPPINE SEA

SAUDI ARABIA

OMAN

ARABIAN SEA

BAY OF BENGAL

VIETNAM

SOUTH CHINA SEA

...HAD

SUDAN

YEMEN

DEM. YEMEN

THAILAND

6

KAMPUCHEA

PHILIPPINES

DJIBOUTI

SOCOTRA (Dem. Yemen)

ETHIOPIA

SRI LANKA

CENTRAL ...RICAN REPUBLIC

SOMALIA

MALDIVES

BRUNEI

MALAYSIA

ZAIRE

UGANDA

KENYA

SINGAPORE

RWANDA

BURUNDI

INDIAN OCEAN

SEYCHELLES

PAPUA NEW GUINEA

SOLOMON ISLANDS

TANZANIA

INDONESIA

10

...GOLA

1

MALAWI

COMOROS

ZAMBIA

CORAL SEA

VANUATU

ZIMBABWE

MOZAMBIQUE

MADAGASCAR

MAURITIUS

NEW CALEDONIA (France)

...BIA

REUNION (France)

1

BOTSWANA

AUSTRALIA

SWAZILAND

SOUTH AFRICA

LESOTHO

NEW ZEALAND

1 President for life
2 Constitutional emirate
3 Traditional sheikdom
4 United emirates
5 Occupied by U.S.S.R.
6 Occupied by Vietnam
7 Self-governing Commonwealth
8 Partially occupied by Turkey
9 Under Islamic principles
10 Limited representative government in which the military plays a dominant role
11 Administered by South Africa in defiance of the United Nations

Equatorial scale 1:80 000 000

WORLD

MAJOR CITIES
(Population in millions)

More than 10
5-9.9
3-4.9
2-2.9

One dot represents 100 000 people

THE WORLD IN PROPORTION TO POPULATION

Canada
U.S.
Mexico
Brazil
U.K.
France
Nigeria
Italy
Pakistan
U.S.S.R.
India
China
Bang.
Vietnam
Japan
Philippines
Indonesia

50 000 000 people

Minneapolis
Detroit
Toronto
Montréal
Chicago
Boston
St. Louis
Pittsburgh
Philadelphia
Baltimore
New York
Washington
Dallas-Fort Worth
Atlanta
San Francisco
Los Angeles
Houston
Habana
México
Guadalajara
Caracas
Bogotá
Lima
Recife
Belo Horizonte
Rio de Janeiro
São Paulo
Pôrto Alegre
Santiago
Buenos Aires
Manchester
Lond
Birmingham
Paris
Madric
Casablanca

THE POPULATION EXPLOSION

Millions

Australia and
Oceania
6000
South America
North and
Central America
5000 U.S.S.R.

Europe
4000
Africa

3000

2000

1000 Asia

0
1850 1875 1900 1925 1950 1975 2000
(projection)

Leningrad
Moskva
Kiev
Budapest
Istanbul
Ankara
El Iskandariya
El Qâhira
Baghdâd
Tehrân
Lahore
Delhi
Karachi
Bombay
Madras
Calcutta
Dhaka
Rangoon
Bangkok
Ho Chi Minh City
Singapore
Jakarta
Surabaya
Kinshasa
Harbin
Shenyáng
Beijing
Lüda
Sŏul
Pusan
Tŏkyŏ
Nagoya
Osaka
Lanzhou
Tianjin
Xi'an
Wuhan
Nanjing
Shanghai
Chengdu
Chongqing
T'aipei
Hanoi
Guangzhou
Hong Kong
Manila
Sydney
Melbourne

Equatorial scale 1: 80 000 000

WORLD

BIRTH RATE

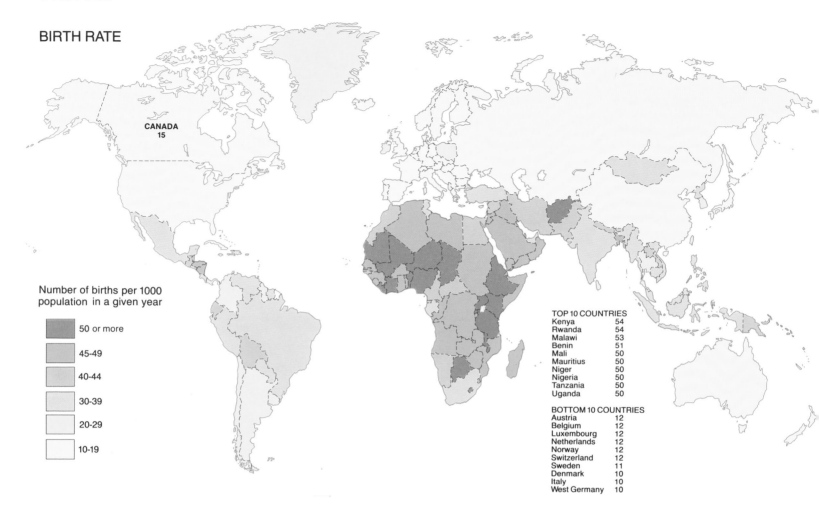

**CANADA
15**

Number of births per 1000
population in a given year

	50 or more
	45-49
	40-44
	30-39
	20-29
	10-19

TOP 10 COUNTRIES
Kenya	54
Rwanda	54
Malawi	53
Benin	51
Mali	50
Mauritius	50
Niger	50
Nigeria	50
Tanzania	50
Uganda	50

BOTTOM 10 COUNTRIES
Austria	12
Belgium	12
Luxembourg	12
Netherlands	12
Norway	12
Switzerland	12
Sweden	11
Denmark	10
Italy	10
West Germany	10

POPULATION DENSITY (TOTAL AREA)

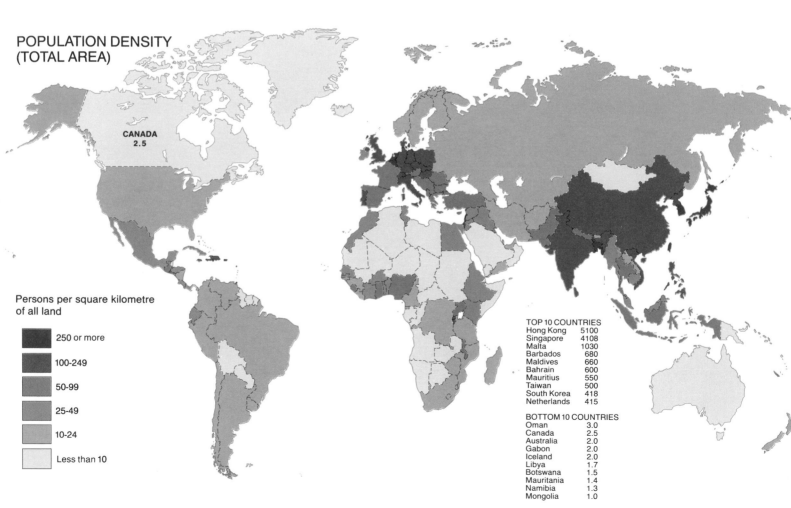

**CANADA
2.5**

Persons per square kilometre
of all land

	250 or more
	100-249
	50-99
	25-49
	10-24
	Less than 10

TOP 10 COUNTRIES
Hong Kong	5100
Singapore	4108
Malta	1030
Barbados	680
Maldives	660
Bahrain	600
Mauritius	550
Taiwan	500
South Korea	418
Netherlands	415

BOTTOM 10 COUNTRIES
Oman	3.0
Canada	2.5
Australia	2.0
Gabon	2.0
Iceland	2.0
Libya	1.7
Botswana	1.5
Mauritania	1.4
Namibia	1.3
Mongolia	1.0

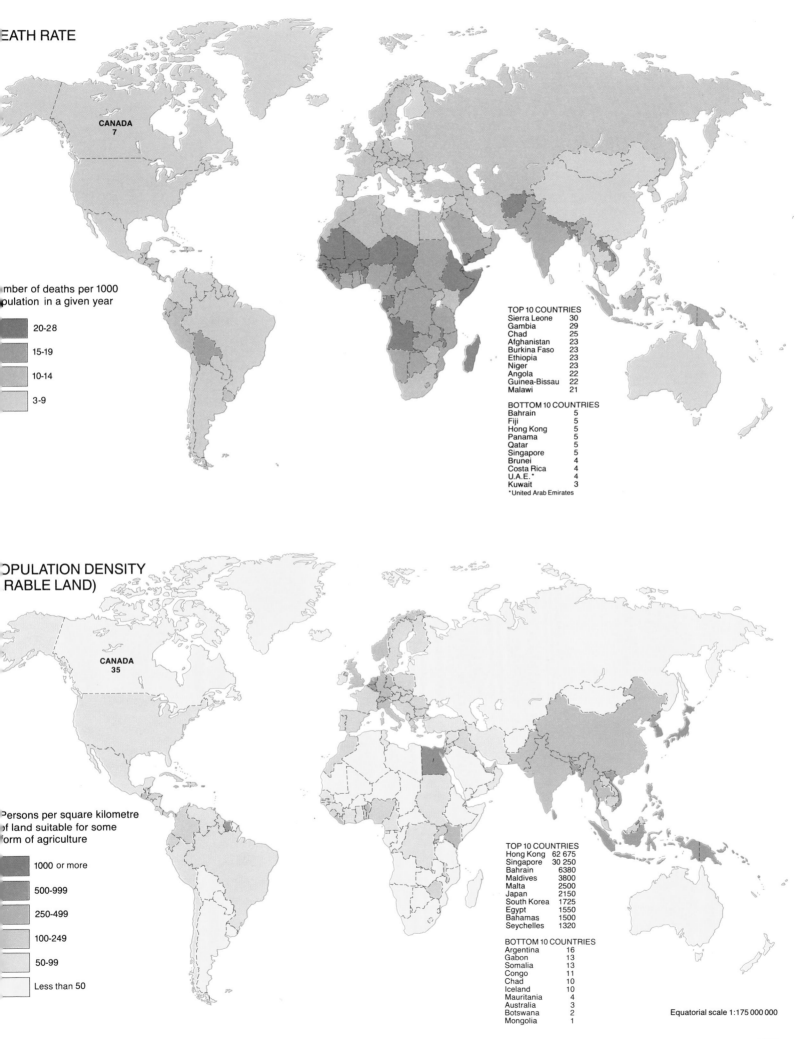

DEATH RATE

Number of deaths per 1000 population in a given year

CANADA 7

- 20-28
- 15-19
- 10-14
- 3-9

TOP 10 COUNTRIES
Sierra Leone	30
Gambia	29
Chad	25
Afghanistan	23
Burkina Faso	23
Ethiopia	23
Niger	23
Angola	22
Guinea-Bissau	22
Malawi	21

BOTTOM 10 COUNTRIES
Bahrain	5
Fiji	5
Hong Kong	5
Panama	5
Qatar	5
Singapore	5
Brunei	4
Costa Rica	4
U.A.E.*	4
Kuwait	3

*United Arab Emirates

POPULATION DENSITY (ARABLE LAND)

Persons per square kilometre of land suitable for some form of agriculture

CANADA 35

- 1000 or more
- 500-999
- 250-499
- 100-249
- 50-99
- Less than 50

TOP 10 COUNTRIES
Hong Kong	62 675
Singapore	30 250
Bahrain	6380
Maldives	3800
Malta	2500
Japan	2150
South Korea	1725
Egypt	1550
Bahamas	1500
Seychelles	1320

BOTTOM 10 COUNTRIES
Argentina	16
Gabon	13
Somalia	13
Congo	11
Chad	10
Iceland	10
Mauritania	4
Australia	3
Botswana	2
Mongolia	1

Equatorial scale 1:175 000 000

WORLD

JANUARY TEMPERATURE

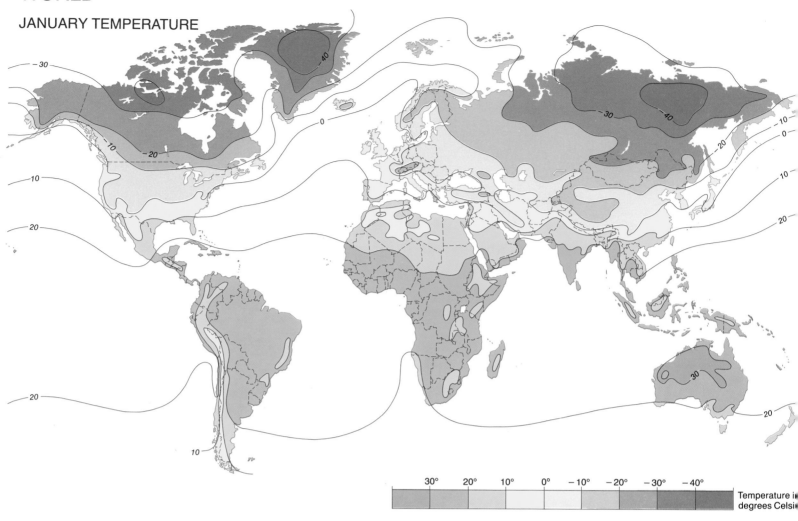

30°	20°	10°	0°	−10°	−20°	−30°	−40°

Temperature in degrees Celsius

ANNUAL PRECIPITATION

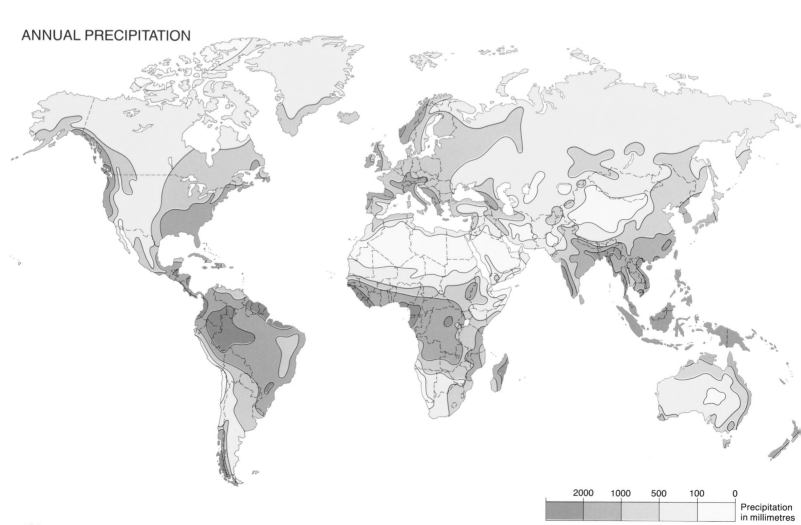

2000	1000	500	100	0

Precipitation in millimetres

JLY TEMPERATURE

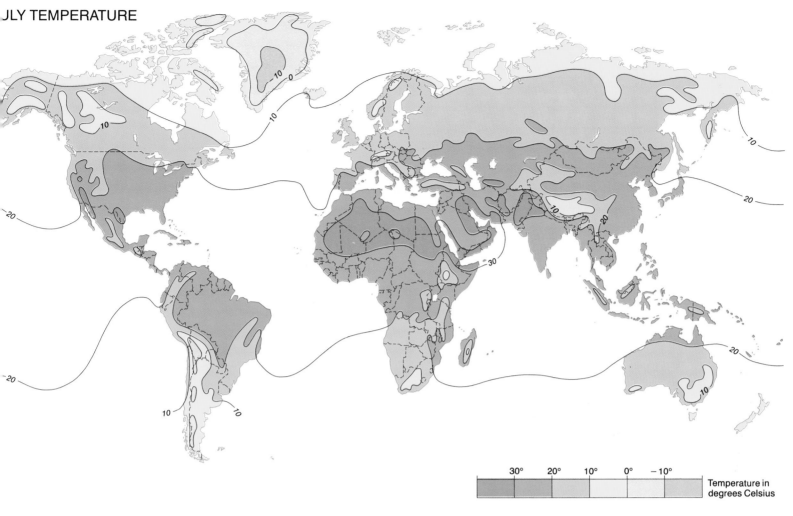

NNUAL SOLAR RADIATION

Isolines are approximate as readings are not available.

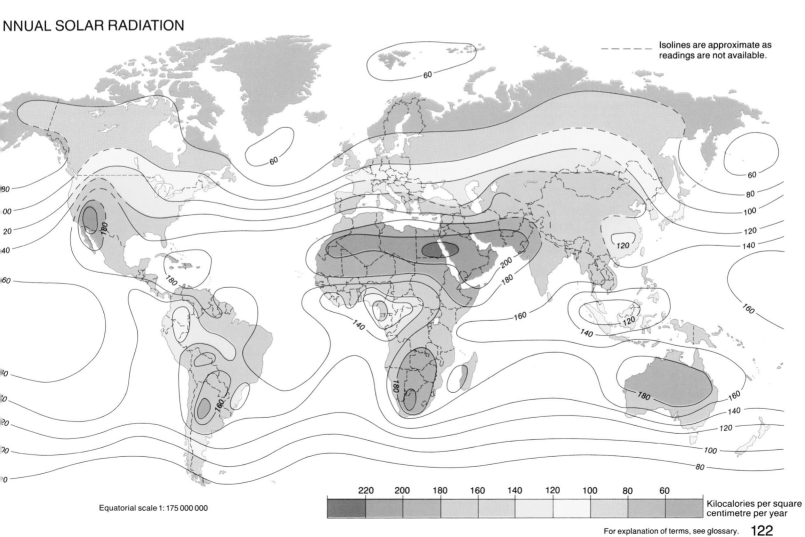

Equatorial scale 1: 175 000 000

WORLD

SOILS

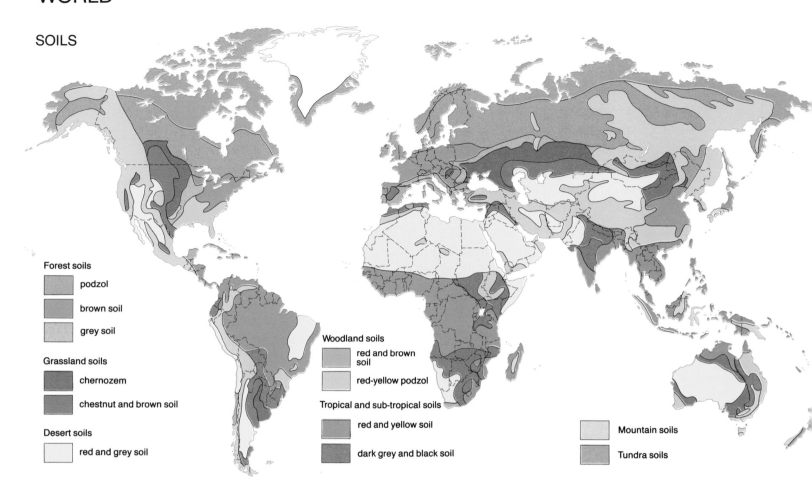

Forest soils

- podzol
- brown soil
- grey soil

Grassland soils

- chernozem
- chestnut and brown soil

Desert soils

- red and grey soil

Woodland soils

- red and brown soil
- red-yellow podzol

Tropical and sub-tropical soils

- red and yellow soil
- dark grey and black soil

- Mountain soils
- Tundra soils

AGRICULTURE

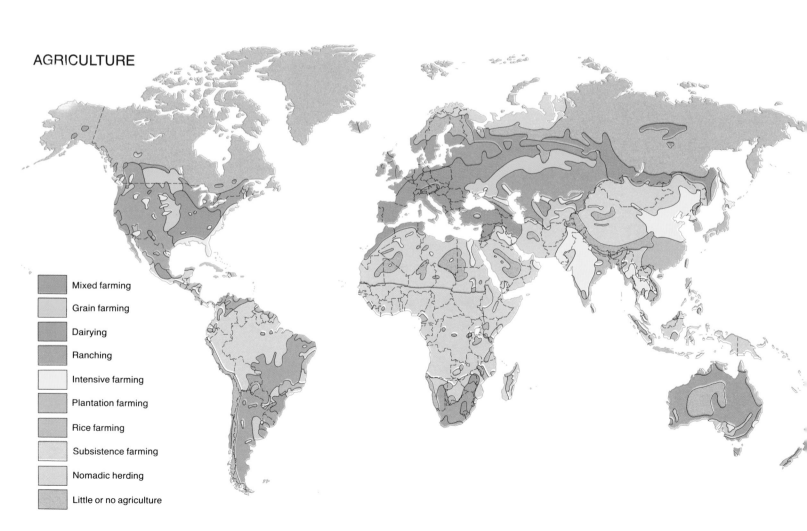

- Mixed farming
- Grain farming
- Dairying
- Ranching
- Intensive farming
- Plantation farming
- Rice farming
- Subsistence farming
- Nomadic herding
- Little or no agriculture

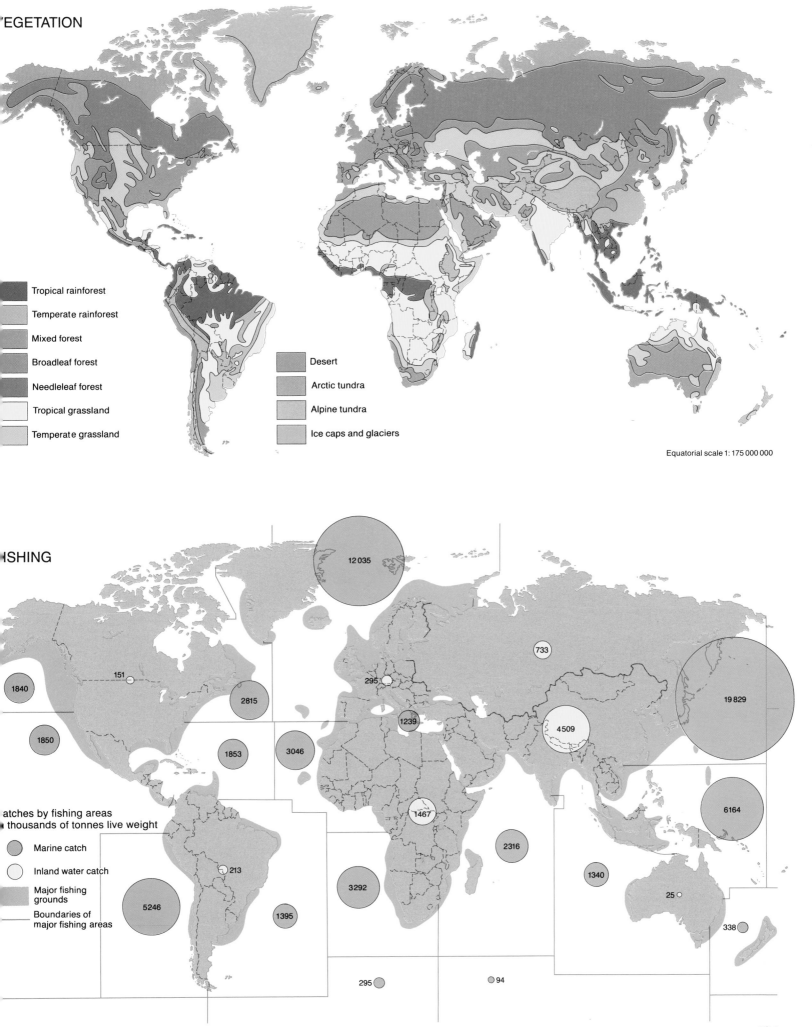

VEGETATION

Tropical rainforest
Temperate rainforest
Mixed forest
Broadleaf forest
Needleleaf forest
Tropical grassland
Temperate grassland

Desert
Arctic tundra
Alpine tundra
Ice caps and glaciers

Equatorial scale 1: 175 000 000

FISHING

Catches by fishing areas
in thousands of tonnes live weight

Marine catch
Inland water catch
Major fishing grounds
Boundaries of major fishing areas

WORLD

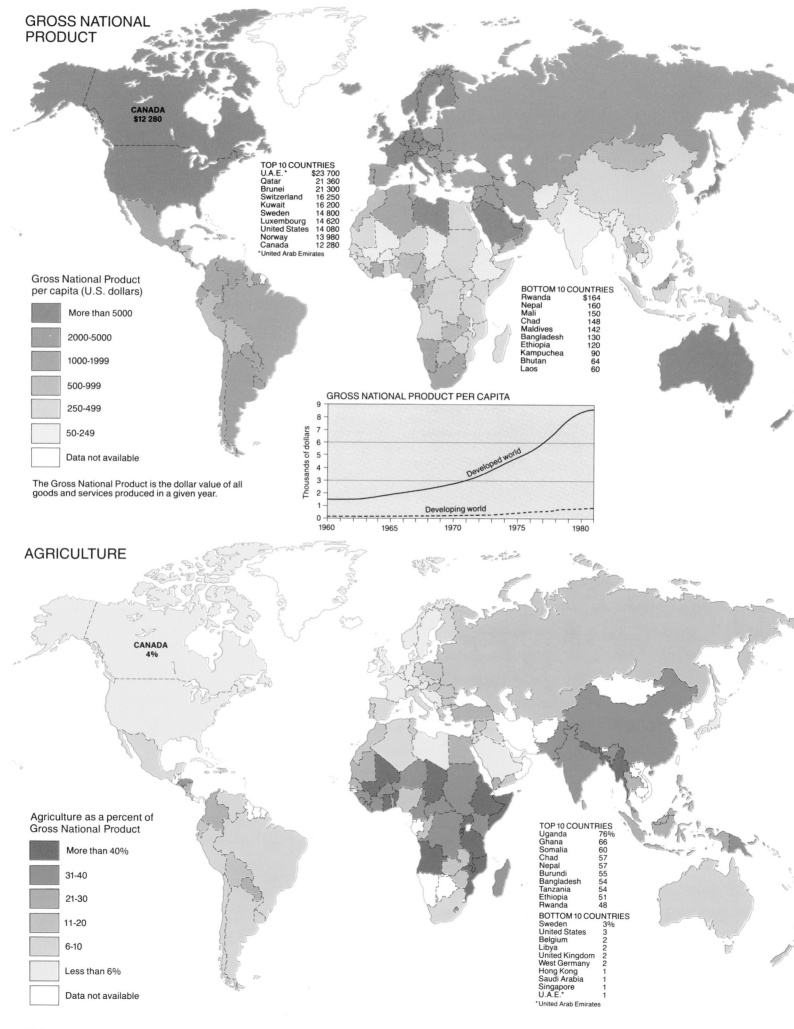

GROSS NATIONAL PRODUCT

CANADA
$12 280

TOP 10 COUNTRIES
U.A.E. *	$23 700
Qatar	21 360
Brunei	21 300
Switzerland	16 250
Kuwait	16 200
Sweden	14 800
Luxembourg	14 620
United States	14 080
Norway	13 980
Canada	12 280

* United Arab Emirates

BOTTOM 10 COUNTRIES
Rwanda	$164
Nepal	160
Mali	150
Chad	148
Maldives	142
Bangladesh	130
Ethiopia	120
Kampuchea	90
Bhutan	64
Laos	60

Gross National Product per capita (U.S. dollars)

- More than 5000
- 2000-5000
- 1000-1999
- 500-999
- 250-499
- 50-249
- Data not available

The Gross National Product is the dollar value of all goods and services produced in a given year.

GROSS NATIONAL PRODUCT PER CAPITA

Thousands of dollars

Developed world

Developing world

1960   1965   1970   1975   1980

AGRICULTURE

CANADA
4%

Agriculture as a percent of Gross National Product

- More than 40%
- 31-40
- 21-30
- 11-20
- 6-10
- Less than 6%
- Data not available

TOP 10 COUNTRIES
Uganda	76%
Ghana	66
Somalia	60
Chad	57
Nepal	57
Burundi	55
Bangladesh	54
Tanzania	54
Ethiopia	51
Rwanda	48

BOTTOM 10 COUNTRIES
Sweden	3%
United States	3
Belgium	2
Libya	2
United Kingdom	2
West Germany	2
Hong Kong	1
Saudi Arabia	1
Singapore	1
U.A.E.*	1

* United Arab Emirates

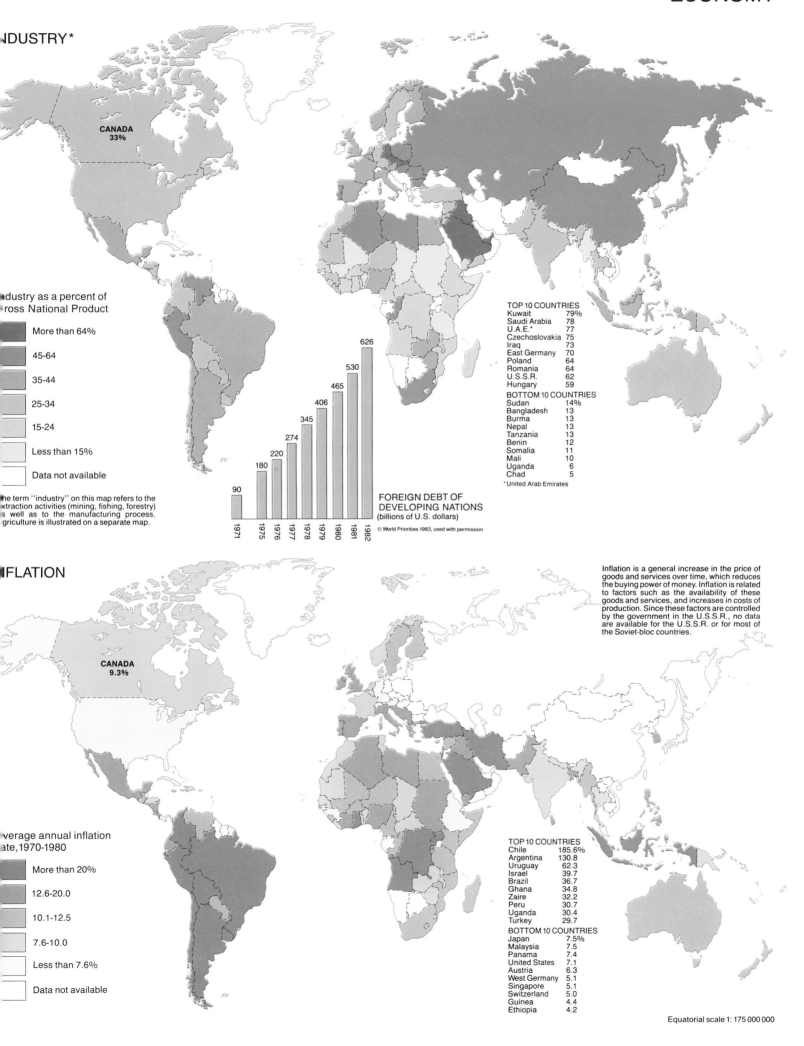

INDUSTRY*

Industry as a percent of Gross National Product

- More than 64%
- 45-64
- 35-44
- 25-34
- 15-24
- Less than 15%
- Data not available

CANADA 33%

The term "industry" on this map refers to the extraction activities (mining, fishing, forestry) as well as to the manufacturing process. Agriculture is illustrated on a separate map.

FOREIGN DEBT OF DEVELOPING NATIONS
(billions of U.S. dollars)

© World Priorities 1983, used with permission

Year	Debt
1971	90
1975	180
1976	220
1977	274
1978	345
1979	406
1980	465
1981	530
1982	626

TOP 10 COUNTRIES
Kuwait	79%
Saudi Arabia	78
U.A.E.*	77
Czechoslovakia	75
Iraq	73
East Germany	70
Poland	64
Romania	64
U.S.S.R.	62
Hungary	59

BOTTOM 10 COUNTRIES
Sudan	14%
Bangladesh	13
Burma	13
Nepal	13
Tanzania	13
Benin	12
Somalia	11
Mali	10
Uganda	6
Chad	5

*United Arab Emirates

INFLATION

Inflation is a general increase in the price of goods and services over time, which reduces the buying power of money. Inflation is related to factors such as the availability of these goods and services, and increases in costs of production. Since these factors are controlled by the government in the U.S.S.R., no data are available for the U.S.S.R. or for most of the Soviet-bloc countries.

CANADA 9.3%

Average annual inflation rate, 1970-1980

- More than 20%
- 12.6-20.0
- 10.1-12.5
- 7.6-10.0
- Less than 7.6%
- Data not available

TOP 10 COUNTRIES
Chile	185.6%
Argentina	130.8
Uruguay	62.3
Israel	39.7
Brazil	36.7
Ghana	34.8
Zaire	32.2
Peru	30.7
Uganda	30.4
Turkey	29.7

BOTTOM 10 COUNTRIES
Japan	7.5%
Malaysia	7.5
Panama	7.4
United States	7.1
Austria	6.3
West Germany	5.1
Singapore	5.1
Switzerland	5.0
Guinea	4.4
Ethiopia	4.2

Equatorial scale 1: 175 000 000

WORLD

SOCIO-ECONOMIC RANKING

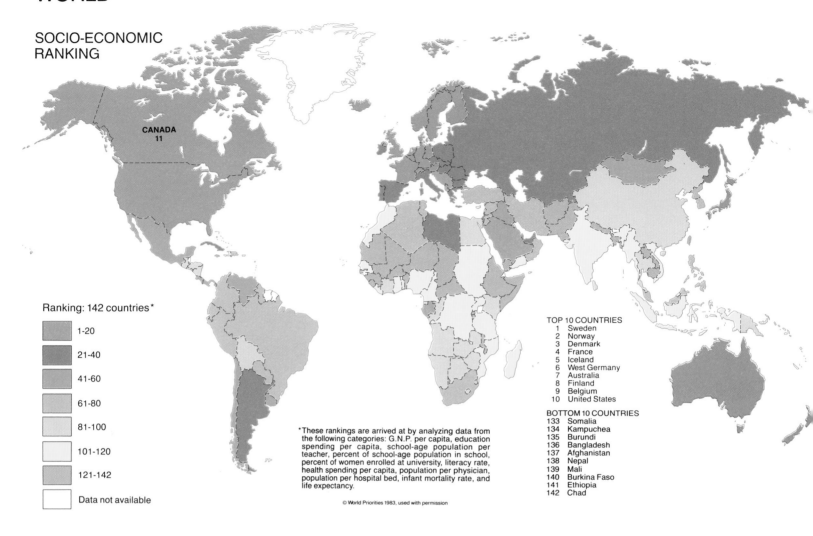

CANADA 11

Ranking: 142 countries*

- 1-20
- 21-40
- 41-60
- 61-80
- 81-100
- 101-120
- 121-142
- Data not available

*These rankings are arrived at by analyzing data from the following categories: G.N.P. per capita, education spending per capita, school-age population per teacher, percent of school-age population in school, percent of women enrolled at university, literacy rate, health spending per capita, population per physician, population per hospital bed, infant mortality rate, and life expectancy.

© World Priorities 1983, used with permission

TOP 10 COUNTRIES
1 Sweden
2 Norway
3 Denmark
4 France
5 Iceland
6 West Germany
7 Australia
8 Finland
9 Belgium
10 United States

BOTTOM 10 COUNTRIES
133 Somalia
134 Kampuchea
135 Burundi
136 Bangladesh
137 Afghanistan
138 Nepal
139 Mali
140 Burkina Faso
141 Ethiopia
142 Chad

FOOD INTAKE

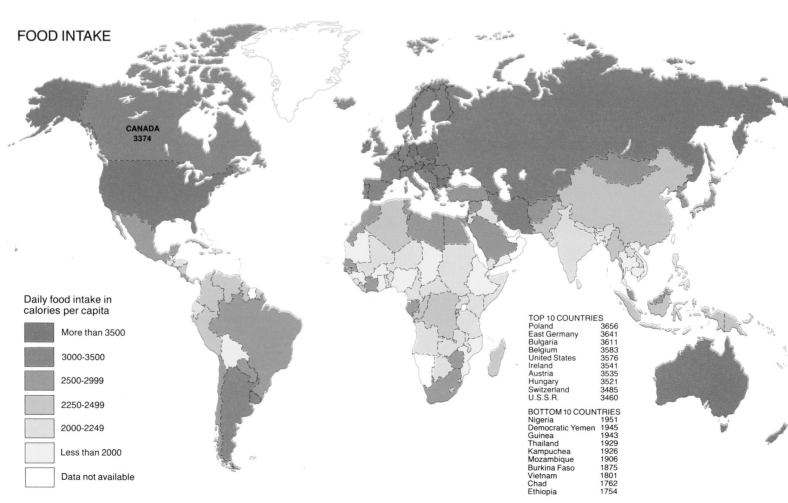

CANADA 3374

Daily food intake in calories per capita

- More than 3500
- 3000-3500
- 2500-2999
- 2250-2499
- 2000-2249
- Less than 2000
- Data not available

TOP 10 COUNTRIES
Poland	3656
East Germany	3641
Bulgaria	3611
Belgium	3583
United States	3576
Ireland	3541
Austria	3535
Hungary	3521
Switzerland	3485
U.S.S.R.	3460

BOTTOM 10 COUNTRIES
Nigeria	1951
Democratic Yemen	1945
Guinea	1943
Thailand	1929
Kampuchea	1926
Mozambique	1906
Burkina Faso	1875
Vietnam	1801
Chad	1762
Ethiopia	1754

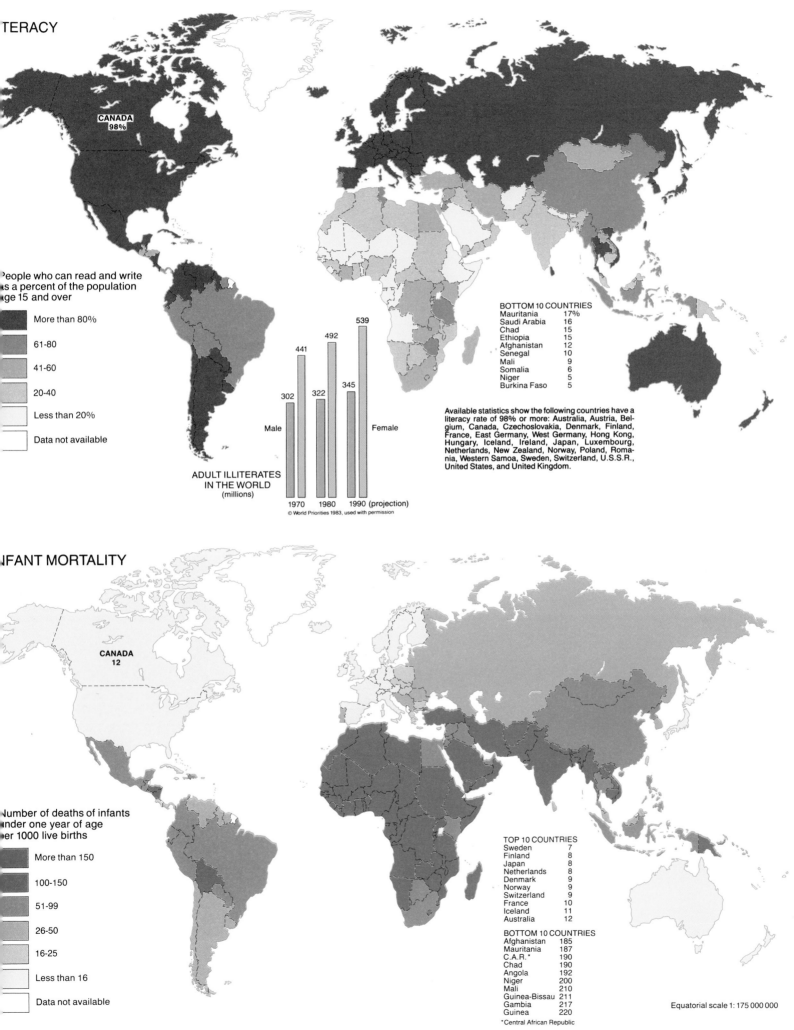

LITERACY

People who can read and write as a percent of the population age 15 and over

- More than 80%
- 61-80
- 41-60
- 20-40
- Less than 20%
- Data not available

ADULT ILLITERATES IN THE WORLD
(millions)

	Male	Female
1970	302	441
1980	322	492
1990 (projection)	345	539

© World Priorities 1983, used with permission

BOTTOM 10 COUNTRIES
Mauritania	17%
Saudi Arabia	16
Chad	15
Ethiopia	15
Afghanistan	12
Senegal	10
Mali	9
Somalia	6
Niger	5
Burkina Faso	5

Available statistics show the following countries have a literacy rate of 98% or more: Australia, Austria, Belgium, Canada, Czechoslovakia, Denmark, Finland, France, East Germany, West Germany, Hong Kong, Hungary, Iceland, Ireland, Japan, Luxembourg, Netherlands, New Zealand, Norway, Poland, Romania, Western Samoa, Sweden, Switzerland, U.S.S.R., United States, and United Kingdom.

CANADA 98%

INFANT MORTALITY

Number of deaths of infants under one year of age per 1000 live births

- More than 150
- 100-150
- 51-99
- 26-50
- 16-25
- Less than 16
- Data not available

CANADA 12

TOP 10 COUNTRIES
Sweden	7
Finland	8
Japan	8
Netherlands	8
Denmark	9
Norway	9
Switzerland	9
France	10
Iceland	11
Australia	12

BOTTOM 10 COUNTRIES
Afghanistan	185
Mauritania	187
C.A.R.*	190
Chad	190
Angola	192
Niger	200
Mali	210
Guinea-Bissau	211
Gambia	217
Guinea	220

*Central African Republic

Equatorial scale 1: 175 000 000

For explanation of terms, see glossary. **128**

WORLD

INDUSTRY

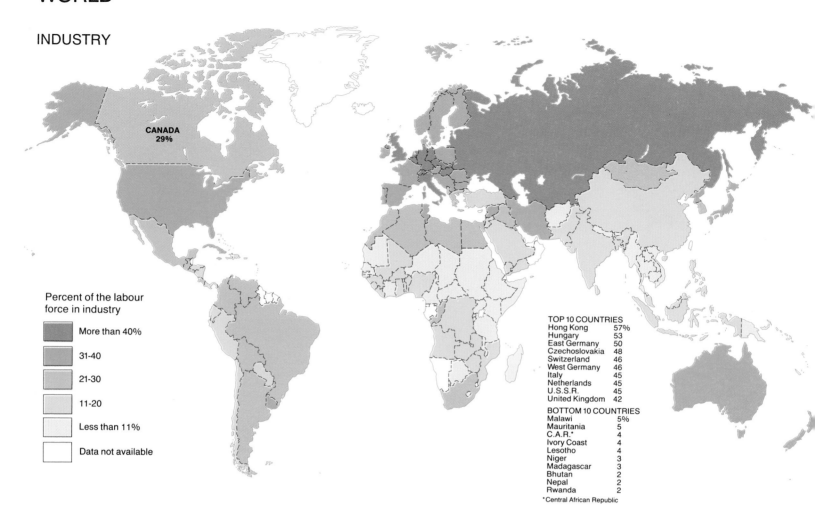

CANADA
29%

Percent of the labour force in industry

- More than 40%
- 31-40
- 21-30
- 11-20
- Less than 11%
- Data not available

TOP 10 COUNTRIES
Hong Kong	57%
Hungary	53
East Germany	50
Czechoslovakia	48
Switzerland	46
West Germany	46
Italy	45
Netherlands	45
U.S.S.R.	45
United Kingdom	42

BOTTOM 10 COUNTRIES
Malawi	5%
Mauritania	5
C.A.R.*	4
Ivory Coast	4
Lesotho	4
Niger	3
Madagascar	3
Bhutan	2
Nepal	2
Rwanda	2

*Central African Republic

SERVICES

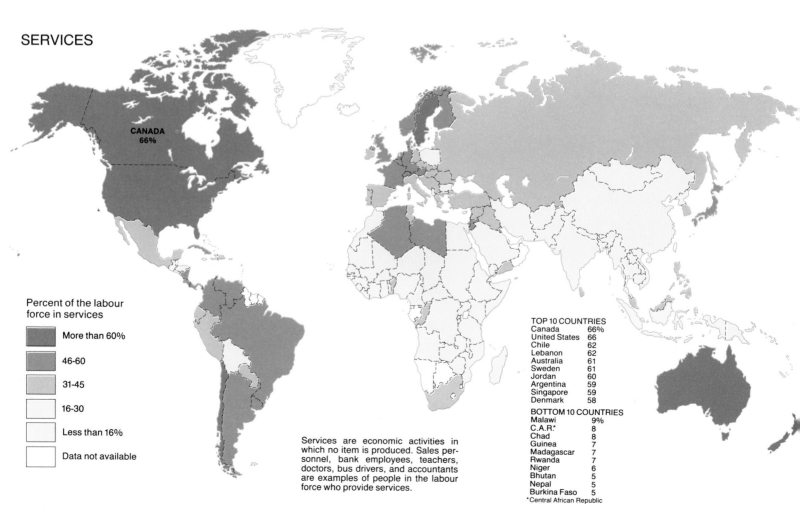

CANADA
66%

Percent of the labour force in services

- More than 60%
- 46-60
- 31-45
- 16-30
- Less than 16%
- Data not available

Services are economic activities in which no item is produced. Sales personnel, bank employees, teachers, doctors, bus drivers, and accountants are examples of people in the labour force who provide services.

TOP 10 COUNTRIES
Canada	66%
United States	66
Chile	62
Lebanon	62
Australia	61
Sweden	61
Jordan	60
Argentina	59
Singapore	59
Denmark	58

BOTTOM 10 COUNTRIES
Malawi	9%
C.A.R.*	8
Chad	8
Guinea	7
Madagascar	7
Rwanda	7
Niger	6
Bhutan	5
Nepal	5
Burkina Faso	5

*Central African Republic

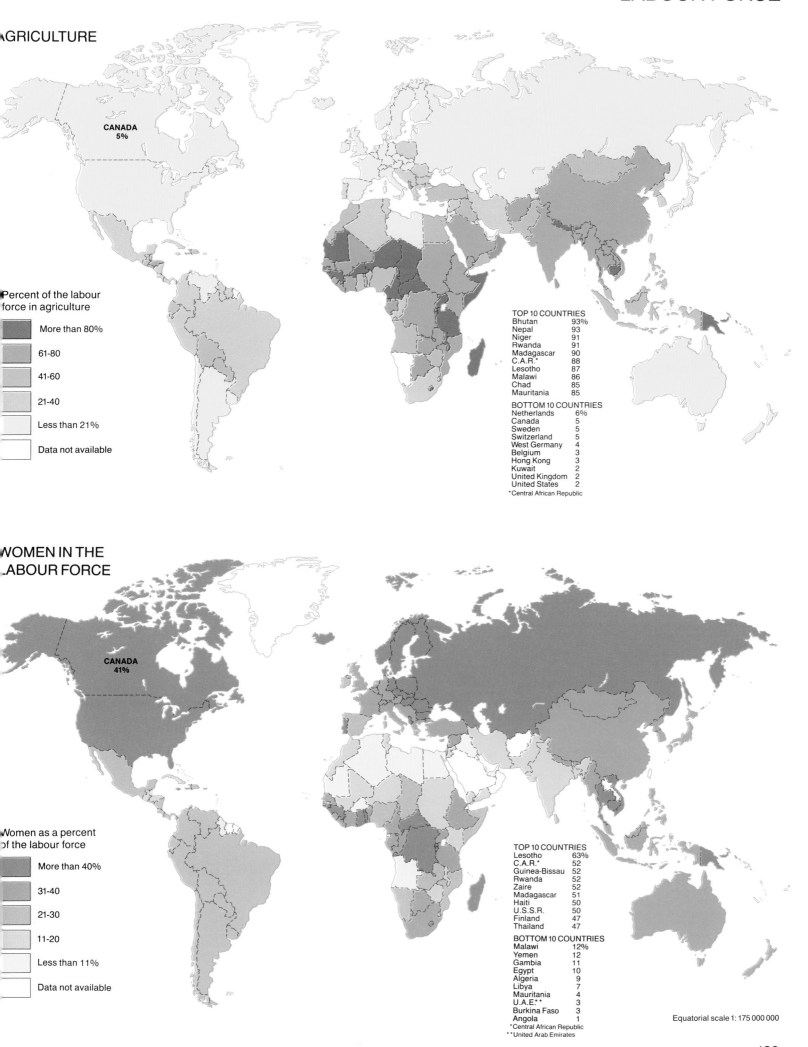

AGRICULTURE

Percent of the labour force in agriculture

- More than 80%
- 61-80
- 41-60
- 21-40
- Less than 21%
- Data not available

CANADA 5%

TOP 10 COUNTRIES
Bhutan	93%
Nepal	93
Niger	91
Rwanda	91
Madagascar	90
C.A.R.*	88
Lesotho	87
Malawi	86
Chad	85
Mauritania	85

BOTTOM 10 COUNTRIES
Netherlands	6%
Canada	5
Sweden	5
Switzerland	5
West Germany	4
Belgium	3
Hong Kong	3
Kuwait	2
United Kingdom	2
United States	2

*Central African Republic

WOMEN IN THE LABOUR FORCE

Women as a percent of the labour force

- More than 40%
- 31-40
- 21-30
- 11-20
- Less than 11%
- Data not available

CANADA 41%

TOP 10 COUNTRIES
Lesotho	63%
C.A.R.*	52
Guinea-Bissau	52
Rwanda	52
Zaire	52
Madagascar	51
Haiti	50
U.S.S.R.	50
Finland	47
Thailand	47

BOTTOM 10 COUNTRIES
Malawi	12%
Yemen	12
Gambia	11
Egypt	10
Algeria	9
Libya	7
Mauritania	4
U.A.E.**	3
Burkina Faso	3
Angola	1

*Central African Republic
**United Arab Emirates

Equatorial scale 1: 175 000 000

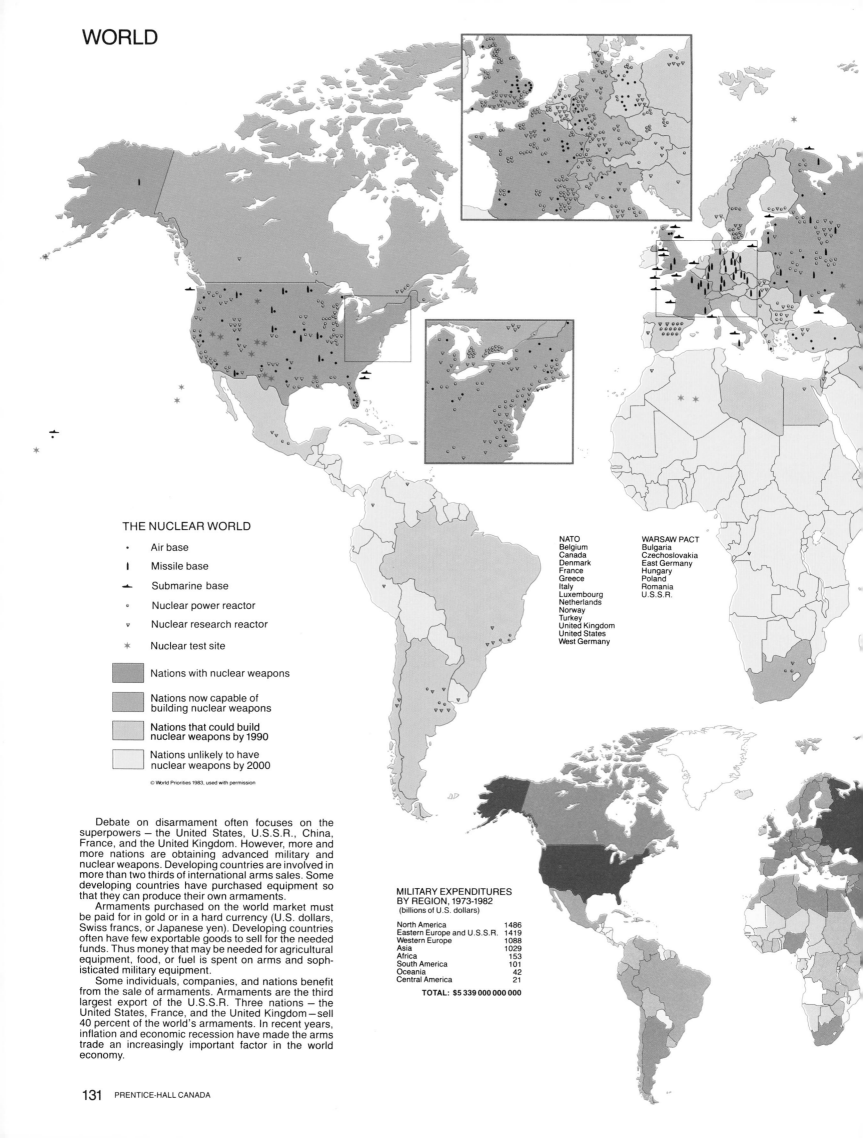

WORLD

THE NUCLEAR WORLD

- ·   Air base
- | Missile base
- ⊥   Submarine base
- ○   Nuclear power reactor
- ▽   Nuclear research reactor
- ✳   Nuclear test site

  Nations with nuclear weapons

  Nations now capable of
  building nuclear weapons

  Nations that could build
  nuclear weapons by 1990

  Nations unlikely to have
  nuclear weapons by 2000

© World Priorities 1983, used with permission

NATO	WARSAW PACT
Belgium	Bulgaria
Canada	Czechoslovakia
Denmark	East Germany
France	Hungary
Greece	Poland
Italy	Romania
Luxembourg	U.S.S.R.
Netherlands	
Norway	
Turkey	
United Kingdom	
United States	
West Germany	

Debate on disarmament often focuses on the superpowers – the United States, U.S.S.R., China, France, and the United Kingdom. However, more and more nations are obtaining advanced military and nuclear weapons. Developing countries are involved in more than two thirds of international arms sales. Some developing countries have purchased equipment so that they can produce their own armaments.

Armaments purchased on the world market must be paid for in gold or in a hard currency (U.S. dollars, Swiss francs, or Japanese yen). Developing countries often have few exportable goods to sell for the needed funds. Thus money that may be needed for agricultural equipment, food, or fuel is spent on arms and sophisticated military equipment.

Some individuals, companies, and nations benefit from the sale of armaments. Armaments are the third largest export of the U.S.S.R. Three nations – the United States, France, and the United Kingdom – sell 40 percent of the world's armaments. In recent years, inflation and economic recession have made the arms trade an increasingly important factor in the world economy.

MILITARY EXPENDITURES
BY REGION, 1973-1982
(billions of U.S. dollars)

North America	1486
Eastern Europe and U.S.S.R.	1419
Western Europe	1088
Asia	1029
Africa	153
South America	101
Oceania	42
Central America	21

TOTAL: $5 339 000 000 000

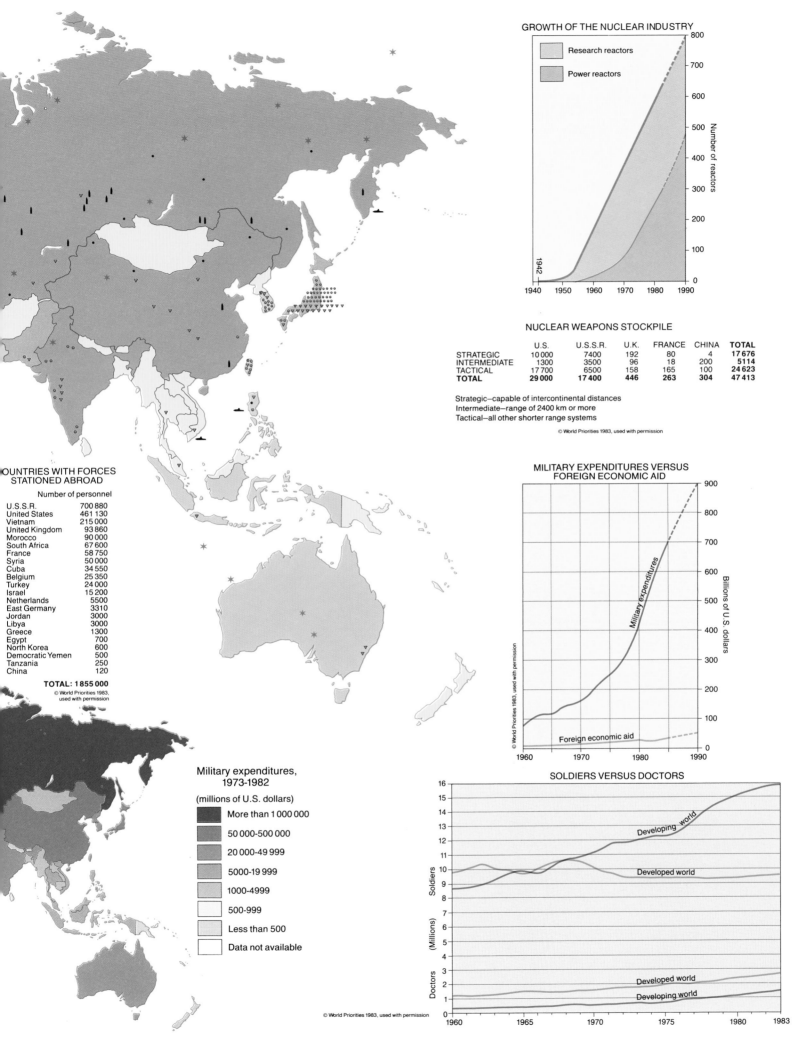

GROWTH OF THE NUCLEAR INDUSTRY

Research reactors
Power reactors

Number of reactors

1942

1940 1950 1960 1970 1980 1990

NUCLEAR WEAPONS STOCKPILE

	U.S.	U.S.S.R.	U.K.	FRANCE	CHINA	TOTAL
STRATEGIC	10 000	7400	192	80	4	17 676
INTERMEDIATE	1300	3500	96	18	200	5114
TACTICAL	17 700	6500	158	165	100	24 623
TOTAL	29 000	17 400	446	263	304	47 413

Strategic—capable of intercontinental distances
Intermediate—range of 2400 km or more
Tactical—all other shorter range systems

© World Priorities 1983, used with permission

COUNTRIES WITH FORCES STATIONED ABROAD

Number of personnel

U.S.S.R.	700 880
United States	461 130
Vietnam	215 000
United Kingdom	93 860
Morocco	90 000
South Africa	67 600
France	58 750
Syria	50 000
Cuba	34 550
Belgium	25 350
Turkey	24 000
Israel	15 200
Netherlands	5500
East Germany	3310
Jordan	3000
Libya	3000
Greece	1300
Egypt	700
North Korea	600
Democratic Yemen	500
Tanzania	250
China	120

TOTAL: 1 855 000

© World Priorities 1983, used with permission

MILITARY EXPENDITURES VERSUS FOREIGN ECONOMIC AID

Billions of U.S. dollars

Military expenditures

Foreign economic aid

© World Priorities 1983, used with permission

1960 1970 1980 1990

Military expenditures, 1973-1982

(millions of U.S. dollars)

- More than 1 000 000
- 50 000-500 000
- 20 000-49 999
- 5000-19 999
- 1000-4999
- 500-999
- Less than 500
- Data not available

SOLDIERS VERSUS DOCTORS

Soldiers (Millions)

Developing world
Developed world

Doctors

Developed world
Developing world

© World Priorities 1983, used with permission

1960 1965 1970 1975 1980 1983

WORLD

ATLANTIC

OCEAN

BERMUDA (U.K.)

WEST INDIES

San Juan
PUERTO RICO (U.S.)

DOMINICAN REPUBLIC
Santo Domingo

NETHERLANDS ANTILLES (Neth.)

VENEZUELA

COLOMBIA

EQUATOR

Bogotá

HAITI
Port-au-Prince

BAHAMAS

CARIBBEAN SEA

ECUADOR
Quito

Boston
New York
Hartford
Philadelphia
Washington
Baltimore
Buffalo
Pittsburgh
Cleveland
Toronto
Lake Ontario
Lake Erie
Richmond
Charleston
Jacksonville
Miami
Tampa

JAMAICA
Kingston

CUBA

PANAMA
Panamá

San José
COSTA RICA
Lake Nicaragua

Nassau

Habana (Havana)

Detroit
Lake Huron
Cincinnati
Indianapolis
Lake Michigan
Milwaukee
Chicago
Atlanta
Nashville
Memphis
New Orleans

NICARAGUA
Managua

HONDURAS
Tegucigalpa

BELIZE
Belmopan

Minneapolis
St. Louis
Kansas City
Wichita

GUATEMALA
Guatemala

SAN SALVADOR
EL SALVADOR

Mérida

Dallas
Fort Worth
Houston
San Antonio

Mississippi

GULF OF MEXICO

BAHIA DE CAMPECHE

Veracruz

UNITED STATES

Missouri
North Platte
Arkansas
Brazos
Pecos

Denver
Albuquerque
El Paso

Rio Grande

Monterrey

MEXICO
México

Acapulco

Great Salt Lake
Salt Lake City
Colorado
Snake

Phoenix
Las Vegas

Guadalajara

GOLFO DE CALIFORNIA

San Francisco
Los Angeles
San Diego

PACIFIC OCEAN

Tropic of Cancer

Longitude West of Greenwich

National capital
Other important city or town
Major international airport
Main railway
Main road
International boundary
Less than 200 m of water
More than 200 m of water

0 km   200   400   600   800   1000
Scale 1:24 500 000   1 cm represents 245 km

134

UNITED STATES

CANADA

Thunder Bay

Lake Superior

Sault Ste. Marie

Québec

MAINE

Augusta

MINNESOTA

Duluth

MICHIGAN

Lake Huron

Ottawa

Montréal

Montpelier

N.H.

Concord

V.T.

St. Paul
Minneapolis

WISCONSIN

Green Bay

Appleton

Lake Michigan

Muskegon
Grand Rapids

Flint

Toronto

Lake Ontario

Syracuse

Albany

MASS.

Boston

CONN.

R.I.

Providence

Rochester

Madison

Milwaukee

Lansing

Detroit

Buffalo

Rochester

NEW YORK

Hartford

LONG ISLAND

Hudson

Waterloo

Cedar Rapids

Rockford

Chicago

South Bend

Toledo

Cleveland

Erie

Lake Erie

Newark

New York

Trenton

IOWA

Des Moines

Davenport

Gary

Fort Wayne

OHIO

Akron

PENNSYLVANIA

Pittsburgh

Harrisburg

Philadelphia

N.J.

Peoria

Indianapolis

Columbus

Dayton

MD.

Baltimore

Dover

DELAWARE

ILLINOIS

Springfield

INDIANA

Cincinnati

Washington D.C.

Annapolis

ATLANTIC OCEAN

Kansas City

Jefferson City

St. Louis

Evansville

Frankfort

Louisville

Lexington

WEST VIRGINIA

Charleston

VIRGINIA

Richmond

Roanoke

Norfolk

MISSOURI

KENTUCKY

Ohio

Roanoke

ARKANSAS

Nashville

Knoxville

NORTH CAROLINA

Winston-Salem

Raleigh

Charlotte

TENNESSEE

Chattanooga

Memphis

Huntsville

Tennessee

SOUTH CAROLINA

Columbia

Charleston

Fort Smith

Little Rock

Atlanta

Augusta

Savannah

Birmingham

GEORGIA

Macon

MISSISSIPPI

ALABAMA

Columbus

Jackson

Montgomery

Savannah

Shreveport

Monroe

Alabama

LOUISIANA

Baton Rouge

Mobile

Pensacola

Tallahassee

Jacksonville

Beaumont

Houston

Lake Charles

New Orleans

Port Arthur

Galveston

GULF OF MEXICO

FLORIDA

St. Petersburg

Tampa

Lake Okeechobee

Fort Lauderdale

Miami

Nassau

BAHAMAS

Key West

STRAITS OF FLORIDA

⊙	National capital
⊚	State capital
•	Other important city or town
✈	Major international airport
+–+	Main railway
—	Main road
—··—	International boundary
—·—	State boundary
	Less than 200 m of water
	More than 200 m of water

0 km 100 200 300 400 500

Scale 1: 10 800 000   1 cm represents 108 km

95° Longitude West of Greenwich

Legend

⊙ National capital
• Other important city or town
✈ Major international airport
┼┼┼ Main railway
─── Main road
▬ ▬ International boundary
Less than 200 m of water
More than 200 m of water

0 km	250	500	750

Scale 1:14 300 000   1 cm represents 143 km

Longitude West of Greenwich

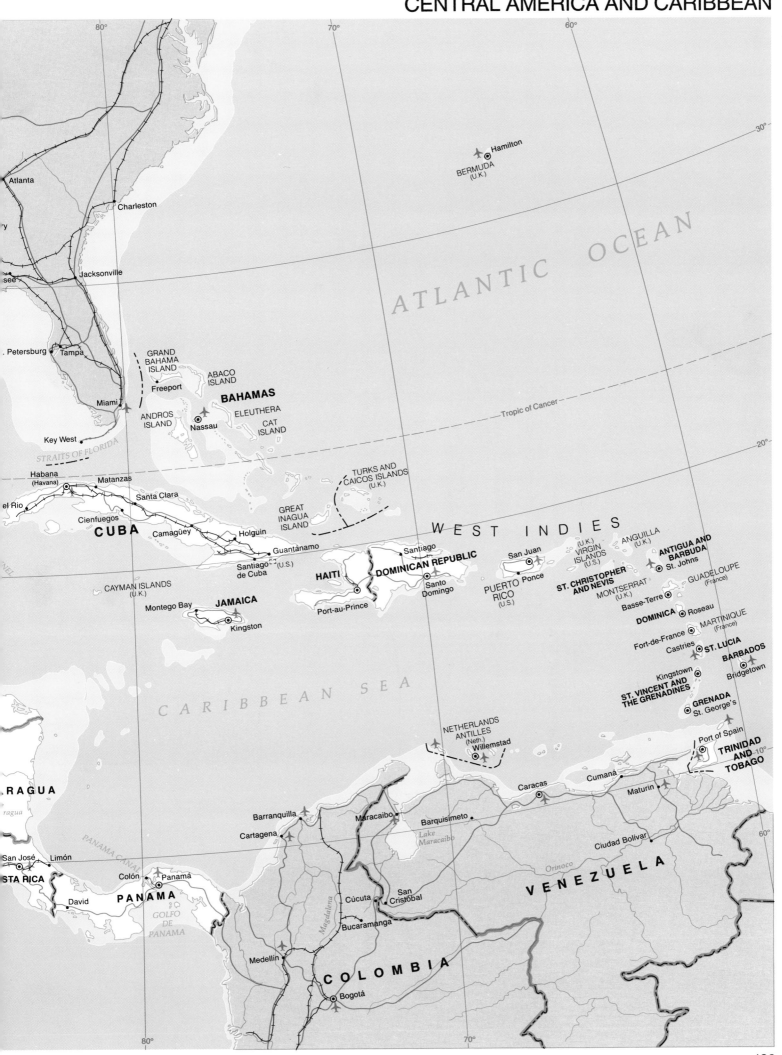

Atlanta

Charleston

ry

. Petersburg | Tampa

Jacksonville

see

Miami

Key West

STRAITS OF FLORIDA

GRAND
BAHAMA
ISLAND

Freeport

ABACO
ISLAND

BAHAMAS

ANDROS
ISLAND

Nassau

ELEUTHERA

CAT
ISLAND

Tropic of Cancer

ATLANTIC OCEAN

Hamilton

BERMUDA
(U.K.)

Habana
(Havana)

Matanzas

el Rio

Santa Clara

Cienfuegos

CUBA

Camagüey

Holguin

Guantánamo

Santiago
de Cuba (U.S.)

CAYMAN ISLANDS
(U.K.)

JAMAICA

Montego Bay

Kingston

TURKS AND
CAICOS ISLANDS
(U.K.)

GREAT
INAGUA
ISLAND

W E S T   I N D I E S

Santiago

HAITI

DOMINICAN REPUBLIC

Port-au-Prince

Santo
Domingo

San Juan

PUERTO
RICO
(U.S.)

Ponce

VIRGIN
ISLANDS
(U.S.)

ANGUILLA
(U.K.)

**ANTIGUA AND
BARBUDA**

St. Johns

**ST. CHRISTOPHER
AND NEVIS**

MONTSERRAT
(U.K.)

GUADELOUPE
(France)

Basse-Terre

DOMINICA

Roseau

MARTINIQUE
(France)

Fort-de-France

Castries

ST. LUCIA

BARBADOS

Bridgetown

Kingstown

**ST. VINCENT AND
THE GRENADINES**

GRENADA

St. George's

C A R I B B E A N   S E A

NETHERLANDS
ANTILLES
(Neth.)

Willemstad

Port of Spain

**TRINIDAD
AND
TOBAGO**

RAGUA

ragua

San José

Limón

STA RICA

Colón

Panamá

David

PANAMA

PANAMA CANAL

GOLFO
DE
PANAMÁ

Barranquilla

Cartagena

Maracaibo

Lake
Maracaibo

Barquisimeto

Cumaná

Caracas

Maturin

Ciudad Bolívar

V E N E Z U E L A

Magdalena

Cúcuta

San
Cristóbal

Orinoco

Bucaramanga

Medellín

C O L O M B I A

Bogotá

WORLD

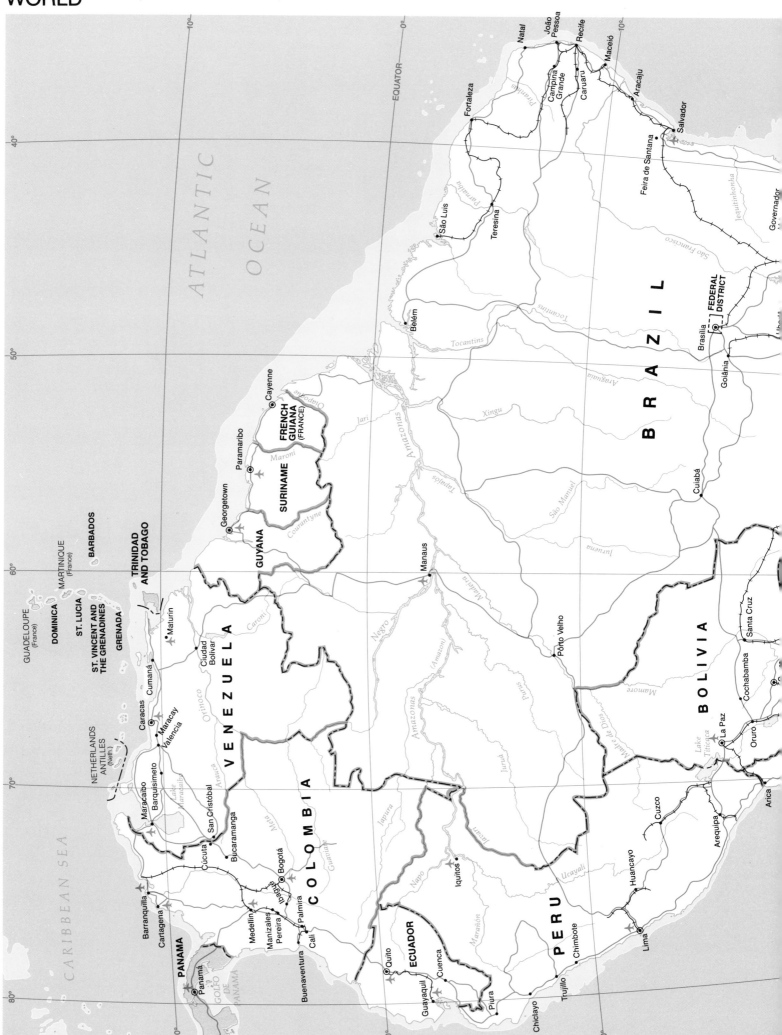

ATLANTIC

OCEAN

EQUATOR

40°

50°

60°

70°

80°

0°

10°

10°

CARIBBEAN SEA

GUADELOUPE
(France)

DOMINICA

MARTINIQUE
(France)

ST. LUCIA

ST. VINCENT AND
THE GRENADINES

BARBADOS

GRENADA

TRINIDAD
AND TOBAGO

NETHERLANDS
ANTILLES
(Neth.)

PANAMA

Panamá

GOLFO
DE
PANAMA

Barranquilla

Cartagena

Maracaibo

Barquisimeto

Lake
Maracaibo

San Cristóbal

Cúcuta

Bucaramanga

Medellín

Manizales

Pereira

Palmira

Ibagué

Bogotá

Cali

Buenaventura

C O L O M B I A

Cumaná

Caracas

Maracay

Valencia

V E N E Z U E L A

Orinoco

Arauca

Meta

Guaviare

Maturín

Ciudad
Bolívar

Caroní

Georgetown

Paramaribo

Cayenne

GUYANA

SURINAME

FRENCH
GUIANA
(FRANCE)

Maroni

Courantyne

Caquetá

Napo

Iquitos

Quito

Cuenca

ECUADOR

Guayaquil

Piura

Chiclayo

Trujillo

Chimbote

Lima

Huancayo

P E R U

Cuzco

Arequipa

Arica

Marañón

Ucayali

Putumayo

Jari

Amazonas

Negro

(Amazon)

Manaus

Pôrto Velho

Madeira

Purus

Juruá

Amazonas

Madre de Dios

Mamoré

B O L I V I A

La Paz

Oruro

Lake
Titicaca

Cochabamba

Santa Cruz

Tapajós

São Manuel

Xingu

Araguaia

Tocantins

Tocantins

Belém

São Luís

Teresina

Fortaleza

Parnaíba

Natal

João
Pessoa

Campina
Grande

Caruaru

Recife

Maceió

Aracaju

Salvador

Feira de Santana

Jequitinhonha

São Francisco

Governador

B R A Z I L

FEDERAL
DISTRICT

Brasília

Goiânia

Cuiabá

Juruena

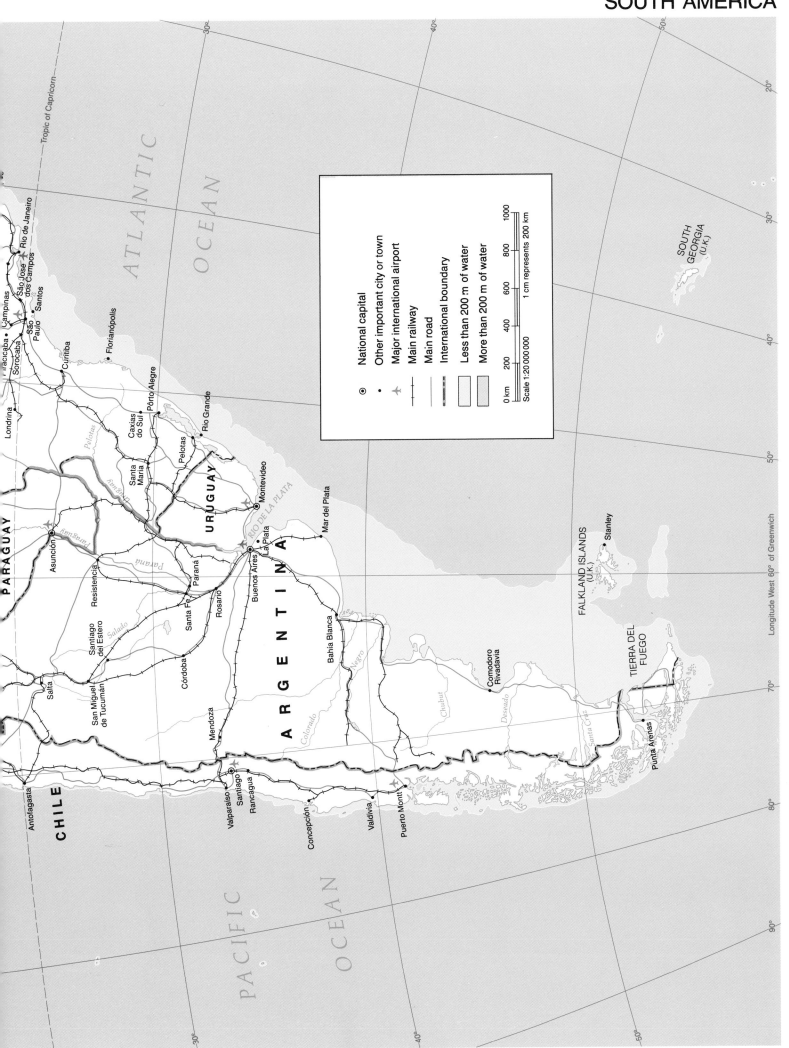

ATLANTIC

OCEAN

PACIFIC

OCEAN

Tropic of Capricorn

Rio de Janeiro
Piracicaba
Campinas
São José dos Campos
Sorocaba
São Paulo
Santos
Londrina
Curitiba
Florianópolis
Caxias do Sul
Pôrto Alegre
Santa Maria
Rio Grande
Pelotas
Pelotas

PARAGUAY

Asunción

URUGUAY

Montevideo

RIO DE LA PLATA
La Plata
Buenos Aires
Mar del Plata

Resistencia
Paraná
Santa Fe
Rosario
Santiago del Estero
Córdoba
Salta
San Miguel de Tucumán
Mendoza

Salado
Salado

ARGENTINA

Bahía Blanca

Colorado
Negro

Chubut

Deseado

Comodoro Rivadavia

Santa Cruz

CHILE

Antofagasta
Valparaíso
Santiago
Rancagua
Concepción
Valdivia
Puerto Montt

TIERRA DEL FUEGO

Punta Arenas

FALKLAND ISLANDS
(U.K.)

Stanley

SOUTH GEORGIA
(U.K.)

Longitude West 60° of Greenwich

| National capital |
| Other important city or town |
| Major international airport |
| Main railway |
| Main road |
| International boundary |
| Less than 200 m of water |
| More than 200 m of water |

0 km 200 400 600 800 1000 km

1 cm represents 200 km

Scale 1:20 000 000

WORLD

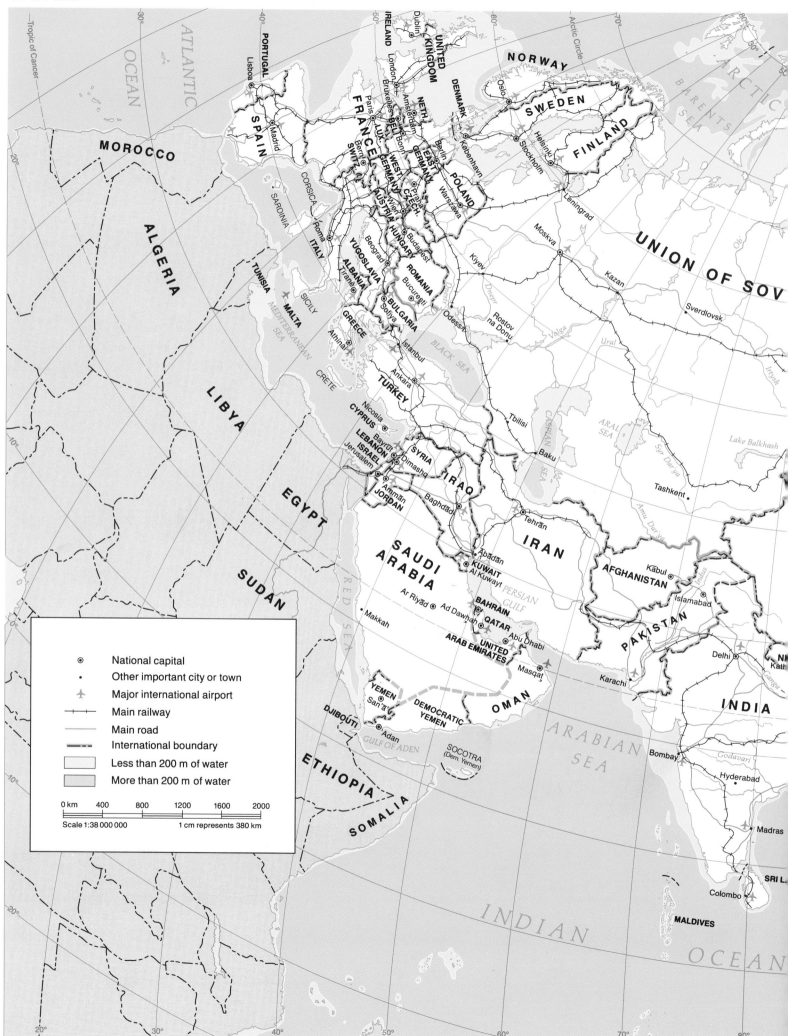

Legend:

- ⊙ National capital
- • Other important city or town
- ✈ Major international airport
- ┼┼┼ Main railway
- ─── Main road
- ▬ ▬ International boundary
- ▢ Less than 200 m of water
- ▨ More than 200 m of water

0 km 400 800 1200 1600 2000

Scale 1:38 000 000   1 cm represents 380 km

OCEAN

150° 130° 110° 90° 80° 70° 60° 50° 40° 30°

Lena

Okhotsk •

BERING SEA

CIALIST REPUBLICS

SEA OF OKHOTSK

MONGOLIA

Lake Baykal

Ulaanbaatar ⊙

Shenyang

Vladivostok

NORTH KOREA

SEA OF JAPAN

JAPAN

P'yŏngyang

Tōkyō

Beijing

Sŏul

SOUTH KOREA

Huang (Yellow)

YELLOW SEA

PACIFIC

CHINA

Shanghai

EAST CHINA SEA

OCEAN

Chang (Yangtze)

(Brahmaputra)

mphu

BHUTAN

T'aipei

TAIWAN

GLADESH

Dhaka

Guangzhou

Mekong

BURMA

Victoria

HONG KONG

(U.K.)

Ha-noi

SOUTH

Saluen

LAOS

CHINA

PHILIPPINES

Irrawaddy

Viangchan

VIETNAM

SEA

Y OF

Manila

NGAL

Rangoon

THAILAND

Krung Thep

KAMPUCHEA

Phnum Pénh

Ho Chi Minh

NEW GUINEA

DAMAN LANDS

PAPUA NEW GUINEA

(India)

NICOBAR ISLANDS

MALAYSIA

BRUNEI

Port Moresby

CORAL SEA

Kuala Lumpur

SINGAPORE

BORNEO

SULAWESI

SUMATRA

INDONESIA

AUSTRALIA

Jakarta

JAVA

TIMOR

EQUATOR 0°

10°

20°

10°

0°

10°

20°

WORLD

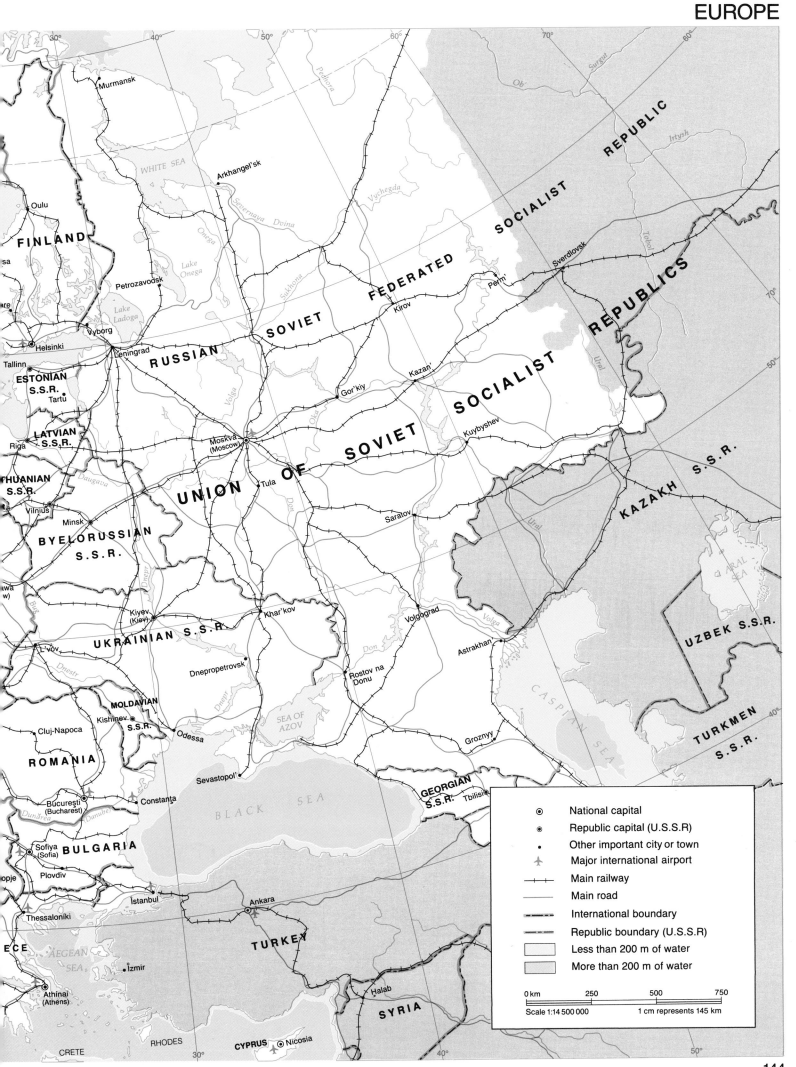

FINLAND

Murmansk

Oulu

WHITE SEA

Arkhangel'sk

Severnaya Dvina

Pechora

Ob

Vychegda

Irtysh

Surgut

SOCIALIST

REPUBLIC

FEDERATED

Sverdlovsk

Perm'

Tobol

Petrozavodsk

Lake Ladoga

Onega

Lake Onega

Sukhona

SOVIET

Kirov

RUSSIAN

Kazan'

Vyborg

Helsinki

Leningrad

Tallinn

ESTONIAN
S.S.R.

Tartu

Volga

Gor'kiy

Oka

REPUBLICS

SOCIALIST

Kuybyshev

Ural

50°

70°

LATVIAN
S.S.R.

Riga

Daugava

UNION

OF

SOVIET

Moskva
(Moscow)

Tula

Don

KAZAKH
S.S.R.

THUANIAN
S.S.R.

Vilnius

Minsk

BYELORUSSIAN
S.S.R.

Saratov

Ural

ARAL
SEA

(wa)

w)

Big

Dnepr

Kiyev
(Kiev)

Khar'kov

Volgograd

Volga

UZBEK S.S.R.

UKRAINIAN S.S.R.

L'vov

Dnestr

Dnepropetrovsk

Dnepr

Don

Rostov na
Donu

Astrakhan

CASPIAN SEA

TURKMEN
S.S.R.

40°

MOLDAVIAN
S.S.R.

Kishinev

Odessa

SEA OF
AZOV

Groznyy

Cluj-Napoca

ROMANIA

Sevastopol'

București
(Bucharest)

Constanța

Dunărea

Danube

BLACK

SEA

GEORGIAN
S.S.R.

Tbilisi

Sofiya
(Sofia)

BULGARIA

Plovdiv

opje

İstanbul

Ankara

Thessaloniki

ECE

AEGEAN
SEA

İzmir

TURKEY

Athínai
(Athens)

Halab

SYRIA

CRETE

RHODES

CYPRUS

Nicosia

	National capital
	Republic capital (U.S.S.R)
•	Other important city or town
✈	Major international airport
┼┼┼	Main railway
──	Main road
▬ ▬	International boundary
▬·▬	Republic boundary (U.S.S.R)
	Less than 200 m of water
	More than 200 m of water

0 km   250   500   750

Scale 1:14 500 000   1 cm represents 145 km

WORLD

ORKNEY
ISLANDS

NORWAY

HEBRIDES

SCOTLAND

Wick

Inverness
Aberdeen
Dundee

UNITED

KINGDOM

NORTHERN
IRELAND

Glasgow
Edinburgh

Londonderry

Belfast

Carlisle
Newcastle

DENMARK

Sligo

Middlesbrough

Esbjerg

Galway
Mullingar

IRELAND

ISLE OF
MAN

IRISH SEA

York
Leeds
Liverpool
Hull

Baile Átha Cliath
(Dublin)

Holyhead

Sheffield

Manchester

Limerick

Stafford
Nottingham

Groningen

Bremerhaven

Bremen

Waterford

ENGLAND

Norwich

Amsterdam

Cork

WALES

Coventry
Birmingham

Cambridge

's-Gravenhage
(The Hague)

NETHERLANDS

Münster

Bielefe

ST. GEORGE'S CHANNEL

Swansea

Oxford

Rotterdam

Dortmund

Cardiff
Bristol

London

Harwich

Essen
Düsseldorf

Kass

Exeter
Southampton

Portsmouth

Oostende

Eindhoven

Köln (Cologne)

Bonn

Plymouth

Brighton

Dover

Calais

Antwerpen
Bruxelles
(Brussels)

Lille

Liège

BELGIUM

Koblenz

WES

Frankfurt

ISLES OF
SCILLY

ENGLISH CHANNEL

Cherbourg

GERM

ATLANTIC

CHANNEL
ISLANDS
(U.K.)

Le Havre
Rouen

Amiens

LUXEMBOURG

Luxembourg

OCEAN

St-Malo

Caen

Reims

Saarbrücken

Mann

Brest

Paris

Metz

Karlsruh

Rennes

Nancy

Strasbourg

Stuttgart

LeMans

Orléans

Troyes

Angers
Tours

Freiburg

Nantes

Dijon

Basel

Zürich

Poitiers

Bourges

Bern

LIECHTENSTEI
Vadu

BAY OF
BISCAY

FRANCE

Lausanne

SWITZERLAN

La Rochelle

Limoges

Clermont-
Ferrand

Vichy

Genève
(Geneva)

Lugano

Lyon

St. Étienne

Torino
(Turin)

Genova
(Genoa)

Bordeaux

Grenoble

La Spe

Bayonne

Nîmes

Avignon

Nice

MONACO

Pamplona

Toulouse

Montpellier

Marseille

Toulon

Andorra

ANDORRA

Perpignan

CORSICA
(France)

Bastia

SPAIN

Zaragoza

Gerona

MEDITERRANEAN

Ajaccio

Vigo

Porto
(Oporto)

PORTUGAL

Legend

◉ National capital
◉ Republic capital (U.S.S.R.)
• Other important city or town
✈ Major international airport
+++ Main railway
— Main road
–·– International boundary
–·– Republic boundary (U.S.S.R.)
☐ Less than 200 m of water
☐ More than 200 m of water

0 km   100   200   300

Scale 1:7 000 000   1 cm represents 70 km

WORLD

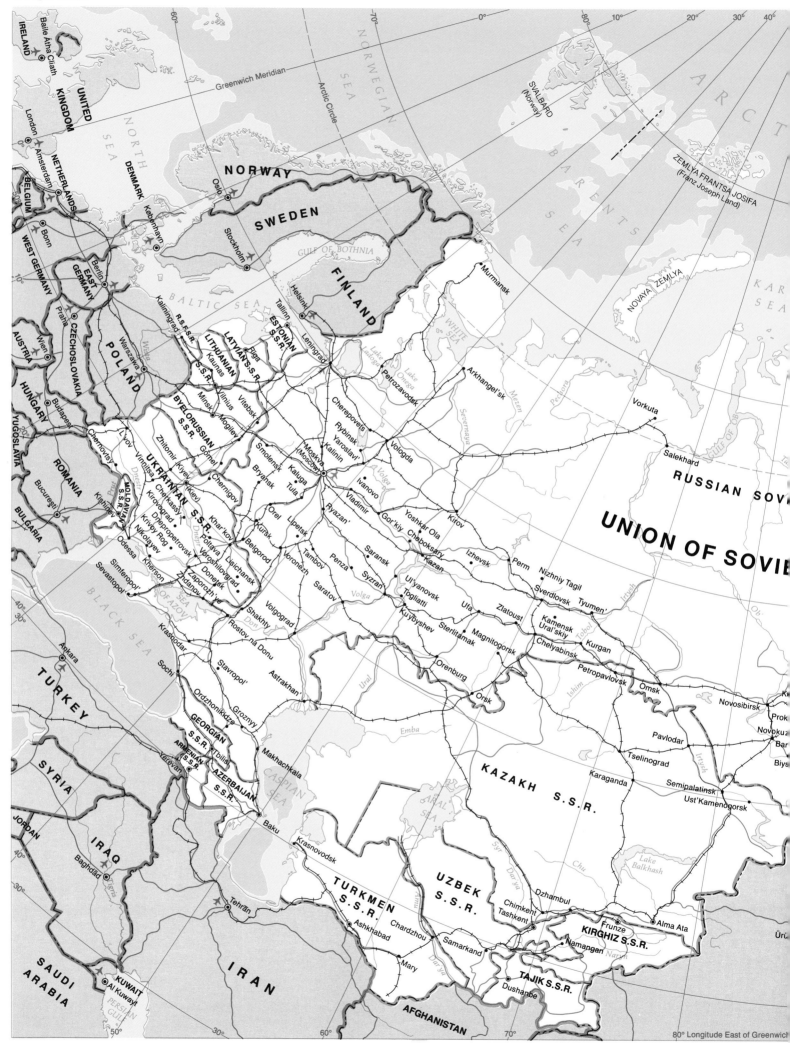

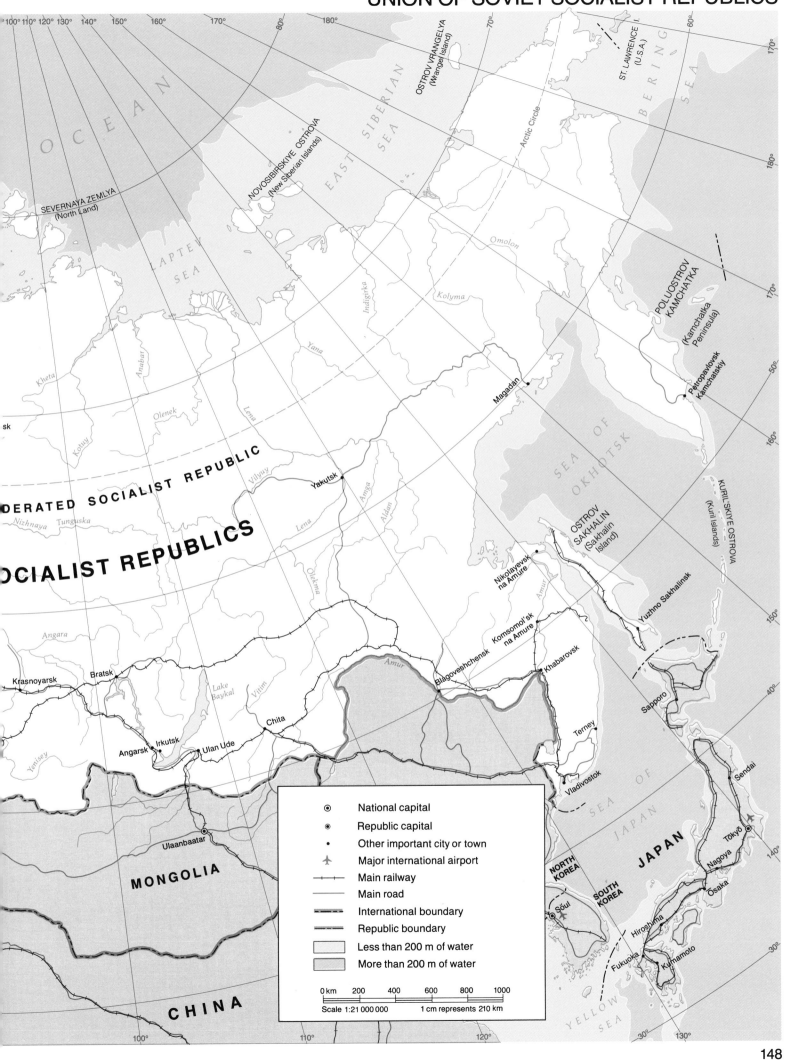

OSTROV VRANGELYA
(Wrangel Island)

ST. LAWRENCE I.
(U.S.A.)

B E R I N G   S E A

O C E A N

SEVERNAYA ZEMLYA
(North Land)

NOVOSIBIRSKIYE OSTROVA
(New Siberian Islands)

E A S T   S I B E R I A N   S E A

Arctic Circle

L A P T E V   S E A

Omolon

Indigirka

Kolyma

POLUOSTROV
KAMCHATKA
(Kamchatka
Peninsula)

Kheta

Olenek

Anabar

Yana

Magadan

Petropavlovsk
Kamchatskiy

S E A   O F
O K H O T S K

Nizhnaya   Tunguska

Vilyuy

Yakutsk

Amga

Aldan

Lena

KURIL'SKIYE OSTROVA
(Kuril Islands)

DERATED SOCIALIST REPUBLIC

OCIALIST REPUBLICS

Lena

Olekma

OSTROV
SAKHALIN
(Sakhalin
Island)

Angara

Vitim

Nikolayevsk
na Amure

Amur

Yuzhno Sakhalinsk

Krasnoyarsk

Bratsk

Lake
Baykal

Amur

Komsomol'sk
na Amure

Blagoveshchensk

Khabarovsk

Sapporo

Yenisey

Chita

Terney

Angarsk   Irkutsk

Ulan Ude

Vladivostok

S E A   O F

Sendai

Ulaanbaatar

J A P A N

Tōkyō

MONGOLIA

NORTH
KOREA

JAPAN

Nagoya

Sŏul

SOUTH
KOREA

Ōsaka

Hiroshima

CHINA

Fukuoka

Kumamoto

YELLOW
SEA

	National capital
⊙	Republic capital
•	Other important city or town
✈	Major international airport
	Main railway
	Main road
	International boundary
	Republic boundary
	Less than 200 m of water
	More than 200 m of water

0 km   200   400   600   800   1000

Scale 1:21 000 000   1 cm represents 210 km

UNION OF SOVIET SOCIALIST REPUBLICS

Irkutsk

Ust'Kamenogorsk

MONGOLIA

Ulaanbaatar
(Ulan Bator)

Alma Ata

Selenge

Dzavhan

Hovd

Ulungur

Ürümqi

Kuqa

Turpan

Hami

Aksu

Ili

Tarim

Kashi

XINJIANG

Kongi

Anxi

Shache
(Yarkant)

Yumen

Hotan

Qarqan

Zhangye

GANSU

Yinchuan

Wuwei

NINGXIA

Xining

QINGHAI

Lanzhou

Huang (Yellow)

CHINA

PAKISTAN

Wei

SHAA

Baoji

Xi
(S

XIZANG

Tongtian

(Yangtze)

Lancang

Nu

(Salween)

(TIBET)

SICHUAN

Yarlung Zangbo

Lhasa
(Lhasa)

Chengdu

Nanchong

Xigazê
Gyangzê

(Brahmaputra)

(Mekong)

Chongqing
(Chungking)

NEPAL

Kanpur

Neijiang

Kathmandu

Zigong

Min

Chang

Thimphu

Yibin

Yangtze

BHUTAN

Jinsha

Jinsha

INDIA

Patna

Yalong

Zunyi

Yachi Wa

BANGLADESH

GUIZHOU

Dhaka

(Yangtze)

Calcutta

Guiyang

Tropic of Cancer

Baoshan

Lancang

Kunming

Raipur

YUNNAN

Yuan (Red)

GUAN

Chittagong

BURMA

Gejiu

Nanning

Hongshui

Mandalay

Da

VIETNAM

(Red)

Sittwe
(Akyab)

BAY OF BENGAL

Hong

(Black)

Hanoi

LAOS

GULF OF

THAILAND

TONKIN

70° 50° 80° 90° 100°

40°

30°

20°

90° 100°

Chita

Heilong

120°

130°

Argun

Blagoveshchensk

140°

50°

OSTROV
SAKHALIN

SEA OF
OKHOTSK

(Kerulen)

Nen

Amur

Khabarovsk

Heilong
Jiang

HEILONGJIANG

Qiqihar

Yichun

Hegang

Jiamusi

Terney

Asahigawa

HOKKAIDO

Sapporo

40°

Songhua

Jixi

Harbin

Mudanjiang

Xar Moron

Hakodate

MONGOL

Changchun

Jilin

JILIN

Liaoyuan

Vladivostok

Aomori

Akita

HONSHU

Sendai

Luan

Fuxin

Shenyang

Fushun
Benxi

Tumen

Ch'ongjin

Niigata

Utsunomiya

Zhangjiakou

**NORTH
KOREA**

Kimch'aek

Kanazawa

Tōkyō

Chiba

Jinzhou

Liaoyang

Anshan

LIAONING

Dandong

Yalu

Hŭngnam

Gifu

Yokohama

Kawasaki
Yokosuka

BEIJING SHI

Beijing
(Peking)

Qinhuangdao

Tangshan

Wŏnsan

Kyōto

Nagoya

Shizuoka

Datong

HEBEI

Tianjin (Tientsin)

TIANJIN SHI

Lüda
(Dairen)

P'yŏngyang

**SOUTH
KOREA**

Sŏul
(Seoul)

Osaka

Hamamatsu

Yangquan

ANXI

Baoding

Shijiazhuang

Ch'ŏngju

Okayama Himeji

Kobe

Wakayama

an

Weifang

Taejŏn

JAPAN

Changzhi

Handan

Jinan
(Tsinan)

Qingdao
(Tsingtao)

YELLOW

Taegu

Kwangju

Pusan

Kurashiki

Hiroshima

Takamatsu

Matsuyama

SHIKOKU

Xinxiang

SHANDONG

Masan

Kitakyūshū

Jiaozuo

Lianyungang
(Xinpu)

SEA

KOREA

Fukuoka

yang

Kaifeng

Zhengzhou

Xuzhou

CHEJU-DO

Kumamoto

Nagasaki

KYŪSHŪ

HENAN

JIANGSU

Bengbu

Taizhou

Huang

Huaian

Taizhou

Kagoshima

UBEI

Hefei

Yangzhou
Changzhou

Nantong

EAST

Wuhu

Nanjing
(Nanking)

Wuxi

Suzhou

Shanghai

Wuhan

ANHUI

SHANGHAI SHI

CHINA

PACIFIC

Chang Jiang

Hangzhou

Ningbo

OCEAN

Yangtze

ZHEJIANG

Jingdezhen

SEA

angsha

Nanchang

Wenzhou

RYUKYU

140°

30°

Xiangtan

Zhuzhou

Gan

JIANGXI

ISLANDS

Hengyang

FUJIAN

Fuzhou

Naha

OKINAWA

Taipei

20°

Min

Xiamen
(Amoy)

TAIWAN

GUANGDONG

T'ainan

T'AIWAN

Guangzhou
(Canton)

Shantou
(Swatow)

Kaohsiung

Bei

MACAU
(Portugal)

Kowloon
Victoria

HONG KONG
(U.K.)

	National capital
	Provincial capital
	Other important city or town
	Major international airport
	Main railway
	Main road
	International boundary
	Provincial boundary
	Less than 200 m of water
	More than 200 m of water

LUZON

BATAN ISLANDS

BABUYAN ISLANDS

NANDAO

iang

SOUTH CHINA

SEA

Longitude East of Greenwich

120°

LUZON

STRAIT

PHILIPPINES

130°

0 km   200   400   600

Scale 1:14 000 000   1 cm represents 140 km

INDIA

C H I N A

Fuzhou

T'aipei

Myitkyina

Kunming

Xiamen

Monywa

TAI

Myingyan • Mandalay

Keng Tung

Guangzhou
(Canton)

Shantou

BURMA

Chiang
Mai

Louangphrabang

Ha-noi

Hai-phong

Zhanjiang

Victoria
HONG KONG
(U.K.)

T'AIWAN

Sittwe
(Akyab)

Nam-dinh

Haikou

LUZON STRAIT

Toungoo

Viangchan
(Vientiane)

Vinh

*GULF OF
TONKIN*

HAINAN

Henzada

LAOS

VIETNAM

Aparri

Bassein

Tak

THAILAND

Hue

LUZON

Rangoon

Moulmein

Da-nang

Baguio

BAY

Ubon
Ratchathani

Angeles

Manila

OF

Tavoy

S O U T H

**ANDAMAN
ISLANDS**
(India)

Mergui

Krung Thep
(Bangkok)

*Tonle
Sap*

KAMPUCHEA

C H I N A

MINDORO

MA

BENGAL

Phnum
Pénh

Nha-trang

S E A

PANAY

Iloilo

A N D A M A N

S E A

Ho Chi Minh
(Saigon)

Can-tho

*GULF OF
THAILAND*

PALAWAN

NEGROS

Surat Thani

SULU SEA

**NICOBAR
ISLANDS**
(India)

Kota Baharu

Zamboanga

BASILAN

Banda Aceh

George Town
(Pinang)

MALAYSIA

Kota Kinabalu
(Jesselton)

Sandakan

SULU ARCHIPELAGO

STRAIT OF MALACCA

MALAYA

NATUNA
BESAR

BRUNEI

Bandar Seri
Begawan

CELEBES

Medan

Kuala
Lumpur

SARAWAK

SEA

SIMEULUE

Malacca

Singapore

SINGAPORE

Paloh

Kuching

NIAS

Bintan

B O R N E O

Gorontalo

S U M A T R A

Pakanbaru

KEPULAUAN
LINGGA

Pontianak

Kapuas

0° Equator

KEPULAUAN
BATU

BANGKA

Samarinda

SIBERUT

Padang

Jambi

Pangkalpinang

Barito

Balikpapan

KEPULAUAN
MENTAWAI

Palembang

BELITUNG

Banjarmasin

SULAWESI

MAKASSAR STRAIT

I N D O

Ujung
Pandang

Telukbetung

INDONESIA

JAVA SEA

N

I N D I A N   O C E A N

Jakarta

Semarang

MADURA

Bandung

Surabaya

Yogyakarta

Malang

BALI

Mataram

Raba

Memboro

FLORES

Ruteng

JAVA

Denpasar

LOMBOK

SUMBAWA

L

SUMBA

Baing

Kupa

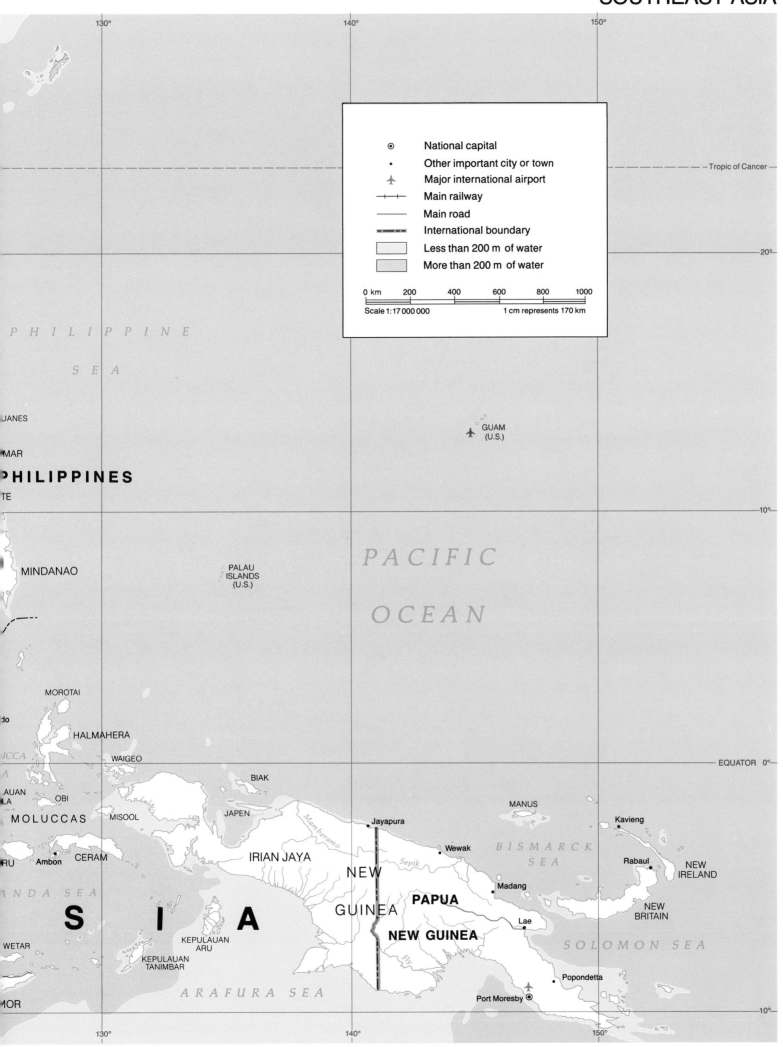

140°

150°

Tropic of Cancer

20°

National capital

Other important city or town

Major international airport

Main railway

Main road

International boundary

Less than 200 m of water

More than 200 m of water

0 km   200   400   600   800   1000

Scale 1:17 000 000   1 cm represents 170 km

PHILIPPINE

SEA

GUAM
(U.S.)

PHILIPPINES

TE

10°

PACIFIC

MINDANAO

PALAU
ISLANDS
(U.S.)

OCEAN

MOROTAI

HALMAHERA

WAIGEO

EQUATOR   0°

ICCA

BIAK

LAUAN
LA

OBI

JAPEN

MANUS

Kavieng

MOLUCCAS

MISOOL

Mamberamo

Jayapura

BISMARCK

RU

Ambon

CERAM

IRIAN JAYA

Sepik

Wewak

SEA

Rabaul

NEW
IRELAND

NDA SEA

NEW

Madang

NEW
BRITAIN

S   I   A

GUINEA

PAPUA

NEW GUINEA

Lae

SOLOMON SEA

WETAR

KEPULAUAN
ARU

KEPULAUAN
TANIMBAR

Popondetta

MOR

ARAFURA SEA

Port Moresby

10°

130°

140°

150°

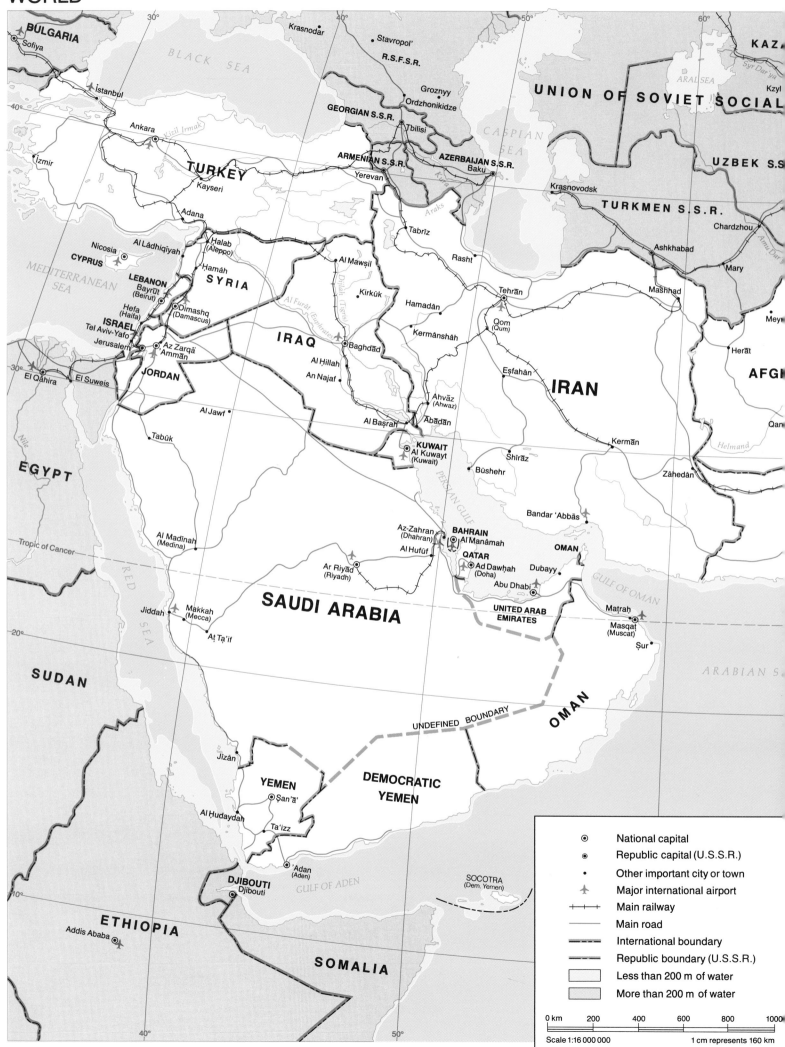

BULGARIA
Sofiya ✈

BLACK SEA

Krasnodar
• Stavropol'

R.S.F.S.R.

istanbul ✈

İzmir •

Ankara ✈
Kizil Irmak

TURKEY

Kayseri •

Adana •

GEORGIAN S.S.R.
Ordzhonikidze
Tbilisi •

Groznyy •

ARMENIAN S.S.R.
Yerevan

AZERBAIJAN S.S.R.
Baku •

CASPIAN SEA

UNION OF SOVIET SOCIAL

ARAL SEA

KAZ

Syr Dar'ya

Kzyl •

UZBEK S.S.

TURKMEN S.S.R.

Krasnovodsk

Ashkhabad ✈

Chardzhou •

Mary •

Halab (Aleppo) •
Al Lâdhiqîyah •

Nicosia ✈
CYPRUS

MEDITERRANEAN SEA

LEBANON
Bayrût (Beirut) ✈

Hefa (Haifa)
ISRAEL
Tel Aviv-Yafo
Jerusalem ✈

Hamâh •

SYRIA

Dimashq (Damascus) ✈

Az Zarqâ •
Ammân ✈
JORDAN

Al Mawsil •

Dijlah (Tigris)

Kirkûk •

Al Furât (Euphrates)

IRAQ

Baghdâd ✈
Al Hillah •
An Najaf •

Tabrîz •

Hamadân •

Kermânshâh •

Rasht •

Tehrân ✈

Qom (Qum) •

Esfahân •

IRAN

Herât •

AFGH

Qar

El Qâhira ✈
EGYPT

Nile

El Suweis •

Al Jawf •

Tabûk •

Ahvâz (Ahwaz) •
Al Basrah •
Âbâdân •

KUWAIT
Al Kuwayt (Kuwait) ⊙

Kermân •

Shîrâz •

Bûshehr •

Zâhedân •

Helmand

Qam

Tropic of Cancer

Al Madînah (Medina) •

Ar Riyâd (Riyadh) ⊙ ✈

Az-Zahran (Dhahran) ✈
Al Hufûf •

BAHRAIN
Al Manâmah ⊙

QATAR
Ad Dawhah (Doha) ⊙

Abu Dhabi ✈

Bandar 'Abbâs ✈

OMAN

GULF OF OMAN

Matrah •
Masqat (Muscat) ✈
Sûr •

RED SEA

Jiddah •
Makkah (Mecca) ✈

At Tâ'if •

SAUDI ARABIA

UNITED ARAB EMIRATES

Dubayy •

ARABIAN S

SUDAN

UNDEFINED BOUNDARY

OMAN

Jizân •

YEMEN
San'â' ⊙

DEMOCRATIC YEMEN

Al Hudaydah •
Ta'izz •

'Adan (Aden) ✈

DJIBOUTI
Djibouti ⊙

GULF OF ADEN

SOCOTRA (Dem. Yemen)

ETHIOPIA
Addis Ababa ⊙ ✈

SOMALIA

⊙	National capital
⊚	Republic capital (U.S.S.R.)
•	Other important city or town
✈	Major international airport
+++	Main railway
——	Main road
– – –	International boundary
— —	Republic boundary (U.S.S.R.)
☐	Less than 200 m of water
☐	More than 200 m of water

0 km   200   400   600   800   1000

Scale 1:16 000 000   1 cm represents 160 km

MONGOLIA

UBLICS

.R.

Lake
Balkhash

Ili

Alma Ata

Frunze

KIRGHIZ S.S.R.

Aksu

Kuqa

Ürümqi

Turpan

Hami

Anxi

Yumen

Zhangye

Wuwei

Huang (Yellow)

Lanzhou

Kashi

Shache

C H I N A

nd

ushanbe

TAJIK S.S.R.

Hotan

Jinsha (Yangtze)

Chengdu

Baghlàn

Kâbul

Peshawar

Islamabad

Rawalpindi

CEASE-FIRE LINE

Srinagar

Indus

Lancang (Mekong)

PAKISTAN

Gujranwala

Lahore

Amritsar

Multan

Sutlej

Xigazê

Lhasa

Gyangzê

Thimphu
Paro Dzong
BHUTAN

Dibrugarh

Delhi

Moràdabad

New Delhi

Ganga (Ganges)

NEPAL

Kathmandu

Darjeeling

Brahmaputra

Baoshan

Kunming

Agra

Lucknow

Kanpur

Ghaghari

Shillong

Jodhpur

Jaipur

Yamuna

Varanasi

Patna

Ganga

BANGLADESH

Dhaka

BURMA

Hyderabad

Allahabad

Asansol

Khulna

Monywa

Mandalay

Jabalpur

Jamshedpur

Calcutta

Myingyan

LAOS

Ahmadabad

Indore

Narmada

Tapti

Raipur

Cuttack

Chittagong

Sittwe

Irrawaddy

Salween

Chiang Mai

Vadodara

Nagpur

Mahanadi

Toungoo

THAILAND

Surat

Raipur

Henzada

Tak

Bombay

Pune
(Poona)

I N D I A

Godavari

BAY OF BENGAL

Bassein

Rangoon

Moulmein

Sholapur

Hyderabad

Guntur

Vishakhapatnam

Tavoy

Kolhapur

Krishna

Tungabhadra

**ANDAMAN
ISLANDS**
(India)

Mangalore

Bangalore

Madras

Mysore

INDIAN

OCEAN

Coimbatore

Tiruchirappalli

LAKSHADWEEP
(India)

Madurai

Trincomalee

**NICOBAR
ISLANDS**
(India)

Trivandrum

Kandy

SRI LANKA

Colombo

Longitude East of Greenwich 90°

SUMATRA

154

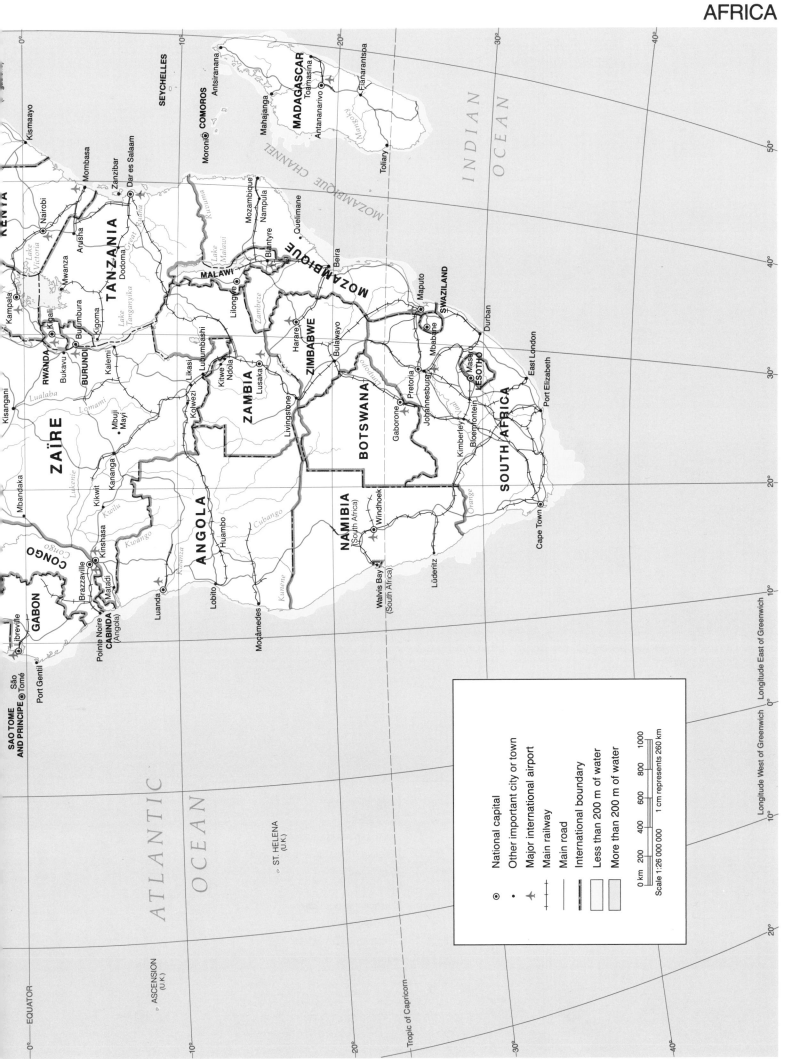

KENYA

Kismaayo
Mombasa
Nairobi
Zanzibar
Dar es Salaam
Arusha
Mwanza
TANZANIA
Dodoma
Kampala
RWANDA
Kigali
Bukavu
Bujumbura
BURUNDI
Kigoma
Kalemi

SEYCHELLES

COMOROS
Moroni

MADAGASCAR
Antsiranana
Mahajanga
Toamasina
Antananarivo
Fianarantsoa
Toliary

MOZAMBIQUE CHANNEL

INDIAN OCEAN

Mozambique
Nampula
Blantyre
MALAWI
Lilongwe
Quelimane
Beira

MOZAMBIQUE

Lake Victoria
Lake Tanganyika
Lake Malawi

Kisangani

ZAÏRE

Lualaba
Lomami
Mbuji Mayi
Kananga
Kikwit
Mbandaka

Lubumbashi
Likasi
Kolwezi
Kitwe
Ndola
ZAMBIA
Lusaka
Livingstone

Harare
ZIMBABWE
Bulawayo

SWAZILAND
Maputo
Mbabane
Durban

Pretoria
Johannesburg
Gaborone
BOTSWANA
Kimberley
Bloemfontein
LESOTHO
Maseru
East London
Port Elizabeth

SOUTH AFRICA

CONGO
Brazzaville
Kinshasa
Matadi
GABON
Libreville
Pointe Noire
CABINDA
(Angola)
Port Gentil

SÃO TOME
AND PRINCIPE
São Tomé

ANGOLA
Huambo
Lobito
Luanda
Moçâmedes

NAMIBIA
(South Africa)
Windhoek
Walvis Bay
(South Africa)
Lüderitz
Cape Town

Kwanza
Kwango
Kwilu
Kasai
Lukenie
Cubango
Kunene
Orange

ATLANTIC OCEAN

ST. HELENA
(U.K.)

ASCENSION
(U.K.)

EQUATOR

Tropic of Capricorn

Longitude West of Greenwich
Longitude East of Greenwich

National capital
Other important city or town
Major international airport
Main railway
Main road
International boundary
Less than 200 m of water
More than 200 m of water

0 km   200   400   600   800   1000
Scale 1:26 000 000   1 cm represents 260 km

INDONESIA

SUMBA SAWU TIMOR ROTI

TIMOR SEA

INDIAN

OCEAN

MELVILLE ISLAND

WESSEL ISLANDS

BATHURST ISLAND

Darwin

GULF OF

GROOTE EYLANDT

CARPENTARIA

Katherine

Roper

Wyndham

Drysdale

Ord

Victoria

Daly

NORTHERN

Derby

Fitzroy Crossing

Halls Creek

Broome

Fitzroy

TERRITORY

Tennant Creek

Mount Isa

Cloncurry

Leichhardt

Flinders

QU

Port Hedland

Lake Mackay

BARROW ISLAND Dampier

Fortescue

Lake Disappointment

Alice Springs

AUSTRAL

Ashburton

Newman

Georgina

Diamantina

Th

Lake McLeod

Gascoyne

WESTERN

Lake Carnegie

Carnarvon

DIRK HARTOG ISLAND

Murchison

Meekatharra

AUSTRALIA

Oodnadatta

Lake Eyre

SOUTH

Lake Torrens

Lake Frome

Geraldton

Lake Barlee

Kalgoorlie

AUSTRALIA

Woomera

Lake Gairdner

Broken Hill

Northam

Ceduna

Whyalla

Port Augusta

Perth

Narrogin

Esperance

GREAT AUSTRALIAN BIGHT

Port Pirie

Bunbury

Port Lincoln

SPENCER GULF

Adelaide

Mildu

Albany

KANGAROO ISLAND

Warrnam

KIN

Lake Mackay

	National capital
⊙	State capital
•	Other important city or town
✈	Major international airport
┼┼┼	Main railway
	Main road
·—··	International boundary
·—·	State boundary
	Less than 200 m of water
	More than 200 m of water

0 km 150 300 450 600 750

Scale 1:15 000 000   1 cm represents 150 km

Longitude East of Greenwich

SOUTHERN OCEAN

150° 160° 170°

TAGULA
ROSSEL
10°

SAN CRISTOBAL

RENNELL
SANTA CRUZ ISLANDS
(U.K.)

CORAL

SEA

TORRES ISLAND

VANUA LAVA
BANKS
SANTA MARIA
ISLANDS

EAT

Cooktown

Cairns

Innisfail

ESPIRITU SANTO
MAÉWO
VANUATU
Luganville
PENTECOST
MALAKULA
AMBRYM
SHEPHERD ISLAND
ÉMAE
ÉFATÉ
Port-Vila

BARRIER

Townsville

REEF

Mackay

ERROMANGO

TANNA

NEW
UVÉA
ANATOM
CALEDONIA
LIFOU
(France)
MARÉ
Nouméa

Beach

Rockhampton

Gladstone

Tropic of Capricorn

A

Bundaberg

FRASER
ISLAND

Neville

Roma

Toowoomba
Brisbane

PACIFIC
OCEAN

Warwick
Gold Coast

Walgett

Bourke
Narrabri

NORFOLK ISLAND
(Aust.)

NEW
SOUTH

Coffs Harbour

Dubbo

Port Macquarie

WALES

LORD HOWE ISLAND
(Aust.)

Maitland
Newcastle

Orange

Wagga Wagga

Sydney

Wollongong

Canberra
AUSTRALIAN
CAPITAL TERRITORY

30°

IA
Albury-Wodonga

TASMAN

Whangarei

elbourne

Bairnsdale

SEA

GREAT BARRIER
ISLAND

Auckland

STRAIT
FLINDERS ISLAND

NORTH
ISLAND

Rotorua

New Plymouth

Burnie

Gisborne

IA
Launceston

Wanganui
Napier

SOUTH
Nelson
Wellington

Hobart
ISLAND
NEW

Cook Strait

Christchurch

ZEALAND

Timaru

CHATHAM
ISLAND (N.Z.)

Invercargill
Dunedin

STEWART ISLAND

150° 160° 170° 180°

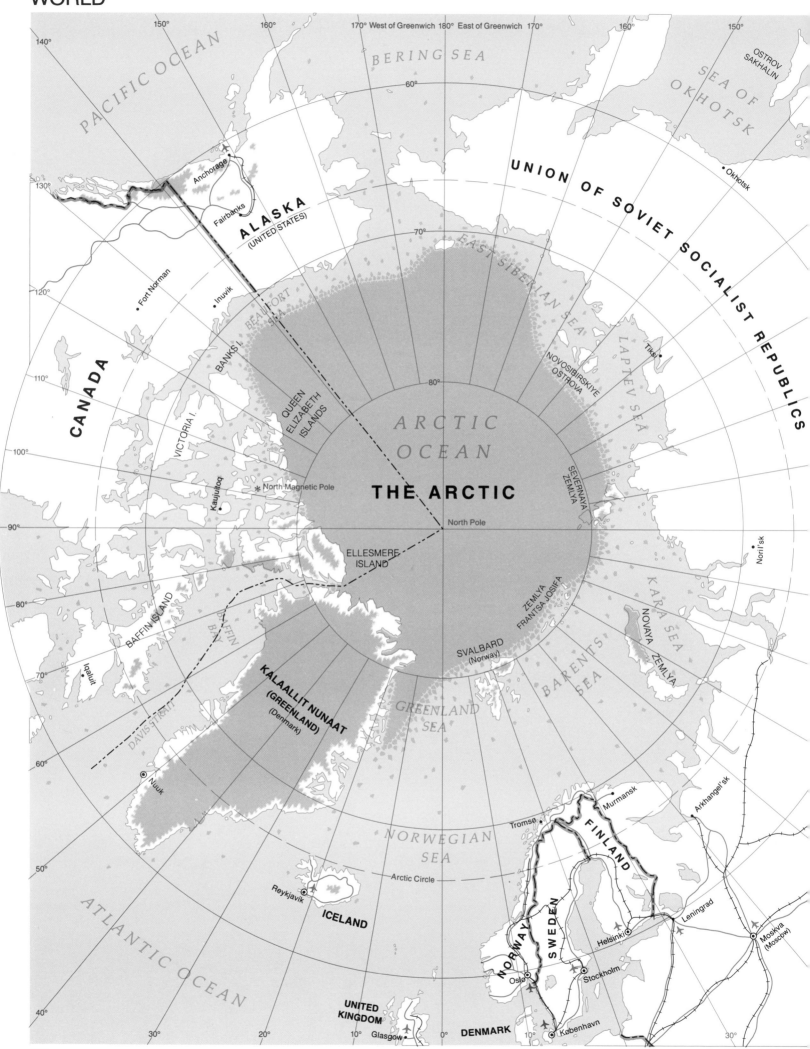

THE ARCTIC

PACIFIC OCEAN

BERING SEA

SEA OF OKHOTSK

OSTROV SAKHALIN

• Okhotsk

UNION OF SOVIET SOCIALIST REPUBLICS

Anchorage •
Fairbanks •

ALASKA
(UNITED STATES)

EAST SIBERIAN SEA

LAPTEV SEA

Tiksi •

• Fort Norman

• Inuvik

BEAUFORT SEA

NOVOSIBIRSKIYE OSTROVA

CANADA

BANKS I.

QUEEN ELIZABETH ISLANDS

ARCTIC OCEAN

SEVERNAYA ZEMLYA

VICTORIA I.

80°

THE ARCTIC

Noril'sk •

Kaujuitoq •

* North Magnetic Pole

North Pole

ZEMLYA FRANTSA JOSIFA

KARA SEA

NOVAYA ZEMLYA

ELLESMERE ISLAND

SVALBARD
(Norway)

BAFFIN ISLAND

BAFFIN BAY

BARENTS SEA

Iqaluit •

KALAALLIT NUNAAT
(GREENLAND)
(Denmark)

GREENLAND SEA

Murmansk •

Arkhangel'sk •

DAVIS STRAIT

⊙ Nuuk

Tromsø •

FINLAND

NORWEGIAN SEA

ATLANTIC OCEAN

Arctic Circle

Reykjavik •

ICELAND

Leningrad •

NORWAY
SWEDEN

Helsinki •

⊙ Moskva
(Moscow)

UNITED KINGDOM

Oslo •
Stockholm •

DENMARK

Glasgow •

⊙ København

140° 150° 160° 170° West of Greenwich 180° East of Greenwich 170° 160° 150°
130° 120° 110° 100° 90° 80° 70° 60° 50° 40° 30° 20° 10° 0° 10° 20° 30°
60° 70°

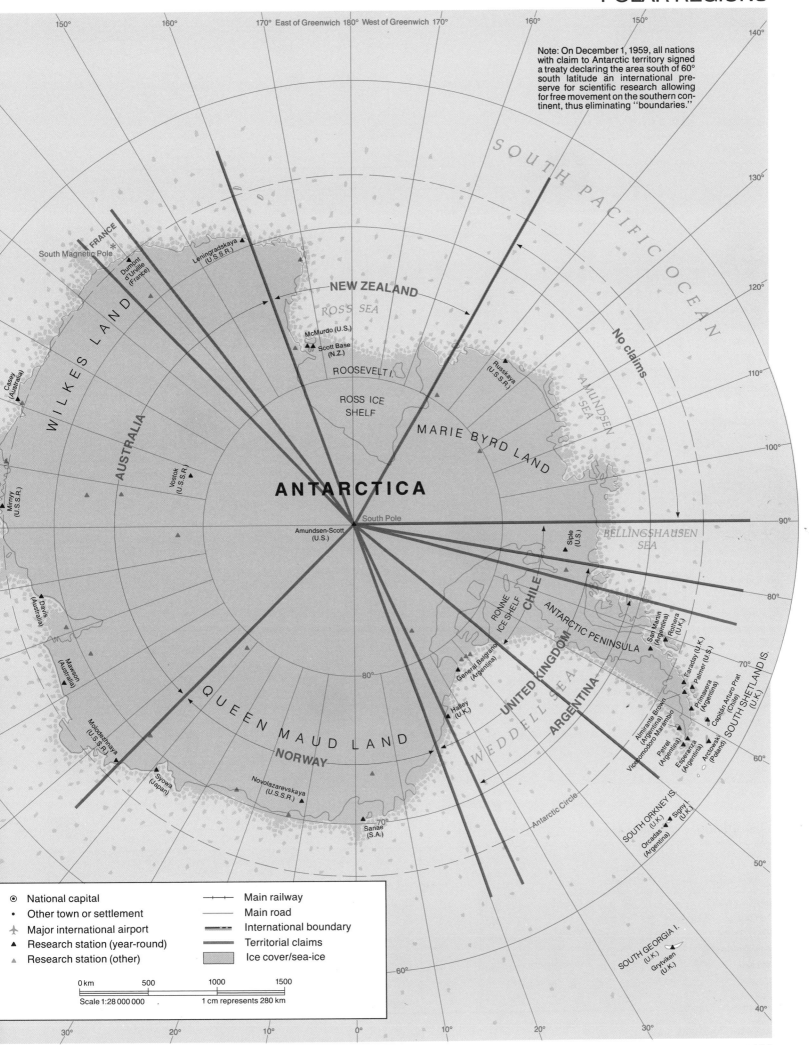

Note: On December 1, 1959, all nations with claim to Antarctic territory signed a treaty declaring the area south of 60° south latitude an international preserve for scientific research allowing for free movement on the southern continent, thus eliminating "boundaries."

SOUTH PACIFIC OCEAN

No claims

NEW ZEALAND

ROSS SEA

McMurdo (U.S.)

Scott Base (N.Z.)

ROOSEVELT I.

ROSS ICE SHELF

Russkaya (U.S.S.R.)

AMUNDSEN SEA

MARIE BYRD LAND

WILKES LAND

FRANCE

South Magnetic Pole

Dumont d'Urville (France)

Leningradskaya (U.S.S.R.)

Casey (Australia)

AUSTRALIA

Vostok (U.S.S.R.)

ANTARCTICA

South Pole

Amundsen-Scott (U.S.)

Siple (U.S.)

BELLINGSHAUSEN SEA

Mirnyy (U.S.S.R.)

Davis (Australia)

RONNE ICE SHELF

CHILE

ANTARCTIC PENINSULA

San Martin (Argentina)

Rothera (U.K.)

Faraday (U.K.)

Palmer (U.S.)

Capitán Arturo Prat (Chile)

SOUTH SHETLAND IS. (U.K.)

Mawson (Australia)

General Belgrano (Argentina)

UNITED KINGDOM

ARGENTINA

Primavera (Argentina)

Almirante Brown (Argentina)

Vicecomodoro Marambio

Petrel (Argentina)

Esperanza (Argentina)

Arctowski (Poland)

Molodezhnaya (U.S.S.R.)

QUEEN MAUD LAND

NORWAY

Halley (U.K.)

WEDDELL SEA

SOUTH ORKNEY IS. (U.K.)

Signy (U.K.)

Orcadas (Argentina)

Syowa (Japan)

Novolazarevskaya (U.S.S.R.)

Sanae (S.A.)

Antarctic Circle

SOUTH GEORGIA I. (U.K.)

Grytviken (U.K.)

⊙ National capital	Main railway
• Other town or settlement	Main road
✈ Major international airport	International boundary
▲ Research station (year-round)	Territorial claims
▲ Research station (other)	Ice cover/sea-ice

0 km   500   1000   1500

Scale 1:28 000 000   1 cm represents 280 km

160

Canada – The Land

1. Climate

Station	Altitude (m)	Temperature (degree Celsius)						Precipitation			Seasonal Changes		
		January Average	July Average	Mean Annual	Record High	Record Low	Heating Degree-Days	Total (mm)	Snowfall (cm)	Days With Precipitation	Frost-Free Days	Last Frost in Spring	First Frost in Autumn
St. John's	141	− 4	15	5	31	− 23	4 798	1 511	364	210	130	June 3	Oct. 12
Goose Bay	44	− 16	16	0	38	− 39	6 494	877	409	176	122	June 4	Oct. 5
Sydney	60	− 4	18	6	35	− 26	4 433	1 340	288	179	145	May 23	Oct. 16
Yarmouth	38	− 3	16	7	30	− 21	4 012	1 283	205	157	174	May 2	Oct. 24
Charlottetown	57	− 7	18	6	34	− 28	4 565	1 128	305	169	150	May 17	Oct. 15
Saint John	30	− 7	17	6	34	− 30	4 693	1 306	217	149	170	May 3	Oct. 21
Chatham (N.B.)	34	− 9	19	5	38	− 35	4 827	1 051	309	152	122	May 22	Sept. 21
Schefferville	512	− 23	13	− 5	32	− 51	8 197	723	335	188	73	June 18	Aug. 31
Québec	75	− 12	19	4	36	− 36	5 024	1 089	326	164	132	May 18	Sept. 28
Montréal (McGill)	57	− 9	22	7	36	− 34	4 437	999	243	164	183	April 22	Oct. 23
Val d'Or	338	− 17	17	2	34	− 44	5 955	902	280	180	98	June 4	Sept. 11
Kapuskasing	229	− 18	17	1	36	− 46	6 330	871	321	186	83	June 13	Sept. 5
Ottawa	126	− 11	21	6	38	− 36	4 635	851	216	152	142	May 11	Oct. 1
Toronto	116	− 4	22	9	41	− 33	3 658	790	141	134	192	April 20	Oct. 30
Windsor	194	− 4	22	9	38	− 26	3 557	836	104	137	173	April 29	Oct. 20
Thunder Bay	196	− 15	18	2	36	− 41	5 708	738	222	141	101	May 31	Sept. 10
Sioux Lookout	374	− 19	18	1	36	− 46	6 205	742	237	165	113	May 29	Sept. 20
Winnipeg	240	− 18	20	2	41	− 45	5 864	535	131	120	118	May 25	Sept. 21
Churchill	35	− 28	12	− 7	33	− 45	9 193	397	192	141	81	June 22	Sept. 12
Regina	574	− 17	19	2	43	− 50	5 909	398	115	112	107	May 27	Sept. 12
Medicine Hat	721	− 12	20	5	42	− 46	4 859	348	121	90	125	May 17	Sept. 20
Calgary	1 079	− 11	17	3	36	− 45	5 948	437	154	113	106	May 28	Sept. 12
Edmonton	676	− 15	18	3	34	− 48	5 600	447	132	124	127	May 14	Sept. 19
Penticton	342	− 3	20	9	41	− 27	3 509	296	69	101	143	May 10	Oct. 1
Vancouver	5	2	17	10	33	− 18	3 031	1 068	52	158	212	March 31	Oct. 30
Victoria	20	3	16	10	36	− 16	2 967	856	45	154	202	April 13	Nov. 2
Estevan Point	6	5	14	9	29	− 14	3 192	3 027	34	202	226	April 5	Nov. 18
Dawson	324	− 29	16	− 5	35	− 58	8 232	326	136	120	92	May 26	Aug. 27
Whitehorse	698	− 19	14	− 1	34	− 52	6 855	260	127	118	87	June 5	Sept. 1
Fort Smith	203	− 27	16	− 4	35	− 54	7 803	331	145	127	64	June 15	Aug. 19
Yellowknife	208	− 29	16	− 6	32	− 51	8 601	250	119	114	108	May 30	Sept. 16
Inuvik	61	− 29	13	− 10	32	− 57	10 183	260	174	128	45	June 26	Aug. 11
Iqaluit	21	− 26	8	− 9	24	− 46	9 820	415	247	135	59	June 30	Aug. 29
Alert	63	− 32	4	− 18	20	− 49	13 093	156	145	99	4	July 14	July 19

Source: Environment Canada, Meteorological Branch, 1978

2. Land and Freshwater Area

Province or Territory	Land (km²)	Fresh Water (km²)	Total (km²)	Percent of Total Area	Province or Territory	Land (km²)	Fresh Water (km²)	Total (km²)	Percent of Total Area
Newfoundland	371 635	34 030	405 720	4.1	Saskatchewan	570 113	81 630	652 330	6.5
Prince Edward Island	5 660	0	5 660	0.1	Alberta	638 233	16 800	661 190	6.6
Nova Scotia	52 841	2 650	55 490	0.6	British Columbia	892 677	18 070	947 800	9.5
New Brunswick	71 569	1 350	73 440	0.7	Yukon Territory	531 844	4 480	483 450	4.8
Québec	1 357 655	183 890	1 540 680	15.5	Northwest Territories	3 246 389	133 300	3 426 320	34.4
Ontario	916 734	177 390	1 068 580	10.7					
Manitoba	547 704	101 590	649 950	6.5	**Canada**	**9 203 054**	**755 180**	**9 970 610**	**100.0**

Source: Energy, Mines and Resources Canada, Geographical Mapping Division, 1983
       Statistics Canada, 1981

3. Basic Demographic Data

Demographic Category	1976	1977	1978	1979	1980	1981	1982	Average
Total Population	**22 992 604**	**23 158 400**	**23 417 400**	**23 644 500**	**23 911 900**	**24 343 181**	**24 513 300**	
Births	360 000	360 700	360 200	366 100	370 700	371 300	369 500	365 500
Deaths	167 000	167 500	168 200	168 200	171 500	171 000	171 000	169 200
Natural Increase	193 000	193 200	192 900	197 900	199 200	200 300	198 500	196 300
Birth Rate (per thousand)	15.7	15.6	15.4	15.5	15.5	15.3	15.1	15.4
Death Rate (per thousand)	7.3	7.2	7.2	7.1	7.2	7.1	7.0	7.2
Natural Increase (per thousand)	8.4	8.3	8.2	8.4	8.3	8.3	8.1	8.3
Immigration	149 400	114 900	86 300	112 100	143 100	128 600	121 100	122 214
Emigration	64 400	61 400	63 500	54 700	45 200	42 000	44 400	53 657
Net Migration	85 000	53 500	22 800	54 400	97 900	86 600	76 700	68 557
Net Migration Rate (percent)	.37	.23	.10	.24	.41	.36	.31	.29
Total Annual Population Increase	**274 500**	**259 000**	**227 100**	**267 400**	**309 400**	**292 000**	**275 700**	**272 157**
Population Growth (percent)	1.20	1.12	0.97	1.13	1.29	1.21	1.12	1.15
Growth from Natural Increase (percent)	70.3	74.6	84.5	74.0	64.4	68.6	72.0	72.6
Doubling Time (years)	58.1	62.3	71.8	61.6	53.9	57.8	62.0	60.6

Source: Statistics Canada, Demography Division, 1983
Statistics Canada, 1981

4. Population Growth by Province and Territory

Province or Territory	1951	1961	1971	1976	1981	1985[1]
Newfoundland	361 416	457 853	522 104	557 725	567 181	578 900
Prince Edward Island	98 429	104 629	111 641	118 229	122 506	126 800
Nova Scotia	642 584	737 007	788 960	828 571	847 442	878 300
New Brunswick	515 697	597 936	634 557	677 250	696 403	717 200
Québec	4 055 681	5 259 211	6 027 764	6 234 445	6 438 403	6 562 200
Ontario	4 597 542	6 236 092	7 703 106	8 264 465	8 625 107	9 023 900
Manitoba	776 541	921 686	988 247	1 021 506	1 026 241	1 065 000
Saskatchewan	831 728	925 181	926 242	921 323	968 313	1 016 400
Alberta	939 501	1 331 944	1 627 874	1 838 037	2 237 724	2 337 500
British Columbia	1 165 210	1 629 082	2 184 021	2 466 608	2 744 467	2 883 000
Yukon Territory	9 096	14 628	18 388	21 836	23 153	22 800
Northwest Territories	16 004	22 998	34 807	42 609	45 741	50 500
Canada	**14 009 429**	**18 238 247**	**21 568 310**	**22 992 604**	**24 343 181**	**25 262 500**
Rural	5 381 176	5 537 857	5 157 525	5 426 408	5 907 254	n.a.[2]
Urban	8 628 253	12 700 390	16 410 785	17 566 196	18 435 927	n.a.

[1] January 1 estimate.
[2] Not available.
Source: Statistics Canada, 1981, 1985

5. Population Distribution

	Percent of Total Population					
Province or Territory	1901	1941	1951	1961	1971	1981
Newfoundland	–	–	2.58	2.51	2.42	2.33
Prince Edward Island	1.92	0.83	0.70	0.58	0.52	0.50
Nova Scotia	8.56	5.02	4.59	4.04	3.66	3.48
New Brunswick	6.16	3.97	3.68	3.28	2.94	2.86
Québec	30.70	28.96	28.95	28.84	27.95	26.44
Ontario	40.64	32.92	32.82	34.19	35.71	35.43
Manitoba	4.75	6.34	5.54	5.05	4.58	4.21
Saskatchewan	1.70	7.79	5.94	5.07	4.29	3.97
Alberta	1.36	6.92	6.71	7.30	7.55	9.19
British Columbia	3.33	7.11	8.32	8.93	10.13	11.27
Yukon Territory	0.51	0.04	0.06	0.08	0.09	0.09
Northwest Territories	0.37	0.10	0.11	0.13	0.16	0.18

Source: Statistics Canada, 1982

6. Projected Population to 2021

		Annual Rate of Population Growth (percent)	Distribution by Age			
Year	Population (10³)		0–14 (percent of total)	15–44 (percent of total)	45–64 (percent of total)	65 + (percent of total)
1986	26 331	1.4	23.1	48.5	18.4	10.0
1991	28 091	1.2	23.7	47.0	18.6	10.7
1996	29 642	1.0	23.4	45.4	20.2	11.0
2001	30 980	0.8	22.1	44.3	22.4	11.2
2006	32 258	0.8	20.9	42.9	25.0	11.2
2011	33 570	0.8	20.4	41.5	26.3	11.8
2016	34 871	0.7	20.6	40.8	25.5	13.1
2021	36 050	0.6	20.7	40.7	24.1	14.5

Source: Statistics Canada, Demography Division, 1976

7. Ethnic Origin[1]

	Nfld.	P.E.I.	N.S.	N.B.	Qué.	Ont.	Man.	Sask.	Alta.	B.C.	Y.T.	N.W.T.	Canada
Single origins	547 640	112 545	767 205	649 420	6 241 115	7 751 615	912 360	853 315	1 940 915	2 407 045	19 580	42 125	22 244 885
African	85	20	3 900	240	6 220	24 895	1 590	500	4 285	3 445	20	25	45 215
Armenian	5	–	20	5	10 385	9 665	10	10	215	840	–	–	21 155
Asian Arabian	190	245	2 880	705	16 850	26 330	885	785	8 285	2 970	–	15	60 140
Austrian	30	15	250	105	2 275	15 145	3 155	4 115	6 400	9 025	60	45	40 630
Balkan	115	10	360	150	6 875	90 975	3 315	1 880	9 340	15 910	60	85	129 075
Baltic	45	20	425	100	4 665	35 600	1 275	435	3 020	4 580	90	30	50 300
Belgian and Luxembourgeois	10	145	465	235	6 585	18 035	6 500	2 830	4 305	3 830	20	35	43 000
British	519 620	93 345	608 685	369 125	487 385	4 487 800	373 995	366 080	962 785	1 385 165	10 060	10 200	9 674 245
Czech and Slovak	40	25	410	185	4 845	33 025	3 590	3 725	11 195	10 470	110	75	67 695
Chinese	635	165	1 545	880	19 255	118 640	7 065	6 970	36 770	96 915	215	200	289 245
Dutch	675	1 340	13 495	4 400	8 055	191 125	33 875	17 215	65 060	72 280	400	315	408 240
Finnish	70	5	260	95	1 140	33 395	1 060	1 275	4 135	10 810	30	45	52 315
French	15 355	14 770	71 350	251 070	5 105 665	652 900	74 050	46 915	111 865	92 310	1 080	1 765	6 439 100
German	1 640	820	33 145	6 490	33 770	373 390	108 140	161 700	233 175	187 630	1 300	1 160	1 142 365
Greek	30	–	1 695	360	49 420	85 960	2 380	1 220	4 820	8 390	30	65	154 365
Magyar (Hungarian)	15	50	470	360	9 745	59 135	4 160	11 080	15 170	15 920	190	100	116 390
Indochinese	75	45	400	525	15 130	12 815	2 020	1 865	6 385	4 410	15	35	43 725
Indo-Pakistani	520	55	940	540	12 195	60 375	2 960	1 140	13 225	29 425	45	30	121 445
Italian	410	100	3 235	1 145	163 735	487 310	9 595	2 755	26 605	52 760	95	220	747 970
Japanese	25	5	40	30	1 395	16 685	1 300	205	5 225	16 040	30	10	40 995
Jewish	285	80	2 090	720	90 355	131 320	14 950	1 515	9 460	13 170	25	55	264 025
Latin American	85	20	690	125	26 315	74 250	3 695	975	6 845	4 525	10	25	117 555
Native Peoples	3 225	435	6 305	4 605	46 855	83 860	59 925	54 720	60 010	64 690	3 415	25 325	413 380
North African Arabian	5	–	20	35	6 090	3 535	125	60	490	185	–	5	10 545
Pacific Island	530	25	1 060	360	6 490	70 220	13 835	2 100	16 645	43 840	50	145	155 290
Polish	180	90	2 455	425	19 755	122 945	28 445	18 335	37 655	23 795	190	205	254 485
Portuguese	245	50	490	315	27 370	129 005	7 830	515	6 125	16 125	5	30	188 105
Romanian	–	5	155	50	2 790	8 170	900	3 905	3 805	2 650	35	25	22 485
Russian	35	10	155	65	2 940	8 715	3 765	6 290	7 715	19 605	50	75	49 435
Scandinavian	640	250	2 175	2 345	4 225	40 335	25 170	42 720	78 565	85 035	745	595	282 795
Spanish	180	5	400	255	15 460	25 185	1 470	730	4 945	4 845	25	40	53 540
Swiss	10	15	440	95	4 320	11 755	870	1 225	4 680	6 335	25	40	29 805
Ukrainian	135	105	1 965	635	14 640	133 995	99 795	76 815	136 710	63 605	635	580	529 615
West Asian	15	–	135	–	1 605	5 445	120	65	895	1 770	–	10	10 055
Other single origins	2 455	280	4 690	2 660	6 315	69 700	10 545	10 645	34 105	33 740	520	515	176 160
Multiple origins	16 110	8 680	72 595	39 950	127 960	782 650	101 345	103 120	272 735	306 570	3 490	3 415	1 838 615
British and French	10 245	5 305	27 650	22 820	62 270	201 415	12 400	9 095	34 995	42 955	540	565	430 255
British and other	3 485	2 440	29 995	11 170	20 645	375 800	46 485	52 985	142 930	171 195	1 560	1 110	859 800
French and other	350	225	3 570	1 910	21 790	45 145	8 820	8 325	19 185	15 290	165	175	124 940
British, French, and other	500	370	4 735	2 100	7 120	50 110	4 320	4 425	15 585	17 475	210	135	107 080
European and other[3]	330	145	5 160	1 040	10 585	83 985	22 965	23 820	48 005	41 705	385	325	238 455
Native Peoples and other[4]	1 200	190	1 485	910	5 540	26 200	6 355	4 480	12 045	17 950	630	1 100	78 085
Total Population[2]	563 750	121 225	839 805	689 375	6 369 065	8 534 265	1 013 705	956 440	2 213 650	2 713 615	23 075	45 540	24 083 500

Note: Totals may not equal the sum of components due to rounding.

[1] This table is based on preliminary data. It includes counts of single and multiple origins. (The 1981 Census was the first to accept more than one ethnic origin for an individual.)

[3] Includes multiple origins involving European, Jewish, and other origins not included elsewhere.

[4] Includes multiple origins involving Native Peoples and British, French, European, Jewish, or other origins.

8. Religion

Religion[1]	Nfld.	P.E.I.	N.S.	N.B.	Que.	Ont.	Man.	Sask.	Alta.	B.C.	Y.T.	N.W.T.	Canada
Catholic	204 465	56 450	310 725	371 245	5 618 365	3 036 245	318 815	310 010	613 930	538 435	5 595	18 330	11 402 605
Roman Catholic	204 430	56 415	310 140	371 100	5 609 685	2 986 175	269 070	279 840	573 495	526 355	5 470	18 215	11 210 385
Ukrainian Catholic	40	30	565	135	8 615	49 305	49 355	30 090	40 280	11 940	125	115	190 585
Protestant	352 695	61 175	487 255	295 785	407 075	4 418 960	573 420	557 315	1 240 000	1 484 925	12 310	23 670	9 914 580
Adventist	775	100	1 370	980	2 420	16 260	1 075	2 205	7 320	9 015	55	20	41 605
Anglican	153 530	6 805	131 130	66 260	132 115	1 164 315	108 220	77 725	202 265	374 055	4 665	15 295	2 436 375
Associated Gospel	–	–	65	20	130	5 760	105	970	565	280	–	–	7 895
Baptist	1 200	6 060	101 585	88 520	25 050	288 465	19 260	16 785	66 375	81 850	1 015	685	696 850
Brethren in Christ	365	225	420	240	570	15 535	490	845	1 040	2 525	5	–	22 260
Christian and Missionary Alliance	–	–	70	55	230	7 215	2 015	6 110	10 095	7 975	30	105	33 895
Church of God	10	30	60	30	475	3 435	440	1 000	3 065	1 500	–	–	10 040
Churches of Christ, Disciples	5	845	1 035	715	185	6 545	920	1 525	2 435	1 110	–	30	15 350
Church of the Nazarene	115	715	745	560	115	3 755	280	860	4 545	1 605	–	60	13 360
Doukhobors	–	–	5	–	45	135	170	1 065	215	5 065	5	5	6 700
Evangelical Free Church	–	–	–	–	55	125	330	395	1 940	2 910	–	–	5 780
Hutterite	–	–	–	–	5	105	5 940	2 980	7 395	105	–	–	16 530
Jehovah's Witnesses	2 020	435	4 920	3 525	19 855	48 460	6 420	9 815	16 195	31 520	120	200	143 485
Latter Day Saints	200	140	1 570	810	2 150	20 095	1 840	3 075	42 980	16 740	160	105	89 865
Church of Latter Day Saints	200	140	1 570	815	2 125	14 505	1 775	2 565	42 190	15 925	160	100	82 060
Reorganized Church of Latter Day Saints	5	–	5	–	35	5 585	60	515	795	815	–	5	7 810
Lutheran	460	210	12 315	1 810	17 665	254 175	58 830	88 785	144 675	122 395	915	665	702 905
Mennonite	90	5	220	185	1 075	46 480	63 495	26 260	20 540	30 895	45	80	189 370
Methodist Bodies	55	55	300	135	1 615	25 360	2 085	4 430	7 360	6 345	60	40	47 840
Evangelical	5	45	65	30	915	5 460	1 375	2 240	5 430	3 415	20	20	19 030
Free Methodist	5	–	15	5	85	8 990	215	1 620	580	740	5	5	12 270
Missionary Church	15	25	–	–	50	6 000	85	150	1 395	260	–	–	7 940
Moravian	2 045	–	25	10	5	305	40	–	1 750	120	5	–	4 350
Pentecostal	37 450	1 315	10 695	21 450	17 420	119 535	15 825	16 435	41 485	55 095	520	1 570	338 790
Plymouth Brethren	35	155	225	40	895	3 270	610	310	550	1 960	–	5	8 060
Presbyterian	2 700	12 620	38 285	12 070	34 625	517 020	23 910	16 065	63 890	89 810	615	505	812 110
Reformed Bodies	5	240	915	100	495	66 910	2 300	515	17 880	14 785	–	35	104 175
Canadian Reformed Church	–	15	5	5	–	6 215	495	–	1 690	2 135	–	–	10 560
Christian Reformed	5	220	890	80	280	50 670	1 390	465	13 460	9 885	–	20	77 370
Salvation Army	45 120	315	4 900	1 965	1 440	45 065	3 695	3 050	7 020	12 275	150	100	125 085
Unitarian	35	50	325	285	1 325	6 120	800	325	1 210	3 955	45	25	14 500
United Church	104 835	29 645	169 605	87 460	126 275	1 655 550	240 395	263 375	525 480	548 360	3 310	3 725	3 758 015
Wesleyan	–	10	1 215	4 265	185	1 995	5	–	35	50	10	–	7 770
Worldwide Church of God	160	5	235	140	695	1 780	620	1 130	1 830	1 525	–	5	8 130
Other Protestant	1 490	1 170	4 995	4 165	19 925	89 160	13 215	11 125	38 460	60 845	585	420	245 550
Eastern Orthodox	65	50	2 345	580	73 270	167 325	21 135	22 495	49 275	24 640	195	195	361 565
Greek Orthodox	50	40	2 020	535	62 265	140 615	19 785	21 065	46 505	21 645	175	180	314 870
Jewish	220	80	2 010	845	102 355	148 255	15 670	1 585	10 655	14 685	20	65	296 425
Eastern Non-Christian	680	230	3 030	1 175	34 325	137 110	7 790	4 185	38 195	78 640	275	255	305 885
Bahai	40	30	415	95	645	3 250	165	465	775	1 815	125	135	7 955
Buddhist	135	50	420	240	12 000	18 595	2 015	985	6 200	11 190	75	50	51 955
Hindu	315	75	1 025	475	6 690	41 655	1 750	1 150	7 360	8 980	–	20	69 500
Islam	100	70	790	315	12 115	52 110	1 925	1 120	16 865	12 715	5	25	98 165
Sikh	65	–	275	50	1 790	16 645	1 685	220	5 985	40 940	45	10	67 710
Para-religious groups[2]	25	–	110	65	745	5 555	590	600	1 580	4 125	5	55	13 445
Non-religious groups[3]	5 605	3 240	34 335	19 685	132 935	620 815	76 285	60 255	260 015	568 170	4 680	2 970	1 788 995
Agnostic	15	10	220	110	420	3 995	595	140	1 520	3 660	50	20	10 770
Atheist	20	5	50	30	370	1 595	190	130	790	1 270	10	5	4 455
No Religion	5 430	3 175	33 690	19 345	131 400	607 830	74 360	59 945	245 515	556 180	4 505	2 895	1 752 385

[1] Preliminary Data based on 1981 census. Totals may not equal the sum of components because data were based on a sample of 20% of the population.
[2] Para-religious groups include the Fourth Way, New Thought, Theosophical, Pagan, and a number of diverse groups such as PSI, EST, and The Farm.
[3] Non-religious groups include Agnostic, Atheist, and individuals who indicated either "no Religion" or "no religious preference"

Source: Statistics Canada, 1981

9. Official Language[1]

Province or Territory		Total Population[2] (number/percent)		English only (number/percent)		French only (number/percent)		Both English and French (number/percent)		Neither French nor English (number/percent)	
Newfoundland	1981	563 750	100.0	550 335	97.6	145	0.0	12 840	2.3	430	0.1
	1971	522 100	100.0	511 620	98.0	510	0.1	9 350	1.8	625	0.1
Prince Edward Island	1981	121 225	100.0	111 205	91.7	200	0.2	9 780	8.1	40	0.0
	1971	111 640	100.0	101 820	91.2	680	0.6	9 110	8.2	30	0.0
Nova Scotia	1981	839 800	100.0	774 760	92.3	1 880	0.2	62 350	7.4	805	0.1
	1971	788 960	100.0	730 700	92.6	4 185	0.5	53 035	6.7	1 035	0.1
New Brunswick	1981	689 375	100.0	417 030	60.5	89 340	13.0	182 555	26.5	455	0.1
	1971	634 560	100.0	396 855	62.5	100 985	15.9	136 115	21.5	600	0.1
Québec	1981	6 369 065	100.0	426 240	6.7	3 826 610	60.1	2 065 100	32.4	51 120	0.8
	1971	6 027 765	100.0	632 515	10.5	3 668 020	60.9	1 663 790	27.6	63 445	1.1
Ontario	1981	8 534 265	100.0	7 401 070	86.7	60 530	0.7	924 480	10.8	148 185	1.7
	1971	7 703 105	100.0	6 724 100	87.3	92 840	1.2	716 065	9.3	170 090	2.2
Manitoba	1981	1 013 705	100.0	915 755	90.3	2 620	0.3	79 990	7.9	15 340	1.5
	1971	988 245	100.0	881 715	89.2	5 020	0.5	80 935	8.2	20 585	2.1
Saskatchewan	1981	956 440	100.0	904 900	94.6	705	0.1	43 650	4.6	7 180	0.8
	1971	926 240	100.0	867 315	93.6	1 825	0.2	45 985	5.0	11 110	1.2
Alberta	1981	2 213 650	100.0	2 045 060	92.4	3 705	0.2	142 465	6.4	22 425	1.0
	1971	1 627 870	100.0	1 525 575	93.7	3 310	0.2	81 000	5.0	17 990	1.1
British Columbia	1981	2 713 615	100.0	2 518 965	92.8	1 445	0.1	154 170	5.7	39 030	1.4
	1971	2 184 620	100.0	2 054 690	94.1	1 775	0.1	101 435	4.6	26 725	1.2
Yukon Territory	1981	23 075	100.0	21 200	91.9	10	0.0	1 820	7.9	45	0.2
	1971	18 385	100.0	17 130	93.2	5	0.0	1 210	6.6	35	0.2
Northwest Territories	1981	45 535	100.0	36 380	79.9	60	0.1	2 750	6.0	6 340	13.9
	1971	34 810	100.0	25 500	73.3	100	0.3	2 120	6.1	7 085	20.4
Canada	**1981**	**24 083 500**	**100.0**	**16 122 900**	**67.0**	**3 987 240**	**16.6**	**3 681 960**	**15.3**	**291 395**	**1.2**
	1971	**21 568 310**	**100.0**	**14 469 540**	**67.1**	**3 879 255**	**18.0**	**2 900 155**	**13.5**	**319 360**	**1.5**

[1] Based on preliminary census data.
[2] Excludes inmates.
Source: Statistics Canada, 1981

10. Family Characteristics

Province or Territory	Husband/Wife Families (percent increase, 1976–1981)	Single Parent Families (percent increase, 1976–1981)
Newfoundland	7.5	17.0
Prince Edward Island	8.0	20.0
Nova Scotia	6.5	16.5
New Brunswick	7.0	26.0
Québec	6.0	26.0
Ontario	8.0	16.0
Manitoba	4.0	15.0
Saskatchewan	9.0	11.0
Alberta	25.0	14.0
British Columbia	15.0	17.0
Yukon Territory	13.5	26.5
Northwest Territories	12.0	22.0
Canada	**9.0**	**19.0**

Source: Statistics Canada, 1981

11. Population Growth Since 1851

Census Year	Population	Increase Since Previous Census	Average Annual Rate of Population Growth (percent)
1851	2 436 297		
1861	3 229 633	793 336	2.9
1871	3 689 257	459 624	1.3
1881	4 324 810	635 553	1.6
1891	4 833 239	508 429	1.1
1901	5 371 315	538 076	1.1
1911	7 206 643	1 835 328	3.0
1921	8 787 949	1 581 306	2.0
1931	10 376 786	1 588 837	1.7
1941	11 506 655	1 129 869	1.0
1951[1]	14 009 429	2 502 774	1.7
1956	16 080 791	2 071 362	2.8
1961	18 238 247	2 157 456	2.5
1966	20 014 880	1 776 633	1.9
1971	21 568 311	1 553 431	1.5
1976	22 992 604	1 424 293	1.3
1981	24 343 181	1 350 576	1.2

1. Includes Newfoundland for the first time. Excluding Newfoundland would reduce growth rate to 1.5%.
Source: Statistics Canada, 1981

12. Education

Province or Territory	Year	Non-Inmate Population, age 15 and over (number)	Less than Grade 9 (number / percent)		Grades 9–13 (number / percent)		University Degree (number / percent)	
Newfoundland	1981	396 485	125 550	31.7	252 475	63.7	18 460	4.7
	1971	326 810	146 775	44.9	173 080	53.0	6 955	2.1
Prince Edward Island	1981	90 825	22 905	25.2	62 415	68.7	5 505	6.1
	1971	75 410	28 475	37.8	44 520	59.0	2 405	3.2
Nova Scotia	1981	641 495	140 845	22.0	453 395	70.7	47 255	7.4
	1971	544 135	176 220	32.4	345 400	63.5	22 510	4.1
New Brunswick	1981	515 945	155 195	30.1	329 635	63.9	31 115	6.0
	1971	428 605	181 305	42.3	232 760	54.3	14 540	3.4
Québec	1981	4 975 830	1 411 265	28.4	3 213 700	64.6	350 860	7.1
	1971	4 208 270	1 778 720	42.3	2 236 550	53.1	193 000	4.6
Ontario	1981	6 649 725	1 282 760	19.3	4 769 115	71.7	597 855	9.0
	1971	5 441 965	1 583 340	29.1	3 572 705	65.6	285 920	5.3
Manitoba	1981	775 940	182 330	23.5	536 000	69.1	57 610	7.4
	1971	694 910	229 315	33.0	433 585	62.4	32 005	4.6
Saskatchewan	1981	718 035	177 075	24.7	496 935	69.2	44 030	6.1
	1971	639 185	232 165	36.3	384 370	60.1	22 650	3.5
Alberta	1981	1 672 620	239 140	14.3	1 273 485	76.1	160 000	9.6
	1971	1 098 375	272 805	24.8	765 445	69.7	60 120	5.5
British Columbia	1981	2 125 735	318 080	15.0	1 633 870	76.9	173 790	8.2
	1971	1 563 095	372 370	23.8	1 113 275	71.2	77 445	5.0
Yukon Territory	1981	16 990	2 490	14.6	12 980	76.4	1 520	8.9
	1971	12 000	2 995	25.0	8 525	71.0	480	4.0
Northwest Territories	1981	29 665	11 565	39.0	15 920	53.7	2 180	7.4
	1971	19 780	10 125	51.2	8 920	45.1	735	3.7
Canada	**1981**	**18 609 285**	**4 069 190**	**21.9**	**13 049 920**	**70.1**	**1 490 185**	**8.0**
	1971	**15 052 530**	**5 014 620**	**33.3**	**9 319 140**	**61.9**	**718 775**	**4.8**

Header: Highest Level of Schooling

Source: Statistics Canada, 1981

13. Destination of Immigrants

Region	1980 (number / percent)		1981 (number / percent)		1982 (number / percent)	
Atlantic Region	3 554	2.5	2 997	2.3	2 576	2.1
Québec	22 538	15.7	21 118	16.4	21 331	17.6
Ontario	62 257	43.5	54 890	42.7	53 031	43.8
Prairie Region	30 226	21.1	27 136	21.1	25 115	20.7
Pacific Region	24 525	17.2	22 126	17.2	19 065	15.8
Not Stated	17	–	351	0.3	29	–
Canada	**143 117**		**128 618**		**121 147**	

Source: Recruitment and Selection Branch, Canadian Employment and Immigration Commission, 1983

14. Origin of Immigrants

Origin	1980 (number / percent)		1981 (number / percent)		1982 (number / percent)	
Asia and Pacific	68 895	48.1	45 716	35.5	38 459	31.8
Europe (excluding U.K.)	22 923	16.0	25 145	19.6	29 711	24.5
Caribbean, South and Central America	13 594	9.5	15 783	12.3	17 196	14.2
United Kingdom	18 245	12.8	21 154	16.4	16 445	13.6
Africa and Middle East	9 534	6.7	10 254	8.0	9 859	8.1
United States	9 926	6.9	10 559	8.2	9 360	7.7
Not Stated	–	–	7	–	117	0.1
Total	**143 117**	**100.0**	**128 618**	**100.0**	**121 147**	**100.0**

Source: Recruitment and Selection Branch, Canadian Employment and Immigration Commission, 1983

15. Family Size

Number of Persons	1976 (percent of total families)	1981 (percent of total families)
1	17	20
2	28	29
3	17	18
4	18	18
5	10	9
6 or more	10	9

Source: Statistics Canada, 1981

Province or Territory	Europe 1981	Europe 1971	Southeast Asia 1981	Southeast Asia 1971	Other Asia 1981	Other Asia 1971	United States 1981	United States 1971	Caribbean 1981	Caribbean 1971	South and Central America 1981	South and Central America 1971	Other Countries 1981	Other Countries 1971	Total Population Born Outside Canada 1981	Total Population Born Outside Canada 1971
Newfoundland	5 660	5 775	425	175	900	640	2 255	1 890	125	75	80	55	335	335	9 785	8 945
Prince Edward Island	2 400	2 165	105	15	185	175	1 740	1 295	15	15	35	10	80	30	4 550	3 705
Nova Scotia	23 880	24 385	940	250	3 415	2 105	11 335	8 780	735	560	260	155	1 150	955	41 710	37 190
New Brunswick	13 820	14 210	815	200	1 140	760	11 005	7 950	200	130	105	150	490	330	27 580	23 735
Québec	325 495	350 415	22 400	4 180	42 010	21 170	40 420	46 480	43 770	15 195	16 290	5 200	35 570	26 280	525 955	468 925
Ontario	1 444 020	1 436 785	62 925	13 520	179 985	57 595	109 325	101 440	110 120	44 550	64 505	20 720	54 875	32 795	2 025 750	1 707 400
Manitoba	99 160	126 310	14 200	1 565	7 545	3 495	11 405	12 090	3 535	2 170	7 515	3 575	2 700	2 050	146 055	151 250
Saskatchewan	53 820	80 775	4 215	395	5 430	3 560	16 555	23 785	895	435	1 305	395	1 425	1 340	83 655	110 690
Alberta	225 115	211 625	20 035	1 930	42 425	11 670	43 820	47 515	7 315	2 205	8 755	1 580	17 355	5 740	364 825	282 260
British Columbia	389 095	370 775	26 300	3 745	107 510	38 385	63 110	57 720	5 480	2 595	9 035	4 270	31 100	19 170	631 620	496 660
Yukon Territory	1 785	1 875	50	5	185	70	660	430	25	25	30	15	150	125	2 885	2 545
Northwest Territories	1 830	1 690	180	45	175	95	380	270	35	25	45	25	135	95	2 780	2 245
Canada	**2 586 080**	**2 626 790**	**152 590**	**26 025**	**390 905**	**139 720**	**312 015**	**309 640**	**172 245**	**67 980**	**107 960**	**36 150**	**145 370**	**89 255**	**3 867 160**	**3 295 530**

Source: Statistics Canada, 1981

17. First Language by Province and Territory

Province or Territory	English	French	Italian	German	Ukrainian	Chinese	Indian, Inuit	Portuguese	Other
Newfoundland	560 460	2 655	90	445	50	725	1 600	205	1 450
Prince Edward Island	115 045	6 080	20	175	35	115	90	20	925
Nova Scotia	793 165	36 030	1 055	1 865	640	1 305	3 055	235	1 440
New Brunswick	453 310	234 030	525	1 220	195	730	2 115	165	4 115
Québec	706 115	5 307 010	133 710	24 060	10 765	15 270	28 080	25 495	187 895
Ontario	6 678 770	475 605	338 980	174 545	81 595	89 355	22 255	114 275	649 725
Manitoba	735 920	52 560	6 170	75 180	58 855	6 075	27 185	6 840	57 455
Saskatchewan	770 815	25 535	1 280	59 625	44 660	5 000	24 265	335	36 795
Alberta	1 810 545	62 145	16 175	91 480	68 130	28 910	27 565	5 560	127 215
British Columbia	2 249 310	45 615	30 595	93 380	26 950	76 270	11 445	12 340	198 560
Yukon Territory	20 245	580	45	495	170	125	835	5	655
Northwest Territories	24 755	1 240	130	385	210	145	18 090	25	765
Canada	**14 918 445**	**6 249 085**	**528 775**	**522 855**	**292 265**	**224 030**	**166 575**	**165 510**	**1 275 830**

Source: Statistics Canada, 1981

18. Labour Force

Province or Territory	Agriculture (number, 1981)	Agriculture (percent change. 1971-1981)	Community, Business, and Personal Service Industries (number, 1981)	Community, Business, and Personal Service Industries (percent change. 1971-1981)	Construction (number, 1981)	Construction (percent change. 1971-1981)	Fishing and Trapping (number, 1981)	Fishing and Trapping (percent change. 1971-1981)	Forestry (number, 1981)	Forestry (percent change. 1971-1981)	Finance, Insurance, and Real Estate (number, 1981)	Finance, Insurance, and Real Estate (percent change. 1971-1981)	Manufacturing (number, 1981)	Manufacturing (percent change. 1971-1981)	Mining (number, 1981)	Mining (percent change. 1971-1981)	Public Administration and Defence (number, 1981)	Public Administration and Defence (percent change. 1971-1981)	Trade (number, 1981)	Trade (percent change. 1971-1981)	Transportation and Communications (number, 1981)	Transportation and Communications (percent change. 1971-1981)
Newfoundland	1 360	15.7	58 985	82.3	16 190	4.2	9 895	45.3	3 920	56.2	6 425	145.2	36 270	106.0	6 610	33.8	19 325	63.7	35 870	55.0	18 775	14.4
Prince Edward Island	5 830	-0.3	15 670	66.3	4 420	57.0	2 790	31.0	295	168.2	1 605	87.7	5 825	38.5	120	140.0	6 075	28.3	8 160	38.3	3 980	28.2
Nova Scotia	8 510	19.7	106 885	61.1	24 185	12.3	7 445	33.2	4 740	51.9	16 000	80.9	54 745	32.7	6 520	5.8	44 580	15.6	63 630	46.3	29 365	22.6
New Brunswick	7 260	8.9	80 130	59.8	21 310	38.7	3 335	31.6	9 235	37.7	10 515	75.8	48 165	32.2	3 890	22.1	28 110	28.5	49 165	42.7	26 575	17.6
Québec	76 805	5.3	876 310	68.0	149 850	25.3	2 485	32.2	24 125	10.1	146 320	61.6	642 035	27.9	30 275	19.5	217 275	55.2	472 135	60.3	234 490	36.5
Ontario	141 630	9.0	1 256 660	59.6	246 075	19.6	2 425	70.2	14 385	69.7	254 945	63.9	1 031 885	25.9	41 885	3.3	304 290	23.0	730 210	46.8	311 390	40.3
Manitoba	41 405	-12.0	140 145	48.3	26 030	16.6	1 270	268.1	1 570	122.7	24 815	57.0	68 850	20.9	6 755	-13.5	42 575	25.2	85 215	30.7	50 590	26.4
Saskatchewan	85 760	-14.8	118 425	45.0	30 845	72.0	215	-23.2	1 485	63.2	19 105	80.3	27 390	37.7	12 730	72.7	34 845	31.8	74 715	44.5	35 760	28.9
Alberta	81 030	-6.5	329 985	95.9	126 335	141.0	280	33.3	3 835	85.3	64 570	155.3	105 435	68.9	75 170	182.6	85 990	58.8	198 130	90.1	98 240	80.1
British Columbia	31 575	37.0	408 415	81.0	105 235	64.7	6 460	68.2	37 035	33.7	75 635	81.2	198 060	34.8	22 590	53.6	96 005	68.2	236 560	60.6	122 730	41.6
Yukon Territory	85	750.0	3 100	71.3	910	64.0	40	60.0	70	0.0	495	167.6	295	90.3	1 330	14.7	2 555	146.9	1 710	93.2	1 590	36.5
Northwest Territories	25	150.0	4 725	108.1	980	120.2	235	-36.5	70	-30.0	690	527.3	420	25.4	2 145	82.6	4 970	100.8	2 095	131.5	2 085	87.0
Canada	**481 275**	**0**	**3 399 435**	**66.5**	**752 370**	**39.8**	**36 865**	**44.9**	**100 765**	**35.5**	**621 120**	**73.5**	**2 219 375**	**30.0**	**210 020**	**51.1**	**886 600**	**38.6**	**1 957 575**	**54.2**	**935 575**	**39.4**

Source: Statistics Canada, 1981

19. Principal Field Crops[1]

Province	Wheat (10³ bushels)	Oats (10³ bushels)	Barley (10³ bushels)	Rye (10³ bushels)	Flaxseed (10³ bushels)	Corn (grain) (10³ bushels)	Soybeans (10³ bushels)	Rapeseed (10³ bushels)	Potatoes (10³ hundred pound bags)	Mustard Seed (10³ pounds)	Sunflower Seed (10³ pounds)	Tame Hay[2] (10³ tons)	Corn (fodder)[2] (10³ tons)	Sugar Beets[2] (10³ tons)
Prince Edward Island	329	2 013	2 736	–	–	–	–	–	17 250	–	–	262	92	–
Nova Scotia	262	1 044	468	180	–	–	–	–	880	–	–	475	130	–
New Brunswick	336	2 000	588	–	–	–	–	–	12 798	–	–	335	52	–
Québec	3 417	20 101	16 535	197	–	35 825	–	–	8 532	–	–	4 740	2 866	220
Ontario	13 852	22 500	34 400	3 319	–	204 520	31 490	–	8 485	–	–	7 634	7 745	–
Manitoba	137 000	37 000	109 000	7 200	17 200	10 000	–	17 700	5 807	23 500	192 500	2 500	530	410
Saskatchewan	630 000	65 000	167 000	14 300	9 200	–	–	32 000	494	93 500	15 000	3 000	–	–
Alberta	225 500	91 000	307 000	9 500	3 000	940	–	41 000	4 230	60 000	–	6 100	450	517
British Columbia	4 200	4 200	8 700	290	–	–	–	2 500	2 070	–	–	1 800	535	–
Canada	**1 014 896**	**244 858**	**646 427**	**34 986**	**29 400**	**251 285**	**31 490**	**93 200**	**60 642**	**177 000**	**207 500**	**28 846**	**12 400**	**1 147**

[1] Excludes Newfoundland and the Territories
[2] Tame Hay, Corn, and Sugar Beets are given in short tons rather than metric tonnes. One short ton is equivalent to 2 000 pounds (907.2 kg).

Source: Statistics Canada, 1982

20. Farm Cash Receipts by Province[1]

Province	Receipts (10³ $) 1980	1981	1982	1983	1984
Newfoundland	n.a.[1]	n.a.	n.a.	35 229	40 937
Prince Edward Island	141 507	186 762	152 398	176 068	186 657
Nova Scotia	202 458	220 567	235 917	234 989	261 175
New Brunswick	153 889	197 493	186 986	195 573	229 354
Québec	2 236 505	2 712 805	2 834 385	2 754 036	3 073 173
Ontario	4 370 039	4 953 437	4 850 484	5 056 896	5 284 328
Manitoba	1 404 568	1 655 215	1 681 228	1 727 713	1 926 405
Saskatchewan	3 149 267	4 010 306	3 883 134	3 961 534	4 221 154
Alberta	3 234 774	3 880 793	3 796 884	3 705 607	3 863 824
British Columbia	749 120	863 940	900 415	898 155	964 547
Canada	**15 642 127**[2]	**18 681 318**[2]	**18 521 831**[2]	**18 745 800**	**20 051 554**

[1] Not available.
[2] Excludes Newfoundland.
Source: Statistics Canada, 1981, 1982, 1984

21. Farm Cash Receipts by Product

Product	Receipts (10⁶ $) 1978	1979	1980	1981	1982
Wheat	1 674.7	1 908.4	2 763.5	3 275.0	3 496.6
Barley	398.2	493.8	546.5	810.1	791.5
Other Grains[1]	1 100.4	1 354.4	1 563.5	1 495.4	1 389.8
Potatoes	151.8	160.1	203.5	316.3	251.4
Fruits	207.2	219.7	226.5	233.1	264.5
Vegetables	281.8	313.4	345.8	405.5	439.0
Floriculture and Nursery	201.2	237.8	262.4	296.5	307.1
Tobacco	267.5	289.7	213.9	380.4	376.8
Cattle and Calves	2 868.8	3 512.0	3 663.3	3 536.6	3 586.4
Hogs	1 155.8	1 302.7	1 402.5	1 614.5	1 957.3
Dairy Products	1 559.6	1 753.9	2 064.9	2 378.9	2 640.3
Poultry	536.7	653.5	663.0	777.0	773.6
Eggs	303.5	339.6	395.0	479.0	462.7
Forest and Maple Products	63.5	84.0	84.0	106.1	99.0

[1] Includes oats, rye, flaxseed, rapeseed, soybeans, and corn.
Source: Statistics Canada, 1983

22. Forest Inventory

Province or Territory	Forest Land (10³ km) Total	Productive	Ownership (10⁶m) Crown provincial	Crown federal	Privately owned	Volume (10⁶ m) Softwoods	Hardwoods	Total
Newfoundland	142	85	135	1	6	429	34	463
Prince Edward Island	3	3	–	–	3	22	11	33
Nova Scotia	41	29	11	1	29	137	66	203
New Brunswick	65	62	31	2	32	338	178	516
Québec	940	849	556	2	66	3 089	1 044	4 133
Ontario	807	426	381	7	44	2 075	1 123	3 198
Manitoba	349	139	231	4	5	439	196	635
Saskatchewan	178	89	118	5	–	293	191	484
Alberta	349	234	297	34	–	781	657	1 438
British Columbia	633	515	543	6	17	7 438	404	7 842
Yukon Territory	242	67	–	242	–	215	40	255
Northwest Territories	615	143	–	615	–	315	131	446
Canada	**4 364**	**2 641**	**2 303**	**919**	**202**	**15 571**	**4 075**	**19 646**

Source: Canadian Forestry Service. *Canada's Forest Inventory, 1981*

23. Volume of Wood Cut

Province or Territory	Volume (10³ m³) 1978	1979	1980	1981
Newfoundland	2 288	2 481	2 795	2 568
Prince Edward Island	159	223	278	333
Nova Scotia	4 157	4 389	4 544	3 986
New Brunswick	8 509	8 750	8 387	7 795
Québec	34 079	35 736	31 687	34 234
Ontario	20 187	21 294	21 322	22 808
Manitoba	1 803	1 903	2 335	1 803
Saskatchewan	2 863	3 579	3 330	3 555
Alberta	5 726	6 208	5 933	6 586
British Columbia	75 164	76 195	74 654	60 780
Yukon Territory and Northwest Territories	167	212	115	124
Canada	**155 102**	**160 970**	**155 380**	**144 572**

Source: Statistics Canada, 1981

24. Leading Minerals

Mineral	Production 1981 (10³ t except where noted)	Production 1982[1]	Production 1981–1982 (percent change)	Value 1981 (10⁶ $)	Value 1982[1]	Value 1981–1982 (percent change)
Metallic Minerals						
Copper	691.3	606.2	− 12.3	1 529.8	1 179.8	− 22.9
Gold (kg)	52 034.0	62 456.0	+ 20.0	922.1	929.4	+ 0.8
Iron Ore	49 551.0	34 496.0	− 30.4	1 748.1	1 211.7	− 30.1
Lead	268.6	290.3	+ 8.1	263.6	210.2	− 20.3
Molybdenum (t)	12 850.0	15 232.0	+ 18.5	218.8	327.1	+ 49.5
Nickel	160.2	88.7	− 44.6	1 238.1	581.1	− 53.1
Silver (t)	1 129.0	1 204.0	+ 6.6	458.1	378.8	− 17.3
Uranium (t)	7 507.0	8 189.0	+ 9.1	794.2	815.2	+ 2.6
Zinc	911.2	1 032.7	+ 13.3	1 089.6	1 108.7	+ 1.8
Industrial Minerals						
Asbestos	1 122.0	822.0	− 26.7	548.4	403.0	− 26.5
Gypsum	7 025.0	5 726.0	− 18.5	46.9	42.6	− 9.2
Potash	6 549.0	5 196.0	− 20.1	990.4	625.7	− 36.8
Salt	7 240.0	8 076.0	+ 11.5	131.6	161.5	+ 22.7
Cement	10 145.0	8 418.0	− 17.0	665.9	610.4	− 8.3
Clay Products	n.a.	n.a.	n.a.	119.1	94.7	− 20.5
Lime	2 555.0	2 191.0	− 14.2	153.9	148.8	− 3.2
Fuels						
Coal	40 088	43 200	+ 7.8	1 072.5	1 297.8	+ 21.0
Natural Gas (10³ m³)	73 824 000	73 783 000	− 0.1	6 420.6	7 081.7	+ 10.3
Petroleum (10³ m³)	74 553	71 095	− 4.6	9 454.1	11 627.9	+ 23.0

[1] Preliminary data

Source: Mineral Policy Sector, Energy, Mines and Resources; Statistics Canada, 1983

25. Selected Dairy Products

Product	1980 Total Production (10³ t)	1980 Per Capita Consumption (kg)	1981 Total Production (10³ t)	1981 Per Capita Consumption (kg)
Products Measured by Weight				
Creamery Butter	102.97	4.51	112.84	4.42
Processed Cheese	67.43	2.92	71.21	2.97
Cheddar Cheese	106.67	1.75	100.73	1.95
Cottage Cheese	29.24	1.21	30.73	1.26
Other Cheeses	71.33	3.67	75.96	3.86
Powdered Skim Milk	109.48	1.80	137.07	1.99

Products Measured by Liquid Volume	Total Production (10³ kL)	Per Capita Consumption (L)	Total Production (10³ kL)	Per Capita Consumption (L)
Evaporated Whole Milk	157.44	2.20	131.92	2.11
Condensed Whole Milk	12.82	.55	13.22	.55
Yogurt	39.32	1.63	43.09	1.77
Ice Cream	311.93	12.95	311.38	12.78

Source: Statistics Canada, 1981

26. Value of Mineral Production

Year	Metallic Minerals (10⁶ $)	Industrial Minerals (10⁶ $)	Fuels (10⁶ $)	Total (10⁶ $)	Per Capita Value ($)
1957	1 159	466	565	2 190	131.87
1958	1 130	460	511	2 101	122.99
1959	1 371	503	535	2 409	137.79
1960	1 407	520	566	2 493	139.48
1961	1 387	542	674	2 603	142.72
1962	1 496	574	811	2 881	155.05
1963	1 510	632	885	3 027	159.91
1964	1 702	690	973	3 365	174.45
1965	1 908	761	1 046	3 715	189.11
1966	1 985	844	1 152	3 981	198.88
1967	2 285	861	1 235	4 381	214.99
1968	2 493	886	1 343	4 722	228.10
1969	2 378	891	1 465	4 734	225.42
1970	3 073	931	1 718	5 722	268.68
1971	2 940	1 008	2 015	5 963	276.46
1972	2 956	1 085	2 367	6 408	293.92
1973	3 850	1 293	3 227	8 370	379.69
1974	4 821	1 731	5 202	11 754	525.55
1975	4 796	1 898	6 653	13 347	588.05
1976	5 315	2 269	8 109	15 693	682.51
1977	5 988	2 612	9 873	18 473	794.26
1978	5 698	2 986	11 577	20 261	863.05
1979	7 951	3 514	14 617	26 081	1 101.81
1980	9 697	4 201	17 944	31 842	1 330.30
1981	8 753	4 611	19 045	32 410	1 328.62
1982[1]	7 035	3 885	22 162	33 082	1 344.62

[1] Preliminary data

Source: Energy, Mines and Resources Canada, 1983

27. Foreign Trade by Product

Product	Imports to Canada (10⁶ $)			Exports from Canada (10⁶ $)		
	1980	1981	1982	1980	1981	1982
Live animals	$ 113	$ 201	$ 142	$ 254	$ 229	$ 326
Food, beverages, tobacco	4 690	5 038	4 798	8 009	9 212	9 894
Meat	273	291	286	521	628	779
Fish	354	360	352	1 252	1 484	1 581
Fruits and vegetables	1 498	1 802	1 874	295	383	399
Wheat	–	–	–	3 862	3 728	4 284
Crude petroleum	6 919	7 861	4 950	2 899	2 505	2 729
Natural gas	–	–	–	3 984	4 370	4 755
Coal	811	834	932	934	1 147	1 269
Sulphur	–	–	–	543	810	720
Wood and paper	919	1 174	871	12 464	12 629	11 712
Textiles	1 276	1 426	1 193	234	267	244
Chemicals	3 354	3 814	3 584	4 056	4 605	4 073
Iron and steel	1 415	2 276	1 238	2 042	2 315	1 969
Aluminium, including alloys	424	445	367	1 533	1 467	1 428
General and industrial machinery	6 752	7 296	5 658	2 181	2 739	2 480
Agricultural machinery	2 092	2 396	1 689	876	885	651
Transportation equipment	16 412	19 476	16 994	13 373	15 747	19 127
Cars and chassis	4 416	5 066	4 042	4 687	5 422	7 053
Trucks, tractors, chassis	1 135	1 386	935	2 445	2 904	3 882
Motor vehicle parts, except engines	6 162	7 331	7 500	3 011	3 635	3 928
Motor vehicle engines	1 162	1 243	1 268	455	640	927
Other equipment and tools	8 078	9 947	9 696	1 976	2 307	2 466
Total	**$69 274**	**$79 129**	**$67 355**	**$74 446**	**$81 203**	**$81 464**

Source: Statistics Canada, 1984

28. Largest Companies

Rank	Name	Sales or Operating Revenue (10⁶)	Number of Employees (10³)	Change In Ranking Since Previous Year	Percent of Foreign Ownership
1.	General Motors of Canada Ltd.	13 805.5	43	+ 1	100
2.	Canadian Pacific Ltd.	12 759.3	121	– 1	0
3.	Imperial Oil Ltd.	8 919.0	15	no change	70
4.	Bell Canada Enterprises Inc.	8 874.7	101	no change	0
5.	Ford Motor Co. of Canada	8 580.6	34	+ 1	90
6.	George Weston Ltd.	7 779.6	60	– 1	0
7.	Alcan Aluminium	6 418.3	70	no change	0
8.	Texaco Canada	5 652.0	4	+ 2	90
9.	Canadian Wheat Board	5 469.0	0.5	no change	0
10.	Shell Canada Ltd.	5 300.0	8	– 2	79
11.	Gulf Canada Ltd.	5 078.0	9	no change	60
12.	Canadian National Railways	4 625.1	63	no change	0
13.	Hudson's Bay Co.	4 370.5	44	no change	0
14.	Chrysler Canada Ltd.	4 325.5	12	+ 2	100
15.	PetroCanada	4 123.8	6	+ 7	0
16.	Provigo Inc.	3 891.2	11	– 1	0
17.	Canada Development Corp.	3 834.7	18	– 3	0
18.	Nova Corp.	3 823.0	8	– 1	0
19.	Ontario Hydro	3 805.1	31	+ 2	0
20.	Hydro-Québec	3 656.0	19	+ 3	0
21.	Brascan Ltd.	3 555.0	0.03	– 2	0
22.	TransCanada PipeLines	3 470.7	1.9	– 4	0
23.	Canada Safeway Ltd.	3 437.7	23	+ 2	100
24.	Hiram Walker Resources Ltd.	3 402.8	10	– 4	12
25.	Steinberg Inc.	3 352.8	32	– 1	0

Source: *The Financial Post 500*, Summer 1984

29. Foreign Trade by Partner

World Regions and Selected Countries	Imports to Canada (10⁶ $)			Exports from Canada (10⁶ $)		
	1980	1981	1982	1980	1981	1982
United States	$48 614	$54 350	$47 362	$46 970	$53 816	$55 477
Western Europe	7 007	8 019	7 023	11 093	10 121	8 528
United Kingdom	1 974	2 377	1 901	3 192	3 293	2 664
West Germany	1 455	1 611	1 383	1 641	1 287	1 231
France	773	879	877	995	976	709
Italy	611	702	725	988	917	691
Netherlands	264	295	268	1 434	1 197	1 077
Belgium and Luxembourg	251	297	263	988	829	763
Asia	5 031	6 881	6 183	7 429	7 460	8 057
Japan	2 796	4 038	3 527	4 357	4 498	4 563
Taiwan	558	729	662	252	233	294
Hong Kong	574	675	669	193	184	238
South Korea	414	608	587	506	445	487
China, People's Republic of	155	220	204	871	1 005	1 229
India	95	107	91	357	346	292
South America	3 015	3 249	2 701	2 315	1 897	1 511
Venezuela	2 217	2 385	1 811	656	545	437
Brazil	348	431	482	955	678	526
Middle East	3 027	2 728	967	1 124	1 524	1 819
Saudi Arabia	2 452	2 273	731	310	455	442
Central America and Antilles	1 035	1 843	1 627	1 534	1 873	1 506
Mexico	345	996	998	484	715	485
Cuba	163	196	95	420	452	324
Jamaica	50	98	125	63	81	67
Africa	538	1 047	659	1 063	1 233	1 152
Oceania	699	661	589	793	940	838
Australia	520	499	441	665	777	650
New Zealand	147	146	140	113	139	157
Eastern Europe	307	350	241	2 125	2 340	2 575
USSR	59	78	43	1 535	1 866	2 066
Total	$69 274	$79 129	$67 355	$74 446	$81 203	$81 464

Source: Statistics Canada, 1984

30. Foreign Ownership of Major Industries

Industry	Percent of Foreign Ownership
Manufacturing	
Beverage	30
Rubber	75
Textile	29
Pulp and Paper	50
Agricultural Machinery	57
Automobile and Auto Parts	92
Transportation Equipment	38
Iron and Steel	9
Aluminium	52
Electrical Equipment	65
Chemical	58
Average	**48**
Petroleum and Natural Gas – Average	**52**
Mining and Smelting – Average	**52**
All Industry – Average	**50**

Source: *Financial Post*, 1984

31. Overview of the Fisheries

Q = Quantity in tonnes live weight
V = Value in thousands of dollars

Sea and Freshwater Fisheries	1981		1982	
	Q	V	Q	V
Total Landings	1 406 935	855 736	1 394 724	889 050
Total Production	719 217	1 910 241	710 979	1 978 507
Total Exports	531 866	1 518 386	550 078	1 611 670
Total Imports	131 569	364 424	112 447	354 014
Per Capita Consumption (kilograms of edible weight)	1981		1982	
	7.2		7.2	

Source: Economic Policy Branch, Department of Fisheries and Oceans, 1982

32. Volume and Value of Fishing Catch

Q = Quantity in tonnes, live weight
V = Value in thousands of dollars

Species	Atlantic Coast		Pacific Coast		Canada	
	Q	V	Q	V	Q	V
Total Groundfish	**764 248**	**275 115**	**62 710**	**36 453**	**826 958**	**311 568**
Cod	506 686	186 329	4 900	2 200	511 586	188 529
Haddock	39 777	24 297	–	–	39 777	24 297
Redfish	58 287	12 841	11 150	6 150	69 437	18 991
Halibut	2 501	7 301	4 410	13 800	6 911	21 101
Flatfishes	77 603	23 499	2 200	1 200	79 803	24 699
Turbot	20 040	5 559	350	100	20 390	5 659
Pollock	33 849	8 703	970	200	34 819	8 903
Hake	13 131	3 151	30 700	5 200	43 831	8 351
Cusk	4 366	1 705	–	–	4 366	1 705
Catfish	6 006	1 223	–	–	6 006	1 223
Other	2 002	507	8 030	7 603	10 032	8 110
Total Pelagic and Other Finfish	**201 785**	**46 757**	**112 293**	**149 228**	**314 078**	**195 985**
Herring	142 425	23 404	38 000	44 200	180 425	67 604
Mackerel	19 324	5 083	–	–	19 324	5 083
Tuna	411	1 086	123	346	534	1 432
Alewife	4 125	940	–	–	4 125	940
Eel	501	925	–	–	501	925
Salmon	1 210	4 797	70 630	104 000	71 842	108 797
Skate	56	2	510	40	566	42
Smelt	1 069	488	0	2	1 069	490
Capelin	31 041	5 958	–	–	31 041	5 958
Other	1 623	4 074	3 030	640	4 653	4 714
Total Shellfish	**141 991**	**294 662**	**7 797**	**12 206**	**149 788**	**306 868**
Clams	4 940	3 930	4 800	5 040	9 740	8 970
Oysters	1 486	1 373	1 600	1 040	3 086	2 413
Scallop	51 255	70 755	–	–	51 255	70 755
Squid	12	4	–	–	12	4
Lobster	27 613	141 883	–	–	27 613	141 883
Shrimps	14 226	19 179	500	2 700	17 726	21 879
Crab	41 514	57 036	830	3 000	42 344	60 036
Other	945	502	67	426	1 012	928
Miscellaneous Items	–	**4 714**	–	**4 303**	–	**9 017**
Total Sea Fisheries	**1 108 024**	**621 248**	**182 800**	**202 190**	**1 290 824**	**823 438**
Inland Fisheries					**50 000**	**50 800**
Grand Total - Canada					**1 340 824**	**874 238**

Source: Department of Fisheries and Oceans, March 1986

33. Consumer Price Index

Year	Consumer Price Index (1971 = 100)							
	All Items	Food	Shelter	Clothing	Transportation	Health, Personal	Recreation, Education	Tobacco, Alcohol
1977	160.8	180.1	159.3	141.0	153.3	155.0	142.7	143.8
1978	175.2	208.0	170.8	146.4	162.2	166.2	148.2	155.5
1979	191.2	235.4	180.5	159.9	178.0	181.2	158.4	166.7
1980	210.6	260.6	192.4	178.7	200.7	199.3	173.5	185.3
1981	236.9	290.4	213.2	191.4	237.6	221.0	191.0	209.2
1982	262.5	311.3	239.2	202.1	271.1	244.4	207.6	241.6
1983 (Jan.)	270.3	315.1	250.7	201.9	278.0	254.4	214.1	258.4

Source: *Canadian Statistical Review*, March 1983

34. Expenditures on Consumer Goods and Services

Goods and Services	Expenditures (10⁶ $)							
	1970	1975	1976	1977	1978	1979	1980	1981
Food and Non-alcoholic Beverages	7 923	15 206	16 567	18 041	20 185	22 683	25 205	25 580
Alcoholic Beverages	1 898	3 501	3 779	4 133	4 465	4 832	5 519	6 342
Tobacco Products	1 396	2 050	2 333	2 582	2 810	3 082	3 524	4 071
Clothing and Footwear	4 034	7 155	8 132	8 773	9 508	10 631	11 618	12 987
Gross Rent, Household Fuel, and Power	9 861	16 445	19 146	21 850	24 299	27 295	30 970	35 792
Furniture, Appliances, and Other Household Furnishing and Services	4 785	9 884	11 117	12 016	13 018	14 345	15 552	17 077
Medical Care and Health Services	1 758	2 896	3 465	3 829	4 372	4 881	5 593	6 544
New and Used Cars	2 337	5 132	5 512	5 942	6 546	7 527	7 787	8 414
Car Repairs and Parts	1 038	1 980	2 239	2 458	2 755	3 139	3 370	3 834
Gasoline, Oil, and Grease	1 383	2 948	3 425	3 766	4 100	4 638	5 574	7 221
Recreation and Reading	3 065	7 249	8 473	9 216	9 986	11 165	12 472	13 958
Educational and Cultural Services	1 402	2 723	3 081	3 475	3 839	4 192	4 709	5 192
Personal Goods and Services	7 133	15 062	17 463	19 308	21 660	24 243	27 605	31 063
Total	**50 327**	**96 995**	**110 886**	**122 530**	**135 153**	**150 521**	**168 395**	**191 025**

Source: Statistics Canada, 1981

35. Value of Non-Farm Dwellings

Province or Territory	Number	Less than $20 000	$20 000- 49 999	$50 000- 64 999	$65 000- 79 999	$80 000- 99 999	$100 000- 149 999	$150 000 or more	Average Value ($)
Newfoundland	119 505	25 780	54 455	19 265	9 950	5 940	2 830	1 285	40 305
Prince Edward Island	26 160	4 420	13 975	4 590	1 690	760	525	200	40 230
Nova Scotia	192 180	34 165	90 930	36 150	15 805	7 840	5 075	2 210	42 995
New Brunswick	154 980	28 105	84 240	26 945	8 910	3 665	2 310	805	38 610
Québec	1 123 880	79 980	542 525	255 745	112 490	58 740	46 660	27 745	51 887
Ontario	1 819 140	63 755	443 180	381 860	288 510	248 765	233 380	159 690	78 218
Manitoba	214 340	21 900	86 300	51 695	27 715	13 950	8 720	4 060	51 755
Saskatchewan	198 520	29 695	65 615	45 455	29 775	15 680	9 150	3 155	51 143
Alberta	433 865	25 265	41 325	43 290	63 505	107 270	102 160	51 050	94 179
British Columbia	628 250	33 615	49 880	45 290	49 455	83 255	155 975	210 775	128 081
Yukon Territory	3 995	655	905	530	700	705	340	160	61 528
Northwest Territories	2 610	885	620	250	205	290	260	95	49 123
Canada	**4 917 430**	**348 225**	**1 473 955**	**911 080**	**608 710**	**546 855**	**567 380**	**461 230**	**73 955**

Source: Statistics Canada, 1981

36. Average Income by Occupation

Occupation	Average Income
Doctors (self-employed)	$62 273
Dentists (self-employed)	55 328
Lawyers (self-employed)	45 921
Accountants (self-employed)	39 317
Engineers (self-employed)	36 477
Teachers and Professors	24 632
Federal Government Employees	19 362
Provincial Government Employees	18 973
Armed Forces	18 193
Other Self-employed Professionals	17 851
Investors	16 560
Municipal Employees	16 286
Salespeople (self-employed)	14 306
Farmers	13 265
Fishers	10 795
Entertainers and Artists	9 188

Source: Statistics Canada, 1980

37. Federal Government Employment

Province or Territory	Total Provincial Labour Force	Federal Gov't Employees	Total Federal Gov't Payroll (10⁶ $)	Average Salary
Newfoundland	221 000	9 889	221.3	$22 300
Prince Edward Island	54 000	3 003	71.5	23 809
Nova Scotia	370 000	34 897	826.6	23 257
New Brunswick	294 000	14 477	336.7	23 600
Québec	2 947 000	82 423	2 000.0	24 205
Ontario	4 519 000	175 294	3 400.0	19 396
Manitoba	499 000	19 260	475.3	24 678
Saskatchewan	462 000	12 940	316.8	24 482
Alberta	1 167 000	32 009	695.0	21 712
British Columbia	1 346 000	45 644	1 000.0	21 908
Yukon Territory	n.a.	1 305	33.9	25 977
Northwest Territories	n.a.	2 542	65.0	25 570

Source: Statistics Canada, 1982

38. Prime Ministers and Governors General

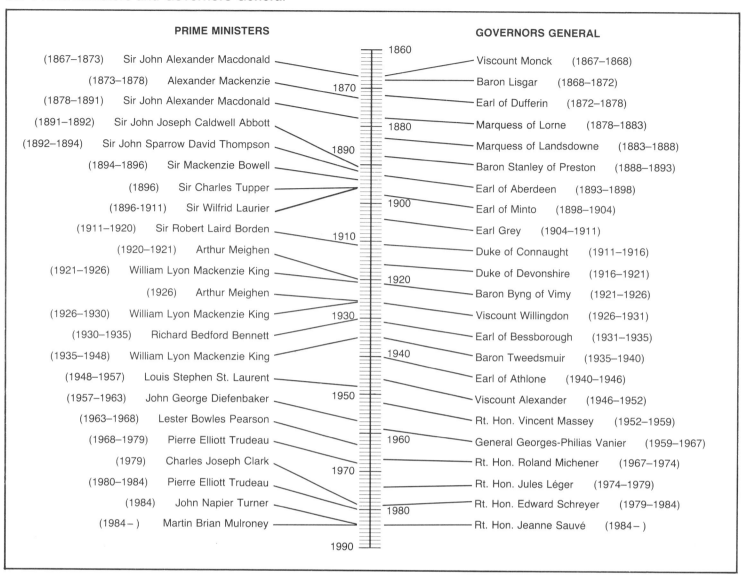

PRIME MINISTERS		GOVERNORS GENERAL
(1867–1873)	Sir John Alexander Macdonald	Viscount Monck (1867–1868)
(1873–1878)	Alexander Mackenzie	Baron Lisgar (1868–1872)
(1878–1891)	Sir John Alexander Macdonald	Earl of Dufferin (1872–1878)
(1891–1892)	Sir John Joseph Caldwell Abbott	Marquess of Lorne (1878–1883)
(1892–1894)	Sir John Sparrow David Thompson	Marquess of Landsdowne (1883–1888)
(1894–1896)	Sir Mackenzie Bowell	Baron Stanley of Preston (1888–1893)
(1896)	Sir Charles Tupper	Earl of Aberdeen (1893–1898)
(1896-1911)	Sir Wilfrid Laurier	Earl of Minto (1898–1904)
(1911–1920)	Sir Robert Laird Borden	Earl Grey (1904–1911)
(1920–1921)	Arthur Meighen	Duke of Connaught (1911–1916)
(1921–1926)	William Lyon Mackenzie King	Duke of Devonshire (1916–1921)
(1926)	Arthur Meighen	Baron Byng of Vimy (1921–1926)
(1926–1930)	William Lyon Mackenzie King	Viscount Willingdon (1926–1931)
(1930–1935)	Richard Bedford Bennett	Earl of Bessborough (1931–1935)
(1935–1948)	William Lyon Mackenzie King	Baron Tweedsmuir (1935–1940)
(1948–1957)	Louis Stephen St. Laurent	Earl of Athlone (1940–1946)
(1957–1963)	John George Diefenbaker	Viscount Alexander (1946–1952)
(1963–1968)	Lester Bowles Pearson	Rt. Hon. Vincent Massey (1952–1959)
(1968–1979)	Pierre Elliott Trudeau	General Georges-Philias Vanier (1959–1967)
(1979)	Charles Joseph Clark	Rt. Hon. Roland Michener (1967–1974)
(1980–1984)	Pierre Elliott Trudeau	Rt. Hon. Jules Léger (1974–1979)
(1984)	John Napier Turner	Rt. Hon. Edward Schreyer (1979–1984)
(1984–)	Martin Brian Mulroney	Rt. Hon. Jeanne Sauvé (1984–)

Timeline: 1860, 1870, 1880, 1890, 1900, 1910, 1920, 1930, 1940, 1950, 1960, 1970, 1980, 1990

39. Income Tax Rates

1983 Rates of Federal Income Tax				
Taxable income		Tax		
$ 1 178 or less		–		
1 179	$ 71	+	16% on next	$ 1 179
2 358	259	+	17% on next	2 358
4 716	660	+	18% on next	2 358
7 074	1 085	+	19% on next	4 716
11 790	1 981	+	20% on next	4 716
16 506	2 924	+	23% on next	4 716
21 222	4 009	+	25% on next	11 790
33 012	6 956	+	30% on next	23 580
56 592	14 030	+	34% on remainder	

[1] Rates are applied to basic federal tax payable. Individual provinces may have additional taxes for larger incomes or tax reductions for lower incomes.

Source: Revenue Canada, 1983

1983 Rates of Provincial Income Tax	
	Tax Rate[1]
Newfoundland	60 %
Prince Edward Island	52.5
Nova Scotia	56.5
New Brunswick	55.5
Québec	n.a.
Ontario	48
Manitoba	54
Saskatchewan	51
Alberta	38.5
British Columbia	44
Yukon Territory and Northwest Territories	43

40. National Political Party Representation

Region	Election Year												
	1949	1953	1957	1958	1962	1963	1965	1968	1972	1974	1979	1980	1984
Atlantic Canada – Total Seats	**34**	**33**	**33**	**33**	**33**	**33**	**32**	**32**	**32**	**31**	**32**	**32**	**32**
Liberal	26	27	12	8	14	20	15	7	10	13	12	19	7
Progressive Conservative	7	5	21	25	18	13	18	25	22	17	17	13	25
New Democratic Party	1	1	0	0	1	0	0	0	0	1	2	0	0
Québec – Total Seats	**70**	**70**	**71**	**75**	**75**	**75**	**73**	**74**	**73**	**74**	**75**	**75**	**75**
Liberal	68	66	62	25	35	47	56	56	56	60	67	74	17
Progressive Conservative	2	4	9	50	14	8	8	4	2	3	2	1	58
Social Credit	0	0	0	0	26	20	9	14	15	11	6	0	0
Ontario – Total Seats	**82**	**85**	**85**	**85**	**85**	**85**	**85**	**88**	**87**	**88**	**95**	**95**	**95**
Liberal	56	51	21	15	44	52	51	64	36	55	32	52	15
Progressive Conservative	25	33	61	67	35	27	25	17	40	25	57	38	66
New Democratic Party	1	1	3	3	6	6	9	6	11	8	6	5	13
Western Canada – Total Seats (including Territories)	**71**	**72**	**72**	**72**	**72**	**72**	**72**	**70**	**68**	**68**	**80**	**80**	**80**
Liberal	43	27	10	1	7	10	9	28	7	13	3	2	2
Progressive Conservative	7	9	21	66	49	47	46	26	42	49	60	51	61
New Democratic Party	11	21	22	5	12	11	12	16	19	6	18	27	17
Social Credit	10	15	19	0	4	4	5	0	0	0	0	0	0
Canada – Total Seats in House of Commons	**262**	**265**	**265**	**265**	**265**	**265**	**265**	**265**	**265**	**265**	**282**	**282**	**282**
Liberal	193	171	105	49	100	129	131	155	109	141	114	147	40
Progressive Conservative	41	51	112	208	116	95	97	72	107	95	136	103	211
New Democratic Party	13	23	25	8	19	17	21	22	31	16	26	32	30
Social Credit	10	15	19	0	30	24	14	14	15	11	6	0	0
Others[1]	5	5	4	0	0	0	2	2	2	1	0	0	1

[1] Includes independents and those who may have broken party ranks and run on a specific issue.

Sources: Beck, J.M. *Pendulum of Power*. Scarborough: Prentice-Hall of Canada, Ltd., 1968.

Public Archives

41. Federal Government Budget

Fiscal Year	Expenditures (10⁶ $)								
	National Defense	Health and Welfare	Agriculture	Post Office	Public Works	Transport	Veterans' Affairs	Payments to Provinces	**Total Expenditures**
1976–77	3 365	10 952	631	1 104	684	1 314	754	3 356	**38 951**
1977–78	3 771	11 635	959	1 237	1 431	1 478	841	3 003	**42 902**
1978–79	4 108	13 024	768	1 275	1 657	1 725	890	3 028	**46 923**
1979–80	4 389	14 038	782	1 412	1 615	1 726	933	3 522	**52 297**
1980–81	5 078	15 792	881	1 597	1 883	2 640	1 006	3 788	**58 813**
1981–82	6 028	17 947	1 125	1 119	2 188	2 279	1 140	4 535	**64 919**

Fiscal Year	Revenue (10⁶ $)								
	Personal Income Tax	Corporation Income Tax	Sales Tax	Other Excise Tax	Excise Duties	Customs Duties	Estate Taxes	Post Office	**Total Budgetary Revenues**
1976–77	14 620	5 377	4 529	1 146	865	2 097	70	615	**32 650**
1977–78	13 439	5 828	5 026	904	882	2 312	66	773	**32 866**
1978–79	14 048	6 262	5 245	827	878	2 747	77	903	**35 216**
1979–80	16 327	7 537	5 119	1 252	895	3 000	96	1 118	**40 159**
1980–81	19 837	8 133	5 882	1 602	1 042	3 188	99	1 109	**46 731**
1981–82	24 046	8 892	6 621	2 079	1 175	3 439	595	479	**54 547**

Source: *Canadian Statistical Review*, 1982

42. Canadian Armed Forces – Strength

Year	Navy	Army	Air Force	Total
1945	92 529	494 258	174 254	761 041
1955	19 207	49 409	49 461	118 077
1965	19 756	46 264	48 144	114 164
1970				91 433
1977				78 091
1978				79 656
1979	(In 1968, the three divisions of the Canadian Armed Forces were combined into a single body.)			78 974
1980				78 909
1981				79 549
1982				82 858
1983				82 905

Source: Statistics Canada, 1983

43. Canadian Armed Forces – Major Conflicts and Peacekeeping Operations

Year(s)	Name or Location of Conflict	Number of Participants	Number Killed
1885	Northwest Rebellion (Canada)	3 323	38
1899-1902	South African War	7 368	89
1914-1918	World War I	626 636	61 332
1939-1945	World War II	1 086 343	32 714
1950-1953	Korean War	25 583	314
1956-1967	Gaza Strip	900	0
1973-1979	Middle East	850	0
1960-1964	Congo	300	0
1983	Cyprus	515	0
1983	Middle East	250	0
1983	Israel	20	0

Source: Statistics Canada, 1983

44. Canada – Census Metropolitan Areas

BOR = Borough
C = City
CM = County (Municipality)
COM = Community
CT = Canton (Municipalité de)
CU = Cantons unis (Municipalité de)
DM = District (Municipality)
HAM = Hamlet
ID = Improvement District
LGD = Local Government District
LID = Local Improvement District
LOT = Township and Royalty
MC = Municipal Corporation
MD = Municipal District
PAR = Parish
P = Paroisse (Municipalité de)
R = Indian Reserve (Réserve indienne)
RM = Rural Municipality
RV = Resort Village
SA = Special area
SCM = Subdivision of County Municipality
SD = Sans designation (Municipalité)
S = Indian Settlement (Établissement indien)
SET = Settlement
SRD = Subdivision of regional district
SUN = Subdivision of Unorganized
SV = Summer village
T = Town
TP = Township
UNO = Unorganized (Non organisé)
V = Ville
VL = Village

Calgary CMA
Calgary (C)

Chicoutimi-Jonquière CMA
Chicoutimi (V)
Jonquière (V)
Kenogami (CT)
Larouche (P)
Laterrière (VL)
Notre-Dame-de-Laterrière (P)
Saint-Honoré (SD)
Shipshaw (SD)
Tremblay (CT)

Edmonton CMA
Alexander 134 (R)
Bon Accord (T)
Edmonton (C)
Fort Saskatchewan (T)
Gibbons (T)
Legal (VL)
Morinville (T)
Redwater (T)
St. Albert (C)
Strathcona County No. 20 (CM)
Sturgeon No. 90 (MD)

Halifax CMA
Bedford (T)
Cole Harbour 30 (R)
Dartmouth (C)
Halifax, Subdivision A (SCM)
Halifax, Subdivision B (SCM)
Halifax, Subdivision C (SCM)
Halifax, Subdivision D (SCM)
Halifax, Subdivision E (SCM)
Shubenacadie 13 (R)

Hamilton CMA
Ancaster (T)
Burlington (C)
Dundas (T)
Flamborough (TP)
Glanbrook (TP)
Grimsby (T)
Hamilton (C)
Stoney Creek (T)

Kitchener CMA
Cambridge (C)
Kitchener (C)
North Dumfries (TP)
Waterloo (C)
Woolwich (TP)

London CMA
Belmont (VL)
Delaware (TP)
London (C)
London (TP)
North Dorchester (TP)
Southwold (TP)
West Nissouri (TP)
Westminster (TP)

Montréal CMA
Anjou (V)
Baie d'Urfé (V)
Beaconsfield (C)
Beloeil (V)
Blainville (V)
Bois-des-Filion (V)
Boisbriand (V)
Boucherville (V)
Brossard (V)
Candiac (V)
Carignan (V)
Chambly (V)
Charlemagne (V)
Chateauguay (V)
Côte-Saint-Luc (C)
Delson (V)
Deux-Montagnes (C)
Dollard-des-Ormeaux (V)
Dorion (V)
Dorval (C)
Greenfield Park (V)
Hampstead (V)
Hudson (V)
Ile Dorval (V)
Ile-Cadieux (V)
Ile-Perrot (V)
Kahnawake 14 (R)
Kirkland (V)
La Prairie (V)
Lachenaie (V)
Lachine (V)
Lasalle (C)
Laval (V)
Le Gardeur (V)
Lemoyne (V)
Léry (V)
Longueuil (V)
Lorraine (V)
Mascouche (V)
McMasterville (VL)
Mercier (V)
Mont-Royal (V)
Mont-Saint-Hilaire (V)
Montréal (V)
Montréal-est (V)
Montréal-nord (V)
Montréal-ouest (V)
Notre-Dame-de-Bon-Secours (P)
Notre-Dame-de-l'Ile-Perrot (P)
Oka (P)
Oka (SD)
Oka 16 (R)
Oka-sur-le-Lac (V)
Otterburn Park (V)
Outremont (V)
Pierrefonds (V)
Pincourt (V)
Pointe-aux-Trembles (V)
Pointe-Calumet (VL)
Pointe-Claire (V)
Pointe-du-Moulin (V)
Repentigny (V)
Richelieu (V)
Rosemère (V)
Roxboro (V)
Saint-Amable (P)
Saint-Basile-le-Grand (V)
Saint-Bruno-de-Montarville (V)
Saint-Constant (V)
Saint-Eustache (V)
Saint-Hubert (V)
Saint-Jean-de-Dieu (P)
Saint-Joseph-du-Lac (P)
Saint-Lambert (V)
Saint-Laurent (V)
Saint-Lazare (P)
Saint-Léonard (V)
Saint-Louis-de-Terrebonne (P)
Saint-Mathias (P)
Saint-Mathieu (SD)
Saint-Mathieu-de-Beloeil (P)
Saint-Philippe (P)
Saint-Pierre (V)
Saint-Raphael-de-l'Ile-Bizard (P)
Saint-Sulpice (P)
Sainte-Anne-de-Bellevue (V)
Sainte-Anne-des-Plaines (P)
Sainte-Catherine (V)
Sainte-Geneviève (V)
Sainte-Julie (V)
Sainte-Marthe-sur-le-Lac (V)
Sainte-Thérèse (V)
Senneville (VL)
Terrasse-Vaudreuil (SD)
Terrebonne (V)
Varennes (V)
Vaudreuil (V)
Vaudreuil-sur-le-Lac (VL)
Verdun (C)
Westmount (C)

Oshawa CMA
Oshawa (C)
Whitby (T)

Ottawa-Hull CMA
In Ontario
Clarence (TP)
Cumberland (TP)
Gloucester (C)
Goulbourn (TP)
Kanata (C)

Nepean (C)
Osgoode (TP)
Ottawa (C)
Rideau (TP)
Rockcliffe Park (VL)
Rockland (T)
In Québec
Aylmer (V)
Gatineau (V)
Hull (V)
Hull, partie ouest (CT)
La Pêche (SD)
Val-des-Monts (SD)

Québec CMA
Ancienne-Lorette (V)
Beauport (V)
Bernières (SD)
Charlesbourg (V)
Charny (V)
Château-Richer (V)
L'Ange-Gardien (P)
Lac-Delage (V)
Lac-Saint-Charles (SD)
Lauzon (V)
Lévis (V)
Lorette 7 (R)
Loretteville (C)
Québec (V)
Saint-Augustin-de-Desmaures (P)
Saint-David-de-L'Auberivière (V)
Saint-Dunstan-du-Lac-Beauport (P)
Saint-Émile (VL)
Saint-Étienne (SD)
Saint-Étienne-de-Beaumont (P)
Saint-Félix-du-Cap-Rouge (P)
Saint-Gabriel-de-Valcartier (SD)
Saint-Gabriel-ouest (SD)
Saint-Jean-Chrysostome (V)
Saint-Jean-de-Boischâtel (VL)
Saint-Joseph-de-la-Pointe-de-Lévy (P)
Saint-Lambert-de-Lauzon (P)
Saint-Louis-de-Pintendre (P)
Saint-Nicolas (V)
Saint-Pierre, Île d'Orléans (P)
Saint-Rédempteur (VL)
Saint-Romuald-d'Etchemin (C)
Sainte-Brigitte-de-Laval (P)
Sainte-Foy (V)
Sainte-Hélène-de-Breakeyville (P)
Sainte-Pétronille (VL)
Shannon (SD)
Sillery (V)
Stoneham and Tewkesbury (CU)
Val-Bélair (V)
Vanier (V)

Regina CMA
Regina (C)
Sherwood No. 159 (RM)

Saint John CMA
East Riverside-Kingshurst (VL)
Fairvale (VL)
Gondola Point (VL)
Grand Bay (VL)
Hampton (VL)
Hampton (PAR)
Musquash (PAR)
Quispamsis (VL)
Renforth (VL)
Rothesay (T)

Rothesay (PAR)
Saint John (C)
Simonds (PAR)
Westfield (VL)
Westfield (PAR)

Saskatoon CMA
Saskatoon (C)

St. Catharines-Niagara CMA
Niagara Falls (C)
Niagara-on-the-Lake (T)
Pelham (T)
Port Colborne (C)
St. Catharines (C)
Thorold (C)
Wainfleet (TP)
Welland (C)

St. John's CMA
Conception Bay South (T)
Division No. 1, Subd. P (SUN)
Division No. 1, Subd. Q (SUN)
Division No. 1, Subd. T (SUN)
Division No. 1, Subd. Z (SUN)
Flatrock (T)
Goulds (T)
Hogan's Pond (T)
Lawrence Pond (T)
Mount Pearl (T)
Paradise (T)
Petty Harbour-Maddox Cove (T)
Portugal Cove (T)
Pouch Cove (T)
St. John's (C)
St. John's Metroplitan Area (T)
St. Phillips (T)
St. Thomas (T)
Torbay (T)
Wedgewood Park (T)

Sudbury CMA
Nickel Centre (T)
Rayside Balfour (T)
Sudbury (C)
Valley East (T)
Walden (T)
Whitefish Lake 6 (R)

Thunder Bay CMA
Fort William 52 (R)
Neebing (TP)
O'Connor (TP)
Oliver (TP)
Paipoonge (TP)
Shuniah (TP)

Toronto CMA
Ajax (T)
Aurora (T)
Brampton (C)
Caledon (T)
East Gwillimbury (T)
East York (BOR)
Etobicoke (BOR)
King (TP)
Markham (T)
Mississauga (C)
Newmarket (T)
North York (C)
Oakville (T)
Pickering (T)
Richmond Hill (T)
Scarborough (C)
Toronto (C)
Vaughan (T)
Whitchurch-Stouffville (T)

York (BOR)

Trois-Rivières CMA
Cap-de-la-Madeleine (C)
Pointe-du-Lac (SD)
Saint-Louis-de-France (P)
Sainte-Marthe-du-Cap-de-la-Madeleine (SD)
Trois-Rivières (V)
Trois-Rivières-Ouest (V)

Vancouver CMA
Barnston Island 3 (R)
Belcarra (VL)
Burnaby (DM)
Burrard Inlet 3 (R)
Capilano 5 (R)
Coquitlam (DM)
Coquitlam 1 (R)
Coquitlam 2 (R)
Delta (DM)
Greater Vancouver Subd. A (SRD)
Katzie 1 (R)
Katzie 2 (R)
Langley (C)
Langley (DM)
Langley 5 (R)
Lions Bay (VL)
Maple Ridge (DM)
McMillan Island 6 (R)
Mission 1 (R)
Musqueam 2 (R)
New Westminster (C)
North Vancouver (C)
North Vancouver (DM)
Pitt Meadows (DM)
Port Coquitlam (C)
Port Moody (C)
Richmond (DM)
Semiahmoo (R)
Surrey (DM)
Tsawwassen (R)
University Endowment Area (SRD)

Vancouver (C)
West Vancouver (DM)
White Rock (C)
Whonnock 1 (R)

Victoria CMA
Belcher Bay 1 (R)
Belcher Bay 2 (R)
Capital, Subd. B (SRD)
Central Saanich (DM)
Cole Bay 3 (R)
East Saanich 2 (R)
Esquimalt (DM)
Esquimalt (R)
New Songhees 1A (R)
North Saanich (DM)
Oakbay (DM)
Saanich (DM)
Sidney (T)
South Saanich 1 (R)
Union Bay 4 (R)
Victoria (C)

Windsor CMA
Belle River (T)
Colchester North (TP)
Essex (T)
Maidstone (TP)
Rochester (TP)
Sandwich South (TP)
Sandwich West (TP)
St. Clair Beach (VL)
Tecumseh (T)
Windsor (C)

Winnipeg CMA
East St. Paul (RM)
Ritchot (RM)
Springfield (RM)
St. François Xavier (RM)
West St. Paul (RM)
Winnipeg (C)

Source: Statistics Canada, 1981

45. Population of Census Metropolitan Areas

Census Metropolitan Area	1981	1984[1]
Calgary CMA	592 743	619 700
Chicoutimi-Jonquière CMA	135 172	138 700
Edmonton CMA	657 057	687 500
Halifax CMA	277 727	285 900
Hamilton CMA	542 095	554 400
Kitchener CMA	287 801	298 400
London CMA	283 668	290 100
Montréal CMA	2 828 349	2 865 900
Oshawa CMA	154 217	166 900
Ottawa-Hull CMA	717 978	756 600
Québec CMA	576 075	589 100
Regina CMA	164 313	173 400
Saint John CMA	114 048	160 100
Saskatoon CMA	154 210	165 100
St. Catharines-Niagara CMA	304 353	307 500
St. John's CMA	154 820	115 500
Sudbury CMA	149 923	148 800
Thunder Bay CMA	121 379	121 700
Toronto CMA	2 998 947	3 140 500
Trois-Rivières CMA	111 453	114 000
Vancouver CMA	1 268 183	1 331 000
Victoria CMA	233 481	242 000
Windsor CMA	246 110	247 900
Winnipeg CMA	584 842	603 500

[1] June 1 estimate.
Source: Statistics Canada, 1981, 1984

Country	Capital	Area (10³km²)	Population (10⁶)	Population Density (persons/km²)	Urban Population (%)	Population Under 15 (%)	Population Over 64 (%)	Birth/Death Rate (per thousand)	Natural Increase (%)	Infant Mortality (per thousand)	Life Expectancy Male/Female (years)	Population Estimate For The Year 2000 (10⁶)
Afghanistan *Democratic Republic of Afghanistan*	Kabul	644	15.4	24	16	45	3	47 / 23	2.4	194	40 / 41	23
Albania *People's Socialist Republic of Albania*	Tiranë	28	3.0	11	37	38	5	26 / 6	2.0	43	69 / 69	3
Algeria *Democratic and Popular Republic of Algeria*	Algiers	2 354	22.8	9	42	46	4	43 / 11	3.2	88	54 / 56	34
Angola *People's Republic of Angola*	Luanda	1 232	8.2	5	14	41	4	47 / 22	2.5	182	39 / 41	12
Argentina *Argentine Republic*	Buenos Aires	2 726	31.2	12	81	30	8	24 / 8	1.6	35	65 / 71	37
Australia *Commonwealth of Australia*	Canberra	7 590	15.8	2	86	24	10	15 / 7	0.8	9	70 / 77	17
Austria *Republic of Austria*	Vienna	83	7.6	90	54	21	15	12 / 12.2	−0.2	11	68 / 75	7
Bahamas *The Commonwealth of the Bahamas*	Nassau	13	0.2	20	75	44	4	24 / 5	1.9	25	64 / 73	0
Bahrain *State of Bahrain*	Manama	0.6	0.4	600	78	44	3	32 / 5	2.7	32	n.a. / n.a.	0
Bangladesh *People's Republic of Bangladesh*	Dhaka	144	103	715	13	47	3	44 / 17	2.7	128	46 / 47	144
Barbados	Bridgetown	0.4	0.3	680	42	29	9	17 / 8	0.9	11	71 / 71	0
Belgium *Kingdom of Belgium*	Brussels	30	9.9	327	95	20	14	12 / 11	0.1	11	69 / 75	9
Belize	Belmopan	22	0.2	6	52	42	4	32 / 7	2.5	27	n.a. / n.a.	0
Benin *People's Republic of Benin*	Porto Novo/Cotonou	111	4.1	37	39	49	5	51 / 21	3.0	120	45 / 45	6
Bhutan *Kingdom of Bhutan*	Thimphu	46	1.4	30	5	40	4	38 / 18	2.0	140	42 / 41	1
Bolivia *Republic of Bolivia*	La Paz/Sucre	1 085	6.4	6	47	42	4	43 / 15	2.8	120	47 / 52	9
Botswana *Republic of Botswana*	Gaborone	574	1.1	1.5	19	45	3	45 / 12	3.3	76	45 / 48	1
Burkina Faso (Upper Volta)	Ouagadougou	274	7.1	28	8	44	3	48 / 23	2.5	150	42 / 43	10
Brazil *Federative Republic of Brazil*	Brasilia	8 412	143.3	18	69	38	4	32 / 9	2.3	71	58 / 62	195
Brunei	Bandar Seri Begawan	5.7	0.2	35	64	38	3	29 / 4	2.5	16	n.a. / n.a.	0
Bulgaria *People's Republic of Bulgaria*	Sofia	109	9.0	80	66	22	11	14 / 11	0.3	17	69 / 74	9
Burma *Socialist Republic of the Union of Burma*	Rangoon	669	37.7	57	27	41	4	33 / 14	2.1	70	49 / 52	48
Burundi *Republic of Burundi*	Bujumbura	27	4.9	170	7	44	3	47 / 17	3.0	124	44 / 46	7.
Cameroon *United Republic of Cameroon*	Yaoundé	460	10.0	21	42	45	3	44 / 17	2.7	103	42 / 45	
Canada	Ottawa	9 976	25.6	2.6	76	22	10	15 / 7	0.8	12	69 / 76	28
Cape Verde *Republic of Cape Verde*	Praia	3	0.3	94	26	31	4	33 / 11	2.4	75	56 / 60	0.
Central African Republic	Bangui	615	2.7	4	41	43	4	47 / 19	2.8	140	35 / 38	4.
Chad *Republic of Chad*	N'Djamena	1 269	5.2	4	22	42	4	45 / 25	2.0	142	30 / 36	7.
Chile *Republic of Chile*	Santiago	748	12.3	16	83	32	6	22 / 6	1.6	20	60 / 66	14.
China *People's Republic of China*	Beijing	9 450	1 050.0	110	32	34	5	18 / 8	1	50	68 / 68	1 200
Colombia *Republic of Colombia*	Bogatá	1 128	30.0	26	67	37	4	28 / 7	2.1	71	65 / 70	38
Congo *People's Republic of the Congo*	Brazzaville	348	1.8	5	48	43	3	45 / 18	2.7	132	47 / 51	2.
Costa Rica *Republic of Costa Rica*	San José	50	2.7	45	48	35	3	30 / 4	2.6	19	66 / 70	
Cuba *Republic of Cuba*	Havana	109	10.2	95	70	28	8	17 / 6	1.1	15	69 / 72	11.
Cyprus *Republic of Cyprus*	Nicosia	9	0.7	69	53	33	2	21 / 8	1.3	12	70 / 73	0.
Czechoslovakia *Czechoslovak Socialist Republic*	Prague	126	15.4	121	74	25	11	15 / 12	0.3	16	67 / 74	16.
Denmark *Kingdom of Denmark*	Copenhagen	42	5.1	120	84	19	15	10 / 11	−0.1	9	71 / 77	5.
Djibouti *Republic of Djibouti*	Djibouti	20	0.3	25	74	46	3	43 / 18	2.6	132	47 / 47	0.
Dominican Republic	Santo Domingo	48	6.4	110	51	41	3	33 / 8	2.5	64	57 / 58	8.
Ecuador *Republic of Ecuador*	Quito	290	9.6	31	45	42	4	36 / 8	2.8	70	55 / 58	13.
Egypt *Arab Republic of Egypt*	Cairo	986	50.5	50	52	39	4	37 / 11	2.6	100	54 / 56	71
El Salvador *Republic of El Salvador*	San Salvador	21	5.1	223	41	35	3	34 / 10	2.4	60	57 / 60	7.
Equatorial Guinea *Republic of Equatorial Guinea*	Malabo	27	0.4	13	60	42	4	42 / 19	2.3	132	42 / 45	0.
Ethiopia	Addis Ababa	1 209	43.9	34	15	46	4	44 / 23	2.1	173	37 / 40	66
Fiji	Suva	18	0.7	34	37	37	3	30 / 5	2.5	21	68 / 72	0.
Finland *Republic of Finland*	Helsinki	333	4.9	14	62	20	12	13 / 9	0.4	7	69 / 77	5.
France *French Republic*	Paris	537	55.4	103	73	22	13	14 / 10	0.4	8	70 / 78	57
Gabon *Gabonese Republic*	Libreville	264	1.2	2	41	36	6	34 / 18	1.6	112	n.a. / n.a.	1.
Gambia *Republic of the Gambia*	Banjul	10	0.8	58	21	43	3	49 / 29	2.0	175	32 / 34	1.
Germany, East *German Democratic Republic*	East Berlin	107	16.7	161	77	19	14	14 / 13	0.04	10	69 / 75	17
Germany, West *Federal Republic of Germany*	Bonn	245	60.7	249	85	17	15	10 / 11	−0.2	10	69 / 76	58
Ghana *Republic of Ghana*	Accra	235	13.6	52	31	46	3	46 / 14	3.2	90	42 / 45	20.

neg. Negligible   n.a. Not available or not applicable

Persons Per Physician	Persons Per Radio	Persons Per Telephone	Persons Per Television	Persons Per Car	Population With Safe Water (%)	Literacy Rate (%)	Daily Newspapers Bought (per thousand population)	G.N.P. Per Capita (U.S.$)	Agricultural Land Cultivated/Pasture (%) (Single figure is total agricultural land.)	Labour Force in Agriculture (%)	People Compared to Arable Land (persons/km²)	Total Highways/Paved Highways (10³ km)	Tourists (10³)	Armed Forces (percent of total population)	Military Expenditures Per Capita (U.S.$)	Military Expenditures (percent of national budget)	Ratio of Military Expenditures to Educational Expenditures	Military Expenditures (percent of G.N.P.)
3 700	14	500	n.a.	7 500	9	12	11	250	12 / 10	53	28	18.7 / 2.96	100	0.6	5	12	1.6 :1	2.1
961	14	n.a.	606	780	n.a.	75	18	740	19 / 24	61	226	5.5 / 1.3	n.a.	1.6	60	11	1.93:1	10.7
5 260	7	60	35	50	77	37	26	1 442	3 / 16	50	44	80 / 46	250	0.35	36	6	0.3 :1	1.9
17 000	57	225	n.a.	47	n.a.	12	85	330	1 / 22	75(e.)	22	75 / 9	n.a.	0.48	n.a.	n.a.	n.a.	3.5
1 080	5	10	5	10	66	94	10	2 510	11 / 46	19	16	210 / 45	1 350	0.55	55	22	1.02:1	3.6
650	1	2.2	3	3	n.a.	99	370	11 460	6 / 58	14	3	845 / 210	800	0.51	207	9	0.4 :1	3
429	3	3	3	4	88	99	412	9 230	20 / 26	14	202	33.6 / 21	12 800	0.49	93	4	0.19:1	1.12
n.a.	3	4	9	8	n.a.	n.a.	140	4 153	1 / 0	9	1 500	3.35 / 1.4	1 100	0	n.a.	n.a.	n.a.	0
1 600	4	10	10	10	99	40	n.a.	10 480	5 / neg.	5	6 380	n.a. / 0.09	n.a.	0.7	141	n.a.	0.78:1	7.1
12 500	n.a.	912	n.a.	3 900	56	30	6	130	64 / neg.	74	960	7.3 / 4.1	45	0.04	1	n.a.	0.74:1	2
1 300	2	6	6	12	98	97	130	3 990	60 / 10	9	700	1.45 / 1.35	371	n.a.	4	n.a.	0.02:1	n.a.
475	2	3	4	3	88	99	418	11 202	28 / 24	3	685	105 / 53	7 623	0.97	322	9	0.54:1	2.9
n.a.	n.a.	n.a.	n.a.	n.a.	n.a.	89	n.a.	1 130	5 / neg.	45	133	2.55 / 0.3	n.a.	n.a.	n.a.	n.a.	n.a.	n.a.
35 000	24	n.a.	n.a.	220	34	20	3	290	11 / 68	90	375	3.4 / 0.7	n.a.	0.05	3	9.7	0.27:1	1.65
4 250	140	1 033	n.a.	n.a.	n.a.	8	n.a.	64	15	93	200	1.3 / 0.4	1.5	0.31	n.a.	0	n.a.	0
2 630	12	44	112	141	34	63	46	540	2 / 1	51	18	38 / 1.15	n.a.	0.45	18	<1	0.54:1	2.57
7 100	13	n.a.	n.a.	270	45	41	23	880	1 / 5	68	2	11 / 0.5	n.a.	0.05	22	6	0.44:1	n.a.
35 000	66	1 939	1 080	727	25	5	0.2	180	10 / 50	95	40	n.a. / n.a.	23	0.04	14	n.a.	1.12:1	3.4
1 700	8	20	12	15	55	75	45	1 870	4 / 13	36	58	1 600 / 80	634	0.17	18	9	0.32:1	1.56
n.a.	n.a.	6	n.a.	n.a.	n.a.	45	n.a.	21 300	3	n.a.	1 225	1.2 / 0.38	n.a.	1.37	n.a.	20	n.a.	n.a.
450	4	9	5	20	n.a.	95	214	3 450	41 / 11	24	144	31 / 6.7	5 100	1.7	77	5	0.64:1	8.66
5 300	50	1 000	n.a.	1 000	17	68	24	180	12 / 16	67	340	27 / 3.0	18	0.43	5	5	2.27:1	4
35 000	42	880	n.a.	862	n.a.	25	0.1	240	25 / 23	85	245	7.8 / 0.3	32	0.16	5	18	1.23:1	4.73
17 000	36	620	n.a.	235	32	19	6	820	11 / 25	80	55	29 / 2.3	96	0.07	7	9	0.5 :1	2.5
560	1	2	3	3	98	99	218	12 280	4 / 2	5	35	829 / 640.9	12 200	0.19	174	8	0.25:1	1.8
7 700	9	200	n.a.	1 000	n.a.	n.a.	n.a.	320	n.a.	n.a.	526	n.a. / n.a.	n.a.	n.a.	n.a.	5	n.a.	n.a.
20 000	32	n.a.	n.a.	250	n.a.	16	n.a.	280	10 / 30(e.)	88	40	21 / 0.29	n.a.	0.04	4	14	0.55:1	1.9
50 000	60	1 250	n.a.	810	26	27	n.a.	148	17 / 35	85	10	27.2 / 0.24	n.a.	0.12	8	33	2.64:1	7.76
1 600	6	20	15	30	70	90	n.a.	1 890	2 / 22	19	63	76 / 9.6	290	0.08	73	22	1.45:1	7.11
3 000	7	n.a.	1 000	20 160	n.a.	70	n.a.	300	11 / 11	85	309	835 / 260	n.a.	0.46	26	n.a.	1.73:1	10.9
2 000	8	20	15	53	64	82	21	1 410	28 / 11	27	120	52.1 / 8.2	826	0.25	7	8	0.33:1	1.35
7 100	18	133	450	123	38	53	n.a.	1 220	2 / 30	90	11	8.3 / 0.56	20	0.23	23	17	0.51:1	5.35
1 400	6	13	15	37	72	90	109	1 300	8 / 22	34	113	26 / 2.1	340	0	11	3	0.10:1	n.a.
1 100	5	35	12	125	55	96	n.a.	1 418	35 / 30	34	185	20.75 / 8.85	n.a.	1.2	49	9	0.58:1	11.9
1 200	3	7	10	12	95	86	96	3 670	47 / 10	20	120	9.7 / 4.6	400	3.1	39	10	0.52:1	5.47
393	4	5	4	8	78	99	286	5 000	42 / 14	12	225	74 / 62	14 400	1.22	143	7.6	0.99:1	5.4
500	3	2	3	4	99	99	367	11 540	64 / 8	8	175	66.48 / 64.55	16 231	0.67	259	n.a.	0.34:1	3.1
n.a.	33	136	142	42	15	n.a.	n.a.	662	1 / 10	n.a.	185	0.99 / 0.22	n.a.	2.44	n.a.	n.a.	n.a.	n.a.
2 000	30	40	15	51	55	62	45	1 175	18 / 17	47	200	11.4 / 5.8	300	0.36	17	n.a.	0.95:1	1.5
1 560	6	32	17	126	36	74	49	1 420	11 / 8	50	160	22.5 / 3.35	280	0.27	22	17	0.62:1	3.03
1 100	8	86	40	130	93	44	102	690	3 / neg.	50	1 550	47.05 / 12.35	1 004	0.79	91	n.a.	3.25:1	7.59
3 700	3	71	34	71	53	63	15	680	32 / 26	47	390	7.25 / 1.55	277	0.12	13	13	0.57:1	1.6
50 000	3	n.a.	n.a.	n.a.	n.a.	20	n.a.	370	n.a.	95	76	0.24 / 0.19	n.a.	1.47	25	14	0.25:1	5
100 000	150	396	1 110	925	8	15	2	120	10 / 55	86	43	10.75 / 3.33	36	0.14	5	33	1.98:1	3.61
2 000	2	17	n.a.	33	n.a.	75	108	1 780	16 / 44	44	220	n.a. / n.a.	188	0.27	n.a.	n.a.	n.a.	n.a.
625	2	2	2	4	72	99	517	10 710	8	6	180	73.5 / 31	259	0.83	102	5	0.21:1	1.79
609	3	3	3	3	97	99	214	10 480	35 / 26	9	170	1 568 / 730	28 000	0.93	350	17	66:1	4.62
3 125	7	60	73	39	1	19	n.a.	3 430	1 / 15	65	13	7 / 0.46	n.a.	0.19	78	5	0.77:1	1.88
12 500	10	223	n.a.	200	12	20	n.a.	312	55 / n.a.	78	105	2.39 / 0.32	n.a.	0	n.a.	n.a.	n.a.	0
510	3	5	3	7	82	99	517	5 335	43 / 15	10	267	127.6 / 47.5	1 100	0.80	218	9	0.97:1	4.80
490	3	3	3	3	99	99	404	11 400	33 / 23	4	465	399 / 161	8 900	0.80	350	18	0.71:1	3.7
10 000	12	181	227	378	35	30	35	420	19	60	90	32.2 / 6.1	58	0.17	5	n.a.	0.33:1	0.85

.) Estimate based on a compilation from a number of sources

Country	Capital	Area (10³km²)	Population (10⁶)	Population Density (persons/km²)	Urban Population (%)	Population Under 15 (%)	Population Over 64 (%)	Birth/Death Rate (per thousand)	Natural Increase (%)	Infant Mortality (per thousand)	Life Expectancy Male/Female (years)	Population Estimate
Greece *Hellenic Republic*	Athens	130	10.0	76	70	22	13	13 / 9	0.4	17	72 / 75	1
Grenada	St. George's	0.3	0.1	317	15	36	6	25 / 7	2.2	22	60 / 66	
Guatemala *Republic of Guatemala*	Guatemala	107	8.6	72	39	45	3	38 / 7	3.1	77	48 / 50	1
Guinea *People's Revolutionary Republic of Guinea*	Conakry	243	6.2	27	22	43	3	47 / 24	2.3	160	39 / 43	
Guinea-Bissau *Republic of Guinea-Bissau*	Bissau	35	0.9	15	27	44	5	41 / 22	1.9	143	37 / 40	
Guyana *Cooperative Republic of Guyana*	Georgetown	210	0.8	4	32	37	4	28 / 6	2.2	35	59 / 63	
Haiti *Republic of Haiti*	Port-au-Prince	27	5.9	198	26	39	6	36 / 13	2.3	108	47 / 50	
Honduras *Republic of Honduras*	Tegucigalpa	112	4.6	35	36	48	3	42 / 10	3.2	82	53 / 56	
Hong Kong	Victoria	1	5.7	5 700	92	24	7	14 / 5	0.9	9	72 / 77	
Hungary *Hungarian People's Republic*	Budapest	93	10.6	118	54	22	12	12 / 14	−0.2	20	66 / 72	10
Iceland *Republic of Iceland*	Reykjavik	103	0.2	2	88	27	10	17 / 7	1.0	6	73 / 79	0
India *Republic of India*	New Delhi	3 168	785	223	22	39	3	35 / 13	2.2	110	42 / 41	1 01
Indonesia *Republic of Indonesia*	Jakarta	1 903	168.4	80	20	40	3	34 / 13	2.1	84	48 / 48	220
Iran *Islamic Republic of Iran*	Tehrān	1 648	46.6	21	50	44	4	42 / 12	3	115	57 / 57	68
Iraq *Republic of Iraq*	Baghdad	438	16.0	30	72	49	4	46 / 13	3.3	77	51 / 54	24
Ireland	Dublin	69	3.6	49	58	31	11	18 / 9	0.9	10	69 / 74	
Israel *State of Israel*	Jerusalem	89	4.2	46	89	33	9	24 / 7	1.7	14	71 / 74	5
Italy *Italian Republic*	Rome	301	57.2	180	72	21	14	10 / 9	0.1	11	69 / 75	58
Ivory Coast *Republic of the Ivory Coast*	Abidjan	322	10.5	29	42	45	2	46 / 16	3.0	110	42 / 45	16
Jamaica	Kingston	11	2.3	205	54	37	6	24 / 5	1.8	21	62 / 66	
Japan	Tokyo	372	121.5	311	76	22	10	13 / 6	0.7	6	72 / 77	128
Jordan *Hashemite Kingdom of Jordan*	'Ammān	96	3.7	35	60	52	3	44 / 7	3.7	63	53 / 53	
Kampuchea *People's Republic of Kampuchea*	Phnum Penh	181	6.4	40	16	33	3	41 / 18	2.3	160	44 / 47	
Kenya *Republic of Kenya*	Nairobi	582	21.0	34	16	53	2	54 / 12	4.2	72	52 / 52	36
Korea, North *Democratic People's Republic of Korea*	P'yŏngyang	123	20.5	160	60	38	4	30 / 7	2.3	30	59 / 63	27
Korea, South *Republic of Korea*	Sŏul	98	43	427	57	32	4	23 / 7	1.6	30	63 / 67	52
Kuwait *State of Kuwait*	Kuwait	24	1.8	54	90	39	1	34 / 3	3.2	23	66 / 71	
Laos *Lao People's Democratic Republic*	Vientiane	237	3.7	16	16	42	3	41 / 18	2.3	129	39 / 42	
Lebanon *Republic of Lebanon*	Beirut	10	2.7	320	76	38	5	29 / 9	2.1	48	61 / 65	
Lesotho *Kingdom of Lesotho*	Maseru	30	1.6	52	6	41	4	42 / 17	2.5	112	46 / 44	
Liberia *Republic of Liberia*	Monrovia	112	2.3	19	39	47	3	48 / 17	3.1	142	46 / 44	
Libya *Socialist People's Libyan Arab Jamahiriya*	Tripoli	1 760	3.9	2	76	47	2	44 / 11	3.3	1100	51 / 54	
Luxembourg *Grand Duchy of Luxembourg*	Luxembourg	2.5	0.4	160	79	19	14	12.0 / 11.9	0.1	12	67 / 74	0
Madagascar *Democratic Republic of Madagascar*	Antananarivo	594	10.3	18	22	44	3	46 / 18	2.1	67	46 / 46	15
Malawi *Republic cf Malawi*	Lilongwe	119	7.3	55	12	48	2	53 / 21	3.2	158	41 / 44	1
Malaysia	Kuala Lumpur	352	15.8	46	32	37	4	31 / 7	2.4	31	66 / 71	2
Maldives *Republic of Maldives*	Male	0.3	0.2	660	27	45	2	45 / 14	3.1	81	53 / 52	0
Mali *Republic of Mali*	Bamako	1 204	7.9	7	17	45	3	49 / 23	2.6	180	40 / 43	11
Malta *Republic of Malta*	Valletta	0.3	0.4	1 030	85	24	9	17 / 9	0.8	12	68 / 73	0
Mauritania *Islamic Republic of Mauritania*	Nouakchott	1 031	1.9	1.5	35	46	3	50 / 21	2.9	137	39 / 43	
Mauritius	Port Louis	1.8	1	550	44	33	4	21 / 7	1.5	25	61 / 65	1
Mexico *The United Mexican States*	Mexico City	1 967	81.7	42	70	42	4	32 / 6	2.6	55	63 / 66	112
Mongolia *Mongolian People's Republic*	Ulaanbaatar	1 565	1.9	1	50	41	3	35 / 10	2.5	46	59 / 62	2
Morocco *Kingdom of Morocco*	Rabat	660	23.7	36	40	46	3	37 / 11	2.6	97	51 / 55	32
Mozambique *People's Republic of Mozambique*	Maputo	785	14	17	13	44	3	46 / 21	2.5	153	42 / 45	21
Namibia	Windhoek	824	1.1	1.3	51	44	3	43 / 14	2.9	110	47 / 50	1
Nepal *Kingdom of Nepal*	Kathmandu	141	17.4	112	5	42	3	42 / 18	2.4	150	42 / 45	24
Netherlands *Kingdom of the Netherlands*	The Hague/Amsterdam	34	14.5	415	88	20	12	12 / 8	0.4	11	72 / 78	15
New Zealand	Wellington	269	3.4	12	85	26	10	16 / 8	0.8	12	69 / 75	3
Nicaragua *Republic of Nicaragua*	Managua	148	3.3	19	53	48	3	44 / 10	3.4	76	51 / 54	5
Niger *Republic of Niger*	Niamey	1 186	6.7	6	13	46	3	50 / 23	2.7	146	40 / 42	11
Nigeria *Federal Republic of Nigeria*	Lagos	924	105.4	108	28	47	2	50 / 20	3	135	48 / 48	160

neg. Negligible   n.a. Not available or not applica

Persons Per Physician	Persons Per Radio	Persons Per Telephone	Persons Per Television	Persons Per Car	Population With Safe Water (%)	Literacy Rate (%)	Daily Newspapers Bought (per thousand population)	G.N.P. Per Capita (U.S.$)	Agricultural Land Cultivated/Pasture (%) (Single figure is total agricultural land.)	Labour Force in Agriculture (%)	People Compared to Arable Land (persons/km²)	Total Highways/ Paved Highways (10³ km)	Tourists (10³)	Armed Forces (percent of total population)	Military Expenditures Per Capita (U.S.$)	Military Expenditures (percent of national budget)	Ratio of Military Expenditures to Educational Expenditures	Military Expenditures (percent of G.N.P.)
452	3	4	6	14	65	95	68	3 910	29 / 40	29	110	38.95 / 16.1	5 200	1.71	220	18	2.96:1	6
n.a.	5	20	n.a.	28	n.a.	n.a.	n.a.	830	44 / 4	31	700	1 / 0.6	32	0	n.a.	0	n.a.	n.a.
2 500	25	89	48	49	39	47	25	1 110	14 / 10	53	285	25.5 / 2.75	444	0.14	9	n.a.	0.65:1	1.08
17 000	47	n.a.	n.a.	560	14	21	2	300	3 / 20(e.)	84	75	7.05 / 5.1	n.a.	0.10	4	n.a.	0.5 :1	0.55
n.a.	58	n.a.	n.a.	n.a.	n.a.	19	11	190	8	86	52	3.3 / 0.45	n.a.	0.8	n.a.	7	n.a.	0.89
4 000	4	30	n.a.	30	84	95	63	563	1 / 3	30	61	5.7 / 0.5	1	0.24	10	5	0.21:1	2.15
16 000	58	309	392	301	12	22	20	290	31 / 18	79	425	3.2 / 0.6	96	0.11	2	8	1.3 :1	1.25
730	23	194	77	180	41	57	37	1 250	7 / 30	56	104	7.3 / 1.5	1	0.13	11	0	0.60:1	2.24
626	n.a.	n.a.	n.a.	n.a.	96	99	n.a.	6 070	14	3	62 675	0.96 / 0.66	2 300	0	n.a.	4	n.a.	0
435	4	10	4	12	44	98	243	2 150	60 / 14	23	160	97.5 / 24.3	7 194	0.96	79	0	0.55:1	2.59
550	4	2	5	3	99	99	554	10 240	neg. / 22	10	10	12.34 / 1.46	72	0	0	16	n.a.	0
4 000	45	303	2 440	848	31	36	20	260	50 / 5	74	381	1 330 / 415	640	0.15	5	13	1.04:1	4.09
16 000	30	469	467	317	11	62	20	550	12	61	524	94 / 26.6	456	0.18	11	n.a.	1.94:1	3.95
2 500	17	41	20	41	51	50	14	1 853	16 / 14	37	66	82 / 36	690	0.9	261	n.a.	2.27:1	10.32
2 350	10	41	31	87	76	30	16	2 214	18 / 10	50	145	21 / 6.5	721	0.98	159	3	2.28:1	8.42
890	4	6	5	5	73	99	220	5 000	17 / 51	23	60	92.3 / 87.5	566	0.47	59	n.a.	0.25:1	1.95
390	6	4	9	13	99	88	231	5 300	20 / 40	7	321	n.a. / 4.6	893	4.43	839	n.a.	2.76:1	32.48
500	4	4	5	4	86	94	97	6 400	50 / 17	15	326	288 / 254.6	14 836	0.65	112	n.a.	0.52:1	2.53
25 000	15	150	34	103	14	41	13	810	8 / 52	75	72	45.6 / 2.46	n.a.	0.06	11	0	0.16:1	2.73
3 800	4	20	20	n.a.	86	86	49	1 363	21 / 23	28	463	11.3 / 7.7	265	0.09	9	5	0.11:1	0.78
840	2	2	4	6	98	99	546	10 200	16 / 3	12	2 150	1 100 / 360	890	0.22	80	22	0.15:1	1.39
2 500	6	62	26	58	77	54	29	1 720	11	23	223	6.35 / 4.9	937	2.3	87	n.a.	2.78:1	14
16 000	70	108	220	283	45	40	n.a.	90	16	85(e.)	150	13.7 / 2.62	16	0.77	n.a.	8	n.a.	13.6
2 600	35	125	360	157	17	54	29	340	13	23	275	51 / 4.6	938	0.05	12	15	0.74:1	5.17
2 500	n.a.	n.a.	n.a.	n.a.	n.a.	85	n.a.	600	17	48	808	21 / 0.36	n.a.	2.66	63	33	2.43:1	12.7
2 000	8	20	18	328	66	91	197	2 010	22 / 1	43	1 725	80 / 33	950	1.64	75	7	2.31:1	10.16
800	3	9	7	5	89	60	159	16 200	neg.	2	1 075	2.6 / 2.3	n.a.	0.97	613	n.a.	1.35:1	6.08
17 000	19	n.a.	n.a.	265	41	41	n.a.	60	8	76	217	18 / 1.3	23	1.28	10	26	5.8 :1	11.2
1 500	2	n.a.	7	88	92	76	93	962	27	18	904	7.4 / 6.2	1 555	0.44	58	6	n.a.	3.43
8 500	61	n.a.	n.a.	1	17	41	25	560	15	87	60	4 / 0.23	n.a.	0.19	n.a.	n.a.	n.a.	0.99
8 400	7	223	213	158	15	18	4	480	20	74	320	8 / 0.66	n.a.	0.24	5	neg.	0.18:1	0.92
1 000	27	n.a.	300	12	87	40	26	8 460	6	20	33	16.3 / 7.75	126	0.89	156	6	0.4 :1	2.64
820	2	2	4	3	98	98	456	14 620	25 / 27	6	n.a.	5.05 / 4.91	n.a.	0.15	103	n.a.	0.14:1	1.28
10 000	15	321	1 150	160	25	45	n.a.	360	5 / 58	90	24	27.5 / 4.55	9	0.06	6	n.a.	0.46:1	1.9
50 000	46	266	n.a.	588	n.a.	25	3	231	10 / 21	86	150	12.68 / 1.88	40	0.02	4	16	0.74:1	3.02
8 000	10	39	27	26	34	75	75	1 870	20 / neg.	48	220	25.25 / 16.75	1 300	0.47	45	20	0.63:1	5.56
15 500	43	n.a.	n.a.	n.a.	n.a.	36	n.a.	142	n.a.	n.a.	3 800	0 / 0	15	n.a.	n.a.	n.a.	n.a.	n.a.
20 000	269	n.a.	n.a.	n.a.	n.a.	9	n.a.	150	20	80	21	15.7 / 1.7	19	0.06	4	22	0.84:1	4.5
756	6	5	6	6	74	85	n.a.	3 480	45	n.a.	2 500	1.27 / 1.16	361	0.8	24	3.5	0.32:1	1.54
16 000	18	n.a.	n.a.	38	17	17	n.a.	480	1 / 10	85	4	6.1 / 0.56	20	0.06	30	22	1.83:1	8.84
2 100	5	33	25	41	60	80	94	1 160	50 / neg.	29	829	1.79 / 1.64	75	0.3	2	3.7	0.03:1	0.7
1 630	5	24	15	67	62	80	55	2 180	12 / 40	41	71	208.1 / 62.93	3 338	0.14	1.8	1(e.)	0.11:1	0.85
486	15	45	472	n.a.	n.a.	89	75	705	1 / 70	52	1	n.a. / n.a.	n.a.	1.55	76	12	1.5 :1	10.85
11 000	15	105	42	63	51	24	7	717	32	50	110	56 / 25	1 428	0.31	42	19	1 :1	3.65
17 000	57	246	n.a.	146	n.a.	33	4	212	1 / 29	74	23	26.5 / 4.35	n.a.	0.17	9	22	2.6 :1	4.13
n.a.	n.a.	n.a.	n.a.	n.a.	n.a.	n.a.	n.a.	1 670	n.a.	n.a.	n.a.	n.a. / n.a.	n.a.	n.a.	n.a.	n.a.	n.a.	n.a.
35 000	100	1 600	n.a.	n.a.	8	19	6	160	16 / 14	93	360	4.2 / 1.75	129	0.15	1	5	0.6 :1	1.26
625	3	2.5	4	3	97	99	290	9 870	70	6	700	104.8 / 86.35	2 939	0.78	304	10	0.41:1	3.99
720	1	2	4	3	93	98	265	7 710	3 / 50	14	22	92.62 / 46.72	390	0.39	93	3.6	0.3 :1	2.2
1 625	21	48	30	84	56	87	51	884	7 / 7	53	52	18.2 / 1.58	207	0.29	28	11	1.17:1	2.5
50 000	40	711	n.a.	585	27	5	1	240	3 / 17	91	47	7.65 / 1.9	n.a.	0.04	2	9	0.17:1	3.29
16 000	14	16	771	540	n.a.	25	630	935	13 / 11	75	180	107.2 / 25.2	7	0.3	28	9.7	0.83:1	6.36

) Estimate based on a compilation from a number of sources

Country	Capital	Area (10³km²)	Population (10⁶)	Population Density (persons/km²)	Urban Population (%)	Population Under 15 (%)	Population Over 64 (%)	Birth/Death Rate (per thousand)	Natural Increase (%)	Infant Mortality (per thousand)	Life Expectancy Male/Female (years)	Population Estimate For The Year 2000 (10⁶)
Norway *Kingdom of Norway*	Oslo	324	4.2	13	71	21	15	12 / 10	0.2	9	72 / 78	4.2
Oman *Sultanate of Oman*	Muscat	260	1.3	3	7	45	3	47 / 14	3.3	117	n.a. / n.a.	2.0
Pakistan *Islamic Republic of Pakistan*	Islāmābād	804	102	121	28	46	3	43 / 15	2.8	120	54 / 49	149
Panama *Republic of Panama*	Panama	77	2.2	25	51	39	4	26 / 5	2.1	29	64 / 67	2.9
Papua New Guinea	Port Moresby	463	3.4	7	13	43	2	40 / 17	2.3	91	51 / 51	4.5
Paraguay *Republic of Paraguay*	Asuncion	407	4.1	8	43	41	4	35 / 7	2.8	45	60 / 63	6
Peru *Republic of Peru*	Lima	1 285	20.2	9	67	42	4	35 / 10	2.5	100	56 / 57	28
Philippines *Republic of the Philippines*	Manila	300	58.1	181	36	41	3	33 / 8	2.5	55	60 / 60	75
Poland *Polish People's Republic*	Warsaw	313	37.5	114	57	24	10	19 / 10	0.9	20	66 / 74	41
Portugal *Portuguese Republic*	Lisbon	92	10.1	108	30	24	12	14 / 9	0.5	20	67 / 72	11
Qatar *State of Qatar*	Doha	11	0.3	20	86	34	1	33 / 5	2.9	53	n.a. / n.a.	0.5
Romania *Socialist Republic of Romania*	Bucharest	238	22.6	96	48	25	10	14 / 10	0.9	24	69 / 72	24
Rwanda *Republic of Rwanda*	Kigali	26	6.5	221	4	47	3	54 / 16	3.8	127	42 / 45	11.1
Samoa (Western)	Apia	2.8	0.2	71	21	44	3	38 / 8	3.0	40	61 / 66	0.3
Saudi Arabia *Kingdom of Saudi Arabia*	Ar Riyād	2 400	11.5	5	70	43	3	42 / 12	3.0	100	51 / 54	18
Senegal *Republic of Senegal*	Dakar	197	6.9	33	42	44	3	48 / 19	2.9	112	41 / 43	10
Seychelles *Republic of Seychelles*	Victoria	0.4	0.1	18	37	37	7	26 / 8	1.8	14	62 / 68	0.1
Sierra Leone *Republic of Sierra Leone*	Freetown	73	3.7	53	28	41	3	47 / 30	1.7	180	44 / 47	4.8
Singapore *Republic of Singapore*	Singapore	0.6	2.6	4 200	100	25	5	16 / 5	1.1	10	65 / 70	3
Solomon Islands	Honiara	30	0.3	8	9	48	3	47 / 10	3.7	52	n.a. / n.a.	0.4
Somalia *Somali Democratic Republic*	Mogadishu	246	7.8	26	30	45	4	47 / 22	2.5	155	39 / 42	12
South Africa *Republic of South Africa*	Pretoria	1 141	33.2	29	53	38	4	33 / 10	2.3	86	57 / 59	45
Spain *Spanish State*	Madrid	505	38.8	75	76	26	11	13 / 8	0.5	10	70 / 75	42
Sri Lanka *Democratic Socialist Republic of Sri Lanka*	Colombo	66	16.6	222	27	36	4	26 / 6	2.0	34	65 / 67	20
Sudan *Democratic Republic of the Sudan*	Khartoum	2 506	22.9	9	25	44	3	46 / 17	2.9	118	62 / 66	34
Suriname *Republic of Suriname*	Paramaribo	163	0.4	3	56	40	4	28 / 8	2	30	62 / 67	0.5
Swaziland *Kingdom of Swaziland*	Mbabane	17	0.7	42	26	45	3	47 / 17	3.0	130	42 / 45	1.0
Sweden *Kingdom of Sweden*	Stockholm	412	8.4	20	83	18	17	11.7 / 11	0.07	8	72 / 78	8
Switzerland *Swiss Confederation*	Bern	41	6.5	152	58	18	14	11.9 / 9.2	0.3	7	72 / 76	6.5
Syria *Syrian Arab Republic*	Damascus	186	10.5	48	50	47	4	47 / 9	3.8	62	55 / 59	17
Taiwan	Taipei	36	19.6	525	77	30	5	20 / 5	1.5	9	66 / 72	22
Tanzania *United Republic of Tanzania*	Dodoma/Dar es Salaam	942	22.4	21	17	46	4	50 / 15	3.5	115	50 / 50	36
Thailand *Kingdom of Thailand*	Bangkok	514	52.8	103	17	37	3	28 / 8	2.0	48	60 / 61	65
Togo *Republic of Togo*	Lomé	56	3.0	55	20	45	3	48 / 17	3.1	107	45 / 46	4.8
Trinidad and Tobago *Republic of Trinidad and Tobago*	Port-of-Spain	5	1.2	240	23	33	5	25 / 7	1.8	24	64 / 68	1.5
Tunisia *Republic of Tunisia*	Tunis	164	7.2	43	52	43	4	33 / 6	2.7	85	54 / 56	9.4
Turkey *Republic of Turkey*	Ankara	780	52.3	65	47	39	5	35 / 10	2.5	92	60 / 60	69
Uganda *Republic of Uganda*	Kampala	39	15.2	370	14	49	3	50 / 17	3.4	112	48 / 52	25
Union of Soviet Socialist Republics (U.S.S.R.)	Moscow	22 402	280	13	65	25	10	20 / 11	0.9	31	64 / 74	310
United Arab Emirates	Abu Dhabi	92	1.4	12	81	26	2	27 / 4	2.3	45	68 / 66	1.9
United Kingdom *U.K. of Great Britain and Northern Ireland*	London	230	56.6	243	90	20	15	13 / 11	0.2	11	68 / 73	57
United States *United States of America*	Washington	9 363	241	26	74	22	12	16 / 9	0.7	11	69 / 76	268
Uruguay *Oriental Republic of Uruguay*	Montevideo	187	3	16	84	27	10	18 / 9	0.9	30	69 / 73	3.4
Venezuela *Republic of Venezuela*	Caracas	912	17.8	22	75	40	3	33 / 6	2.7	39	66 / 66	25
Vietnam *Socialist Republic of Vietnam*	Hanoi	330	62.0	182	19	41	4	34 / 9	2.5	60	53 / 53	85
Yemen *Yemen Arab Republic*	San'a	195	6.3	33	15	47	4	49 / 18	3.1	135	41 / 41	10
Yemen, Democratic *People's Democratic Republic of Yemen*	Aden	160	2.3	12	37	49	4	47 / 17	3.0	135	44 / 44	3.4
Yugoslavia *Socialist Federal Republic of Yugoslavia*	Belgrade	256	23.2	90	47	25	8	16 / 9	0.7	30	66 / 71	25
Zaire *Republic of Zaire*	Kinshasa	2 344	31.3	13	34	46	3	42 / 14	2.8	106	42 / 46	47
Zambia *Republic of Zambia*	Lusaka	291	7.1	26	43	47	3	48 / 15	3.3	88	46 / 49	11.1
Zimbabwe	Harare	151	9.0	61	24	51	2	47 / 12	3.5	80	53 / 56	15

neg. Negligible   n.a. Not available or not applicable

Persons Per Physician	Persons Per Radio	Persons Per Telephone	Persons Per Television	Persons Per Car	Population With Safe Water (%)	Literacy Rate (%)	Daily Newspapers Bought (per thousand population)	G.N.P. Per Capita (U.S.$)	Agricultural Land Cultivated/Pasture (%) (Single figure is total agricultural land.)	Labour Force in Agriculture (%)	People Compared to Arable Land (persons/km²)	Total Highways/Paved Highways (10³ km)	Tourists (10³)	Armed Forces (percent of total population)	Military Expenditures Per Capita (U.S.$)	Military Expenditures (percent of national budget)	Ratio of Military Expenditures to Educational Expenditures	Military Expenditures (percent of G.N.P.)
575	3	3	4	4	98	99	430	13 980	3 / 2	17	450	78.12 / 17.7	448	0.94	322	8.7	0.44:1	3.9
2 000	n.a.	70	n.a.	n.a.	52	33	n.a.	6 230	neg.	83	89	2.82 / 0.01	n.a.	2.68	914	n.a.	9.71:1	32.46
760	65	243	n.a.	400	25	23	11	249	24 / 16	60	365	87.5 / 26.85	221	0.5	12	24	2.54:1	6.64
1 300	8	12	10	30	77	79	79	2 110	4 / 11	40	109	7.7 / 2.5	361	0.11	9	n.a.	0.14:1	1.48
16 000	n.a.	100	n.a.	186	20	32	9	760	neg.	53	700	19.2 / 0.65	n.a.	0.12	9	3.7	0.21:1	1.65
1 340	15	77	40	223	13	82	39	1 363	2 / 24	49	20	8.8 / 1.1	3	0.48	13	15	0.98:1	1.96
1 600	9	45	26	56	47	72	51	1 080	2 / 14	43	60	52.4 / 5.4	264	0.4	33	n.a.	1.91:1	2.1
3 150	26	101	68	153	50	79	20	750	30 / 5	57	540	120 / 18.55	730	0.18	11	n.a.	0.98:1	3.67
675	4	12	5	17	47	98	240	3 750	49 / 10	28	190	305.9 / 65	10 544	0.77	99	n.a.	0.98:1	5.72
780	5	8	13	10	n.a.	72	54	2 024	48 / 6	31	245	44.7 / 40	1 409	0.6	64	10	0.88:1	3.9
980	5	7	n.a.	n.a.	97	20	n.a.	21 360	neg.	10	442	0.81 / 0.45	n.a.	1.2	1 194	7.3	0.6 :1	n.a.
790	7	16	8	154	n.a.	98	171	2 986	44 / 19	40	150	80.4 / 28.5	3 684	0.75	56	3.5	0.54:1	4.09
7 000	65	1 310	n.a.	960	68	25	0.1	164	33 / 34	91	360	9 / 0.32	n.a.	0.09	3	15	0.74:1	2.06
2 884	3	40	n.a.	80	n.a.	98	n.a.	320	n.a.	67	131	n.a. / n.a.	22	n.a.	n.a.	n.a.	n.a.	n.a.
1 700	44	60	70	170	97	16	20	12 220	neg. / 1	40	12	30.1 / 16.5	n.a.	0.65	1 004	n.a.	1.98:1	22.64
50 000	18	150	300	146	n.a.	10	5	440	12 / 28	70	72	13.9 / 2.9	168	0.11	10	7	0.9 :1	3.41
2 857	5	14	n.a.	23	96	58	65	2 430	54 / neg.	19	1 320	0.22 / 0.15	50	n.a.	n.a.	neg.	n.a.	n.a.
16 500	58	260	400	233	12	15	18	330	6 / 27	75	130	7.4 / 1.2	24	0.06	2	8.5	0.23:1	1.73
1 610	6	6	7	17	96	76	215	6 660	22 / neg.	2	30 250	2.22 / 1.81	1 506	0.98	186	16.8	2.22:1	6.18
n.a.	20	110	n.a.	n.a.	96	n.a.	n.a.	391	n.a.	n.a.	260	0.84 / 0.25	n.a.	n.a.	n.a.	neg.	n.a.	n.a.
35 000	53	n.a.	n.a.	5 520	38	6	2	250	0.3 / 12.7	60	13	13.5 / 1.8	neg.	0.96	12	28	1.75:1	10.19
12 000	12	14	n.a.	14	50	66		2 240	12	30	30	203 / 58	n.a.	0.19	80	17.5	1.2 :1	5.01
675	4	4	5	6	78	93	128	4 770	41 / 27	19	120	146 / 69.2	34 266	0.82	67	23.8	0.79:1	3.62
6 700	20	223	n.a.	150	19	81	n.a.	330	25	53	600	66.2 / 24.4	154	0.06	1	6	0.28:1	0.77
2 000	12	300	190	530	50	20	2	442	3 / 10	86	65	10.55 / 0.67	37	0.21	14	n.a.	3.2 :1	5.67
2 030	3	19	11	15	n.a.	65	74	3 310	neg.	29	760	2.5 / 0.5	55	0.26	n.a.	n.a.	n.a.	n.a.
9 000	10	60	n.a.	67	37	36	10	870	15 / 73	60	40	2.8 / 0.4	n.a.	0.09	2	n.a.	0.05:1	0.89
560	3	2	3	3	99	99	528	14 801	7 / 2	5	220	404 / 73.4	n.a.	1	365	8	0.39:1	3.8
498	3	1.5	4	4	96	99	414	16 250	10 / 43	5	310	62.15 / 62.15	8 341	0.5	280	19.5	0.4 :1	2.52
2 560	6	46	36	145	71	45	7	1 790	48 / 29	51	66	17 / 12.05	681	2.09	147	n.a.	2.67:1	14.8
3 000	6	11	6	102	n.a.	85	83	2 172	24 / 6	34	n.a.	16.9 / 7.8	1270	2.75	106	41.5	1.92:1	6.9
5 000	56	235	n.a.	378	39	37	8	229	15 / 31	90	38	34.23 / 3.6	93	0.1	10	n.a.	0.88:1	5.23
8 000	9	127	61	155	25	82	21	820	24	76	275	34.98 / 16.25	1 220	0.4	18	18.6	1.06:1	5.25
16 000	49	540	n.a.	195	16	18	3	273	15 / 35	78	162	7 / 1.24	n.a.	0.05	8	9.8	0.37:1	2.55
1 850	6	15	13	9	93	92	125	6 860	26 / 2	13	700	7.9 / 3.6	158	0.09	11	4.8	0.07:1	1.51
25 000	8	44	31	62	49	40	36	1 290	28 / 23	45	89	17.14 / 7.95	1 016	0.25	30	5.7	0:48:1	2.68
1 920	11	35	26	197	68	60	n.a.	1 251	35 / 25	56	85	60 / 21	1 661	1.13	64	16	0.91:1	5.11
5 000	53	275	186	490	35	25	3	220	21	90	135	6.76 / 1.94	10	0.16	11	n.a.	1.12:1	8.01
289	2	14	4	40	n.a.	99	396	6 760	10 / 16	23	44	1 565 / 330	4 399	1.44	394	6.2	2.08:1	12.66
770	21	10	n.a.	n.a.	n.a.	21	8	23 770	neg.	5	470	n.a. / 0.78	n.a.	3.6	836	36	2.39:1	0.55
653	1	2	3	3	99	99	410	9 180	30 / 50	2	304	358.5 / 358.5	11 490	0.6	262	n.a.	0.88:1	5.25
568	0.5	1	2	2	98	99	287	14 080	19 / 27	2	53	6 366 / 6 366	18 609	1.36	499	12.2	0.88:1	5.98
719	2	14	10	23	92	94	n.a.	2 500	11 / 73	8	19	49.9 / 6.7	491	1.02	40	14	1.22:1	2.58
910	4	22	13	20	75	82	178	3 830	4 / 18	20	70	59 / 21.9	652	0.32	44	6.7	0.29:1	1.81
5 550	20	n.a.	n.a.	n.a.	14	75	5	170	14 / neg.	70	516	41.1 / 5.5	n.a.	1.42	18	n.a.	5 :1	4.21
12 500	66	n.a.	n.a.	n.a.	4	12	10	550	1 / 19	55	63	3.5 / 0.48	n.a.	0.29	52	22	5.38:1	3.09
9 300	20	n.a.	63	168	93	20	12	520	<1 / 6(e.)	28	21	5.3 / 0.33	18	0.92	43	22.4	3.25:1	11.2
763	5	14	6	12	n.a.	85	96	2 490	32 / 25	48	160	105 / 45	5 625	1.1	105	6.2	0.77:1	4.87
50 000	13	645	4 430	310	19	30	9	170	1 / 13	78	97	169 / 2.66	24	0.13	10	n.a.	1.55:1	4.09
20 000	51	104	225	61	42	49	20	580	5 / 10	57	17	35.8 / 5.4	56	0.12	41	n.a.	1.7 :1	3.16
10 800	26	37	100	41	n.a.	30	12	740	6 / 34	35	104	79 / 8	n.a.	0.06	31	n.a.	1.63:1	4.74

) Estimate based on a compilation from a number of sources

GLOSSARY

Aboriginal rights Rights claimed by Native peoples because they are the original inhabitants of a country

Absolute monarchy A form of government that has a hereditary chief of state with full powers over government and its operation

Abyssal plain A large, generally flat area of the ocean floor at a depth of 4000 m or more

Acid rain A type of precipitation created by pollution of the atmosphere. Sulphur dioxide and nitric oxides combine with water vapour to produce a mild acid which falls and kills vegetation, fish, and wildlife.

Adhesion A region added on to a previous treaty

Agricultural Land Reserve An area of land set aside for agricultural uses only (grazing or crops). British Columbia has developed these reserves to prevent urban growth from taking over prime farm land.

Air mass A large body of air with generally the same temperature and moisture conditions throughout. It usually develops over large bodies of water (warm and moist or cool and moist) or over large land areas (hot and dry or cold and dry).

Alluvial soil An azonal soil developed from the materials deposited by moving water. Alluvial soil is often found in the delta areas of rivers. It is usually young in age, rich in minerals, and therefore suitable for agriculture.

Alpine Referring to high altitudes

Annexation The addition of property to a town, city, province, or country

Anthracite A high quality coal which is black or blue-black in colour, very hard, and approximately 90 percent carbon

Anticline An arch-like upfolding of rock which results from pressure in the earth's crust

Aquifer An underground layer of porous rock, such as sandstone or limestone, that contains water and allows it to percolate. When blocked by nonporous layers, an aquifer may become a groundwater reservoir.

Arable land Land suitable for ploughing and cultivation. (Does not include pastureland or forested areas not capable of being used for growing crops.)

Arctic Referring to high latitudes

Arctic Climatic Region A climatic region in Canada's Far North, characterized by low precipitation, very cold winters, and cool summers. The average temperature is rarely above freezing.

Armaments The military forces and equipment of a nation. The term is also used to describe the arms and military equipment of a ship, plane, tank, fort, or other military vehicle or installation.

Arms Weapons. For example, machine guns and rifles.

Assemblyman An elected member of the provincial legislature in Prince Edward Island

Asthenosphere A layer in the earth's interior, 80 to 250 km beneath the surface. The asthenosphere is partially molten and has some movement caused by convection currents within the earth's interior.

Atmosphere The envelope of gases that surrounds the earth, containing mostly nitrogen, oxygen, and carbon dioxide. Other gases and water vapour are also present.

Azonal soil One of the three major soil orders. Soils in this group are usually very young therefore distinct horizons have not yet developed.

Badlands An area in a semi-arid environment where deep gullies and ravines have been formed by water erosion. In Canada, the largest area of badlands is in southern Alberta.

Bank Rate (Bank of Canada) The interest rate charged by the Bank of Canada on loans it makes to chartered banks. The rate is usually set each Thursday. As the bank rate changes, so does the rate charged by chartered banks and other financial institutions.

Bankruptcy A legal term defining the state of the finances of an individual or a company unable to repay debts

Barometric pressure Atmospheric pressure measured by a barometer

Barrel A unit in the imperial system equal to approximately 160 L or 0.16 mL^3

Bathymetric contour See *Isobath*

Bathymetry The science of measuring the depth of a body of water (ocean, sea, or lake)

Bedrock The solid material, usually rock, which lies beneath soil

Beothuk Indians An Indian group that once lived in Newfoundland but is now extinct. Disease and conflicts destroyed the Beothuks early in the nineteenth century.

Billion In North America, one thousand million; elsewhere in the world, one million million. It is preferable to use the words *one thousand million* to avoid confusion.

Biosphere The part of the earth that supports life. It consists of two layers, the atmosphere and the lithosphere (crust).

Birth rate The number of live births per 1000 people, usually measured over a period of one year

Bituminous coal A type of coal which is dark grey in colour, medium hard, and approximately 80 percent carbon

Boreal Referring to the coniferous forest area in the Northern Hemisphere (Canada, the U.S.S.R., and Scandinavia). It means "of the north".

Boreal Climatic Region A climatic region that stretches across Canada, south of the Arctic Climatic Region. Moderate precipitation and a broad temperature range are the key characteristics.

Broadleaf trees Trees with leaves rather than needles. In Canada, most broadleaf trees lose their leaves in winter. Examples include oak, maple, birch, and poplar.

Cabinet A political group made up of members of parliament, or other people chosen by the Prime Minister. The federal cabinet develops policies to govern the country. Each cabinet member is usually responsible for a specific Ministry within the governmental organization.

Calorie (cal) An imperial unit of energy defined as the amount of heat required to raise the temperature of one kilogram of water one celsius degree. 1 cal = 4.187 J (joules).

Cambium The layer of tissue in trees between the bark and the wood, from which new wood and bark are developed

Cambrian period The first geological period of the Paleozoic Era, extending from about 600 000 000 to 500 000 000 (a) years ago

Canadian International Development Agency (CIDA) A Canadian government organization formed to assist developing nations with technical advice and loans of both money and personnel

Canadian Shield An area of Precambrian rock, mostly igneous, that covers almost half of Canada. It is the dominant physical feature in the Near North region

CANDU nuclear power reactor The system developed in Canada for nuclear power production. CANDU reactors have been sold overseas.

Canyon A steep-walled gorge on land, or a deep trough in the ocean

Capital Assets, in the form of money, property, or goods that are owned or used by a person, company, or country

Cash receipts Money obtained from selling goods or services

C.B.D. See *Central Business District*

Census Division An area used to compile statistics about the people and activities found there

Census Metropolitan Area (C.M.A.) In Canada, a city with a population of over 100 000

Central Business District (C.B.D.) The downtown area of a town or city. Land use is mostly commercial and governmental.

Central Mortgage and Housing Corporation (C.M.H.C.) A government Crown Corporation set up to provide loans (mortgages) for home buyers

Charter flight A flight organized for a group of people. Charter flights in Canada often go to Hawaii, Mexico, Florida, the Caribbean, and Europe.

Chernozem A fertile black or dark brown pedocal soil which is rich in humus. Chernozems are found in the Canadian Prairies, the Ukraine, Eastern Europe, and the United States.

CIDA See *Canadian International Development Agency*

Clay Belts Areas in northern Ontario and Québec that were covered by post-glacial lakes. The lake-bed deposits make the areas suitable for general mixed farming.

Clear cutting The harvesting of all trees in a given area that are large enough for commercial use

Climograph A graph used to illustrate temperature and precipitation. Temperature is shown as a line graph and precipitation as a series of bar graphs, one for each month of the year.

C.M.A. See *Census Metropolitan Area*

C.M.H.C. See *Central Mortgage and Housing Corporation*

Commercial land use A type of land use involving retail and wholesale trade. Stores, offices, banks, and warehouses are classified as commercial land use.

Communist nation A nation in which all property is owned by the state, and all efforts (labour, industry, agriculture) are organized for the benefit of the people. Examples include the U.S.S.R. and Cuba.

Communist/Socialist republic A nation with a government whose main interests are in social and economic equality for all persons. The state owns the major industries and controls the economic, social, and political life of society.

Computerized mapping Maps of weather and land use produced by computers. The computer takes the data, extracts the information required, and plots the information in a map format.

Confederation In Canada,the uniting of the provinces to form one nation. Canada's Confederation took place on July 1, 1867 when the British North America Act established the Dominion of Canada by joining Ontario, Québec, Nova Scotia, and New Brunswick.

Coniferous forest A type of forest containing trees that have needles, cones, and generally softwood trunks

Constant dollars Dollars which are changed to reflect the value of the dollar at a specific time. They are used when comparing the value of an item over a period of time. Inflation is not considered.

Constitution The system of fundamental laws and principles of a government, often in written form. Canada repatriated its constitution in April 1982.

Constitutional monarchy A form of government that has a hereditary chief of state with powers outlined in a constitution

Consulate The office of an official government representative in a foreign country. It usually has specific duties or interests, such as trade.

Consumer Price Index (C.P.I.) A measure of the changes in market prices of specific goods and services such as food, energy, housing, and transportation. It is one indication of the rate of inflation.

Containerization A method of shipping materials by packing them into containers of a specific size and shape. The containers are not opened (except for customs' checks) until they reach their final destination. They fit onto trucks, trains, airplanes, and ships. Special port facilities have been developed to handle these containers.

Continental climate A type of climate that occurs when there is little effect on temperature by a large body of water. It is characterized by low precipitation (most occurring in the summer) and a wide temperature range. Winnipeg and Fort Smith have this type of climate.

Continental crust The solid layer, above the lithosphere, that underlies the major continents. It is thicker than the solid layer under the oceans.

Continental drift The movement of the large, rigid plates in the earth's lithosphere. The theory of continental drift was developed by Alfred Wegener.

Continentality The influence of a large land mass on climate. See *Continental Climate.*

Continental shelf The border of a continent, covered by water, which slopes gently from the coastline to the steep continental slope. The change in slope usually takes place at a depth of 200 m.

Continental slope The slope which leads from the outer edge of the continental shelf, at a depth of 200 m to the ocean floor

Convection One of the basic methods of heat movement or transfer. Circulation is caused by heating which causes the material to rise and be replaced. *Convection currents* occur in the atmosphere and in the asthenosphere.

Co-operative An organization involved with the production or sale of a product or service. The organization is owned collectively by its members who share the profits.

Cordilleran Climatic Region A climatic region along the west coast of Canada, characterized by variations in precipitation and temperature. These variations are caused by differences in altitude, relief, and exposure within the region.

Core The centre of the earth. The temperature of the inner part, the *solid core*, is in excess of 4000°C. The *liquid core*, which surrounds the solid core, is not actually liquid, but is in a more fluid state than the solid core.

C.P.I. See *Consumer Price Index*

Cropland Land used to raise field crops such as wheat, oats, and barley

Crown land Land owned by the nation. Income from the sale or lease of this land goes to the government of the nation.

Crude oil Oil in its natural form, as it comes out of the earth

Crustacean A class of invertebrates with a hard outer shell and jointed appendages. Examples include shrimps, crabs, and lobsters.

Cultural mosaic The coexistence of many different customs, arts, and languages in a region or country

Cyclonic storm A low pressure area, often accompanied by warm and cold fronts, which brings precipitation to many middle-latitude areas

Death rate The number of deaths per 1000 people, usually measured over a period of one year

Deciduous forest A type of forest containing trees which shed their leaves, usually in the autumn. The leaves fall as the tree prepares for a period (winter) during which little ground moisture will be available.

Democratic parliamentary system A system of government in which the ultimate power is held by the people, who elect representatives to a parliament

Deposition The laying down of materials carried by water, ice, or wind

Developed countries One of two basic classifications of countries, determined by examining factors such as economic development, G.N.P. per capita, income per capita, potential for development, energy use, literacy, and quantity and quality of food

Developing countries One of the two basic classifications of countries, determined in comparison to developed countries

Devonian Period The fourth geological period of the Paleozoic Era, extending from 400 000 000 to 345 000 000 a (years) ago

Disposable income The amount of money that an individual has to spend after taxes and other deductions have been subtracted from the basic salary

Drainage basin An area drained by a single river system. Examples include the MacKenzie drainage basin and the St. Lawrence drainage basin.

Drumlin A hill, usually oval in shape, formed by glaciers. Drumlins are often found in groups or *fields*. Many are found near Peterborough and Guelph in Ontario.

Eastern Europe In this atlas: Czechoslovakia, Poland, Hungary, Romania, Bulgaria, Yugoslavia, and Albania. These countries lie behind the Iron Curtain and are more or less under Soviet influence.

Ecumene Any populated area with an integrated transportation system. (The word is from the Ancient Greek and referred to the "habitable world".)

EEC See *European Economic Community*

Electoral district An area which elects one person to the provincial legislature or Canadian parliament. Provincial and federal electoral districts do not necessarily coincide.

Electorate All people qualified to vote in an election

Embassy The official offices and residence of the ambassador of one country in another country

Emigration The movement of people out of an area or country

Emirate A Moslem country. Seven Emirates joined together in 1971 to become an independent country called the United Arab Emirates.

Equatorial scale A scale that is accurate near or at the equator. The earth cannot be represented exactly on a flat surface because of its shape. In some map projections, the scale varies with the distance from the equator.

Erosion The wearing down and carrying away of materials on the earth's surface by water, ice, or wind

Escarpment A steep slope or cliff formed by faulting or differential erosion. For example, the Niagara Escarpment was formed by the erosion of several types of rock with differing resistance.

Esker A long narrow ridge of rounded and sorted materials, usually sand or gravel. Eskers are formed under or in glaciers as meltwaters create streams and deposit materials.

Ethnicity The designation of the basic divisions or groups of people as distinguished by their customs, language, and background

European Economic Community (EEC) Also called the Common Market. An economic alliance involving ten full members — Belgium, Denmark, France, West Germany, Greece, Ireland, Italy, Luxembourg, the Netherlands, and the United Kingdom. It's aims are to have an integrated economy, coordinated social development, and eventual political unity.

Exports Goods and services sold to other countries. Canada's main exports include automobile parts, grains, minerals, and forest products.

External aid Assistance provided for other nations, usually in the form of goods, money, or technical expertise

External trade Trade with other countries

Extractive industry A type of industry that takes raw materials from the natural environment for refining or manufacturing. Mining, fishing, and lumbering are considered extractive industries.

Extrusive rock Igneous rock formed on the earth's surface from lava or ash that has cooled quickly. Examples include basalt, pumice, and breccia.

Farm cash receipts Money obtained by the sale of agricultural goods

Fast ice Ice which covers a body of water and has little or no movement during the winter season

Fault A fracture in the earth's crust along which rock strata have moved vertically or horizontally. Faults may trap oil or gas deposits in a specific area.

Faulting See *Fault*

Federal statute A law passed by the Canadian parliament

Field (Oil or Gas) An area in which oil or gas has been discovered. New oil and gas fields in Canada have been found off the east coast and in the Beaufort Sea.

Flaw lead An area, in winter, that winds keep generally free of ice. It is usually close to shore.

Flora The plant life associated with a specific region

Folding The bending of rock layers, often resulting in mountain formation. The Rocky Mountains and the Andes are examples of folded mountains.

Food chain A pattern of feeding relationships in an ecosystem. For example, plankton are eaten by small fish, the small fish are eaten by larger fish, and the larger fish are eaten by people.

Forage crops Crops grown to be used as food for animals. Corn is an important forage crop.

Foreign debt One nation's debt to another. Nations often borrow money from each other. In most cases, the money is used to develop resources or to supply necessary material goods.

Foreign investment The investment of money in one country's stocks and bonds by individuals or companies who are citizens of another country

Fossil The imprint or the remains of a prehistoric plant or animal. Fossils are almost always found in sedimentary rock.

Fossil fuel Any energy source originating from prehistoric plants and animals, mostly found in or associated with sedimentary rock. The main fossil fuels are coal, peat, natural gas, and petroleum.

Fractionating tower A column in a petroleum refinery used to separate petroleum into *fractions* (parts of a distilled material) based on their boiling points

Front The surface or line between masses of air with different characteristics. The type of front (warm or cold) depends on which mass of air is moving into an area.

Frost-free period The total number of days between the average date of the last frost in spring and the average date of the first frost in autumn

Gauging station A station at which information on water flows is kept. The data collected are used to interpret patterns in stream flow, and their consequences.

Generating station A plant where electrical power is produced by falling water, coal, petroleum, natural gas, nuclear fission, or any other energy source

Generator A machine used to convert mechanical energy (for example, falling water) into electrical energy

Geological Province A large area that has common characteristics of rock structure, rock type, and/or rock age

Glacier A slow-moving mass of ice found at high latitudes and high altitudes

G.N.P. See *Gross National Product*

Grassland A vegetation type comprised mainly of grasses because there is insufficient moisture to support trees. Grassland areas are often called prairies, steppes, velds, savannas, and pampas.

Grid A network of power transmission lines into which all power is fed and from which consumers, such as industries and homes, receive electricity

Gross National Product (G.N.P.) The dollar value of all goods and services produced in a country in a given year

Ground water The water in the soil and in the bedrock underlying the soil

Growing degree days A figure compiled by adding the number of degrees by which the average temperature of each day in a year exceeds 6°C

Growing season The period of the year with enough warmth and moisture for crops to grow

Hard currency One of the world's more stable currencies, in which most international transactions are carried out — American dollars, Japanese yen, Swiss or French francs, or German marks

Hardwood Wood generally produced from broadleaf trees, including maple, oak, and elm

Heartwood The column of hard wood at the centre of a tree which supports the tree. Although the heartwood is dead, it will not decay as long as the tree's outer layers remain intact.

Heath An open area, often found in high altitudes and high latitudes, that is usually covered in grasses or short shrubs

Heating degree days A figure compiled by adding the number of degrees by which the temperature of each day in a year goes below 18°C. At 18°C, the furnace is usually turned on in a home or an industry.

Heavy water A compound, like water, but with a heavier atomic weight. It is composed of oxygen and the isotope of hydrogen (H_2O_2). Heavy water is used in nuclear power reactors.

High Commission The office of the representative of a British Commonwealth country in another Commonwealth country. Canada has High Commissions in most Commonwealth countries.

Horizon A distinct layer in a soil profile. Most soil profiles have A, B, and C horizons.

Housing starts The number of new houses that began to be constructed in a specific period. In a healthy economy, housing starts are usually high in number.

Humidity The amount of moisture in the air. Humidity is usually expressed as a percent of the total amount of moisture the air is capable of carrying. For example, 95 percent humidity usually indicates that precipitation will occur shortly.

Hydrocarbon A compound containing only compounds of carbon and hydrogen. There are thousands of these compounds, including methane and crude petroleum.

Hydro-electric energy Electricity produced by the natural movement of falling water. For example, hydro-electric energy is produced by Churchill Falls and Niagara Falls.

Ice-cap A large mass of ice, smaller than an ice sheet. The largest ice-cap today is found in Greenland.

Ice floe An area of floating ice detached from the main polar ice mass

Ice sheet A very large mass of ice. The last continental ice sheet to cover parts of North America was the Wisconsin Ice Sheet.

Igneous rock Rock formed from the cooling of molten materials. See also *intrusive rock* and *extrusive rock*.

Immigration The movement of people into an area or country

Impermeable rock See *Non-porous rock*

Imports Goods and services bought from other countries and brought into a country. Canada's main imports include automobiles, petroleum, and electrical goods.

Improved hectare Land that has been either cleared of trees or ploughed for the growing of crops

Indian Act A federal statute specifying government responsibilities regarding Native peoples. Many amendments have been made since it was passed in 1876. Since 1969 there have been many discussions between the government and Native associations about major changes in the Act.

Industrial mineral A mineral such as stone, sand, or gravel, used for general building purposes

Industry Refers to extractive processes (mining, forestry, fishing) and manufacturing. Agriculture is not included. Some countries, including Canada, place service industries such as commerce and insurance in this broad category.

Infant mortality rate The number of deaths of children less than one year of age per 1000 births, usually measured over the period of one year

Inflated dollars Dollars which are adjusted in their value as inflation rises. They are used for most statistical comparisons because inflation causes dollars to have less *real value* (buying power).

Inflation A general increase in the price of goods and services over time. In periods of high inflation, the purchasing power of money decreases.

Inorganic materials Materials such as rock fragments, liquids, and gases. Inorganic and organic materials combine to produce soil.

Inshore fishery The sector of the fishing industry that usually operates less than 15 km from the shore. It involves small boats (under 10 t [tonnes]) that return to the home port each day.

Intensive farming A type of farming that obtains very high yields per hectare by using much labour and capital. In Canada, examples include market gardening of vegetables, and the use of greenhouses, feed-lots, or irrigation.

Internal drainage A system of drainage that has no outlet to the ocean. It is usually caused by land in the interior of a continent that is lower than sea level. Examples include the Dead Sea, the Caspian Sea, and Lake Eyre.

International date line An imaginary line which approximately follows 180° longitude. The area of the world just east of the line is one day ahead of the area just west of the line. The line varies from 180° slightly to avoid splitting islands or countries into separate days.

Intrazonal soil One of the three major soil orders. Soils in this group develop in areas where bedrock or drainage has more influence on development than climate or natural vegetation.

Intrusion The penetration of molten material into the earth's crust, usually along a fracture or fault

Intrusive rock Igneous rock formed within the earth's crust from magma (molten rock that has not reached the earth's surface). Examples include granite, gabbro, and serpentine.

Inuit The Native peoples who live in the Far North Region of Canada, and Greenland

Islamic republic A country in which the people elect representatives to the government, but where the rules of Islam are superimposed on the system of government

Isobath A contour line showing relief on the floor of a body of water

Isoline A line on a map joining points with the same numerical value. (The word *isos* is Greek for "equal".)

Isostatic rebound The vertical movement of parts of the earth's crust in an attempt to maintain equilibrium. When glaciers recede, continents often rise after the weight of the ice has gone.

Isotherm A line joining all places having the same temperature

Jet stream A tube-like band of high velocity wind found in the upper atmosphere

Joule (J) A metric unit of energy defined as the work done by the force of one newton when it moves its point of application a distance of one metre

Labour force The total number of people working or looking for work in an area, province, or country

Land claims The case presented by the Native peoples for ownership and control of lands on which they live or have lived. Some claims have already been settled, but many more will be settled through the government or the courts.

Landed value The dollar value of fish caught before marketing and processing

Landform Any feature of the earth's surface formed by earth movements or by the wearing down of the surface by the atmosphere

Land use The type of human activity carried out on the land. Common land uses include agricultural, residential, commercial, and industrial.

Latitude Distance, measured in degrees, north and south of the equator. The north pole is at 90°N and the south pole is at 90°S. All lines of latitude are parallel.

Leaching The removal of soluble materials in soil from the A horizon to the B horizon by percolating water. Leaching is most significant in humid climates.

Legislature The group of people given the responsibility and power to make laws for a province, state, or country. In Canada, there is a legislature for each province and territory, as well as a federal legislature.

Lichen A living partnership between an algae and a fungus, existing in a great range of forms. Lichens are common to many tundra areas.

Life expectancy The average number of years that an individual is expected to live. The availability of food and health care are major factors in determining the life expectancy of the people in a country.

Lignite A low-grade coal which is brownish in colour and has a high water content

Literacy The ability to read and write. Various international organizations are trying to raise the literacy rates in the world.

Lithosphere The crust of the earth

Logarithmic scale A scale using logarithms, or diminishing distances between lines. It is a condensed way of showing large numerical increases.

Longitude The distance, measured in degrees, east and west of the Prime Meridian. The lines of longitude, called *meridians*, join the north and south poles.

Mantle A concentric layer of the earth's interior, about 2900 km thick, between the crust and the core

Manufacturing A type of industry that involves the changing of raw materials into finished products, usually with the assistance of machinery

Marketing Board An organization that buys products from producers and then collectively distributes these products to wholesalers or retailers. Canada has marketing boards for wheat, eggs and dairy products, and other agricultural goods.

Market trend The general direction of the stock market. In Canada, the "300 Index" in Toronto is often used to gauge general market trends.

Mass transit The movement of people, usually in an urban area, by bus, streetcar, subway, or commuter train

Meltwater Water produced by the thawing of snow or ice. Meltwaters from the last glacial period covered large areas in Manitoba, southern Ontario and Québec, and the Clay Belt area of northern Ontario.

Member of Parliament (M.P.) An elected representative of a federal electoral district, who is a member of Canada's federal legislative body, the House of Commons

Member of the Legislative Assembly (M.L.A.) An elected representative of a provincial electoral district in most Canadian provinces, who is a member of a provincial Legislative Assembly

Metallic mineral A mineral belonging to a particular class of chemical elements that yield a metal when processed. Examples include iron, gold, silver, and uranium.

Metamorphic rock A type of rock that results from changes in other rock types caused by heat and/or pressure. Examples include marble, gneiss, and quartzite.

Meteorologist A person who studies the phenomena of the atmosphere. One of the main functions of many meteorologists is weather forecasting.

Métis A person of mixed European and Indian descent

Mid Atlantic Ridge A system of submarine mountains that thrust up from the abyssal plain. The ridge runs parallel to the ocean margins, and marks the edge of plates.

Mid Atlantic Rift A steep-sided trough within the Mid Atlantic Ridge

Middle East In this atlas: the countries of southeast Asia and northeast Africa, including Afghanistan, Bahrain, Egypt, Iran, Iraq, Israel, Jordan, Kuwait, Lebanon, Libya, Oman, Qatar, Saudi Arabia, Syria, Turkey, United Arab Emirates, Yemen (Republic), and Democratic Yemen

Migration The movement of people, birds, or animals from one location to another

Military regime A type of government controlled by the army or other military personnel. It often results from an overthrow of the previous government.

Millibar (mbar) A unit of atmospheric pressure used on weather maps. 1000 mbar = 1 bar.

Mineral A naturally occurring crystalline substance with a specific chemical composition and regular internal structure. Rocks are made up of combinations of different minerals. See also *industrial mineral* and *metallic mineral*.

Mineral fuel An energy source made from minerals. Examples include the fossil fuels and uranium.

Mississippian Period A geological period in the Carboniferous Period, extending from 345 000 000 to 280 000 000 a (years) ago

Mixed farming A type of farming in which both livestock and crops are produced

M.L.A. See *Member of the Legislative Assembly*

Moisture deficiency The amount of moisture needed for plant growth which is not provided by precipitation. When high temperatures increase evaporation, there is usually a moisture deficiency. Irrigation can help to solve this problem.

Moraine Material deposited by a glacier, often in the form of hills. End moraines are found at the farthest point of advance of a glacier.

Mortgage A long-term loan, usually for a costly item such as a house or building

Motion graphics A technique used on television to illustrate how weather changes with the movement of frontal systems.

M.P. See *Member of Parliament*

Municipality A town or city with its own government

Munitions Military supplies, particularly weapons and ammunition

Native peoples All peoples who are descendants of Canada's original inhabitants. Native peoples include registered Indians, non-registered Indians, Métis, and Inuit.

NATO See *North Atlantic Treaty Organization*

Natural increase The difference between the number of births and deaths, often given per 1000 people. Data is usually kept for countries but more detailed information is sometimes available for parts of a country (state, province, city).

Natural resource An item, usually having economic value for society, found in or on the land or in the water. Examples include fish, forests, water, minerals, and fur-bearing animals.

Nautical mile A unit of distance used in navigation, equal to 1.853 km. The distance is one minute of an arc on a Great Circle drawn on a sphere the same size as the earth.

Needleleaf Trees with needles rather than leaves. The needles fall throughout the year, not only in the autumn. Most needleleaf trees are evergreens such as pine, fir, and spruce.

Net immigration The difference between immigration and emigration

NGO See *Non-Governmental Organization*

Nomadic Without a permanent residence. Most nomadic peoples are hunters and follow the movement of game.

Non-Governmental Organization (NGO) A private group that raises funds to provide assistance to others, particularly to developing nations. Examples include C.U.S.O., Oxfam, and Save the Children.

Non-porous rock Also called *impermeable rock*. A dense type of rock, with few pore spaces, that does not allow liquids to pass through.

Non-registered Indian A person who is Indian by birth, heritage, and culture but who is not classified as "Indian" according to the definition in the Indian Act

Non-renewable resource A resource that, once taken from the sea or the land, cannot be returned. Examples include minerals and fossil fuels.

North Atlantic Treaty Organization (NATO) A military alliance involving thirteen nations on both sides of the North Atlantic Ocean — Belgium, Canada, Denmark, France, Greece, Italy, Luxembourg, the Netherlands, Norway, Turkey, the United Kingdom, the United States, and West Germany

Northwest Passage A route across Canada's north by water. Early explorers searched for this route to Cathay (China). The route is difficult to traverse due to ice conditions.

Nuclear energy Electricity produced by using the heat from nuclear fission to make steam to drive a generator

Nuclear reactor A device designed to produce electricity by using the heat from nuclear fission. There are a few small research reactors in Canada, and several reactors, mostly in Ontario, involved in the active production of power.

Nuclear test site A location used to experiment with nuclear devices

Occupied hectare Land that has been claimed or sold in an area. A farm is usually established on the property, but not all of the land must be ploughed or improved to be considered occupied.

Oceania In this atlas: the islands in the South Pacific Ocean, including Australia, New Zealand, Papua New Guinea, Fiji, Tahiti, Western Samoa, and the many island states of Polynesia

Offshore fishery The sector of the fishing industry that usually operates more than 80 km from the shore. It involves large boats (more than 50 t [tonnes]) that stay at sea for several days before returning to the home port.

Oil sands Sands saturated with heavy crude oil. Large oil sands are found near Athabasca in Alberta.

One party republic A country with a chief of state who is not a monarch (usually a president). It has only one political party.

Open pit mine Ore found near the surface that is mined through a large excavated pit rather than underground

Oregon Territory One of the last areas to be designated as belonging to Canada or to the United States. The area included what is now southern British Columbia, Oregon, and Washington State.

Organic soil An incompletely developed soil containing mostly dead organic materials. This soil is often found in areas of poor drainage.

Orogen A mountain system formed primarily by folding. In Canada, the Rocky Mountains, Coast Mountains, and Appalachians were all formed by folding.

Outcrop Bedrock that protrudes from the land surface, usually without vegetation or soil covering

Pacific Rim the countries around the Pacific Ocean, from Chile to Canada on the east side, and from Australia to Japan on the west side

Pack ice Seasonal ice formed by the joining of several ice floes

Pangaea In the theory of continental drift, the original land mass that broke apart to create the present continents

Parkland A transitional vegetation region between grassland and boreal forest

Pedalfer A major zonal soil group found in areas with a humid climate. Soils in this group contain mainly aluminium and iron oxides. Examples include laterites and podzols.

Pedocal A major zonal soil group found in areas with a dry climate. Soils in this group are rich in calcium because leaching is not significant. Fertility is related to the amount of precipitation. Examples include chernozems and dark brown soils.

Percolation The downward movement of water through the soil or through joints in the bedrock

Permafrost Ground that does not completely thaw in summer. The surface layer often thaws but the ground underneath remains frozen and does not allow much drainage. Boggy conditions usually result.

Permeable rock Also called *porous rock*. A rock with many pore spaces that allow liquids to pass through.

PetroCanada A company formed by the federal government to develop Canada's oil reserves, process the materials, and market the products

Petroleum basin A large natural downfold where oil and gas deposits have often accumulated

Phloem Plant tissue that serves as a pathway for the distribution of food material in plants

Plankton Microscopic plant and animal life found in water. They are an important food source for fish and whales.

Plantation farming The extensive use of land for a single crop. The term generally refers to the growing of tea, rubber, coffee, or sugar in the tropics.

Plate Section of the earth's crust that "floats" in the earth's mantle in much the same way as an iceberg floats in water. Plate movement (continental drift) can cause earthquakes and volcanoes.

Plateau An upland area with a fairly flat surface and steep slopes. Rivers often dissect plateau surfaces.

Plate tectonics The study of the plate movements in the lithosphere

Platform A large geological block forming the base of a continent. For example, the Canadian Shield is a platform.

Podzol A pedalfer soil associated with coniferous forests. Although generally poor for agriculture, podzols can be improved by adding lime. Much of the Near North has podzolic soils.

Population density Determined by comparing the total population of a region with the total area.

$$\text{Population Density} = \frac{\text{Population}}{\text{Area (km}^2)}$$

Population distribution The pattern of where people live in an area

Population profile A diagram showing the structure of a population according to age and sex

Porous rock See *Permeable rock*

Post-glacial lake A lake formed by meltwaters as a glacier receded. Ice blocked the normal drainage routes and caused extensive ponding. Lake Agassiz in Manitoba was an example.

Precipitation Moisture which accumulates in clouds and then falls to earth as rain, snow, hail, sleet, or ice pellets

Premier The political leader of a province, usually the leader of the political party in power in that province

Prevailing winds Winds that are most common in a location. In most parts of Canada, the westerlies are the prevailing winds.

Primary family Also called *nuclear family*. A group composed of one or more adults and one or more children. A primary family usually lives in one household.

Primary industry Industry involved with natural resources. Examples include fishing, agriculture, mining, and forestry.

Prime meridian An imaginary line at zero degrees longitude. It passes through Greenwich, England. All meridians are numbered east and west of this line.

Processor A company or individual that takes a raw material and changes it into another product. For example, a flour mill processes wheat into flour and a bakery processes flour into bread.

Provincial Statute A law passed by a provincial legislature

Pulp Ground-up, wet cellulose used to make paper. Pulp is usually made from wood, but also from linen or rags. It has a consistency similar to porridge.

Quaternary The most recent period of the Cenozoic Era, also known as the age of man

Quota The number or proportion that is allowed or permitted. For an example, an import quota limits the quantity of a product that will be accepted into a country.

Rainforest A vegetation type comprised mainly of thick, luxuriant evergreen forest, found in areas with high precipitation distributed evenly throughout the year. Tropical rainforests are found in areas such as the Amazon and Congo Basins. Temperate rainforests are found in China, Australia, New Zealand, and southeastern parts of the United States.

Rangeland Land used for grazing cattle

Raw material Something that is changed by manufacturing into a more finished state. For example, iron is a raw material for the steel industry, and steel is a raw material for the ship-building industry.

Real Gross National Product The Gross National Product expressed in constant dollars rather than inflated dollars

Reef A ridge or strip of coral lying close to the surface of an ocean

Refinery A plant where raw materials such as oil, sugar, or metals are processed

Regeneration The process of reproducing or renewing. Regeneration in the forest industry refers to the replanting of trees.

Registered Indian A person who is registered under and subject to the Indian Act

Relief 1) The general physical variations of the land
2) The difference between the highest and lowest points in a given area

Reserve An area of land belonging to the federal government. Registered Indians have the right to occupy and use the land.

Retail Referring to the sale of products or services to consumers

Ridge An upland area, usually long and narrow with steep sides. Ridges are found both on land and in the ocean.

Rift A depression in the land, also called a *rift valley*. Rifts occur in the ocean when plates separate. An example is the Mid Atlantic Rift.

Rock strata (singular, *stratum*) Layers or beds of one kind of rock, usually sedimentary

Roundwood The forest output of unprocessed wood, used for products such as pulpwood, saw logs, veneer logs, and firewood. When volume figures are compiled, they do not usually include bark.

Runoff Moisture, either from precipitation or from melting snow, that flows over the surface, eventually joining streams and rivers

Rural Concerning the area outside towns and cities

Sapwood The soft wood just beneath the bark of a tree through which water moves from the roots to the leaves

Satellite image An image similar to a photograph but recorded on bands of the electro-magnetic spectrum. It is taken from a satellite. Landsat images, taken from 900 km above the earth, are of value to foresters, geographers, hydrologists, and wildlife and agriculture specialists.

Sea floor spread The movement of plates away from a central rift on the sea floor

Sea-ice A covering of thick ice over a large area of water. Sea-ice is common in the Arctic Ocean.

Seamount An individual mountain which rises from the sea floor but does not break the surface. Seamounts are often underwater volcanoes with steep slopes and pointed peaks or crests.

Sedges Coarse, grass-like plants that grow in clumps, usually in areas of poor drainage

Sedimentary rock A type of rock formed by the compression of deposits of water, wind, and ice. Examples include shale, sandstone, limestone, and conglomerate.

Seismic zone An area of the earth's crust which experiences horizontal or vertical movement, often associated with earthquakes and volcanoes. Areas of high seismic activity are found along fault lines and the edges of plates.

Self-determination Determination or decision for one's self without outside influence. The term is often used for a group of people who wish to decide upon their own political status or form of government.

Self-governing Commonwealth The term used to describe the status of Puerto Rico within the political framework of the United States. Puerto Rico has its own constitution but has a resident non-voting commissioner in the United States Congress.

Services Economic activities in which no item is produced. Examples of people in the labour force who provide services are sales personnel, bank employees, teachers, doctors, bus drivers, and accountants.

Seven Years' War A European war (1756-1763) that involved many countries including Austria, England, France, Prussia, Russia, Sweden, and Saxony. In Canada, the battle between Wolfe and Montcalm on the Plains of Abraham above Québec led to the conquest of Canada by England.

Shaded relief map A map illustrating the general physical variations of land using a graphic representation of these features

Sheikdom A region under the rule of a sheik, the head of an Arab family, clan, tribe, or village

Snow belts Areas that have higher than average snowfall due to the prevailing winds, elevation, and the presence of a body of water. There is a snow belt in southern Ontario in the lee of the Great Lakes.

Softwood Wood produced by most conifers, such as pine.

Solar energy Energy from the sun

Solar radiation Radiant heat from the sun, emitted in the form of short waves. It is measured in megajoules per square metre.

Soluble Able to be dissolved

Specialty crop A crop associated with a particular area, such as peaches in the Niagara Fruit Belt of Ontario, or vegetables in the Fraser Delta area of British Columbia

Stock Market Index An index that measures the value of stocks traded on an exchange. Examples include TSE 300 (Toronto Stock Exchange) and the Dow-Jones Industrial Index (New York).

Stockpile A reserve of materials, often used in the context of nuclear weapons

Stratigraphic trap A reservoir containing oil or gas or both, formed by a layer of impermeable rock that traps the oil and gas

Strip mine See *Open pit mine*

Subbituminous coal A type of coal which is grey in colour, fairly soft, and less than 50 percent carbon

Submarine cable A cable under an ocean used to transmit telephone calls. Submarine cables will probably be replaced by satellites in the next few years.

Subsistence farming A type of farming that involves the raising of livestock or cultivation of crops for consumption rather than for sale

Superpower A nation with political influence over other nations. The United States, the U.S.S.R., France, the United Kingdom, and China are considered superpowers.

Surface current The movement of water near the surface, caused by differences in water density and salinity, and the rotation of the earth

Sustained yield The use of a renewable resource, such as fish, trees, air, and water, at a rate that allows the resource to renew itself

Temperate Referring to the region of the world outside the tropics, south of the Arctic Circle, and north of the Antarctic Circle

Tertiary Period The first period of the Cenozoic Era, extending from about 65 000 000 a (years) ago to the beginning of the glacial periods 1 000 000 a (years) ago

Thermal energy Electricity produced by burning fossil fuels

Till A mixture of unsorted materials deposited by glaciers underneath the ice. These materials may vary in size from clay-sized particles to boulders.

Time zone A geographical area within which the same standard time is used. Canada has seven of the world's time zones.

Trading price The dollar value at which items are bought or sold

Transformer A machine used for changing the voltage of an electrical current

Transform fault A fracture in the earth's surface, associated with plate movements. It occurs at right angles to the rifts between plates.

Transmission line A power line along which electricity moves

Tropical Referring to the region of the world between the Tropic of Cancer and the Tropic of Capricorn

Tundra A term used to describe the climate, vegetation, or soil of the Arctic and Sub-arctic regions between the forested areas and those with permanent snow and ice

Turbine An engine or motor driven by the pressure of steam, water, or air

Unconsolidated materials Loose materials on the earth's surface, including glacial deposits, boulders, sand, gravel, soil, muskeg, and bogs

Undifferentiated glacial deposits Varied glacial deposits over a small area. Maps group different materials of varied origin and structure in this category.

Unemployment rate Persons in the total labour force who are presently seeking but are unable to find work, usually expressed as a percent

Upper mantle see *Lithosphere*

Urban Referring to a city or town. Canada's definition of an urban area is an area of 1000 people and a population density of 400 or more per square kilometre.

Urbanization The process of an area changing from rural to urban

Value added The total change in the monetary value of an item at each stage of the manufacturing process

Volcanic rock See *Igneous rock*

Warsaw Pact A military alliance involving the U.S.S.R. and the Soviet bloc countries — Bulgaria, Czechoslovakia, East Germany, Hungary, Poland, Romania

Watt The power that produces energy at the rate of one joule per second

Weather station A location equipped with instruments to record atmospheric conditions. In Canada, continuous data is relayed to Environment Canada for analysis and forecasting.

Western Europe In this atlas: the United Kingdom, Ireland, Norway, Sweden, Finland, Denmark, the Netherlands, Belgium, Luxembourg, Spain, France, Portugal, West Germany, Switzerland, Austria, Italy, Greece, Cyprus, and Iceland

Wholesale Concerning the sale of products and services in large quantities, usually to retailers who then sell them to consumers

Wildland An area which has not been developed for human use, including forested areas, parkland, open woodland, and areas north of the treeline

Wind chill factor A measurement combining the effect of low temperatures and high winds. This combination can cause frostbite or hypothermia (loss of body heat leading to death).

Wisconsin Ice Sheet The most recent continental ice sheet that began to retreat about 15 000 a (years) ago. It covered much of North America with ice up to 2000 m deep.

Zonal soil The most predominant of the three major soil orders. Soils in this group are well developed with distinct horizons. They reflect the influence of climate and natural vegetation. Examples include pedalfers and pedocals.

GAZETTEER

The names of places and features in this atlas are listed in alphabetical order. The number printed in boldface type immediately to the left of the name is the number of the page where the place or feature is best shown (some names can be found on several pages). The latitude and longitude are given for the location of the name on the map. They are listed in the two columns to the left of the page number.

Slashes are used to indicate two names for a single entry. For example, Cairo is listed twice as Cairo/El Qâhira and as El Qâhira/Cairo. When two or more entries have the same name, the country or Canadian province is given in parentheses. For example, London is listed twice, as London (U.K.) and as London (Ont.). A closed square (■) indicates a country, and an open square (□) indicates an administrative division within a country, for example, a province or state.

Abbreviations

The following abbreviations have been used on the map plates and in the Gazetteer.

Alb.	Albania
Alta.	Alberta
Aust.	Austria
Austral.	Australia
Assoc.	Association
Bang.	Bangladesh
B.C.	British Columbia
Bel.	Belgium
Bulg.	Bulgaria
C.	Cemetery
Cam.	Cameroon
C.A.R.	Central African Republic
C.B.D.	Central Business District
C.M.A.	Census Metropolitan Area
C.M.H.C.	Central Mortgage and Housing Corporation
Co.	Company
Corp.	Corporation
C.P.	Canadian Pacific
C.P.I.	Consumer Price Index
CUSO	Canadian University Services Overseas
Czech.	Czechoslovakia
Dem. Yemen	Democratic Yemen
Den.	Denmark
D.N.D.	Department of National Defence
Dom. Rep.	Dominican Republic
D.P.R.	Democratic People's Republic
(e.)	Estimate based on a compilation from a number of sources
E.E.C.	European Economic Community
Eq. Guinea	Equatorial Guinea
Est.	Estimated
Fr.	France
Fr. Guiana	French Guiana
Germ.	Germany
G.N.P.	Gross National Product
Hond.	Honduras
Hung.	Hungary
I.	Island
Is.	Islands
Inc.	Incorporated
Int.	International
Jam.	Jamaica
L.	Lake
Leb.	Lebanon
Ltd.	Limited
Lux.	Luxembourg
Man.	Manitoba
M.L.A.	Member of the Legislative Assembly
M.P.	Member of Parliament
Mt.	Mount or Mountain
Mts.	Mountains
Mun.	Municipal
n.a.	Not available or not applicable
NATO	North Atlantic Treaty Organization
N.B.	New Brunswick
neg.	Negligible
Neth.	Netherlands
Nfld.	Newfoundland
N.S.	Nova Scotia
N.W.T.	Northwest Territories
N.Z.	New Zealand
Ont.	Ontario
P.	Post Office
P.D.R.	People's Democratic Republic
P.E.I.	Prince Edward Island
Port.	Portugal
P.R.	Puerto Rico
Que.	Quebec
R.	River
Rom.	Romania
R.S.F.S.R.	Russian Soviet Federated Socialist Republic
S.A.	South Africa
Sask.	Saskatchewan
Soc. Rep.	Socialist Republic
S.S.R.	Soviet Socialist Republic
Switz.	Switzerland
U.A.E.	United Arab Emirates
U.K.	United Kingdom
U.S.	United States
U.S.S.R.	Union of Soviet Socialist Republics
Y.T.	Yukon Territory
Yugo.	Yugoslavia

26N	77W	138	Abaco I.
30N	48E	153	Ābādān
57N	2W	145	Aberdeen
5N	4W	155	Abidjan
48N	79W	20	Abitibi, Lac
49N	82W	84	Abitibi R.
24N	54E	153	Abu Dhabi
17N	100W	137	Acapulco
5N	0	155	Accra
12N	45E	153	ʿAdan / Aden
37N	35E	153	Adana
25N	51E	153	Ad Dawḩah / Doha
9N	38E	155	Addis Ababa
35S	138E	157	Adelaide
12N	45E	153	Aden / ʿAdan
13N	50E	153	Aden, Gulf of
43N	16E	146	Adriatic Sea
33N	65E	153	Afghanistan ■
17N	8E	155	Agadez
30N	9W	155	Agadir
27N	78E	154	Agra
22N	102W	137	Aguascalientes
23N	72E	154	Ahmadabad
31N	49E	153	Ahvāz / Ahwāz
51N	114W	93	Airdrie
42N	8E	145	Ajaccio
52N	81W	78	Akimiski I.
39N	140E	150	Akita
68N	135W	77	Aklavik
41N	81W	136	Akron
41N	80E	149	Aksu
61N	79W	78	Akulivik
32N	87W	136	Alabama □
31N	88W	136	Alabama R.
65N	150W	134	Alaska □
58N	145W	133	Alaska, Gulf of
46N	23E	146	Alba Iulia
41N	20E	143	Albania ■
35S	118E	157	Albany (Australia)
42N	73W	136	Albany (U.S.)
52N	84W	84	Albany R.
30N	47E	153	Al Baṣrah
54N	115W	93	Alberta □
57N	10E	145	Ålborg
35N	106W	135	Albuquerque
36S	147E	158	Albury - Wodonga
59N	132E	148	Aldan R.
46N	37E	144	Aleppo / Ḩalab
82N	62W	78	Alert
45N	74W	98	Alexandria (Ont.)
31N	30E	155	Alexandria / El Iskandariya (Egypt)
34N	42E	153	Al Furāt R. / Euphrates R.
36N	3E	155	Alger / Algiers
35N	3E	155	Algeria ■
36N	3E	155	Algiers / Alger
45N	78W	84	Algonquin Provincial Park
23N	46E	153	Al Hillah
14N	43E	153	Al Hudaydah
25N	49E	153	Al Hufūf
23S	153E	157	Alice Springs
24N	23E	153	Al Jawf
29N	48E	153	Al Kuwayt / Kuwait
35N	36E	153	Al Lādhiqīyah
25N	82E	154	Allahabad
44N	80E	97	Alliston
48N	71W	84	Alma
43N	77E	147	Alma Ata
24N	40E	153	Al Madīnah / Medina
26N	50E	153	Al Manāmah
36N	43E	153	Al Mawṣil
65S	63W	160	Almirante Brown (research station)
45N	76W	98	Almonte
64N	72W	78	Amadjuak L.
35N	101W	135	Amarillo
24N	118E	150	Amoy / Xiamen
2S	54W	139	Amazonas R. / Amazon R.
3S	128E	152	Ambon
16S	168E	158	Ambrym, I.
61N	131E	148	Amga R.
45N	64W	103	Amherst
49N	2E	145	Amiens
32N	36E	153	ʿAmmān
31N	75E	154	Amritsar
52N	5E	145	Amsterdam
40N	62E	147	Amu Dar'ya (river)
71N	124W	77	Amundsen Gulf
72N	115W	160	Amundsen Sea
90S	0	160	Amundsen – Scott (research station)
52N	139E	148	Amur R.
72N	113E	148	Anabar R.
20S	169E	158	Anatom, I.
62N	150W	133	Anchorage
43N	13E	146	Ancona
12N	92E	154	Andaman Is.
13N	96E	151	Andaman Sea
42N	1E	145	Andorra ■
25N	78W	138	Andros I.
58N	97E	148	Angara R.
52N	104E	148	Angarsk
15N	120E	151	Angeles
47N	1W	145	Angers
12S	18E	156	Angola ■
18N	63W	138	Anguilla
32N	117E	150	Anhui □
40N	33E	153	Ankara
36N	7E	155	Annaba
32N	44E	153	An Najaf
38N	76W	136	Annapolis
52N	55W	104	Anse aux Meadows, L', National Park
41N	123E	150	Anshan
19S	47E	156	Antananarivo
90S	0	160	Antarctica
67S	60W	160	Antarctic Peninsula
49N	63W	103	Anticosti, Île d'
49N	63W	103	Anticosti National Park
45N	62W	103	Antigonish
17N	61W	138	Antigua and Barbuda ■
24S	70W	140	Antofagasta
12S	49E	156	Antsiranana
51N	4E	145	Antwerpen / Antwerp
11N	96E	149	Anxi
40N	140E	150	Aomori
18N	121E	151	Aparri
44N	88W	136	Appleton
42N	13E	146	Aquila, L'
16N	65E	153	Arabian Sea
11S	37W	139	Aracaju
46N	21E	146	Arad
9S	135E	152	Arafura Sea
5S	48W	139	Araguaia R.
39N	47E	153	Araks R.
44N	60E	147	Aral Sea
7N	69W	139	Arauca R.
64N	41E	147	Archangel'sk
73N	85W	78	Arctic Bay
78N	160W	159	Arctic Ocean
62S	59W	160	Arctowski (research station)
41N	26E	146	Arda R.
16S	71W	139	Arequipa
47N	54W	104	Argentia
35S	66W	140	Argentina ■
44N	26E	146	Argeş R.
56N	10E	146	Århus
18S	70W	139	Arica
34N	111W	135	Arizona □
35N	92W	136	Arkansas □
33N	91W	136	Arkansas R.
40N	44E	147	Armenian S.S.R. □
43N	11E	146	Arno R.
48N	54W	104	Arnold's Cove
45N	76W	84	Arnprior
24N	46E	153	Ar Riyāḑ / Riyadh
48N	90W	88	Arrow Lake
44N	80W	97	Arthur
8S	133E	152	Aru, Kepulauan (islands)
3S	36E	156	Arusha
43N	142E	150	Asahigawa
23N	87E	154	Asansol
45N	72W	98	Asbestos
8S	14W	156	Ascension I.
51N	103W	94	Asessippi Provincial Park
23S	117E	157	Ashburton R.
50N	121W	98	Ashcroft
38N	58E	147	Ashkhabad
15N	39E	155	Asmera
49N	106W	94	Assiniboia
50N	101W	94	Assiniboine R.
50N	115W	88	Assiniboine, Mt., Provincial Park
49N	48E	147	Astrakhan'
25S	57W	140	Asunción
24N	33E	155	Aswān
27N	31E	155	Asyūt
17N	35E	155	Atbara R.
54N	113W	93	Athabasca
58N	112W	93	Athabasca R.
38N	23E	144	Athens / Athinai
38N	23E	144	Athinai / Athens
48N	91W	83	Atikokan
34N	84W	136	Atlanta
59N	133W	87	Atlin
60N	134W	87	Atlin L.
59N	134W	87	Atlin Provincial Park
21N	40E	153	Aṭ Ṭaʾif
37S	174E	158	Auckland
33N	82W	136	Augusta (Georgia)
44N	69W	136	Augusta (Maine)
39N	105W	135	Aurora (Colorado)
44N	79W	97	Aurora (Ont.)
30N	97W	135	Austin
23S	135E	157	Australia ■
35S	149E	158	Australian Capital Territory □
47N	14E	146	Austria ■
67N	67W	78	Auyuittuq National Park
47N	53W	104	Avalon Peninsula
43N	5E	145	Avignon
80N	90W	77	Axel Heiberg I.
42N	80W	97	Aylmer
40N	48E	147	Azerbaijan S.S.R. □
46N	36E	147	Azov, Sea of
26N	50E	153	Az-Zahran / Dhahran
32N	36E	153	Az Zarqā'
54N	126W	87	Babine L.
19N	122E	150	Babuyan Is.
65N	104W	77	Back R.
68N	75W	78	Baffin I.
33N	44E	153	Baghdād
36N	69E	154	Baghlān
16N	120E	151	Baguio
24N	75W	138	Bahamas ■
26N	50E	153	Bahrain ■
38S	62W	140	Bahía Blanca
7N	31E	155	Bahr el Jebel / White Nile R.
48N	70W	84	Baie, La
49N	68W	84	Baie-Comeau
47N	70W	98	Baie-St. Paul
50N	56W	104	Baie Verte
53N	6W	145	Baile Atha Cliath / Dublin
10S	120E	151	Baing
37S	147E	158	Bairnsdale
64N	96W	77	Baker L.
35N	119W	135	Bakersfield
40N	49W	147	Baku
47N	17E	146	Balaton, L.
48N	66W	103	Baldwin Provincial Park
39N	3E	143	Balearic Is. / Islas Baleares
57N	67W	78	Baleine, Riv. à la
8S	115E	151	Bali, I.
1S	117W	151	Balikpapan
46N	75E	147	Balkhash, L.
37S	144E	157	Ballarat

45N 79W **97** Balsam L.
18N 101W **137** Balsas R.
56N 20E **146** Baltic Sea
39N 76W **136** Baltimore
12N 8W **155** Bamako
5N 20E **155** Bambari
5N 95E **151** Banda Aceh
6S 130E **152** Banda Sea
27N 56E **153** Bandar 'Abbās
5N 115E **151** Bandar Seri Begawan
7S 107E **151** Bandung
51N 115W **88** Banff
51N 116W **93** Banff National Park
13N 77E **154** Bangalore
32N 20E **155** Banghāzī / Benghazi
1N 125E **151** Bangka, I.
13N 100E **151** Bangkok / Krung Thep
24N 90E **154** Bangladesh ■
4N 18E **155** Bangui
44N 17E **146** Banja Luka
3S 114E **151** Banjarmasin
13N 16W **155** Banjul
73N 121W **77** Banks I. (N.W.T.)
10S 142E **158** Banks Is. (Vanuatu)
54N 6W **145** Bann R.
48N 19E **146** Banská Bystrica
39N 115E **150** Baoding
34N 107E **149** Baoji
25N 99E **149** Baoshan
40N 110E **149** Baotou
48N 58W **104** Barachois Pond Provincial Park
53N 25E **146** Baranovichi
13N 59W **138** Barbados ■
42N 2E **143** Barcelona
73N 39E **159** Barents Sea
41N 17E **143** Bari
2S 114E **151** Barito R.
29S 119E **157** Barlee, L.
53N 83E **147** Barnaul
10N 69W **139** Barquisimeto
11N 74W **139** Barranquilla
54N 114W **93** Barrhead
44N 79W **97** Barrie
20S 115E **157** Barrow I.
47N 7E **145** Basel
6N 122E **151** Basilan, I.
17N 95E **151** Bassein
16N 61W **138** Basse-Terre
39S 146E **158** Bass Strait
42N 9E **145** Bastia
11S 130E **157** Bathurst I. (Australia)
76N 100W **77** Bathurst I. (N.W.T.)
47N 65W **103** Bathurst
30N 91W **136** Baton Rouge
53N 110W **93** Battle R.
20N 122E **150** Batan Is.
70N 128W **77** Bathurst, Cape
0 98E **151** Batu, Kepulauan (islands)
22S 49W **140** Bauru
53N 108E **148** Baykal, L.
43N 1W **145** Bayonne
33N 35E **153** Bayrūt / Beirut
43N 82W **97** Bear Creek
46N 70W **98** Beauceville
72N 140W **77** Beaufort Sea
30N 94W **136** Beaumont
55N 107W **94** Beauval
55N 119W **93** Beaverlodge
44N 79W **97** Beaverton
46N 72W **98** Bécancour
31N 2W **155** Béchar
24N 113E **150** Bei R.
39N 116E **150** Beijing / Peking
39N 116E **150** Beijing Shi □
19S 35E **156** Beira
33N 35E **153** Beirut / Bayrūt
56N 78W **78** Belcher Is.
1S 48W **139** Belém
54N 6W **145** Belfast
50N 5E **145** Belgium ■
51N 37E **147** Belgorod
44N 20E **146** Belgrade / Beograd
3S 108E **151** Belitung, I.
17N 88W **137** Belize ■
17N 88W **137** Belize (city)
52N 55W **104** Belle Isle
51N 56W **104** Belle Isle, Strait of
44N 77W **97** Belleville
66S 80W **160** Bellingshausen Sea
17N 88W **137** Belmopan
20S 44W **139** Belo Horizonte
21S 146E **158** Belyando R.
36S 144E **158** Bendigo
15N 90E **154** Bengal, Bay of
32N 20E **155** Benghazi / Banghāzī
33N 117E **150** Bengbu
10N 2E **155** Benin ■
9N 11E **155** Benue R.
41N 123E **150** Benxi
44N 20E **146** Beograd / Belgrade
.52N 97W **83** Berens River
54N 28E **146** Berezina R.
60N 5E **143** Bergen
58N 167E **159** Bering Sea
52N 13E **146** Berlin
32N 65W **138** Bermuda □
47N 7E **145** Bern
27N 90E **154** Bhutan ■
1S 136E **152** Biak, I.
53N 23E **146** Bialystok
55N 112W **93** Biche, Lac La
52N 8E **145** Bielefeld
44N 76W **98** Big Rideau L.
54N 89W **83** Big Trout Lake
43N 3W **143** Bilbao
45N 108W **135** Billings
1N 104E **151** Bintan, I.
50N 97W **94** Birds Hill Provincial Park
50N 122W **88** Birkenhead Lake Provincial Park
52N 2W **145** Birmingham (U.K.)
33N 86W **136** Birmingham (U.S.)
45N 2W **145** Biscay, Bay of
34N 5E **155** Biskra
46N 100W **135** Bismarck
4S 146E **152** Bismarck Sea
11N 15W **155** Bissau
52N 85E **147** Biysk
21N 105E **151** Black Da R.
44N 79W **97** Black R.
45N 66W **103** Blacks Harbour
50N 127E **148** Blagoveshchensk
15S 35E **156** Blantyre
42S 82W **97** Blenheim
29S 26E **156** Bloemfontein
52N 97W **83** Bloodvein River
15N 32E **155** Blue Nile R. / El Bahr el Azraq
7N 11W **155** Bo
10N 7W **155** Bobo Dioulasso
58N 29E **146** Bobruysk
57N 17E **143** Böde
47N 9E **145** Bodensee
4N 74W **139** Bogotá
43N 116W **135** Boise
17S 64W **139** Bolivia ■
44N 11E **146** Bologna
46N 11E **146** Bolzano
19N 72E **154** Bombay
48N 53W **104** Bonavista
48N 53W **104** Bonavista Bay
48N 53W **104** Bonavista, Cape
45N 77W **98** Bon Echo Provincial Park
50N 7E **146** Bonn
71N 90W **77** Boothia, Gulf of
71N 94W **77** Boothia Peninsula
44N 0 **145** Bordeaux
1N 115E **151** Borneo
46N 63W **97** Borden
55N 15E **146** Bornholm
42N 71W **136** Boston
22S 24E **156** Botswana ■
7N 5W **155** Bouaké
47N 2E **145** Bourges
30S 146E **158** Bourke
51N 112W **93** Bow R.
53N 121W **88** Bowron Lake Provincial Park
45N 79W **84** Bracebridge
44N 79W **97** Bradford
27N 93E **154** Brahmaputra R.
45N 28E **146** Brăila
43N 75W **97** Brampton
49N 100W **94** Brandon
43N 80W **97** Brantford
46N 61W **103** Bras d'Or L.
15S 48E **139** Brasília
45N 25E **146** Braşov
48N 17E **146** Bratislava
56N 101E **148** Bratsk
52N 10E **146** Braunschweig
52N 117W **91** Brazeau
10S 50W **140** Brazil ■
34N 102W **135** Brazos R.
4S 15E **156** Brazzaville
53N 8E **145** Bremen
53N 8E **145** Bremerhaven
45N 10E **146** Brescia
51N 17E **146** Breslau / Wroclaw
48N 4W **145** Brest (France)
52N 23E **146** Brest (U.S.S.R.)
45N 65W **103** Bridgetown (N.S.)
13N 59W **138** Bridgetown (Barbados)
44N 64W **103** Bridgewater
44N 77W **97** Brighton (Ont.)
51N 0 **145** Brighton (U.K.)
27S 153E **158** Brisbane
51N 2W **145** Bristol
55N 125W **88** British Columbia □
49N 16E **146** Brnö / Brünn
57N 101W **83** Brochet
44N 75W **98** Brockville
32S 141E **157** Broken Hill
45N 72W **98** Brome, Lac
50N 112W **93** Brooks
18S 122E **157** Broome
45N 74W **98** Brownsburg
26N 98W **135** Brownsville
47N 15E **146** Bruck
4N 115E **151** Brunei ■
51N 4E **145** Bruxelles / Brussels
53N 34E **147** Bryansk
7N 73W **139** Bucaramanga
48N 56W **104** Buchans
44N 26E **146** Bucharest / Bucureşti
45N 75W **98** Buckingham
44N 26E **146** Bucureşti / Bucharest
47N 19E **146** Budapest
4N 77W **139** Buenaventura
34S 58W **140** Buenos Aires
43N 78W **136** Buffalo
51N 105W **94** Buffalo Pound Provincial Park
3S 29E **156** Bujumbura
51N 23E **146** Bug R.
2S 29E **156** Bukavu
20S 28E **156** Bulawayo
42N 25E **146** Bulgaria ■
2N 22E **156** Bumba
33S 115E **157** Bunbury
25S 152E **158** Bundaberg
42N 27E **146** Burgas
42N 4W **143** Burgeo
47N 55W **104** Burin
47N 55W **104** Burin Peninsula
12N 1W **155** Burkina Faso / Upper Volta ■
43N 79W **97** Burlington
21N 96E **151** Burma ■
41S 146E **158** Burnie
44N 78W **97** Burnt R.
31N 32E **155** Bûr Sa'îd / Port Said
3S 126E **152** Buru, I.
3S 30E **156** Burundi ■
29N 51E **153** Büshehr
46N 112W **135** Butte
47N 53W **104** Butter Pot Provincial Park
5S 122E **151** Butung, I.
53N 18E **146** Bydgoszcz
53N 27E **147** Byelorussian S.S.R. □
47N 59W **103** Cabot Strait
5S 12E **156** Cabinda ■
44N 20E **146** Čačak
36N 6W **143** Cadiz
49N 0 **145** Caen
39N 9E **143** Cagliari
17S 145E **157** Cairns
30N 31E **155** Cairo / El Qâhira
51N 2E **145** Calais
22N 88E **154** Calcutta
44N 80W **97** Caledon
51N 114W **93** Calgary C.M.A.
3N 76W **139** Cali
37N 120W **135** California □
27N 111W **137** California, Golfo de
21N 78W **138** Camaguey
43N 80W **97** Cambridge (Ont.)
52N 0 **145** Cambridge (U.K.)
69N 105W **77** Cambridge Bay
6N 12E **155** Cameroon ■
50N 125W **87** Campbell River
47N 66W **103** Campbellton
19N 90W **137** Campeche
19N 93W **137** Campeche, Bahia de
7S 35W **139** Campina Grande
22S 47W **140** Campinas
20S 54W **139** Campo Grande
21S 41W **140** Campos
53N 113W **93** Camrose
35N 95W **135** Canadian R.
46N 66W **103** Canaan R.
60N 95W **133** Canada ■
35S 149E **158** Canberra
29N 17W **155** Canary Is.
20N 88W **137** Cancun
55N 69W **78** Caniapiscau, Riv.
51N 115W **93** Canmore
45N 61W **103** Canso
10N 105E **151** Can-tho
49N 66W **103** Cap Chat
46N 61E **103** Cape Breton Highlands National Park
46N 60W **103** Cape Breton I.
64N 76W **78** Cape Dorset
55N 82W **78** Cape Henrietta Maria
61N 70W **78** Cape Hopes Advance
34S 18E **156** Cape Town
50N 128W **87** Cape Scott Provincial Park
63S 61W **160** Capitán Arturo Prat (research station)
10N 67W **139** Caracas
47N 53W **104** Carbonear
51N 3W **145** Cardiff
15N 75W **138** Caribbean Sea
45N 76W **98** Carleton Place
54N 3W **145** Carlisle
62N 136W **77** Carmacks
24S 113E **157** Carnarvon
26S 122E **157** Carnegie, L.
5N 62W **139** Caroni R.
14S 139E **157** Carpentaria, Gulf of
55N 123W **88** Carp Lake Provincial Park
39N 119W **135** Carson City
10N 75W **139** Cartagena (Colombia)
37N 1W **143** Cartagena (Spain)
53N 57W **84** Cartwright
8S 36W **139** Caruaru
33N 7W **155** Casablanca
48N 66W **103** Cascapédia R.
66S 110E **160** Casey (research station)
42N 106W **135** Casper
43N 53E **147** Caspian Sea
59N 129W **87** Cassiar
49N 117W **88** Castlegar
14N 61W **138** Castries
48N 53W **104** Catalina
14N 124E **152** Catanduanes, I.
24N 75W **137** Cat Island
29S 51W **140** Caxias do Sul
5N 52W **139** Cayenne
19N 80W **138** Cayman Is. □
10N 124E **151** Cebu
53N 100W **94** Cedar Lake
42N 91W **136** Cedar Rapids
32S 133E **157** Ceduna
3N 123E **151** Celebes Sea
7N 20E **155** Central African Republic ■
3S 129E **152** Ceram, I.
49N 14E **146** České Budějovice
36N 5W **155** Ceuta
15N 17E **155** Chad ■
13N 14E **155** Chad, L.
48N 65W **103** Chaleur Bay
48N 64W **103** Chandler
31N 117E **150** Chang Jiang / Yangtze R.
43N 124E **150** Changchun
28N 113E **150** Changsha
36N 113E **150** Changzhi
31N 120E **150** Changzhou
49N 2W **145** Channel Is. □
47N 59W **104** Channel-Port aux Basques
10N 16E **155** Chari R.
39N 63E **147** Chardzhou
30N 93W **136** Charles, L.
32N 80W **136** Charleston (South Carolina)
38N 81W **136** Charleston (West Virginia)
26S 146E **158** Charleville
35N 80W **140** Charlotte
46N 63W **103** Charlottetown
45N 74W **98** Châteauguay R.
50S 74W **158** Chatham I.
47N 65W **103** Chatham (N.B.)
42N 82W **97** Chatham (Ont.)
35N 85W **136** Chattanooga
46N 71W **98** Chaudière R.
56N 47E **147** Cheboksary
45N 61W **103** Chedabucto Bay
33N 126E **150** Cheju-do
55N 61E **147** Chelyabinsk
34N 104E **149** Chengdu
47N 2E **145** Cher R.
49N 1W **145** Cherbourg
59N 38E **147** Cherepovets
49N 32E **147** Cherkassy
51N 31E **147** Chernigov
48N 26E **147** Chernovtsy
44N 81W **97** Chesley
63N 90W **77** Chesterfield Inlet
46N 61W **103** Chéticamp
41N 104W **135** Cheyenne
18N 99E **151** Chiang Mai
35N 140E **180** Chiba
50N 74W **84** Chibougamau
49N 73W **84** Chibougamau Provincial Park
42N 87W **136** Chicago
48N 66W **103** Chic-Chocs Provincial Park
6S 80W **139** Chiclayo
48N 71W **84** Chicoutimi-Jonquière C.M.A.
45N 64W **103** Chignecto Bay
28N 106W **137** Chihuahua
35S 72W **140** Chile ■
51N 124W **88** Chilko L.
52N 124E **88** Chilcotin R.
49N 122W **88** Chilliwack
9S 78W **139** Chimbote
42N 69E **147** Chimkent
30N 110E **149** China ■
54N 79W **78** Chisasibi (Fort George)
52N 113E **148** Chita
22N 91E **154** Chittagong
41N 129E **150** Ch'ongjin
29N 106E **149** Chongqing / Chungking
39N 125E **150** Ch'ŏngju
43S 172E **158** Christchurch
45N 71E **147** Chu R.
43S 65W **140** Chubut R.
29N 106E **149** Chungking / Chongqing
22S 69W **140** Chuquicamata
58N 94W **84** Churchill
53N 64W **84** Churchill Falls
58N 95W **83** Churchill R. (Man.)
53N 62W **84** Churchill R. (Nfld.)
22N 80W **138** Cienfuegos
39N 84W **136** Cincinnati
8N 63W **139** Ciudad Bolivar
31N 106W **137** Ciudad Juárez
27N 110W **137** Ciudad Obregón
23N 99W **137** Ciudad Victoria
58N 112W **93** Claire, L.
54N 101W **94** Clearwater Lake Provincial Park
45N 3E **145** Clermont-Ferrand
41N 81W **136** Cleveland
43N 81W **97** Clinton
20S 140E **157** Cloncurry
46N 23E **146** Cluj-Napoca
45N 71W **98** Coaticook
62N 83W **78** Coats I.
18N 94W **137** Coatzacoalcos
43N 78W **97** Cobourg
17S 66W **139** Cochabamba
30S 153E **158** Coffs Harbour
11N 77E **154** Coimbatore
38S 143E **157** Colac
54N 110W **93** Cold Lake
44N 80W **97** Collingwood
51N 7E **145** Cologne / Köln
3N 73W **139** Colombia ■
7N 80E **154** Colombo
9N 80W **138** Colón
37N 106W **135** Colorado □
37S 68W **140** Colorado R. (Argentina)
34N 114W **135** Colorado R. (California)
32N 100W **135** Colorado R. (Texas)
39N 105W **135** Colorado Springs
34N 81W **136** Columbia
46N 121W **135** Columbia R.
38N 77W **136** Columbia, District of □
32N 85W **136** Columbus
45N 9E **145** Como
46N 9E **145** Como, Lago di
46S 67W **140** Comodoro Rivadavia
12N 44E **156** Comoros Is. ■
49N 125W **87** Comox
9N 13W **155** Conakry
37S 73W **140** Concepción
48N 53W **104** Conception Bay
27N 106W **137** Conchos (river)
43N 71W **136** Concord
1S 16E **156** Congo ■
1S 16E **156** Congo R.
41N 72W **136** Connecticut □
44N 28E **146** Constanţa
36N 6E **155** Constantine
41S 174E **158** Cook Strait
15S 145E **157** Cooktown
55N 12E **146** Copenhagen / København
68N 15W **77** Coppermine
66N 115W **77** Coppermine R.
64N 83W **78** Coral Harbour
15S 150E **158** Coral Sea
31S 64W **140** Córdoba (Argentina)
38N 5W **143** Córdoba (Spain)
52N 8W **145** Cork
49N 58W **104** Corner Brook
45N 74W **98** Cornwall
75N 95W **77** Cornwallis I.
52N 111W **93** Coronation
28N 97W **135** Corpus Christi
42N 9E **145** Corse / Corsica
43N 8W **143** Coruña, La
10N 84W **138** Costa Rica ■
4N 58W **139** Courantyne R.
49N 125W **87** Courtenay
45N 72W **98** Cowansville
49N 58W **104** Cox's Cove
44N 23E **146** Craiova
49N 115W **88** Cranbrook
57N 106W **83** Cree L.
44N 80W **97** Creemore
49N 116W **88** Creston
35N 25E **144** Crete / Kriti
52N 115W **93** Crimson Lake Provincial Park
54N 97W **83** Cross Lake
50N 115W **88** Crowsnest Pass
22N 79W **138** Cuba ■
16S 18E **156** Cubango R.
8N 72W **139** Cúcuta
3S 79W **139** Cuenca
19N 99W **137** Cuernavaca
15S 56W **139** Cuiaba R.
24N 107W **137** Culiacán
10N 64W **139** Cumana
65N 66W **78** Cumberland Sound
25S 49W **140** Curitiba
20N 86E **154** Cuttack
13S 72W **139** Cuzco
50N 110W **93** Cypress Hills Provincial Park (Alta.)

34N	62E	**153**	Herāt
48N	113E	**150**	Herlen R. / Kerulen R.
29N	111W	**137**	Hermosillo
58N	117W	**93**	High Level
55N	116W	**93**	High Prairie
35N	134E	**150**	Himeji
53N	117W	**93**	Hinton
34N	132E	**150**	Hiroshima
43S	147E	**158**	Hobart
11N	107E	**151**	Ho Chi Minh / Saigon
41N	111E	**150**	Hohhot
43N	143E	**150**	Hokkaidō □
21N	76W	**138**	Holguin
70N	117W	**77**	Holman
53N	4W	**145**	Holyhead
14N	86W	**138**	Honduras ■
22N	114E	**150**	Hong Kong (U.K.) □
25N	107E	**149**	Hongshui R.
49N	64W	**103**	Honguédo, Détroit d'
36N	138E	**150**	Honshū
21N	158W	**135**	Honolulu
49N	121W	**88**	Hope
55N	60W	**84**	Hopedale
50N	55W	**104**	Horse Is.
37N	80E	**149**	Hotan
54N	126W	**87**	Houston (B.C.)
30N	95W	**136**	Houston (U.S.)
49N	91E	**149**	Hovd R.
50N	16E	**146**	Hradec Králové
40N	114E	**150**	Huainan
12S	16E	**156**	Huambo
12S	75W	**139**	Huancayo
38N	111E	**150**	Huang R. / Yellow R.
31N	112E	**150**	Hubei □
60N	86W	**78**	Hudson Bay
53N	102W	**94**	Hudson Bay (town)
43N	74W	**136**	Hudson R.
62N	70W	**78**	Hudson Strait
56N	121W	**93**	Hudson's Hope
16N	107E	**151**	Hue
45N	75W	**98**	Hull (Qué.)
53N	0	**145**	Hull (U.K.)
41N	116W	**135**	Humboldt R.
27N	112E	**150**	Hunan □
51N	121W	**88**	100 Mile House
39N	127E	**150**	Hŭngnam
45N	74W	**98**	Huntingdon
45N	79W	**84**	Huntsville (Ont.)
34N	87W	**136**	Huntsville (U.S.)
45N	83W	**97**	Huron, L.
17N	78W	**154**	Hyderabad (India)
25N	68E	**154**	Hyderabad (Pakistan)
44N	27E	**146**	Ialomiţa R.
7N	4E	**155**	Ibadan
4N	75W	**139**	Ibagué
45N	73W	**98**	Iberville
65N	19W	**159**	Iceland ■
44N	114W	**135**	Idaho □
69N	81W	**78**	Igloolik
49N	91W	**83**	Ignace
52N	5W	**145**	IJssel Meer
55N	108W	**94**	Île-à-la-Crosse, Lac, Provincial Park
43N	78E	**153**	Ili R.
40N	89W	**136**	Illinois □
10N	123E	**151**	Iloilo
8N	4E	**155**	Ilorin
20N	78E	**154**	India ■
5S	75E	**154**	Indian Ocean
40N	86W	**136**	Indiana □
39N	86W	**136**	Indianapolis
68N	145E	**148**	Indigirka R.
5S	115E	**151**	Indonesia ■
22N	75E	**154**	Indore
32N	71E	**154**	Indus R.
43N	81W	**97**	Ingersoll
52N	114W	**93**	Innisfail
47N	11E	**146**	Innsbruck
58N	78W	**78**	Inukjuak
68N	133W	**77**	Inuvik
46S	168E	**158**	Invercargill
50N	116W	**88**	Invermere
46N	61W	**103**	Inverness (N.S.)
57N	4W	**145**	Inverness (U.K.)
42N	93W	**136**	Iowa □
53N	32E	**146**	Iput R.
62N	66W	**78**	Iqaluit (Frobisher Bay)
3S	73W	**139**	Iquitos
33N	53E	**153**	Iran ■
20N	101W	**137**	Irapuato
33N	44E	**153**	Iraq ■
53N	8W	**145**	Ireland ■
4S	137E	**152**	Irian Jaya □
54N	5W	**145**	Irish Sea
52N	106E	**148**	Irkutsk
45N	75W	**98**	Iroquois
48N	80W	**84**	Iroquois Falls
23N	106E	**151**	Irrawaddy R.
59N	68E	**147**	Irtysh R.
78N	104W	**77**	Isachsen
53N	66E	**147**	Ishim R.
43N	24E	**146**	Iskŭr R.
57N	131W	**87**	Iskut R.
33N	73E	**154**	Islamabad
39N	3E	**143**	Islas Baleares / Balearic Is.
54N	4W	**145**	Isle of Man
32N	35E	**153**	Israel ■
41N	29E	**153**	İstanbul
42N	14E	**144**	Italy ■
48N	24E	**146**	Ivano Frankovsk
56N	41E	**147**	Ivanovo
7N	5W	**155**	Ivory Coast ■
62N	77W	**78**	Ivujivik
56N	53E	**147**	Izhevsk
38N	27E	**153**	İzmir
28N	80E	**154**	Jabalpur
32N	90W	**136**	Jackson
30N	81W	**136**	Jacksonville
50N	63W	**103**	Jacques-Cartier, Détroit de
27N	76E	**154**	Jaipur
6S	106E	**151**	Jakarta
18N	77W	**138**	Jamaica ■
1S	103E	**151**	Jambi
51N	80W	**78**	James Bay
22N	86E	**154**	Jamshedpur
36N	136E	**150**	Japan ■
1S	136E	**152**	Japen, I.
1S	72W	**139**	Japura R.
1N	53W	**139**	Jari R.
52N	118W	**88**	Jasper
52N	118W	**93**	Jasper National Park
7S	110E	**151**	Java □
4S	115E	**151**	Java Sea
5S	73W	**139**	Javari R.
2S	140E	**152**	Jayapura
38N	92W	**136**	Jefferson City
16S	42W	**139**	Jequitinhonha R.
41N	35E	**153**	Jerusalem
6N	116E	**151**	Jesselton / Kota Kinabalu
32N	106E	**149**	Jialing R.
46N	130E	**150**	Jiamusi
33N	120E	**150**	Jiangsu □
27N	116E	**150**	Jiangxi □
35N	113E	**150**	Jiaozuo
21N	39E	**153**	Jiddah
43N	126E	**150**	Jilin
36N	117E	**150**	Jinan
29N	117E	**150**	Jingdezhen
27N	100E	**149**	Jinsha R. / Yangtze R.
41N	121E	**150**	Jinzhou
45N	131E	**150**	Jixi
17N	42E	**153**	Jizān
7S	35W	**139**	João Pessoa
26N	73E	**154**	Jodhpur
26S	28E	**156**	Johannesburg
57N	14E	**146**	Jönköping
48N	71W	**84**	Jonquière
31N	36E	**153**	Jordan ■
1N	42E	**156**	Juba, R.
21S	43W	**140**	Juiz de Fora
7S	69W	**139**	Juruá R.
11S	58W	**139**	Juruena R.
34N	69E	**154**	Kābul
10N	7E	**155**	Kaduna
31N	130E	**150**	Kagoshima
34N	114E	**150**	Kaifeng
66N	45W	**159**	Kalaallit Nunaat (Greenland) □
6S	29E	**156**	Kalemi
30S	121E	**157**	Kalgoorlie
57N	36E	**147**	Kalinin
54N	20E	**147**	Kaliningrad
56N	16E	**146**	Kalmar
54N	36E	**147**	Kaluga
57N	160E	**148**	Kamchatka Peninsula
48N	27E	**146**	Kamenets Podol'skiy
56N	62E	**147**	Kamensk Ural'skiy
50N	120W	**88**	Kamloops
0	32E	**156**	Kampala
13N	105E	**151**	Kampuchea ■
51N	116W	**88**	Kananaskis Provincial Park
6S	22E	**156**	Kananga
36N	136E	**150**	Kanazawa
7N	80E	**154**	Kandy
21N	158W	**135**	Kaneohe
35S	137E	**157**	Kangaroo I.
58N	66W	**78**	Kangiqsualujjuaq
62N	72W	**78**	Kangiqsujuaq
60N	70W	**78**	Kangirsuk
70N	68W	**78**	Kangirtugaapik (Clyde River)
10N	9W	**155**	Kankan
12N	8E	**155**	Kano
26N	80E	**154**	Kanpur
38N	98W	**135**	Kansas □
39N	94W	**136**	Kansas City
22N	120E	**150**	Kaohsiung
0	110E	**151**	Kapuas R.
49N	82W	**84**	Kapuskasing
75N	70E	**159**	Kara Sea
25N	67E	**154**	Karachi
50N	73E	**147**	Karaganda
45N	15E	**146**	Karlovac
56N	15E	**146**	Karlskrona
49N	8E	**145**	Karlsruhe
52N	82W	**78**	Kashechewan
39N	76E	**149**	Kashi
16N	36E	**155**	Kassala
51N	9E	**145**	Kassel
14S	132E	**157**	Katherine
27N	85E	**154**	Kathmandu
50N	19E	**146**	Katowice
57N	11E	**146**	Kattegat
75N	95W	**77**	Kaujuitoq (Resolute)
55N	24E	**147**	Kaunas
22N	159W	**135**	Kavai
2S	151E	**152**	Kavieng
35N	139E	**150**	Kawasaki
14N	11W	**155**	Kayes
38N	35E	**153**	Kayseri
50N	70E	**147**	Kazakh S.S.R. □
55N	49E	**147**	Kazan
59N	127W	**87**	Kechika R.
63N	95W	**77**	Keewatin, District of, □
43N	65W	**103**	Kejimkujik National Park
50N	119W	**88**	Kelowna
55N	86E	**147**	Kemerovo
45N	75W	**98**	Kemptville
20N	98E	**151**	Keng Tung
37N	85W	**136**	Kentucky □
45N	64W	**103**	Kentville
1N	38E	**156**	Kenya ■
8S	133E	**152**	Kepulauan Aru (islands)
0	98E	**151**	Kepulauan Batu (islands)
0	105E	**151**	Kepulauan Lingga (islands)
3S	99E	**151**	Kepulauan Mentawai (islands)
2S	126E	**152**	Kepulauan Sula (islands)
8S	132E	**152**	Kepulauan Tanimbar (islands)
30N	57E	**153**	Kermān
34N	47E	**153**	Kermānshāh
48N	113E	**150**	Kerulen R. / Herlen R.
25N	82W	**136**	Key West
48N	135E	**148**	Khabarovsk
50N	36E	**147**	Kharkhov
15N	32E	**155**	Khartoum
46N	32E	**147**	Kherson
72N	98E	**148**	Kheta R.
49N	27E	**146**	Khmel'nitskiy
22N	89E	**154**	Khulna
52N	116W	**88**	Kicking Horse Pass
54N	10E	**145**	Kiel
51N	20E	**146**	Kielce
50N	30E	**147**	Kiev / Kiyev
2S	30E	**156**	Kigali
5S	30E	**156**	Kigoma
5S	18E	**156**	Kikwit
46N	81W	**84**	Killarney Provincial Park
51N	126W	**87**	Kimaklini R.
49N	116W	**88**	Kimberley (B.C.)
28S	24E	**156**	Kimberley (S. Africa)
41N	129E	**150**	Kimch'aek
44N	81W	**97**	Kincardine
51N	109W	**93**	Kindersley
39S	144E	**157**	King I.
18N	77W	**138**	Kingston (Jamaica)
44N	76W	**98**	Kingston (Ont.)
13N	61W	**138**	Kingstown
42N	82W	**97**	Kingsville
4S	15E	**156**	Kinshasa
42N	75E	**147**	Kirghiz S.S.R. □
48N	80W	**84**	Kirkland Lake
35N	44E	**153**	Kirkūk
58N	49W	**147**	Kirov
48N	35E	**147**	Kirovograd
0	25E	**156**	Kisangani
47N	29E	**147**	Kishinev
0	42E	**155**	Kismaayo
34N	131E	**150**	Kitakyūshū
43N	80W	**97**	Kitchener C.M.A.
54N	128W	**87**	Kitimat
13S	28E	**156**	Kitwe
50N	30E	**147**	Kiyev / Kiev
51N	30E	**146**	Kiyevskoye Reservoir
41N	34E	**153**	Kizil Irmak R.
46N	14E	**146**	Klagenfurt
56N	21E	**146**	Klaipėda
61N	138W	**77**	Kluane National Park
36N	84W	**136**	Knoxville
34N	135E	**150**	Kōbe
55N	12E	**146**	København / Copenhagen
50N	7E	**145**	Koblenz
49N	117W	**88**	Kokanee Glacier Provincial Park
55N	9E	**146**	Kolding
16N	74E	**154**	Kolhapur
51N	7E	**145**	Köln / Cologne
10S	25E	**156**	Kolwezi
66N	152E	**148**	Kolyma R.
50N	137E	**148**	Komsomol'sk na Amure
41N	88E	**149**	Konqi R.
50N	117W	**88**	Kootenay L.
50N	116W	**88**	Kootenay R.
51N	116W	**88**	Kootenay National Park
40N	127E	**150**	Korea, North ■
37N	127E	**150**	Korea, South ■
35N	128E	**150**	Korea Strait
9N	5W	**155**	Korhogo
48N	21E	**146**	Košice
6N	102E	**151**	Kota Baharu
6N	116E	**151**	Kota Kinabalu / Jesselton
68N	102E	**148**	Kotuy R.
47N	65W	**103**	Kouchibouguac National Park
22N	114E	**150**	Kowloon
44N	21E	**146**	Kragujevac
50N	20E	**146**	Kraków
40N	53E	**147**	Krasnovodsk
56N	93E	**148**	Krasnoyarsk
16N	78E	**154**	Krishna R.
58N	8E	**145**	Kristiansand
56N	14E	**146**	Kristianstad
35N	25E	**144**	Kríti / Crete
47N	33E	**147**	Krivoy Rog
13N	100E	**151**	Krung Thep/ Bangkok
3N	101E	**151**	Kuala Lumpur
1N	110E	**151**	Kuching
32N	130E	**150**	Kumamoto
6N	1W	**155**	Kumasi
17S	12E	**156**	Kunene R.
25N	102E	**149**	Kunming
10S	123E	**151**	Kupang
42N	83E	**149**	Kuqa
34N	134E	**150**	Kurashiki
55N	65E	**147**	Kurgan
45N	150E	**148**	Kuril Is. / Kuril'skiye Ostrova
51N	36E	**147**	Kursk
58N	67W	**78**	Kuujjuaq
55N	78W	**77**	Kuujjuarapik (Poste-de-la-Baleine)
29N	47E	**153**	Kuwait / Al Kuwayt ■
53N	50E	**147**	Kuybyshev
58N	125W	**87**	Kwadacha Wilderness Provincial Park
35N	127E	**150**	Kwangju
7S	16E	**156**	Kwango R.
10S	15E	**156**	Kwanza R.
5S	18E	**156**	Kwilu R.
35N	135E	**150**	Kyōto
33N	131E	**150**	Kyūshū □
11N	12W	**155**	Labé
50N	14E	**146**	Labe R. / Elbe R.
48N	70W	**84**	La Baie
55N	112W	**93**	La Biche, Lac
53N	67W	**84**	Labrador City
53N	58W	**84**	Labrador Sea
45N	72W	**98**	Lac-Brome
34S	144E	**157**	Lachlan R.
45N	74W	**98**	Lachute
55N	108W	**94**	Lac Île-à-la-Crosse Provincial Park
55N	112W	**93**	Lac la Biche
55N	104W	**94**	Lac La Ronge
55N	104W	**94**	Lac La Ronge Provincial Park
45N	71W	**98**	Lac-Mégantic
52N	113W	**93**	Lacombe
43N	8W	**143**	La Coruña
61N	30E	**147**	Ladoga, L.
6S	147E	**152**	Lae
57N	14E	**146**	Lagan R.
53N	75W	**78**	La Grande Rivière
31N	74E	**154**	Lahore
62N	70W	**78**	Lake Harbour
49N	95W	**83**	Lake of the Woods
47N	84W	**84**	Lake Superior Provincial Park
56N	109W	**93**	La Loche
47N	73W	**84**	La Mauricie National Park
25N	100E	**149**	Lancang R. / Mekong R.
74N	84W	**77**	Lancaster Sound
52N	55W	**104**	L'Anse aux Meadows National Park
42N	84W	**140**	Lansing
36N	104E	**149**	Lanzhou
17N	105E	**151**	Laos ■
16S	68W	**139**	La Paz (Bolivia)
24N	111W	**137**	La Paz (Mexico)
35S	58W	**140**	La Plata
76N	125E	**148**	Laptev Sea
42N	13E	**146**	L'Aquila
8S	123E	**151**	Larantuka
27N	99W	**135**	Laredo
55N	105W	**94**	La Ronge, Lac
29N	91E	**149**	Lasa / Lhasa
49N	79W	**84**	La Sarre
50N	55W	**104**	La Scie
44N	10E	**145**	La Spezia
36N	115W	**135**	Las Vegas
47N	73W	**84**	La Tuque
57N	24E	**147**	Latvian S.S.R. □
41S	147E	**158**	Launceston
47N	71W	**84**	Laurentides Provincial Park
46N	6E	**145**	Lausanne
47N	77W	**84**	La Vérendrye Provincial Park
34N	98W	**135**	Lawton
57N	100W	**83**	Leaf Rapids
42N	82W	**97**	Leamington
34N	36E	**153**	Lebanon ■
48N	11E	**146**	Lech R.
53N	113W	**93**	Leduc
53N	1W	**145**	Leeds
49N	0	**145**	Le Havre
19S	140E	**157**	Leichardt R.
51N	12E	**146**	Leipzig
48N	0	**145**	Le Mans
46N	6E	**145**	Léman, Lac
67N	124E	**148**	Lena R.
60N	30E	**147**	Leningrad
69S	159E	**160**	Leningradskaya (research station)
44N	1W	**137**	Leon
46N	73W	**98**	L'Epiphanie
29S	28E	**156**	Lesotho ■
55N	115W	**93**	Lesser Slave Lake Provincial Park
49N	112W	**93**	Lethbridge
38N	84W	**136**	Lexington
11N	125E	**152**	Leyte, I.
29N	91E	**149**	Lhasa / Lasa
34N	119E	**150**	Lianyungang / Xinpu
42N	122E	**150**	Liaoning □
41N	123E	**150**	Liaoyang
43N	125E	**150**	Liaoyuan
61N	130W	**77**	Liard R.
6N	9W	**155**	Liberia ■
0	9E	**156**	Libreville
27N	17E	**155**	Libya ■
47N	9E	**145**	Liechtenstein ■
50N	5E	**145**	Liège
57N	21E	**146**	Liepāja
21S	168E	**158**	Lifou, I.
43N	9E	**145**	Ligurian Sea
11S	26E	**156**	Likasi
50N	3E	**145**	Lille
49N	122W	**88**	Lillooet
12S	77W	**139**	Lima
52N	8W	**145**	Limerick
57N	9E	**145**	Lim Fjorden
45N	1E	**145**	Limoges
39N	103W	**138**	Limon
23S	28E	**156**	Limpopo R.
41N	96W	**135**	Lincoln
0	105E	**151**	Lingga, Kepulauan (islands)
48N	14W	**146**	Linz
43N	4E	**145**	Lion, Golfe du
52N	39E	**147**	Lipetsk
38N	9W	**143**	Lisboa / Lisbon
49N	38E	**147**	Lisichansk
43N	80W	**97**	Listowel
55N	24E	**147**	Lithuanian S.S.R. □
34N	92W	**136**	Little Rock
24N	109E	**150**	Liuzhou
53N	3W	**145**	Liverpool
17S	26E	**156**	Livingstone
46N	14E	**146**	Ljubljana
53N	110W	**93**	Lloydminster
12S	13E	**156**	Lobito
56N	109W	**93**	Loche, La
43N	65W	**103**	Lockeport
51N	19E	**146**	Łódź
50N	121W	**88**	Logan Lake
47N	2E	**145**	Loire R.
5S	25E	**156**	Lomami R.
8S	116E	**151**	Lombok, I.
6S	1E	**155**	Lomé
43N	81W	**97**	London C.M.A. (Ont.)
51N	0	**145**	London (U.K.)
55N	7W	**145**	Londonderry
23S	51W	**140**	Londrina
41N	73W	**135**	Long Island
49N	86W	**84**	Longlac
42N	80W	**97**	Long Point Provincial Park
23S	144E	**158**	Longreach
31S	159E	**158**	Lord Howe I.
34N	118W	**135**	Los Angeles
20N	103E	**151**	Louangphrabang
46N	60W	**103**	Louisbourg National Park
31N	92W	**136**	Louisiana □
38N	85W	**136**	Louisville
49N	118W	**88**	Lower Arrow L.
0	25E	**156**	Lualaba R.
42N	117E	**150**	Luan R.
9S	13E	**156**	Luanda
33N	102W	**135**	Lubbock
54N	10E	**146**	Lübeck
51N	22E	**146**	Lublin
11S	27E	**156**	Lubumbashi
27N	81E	**154**	Lucknow (India)
44N	81W	**97**	Lucknow (Ont.)
39N	121E	**150**	Luda / Dairen
26S	15E	**156**	Lüderitz
3S	20E	**156**	Lukenie R.
50N	105W	**94**	Lumsden
44N	64W	**103**	Lunenburg
31N	104E	**150**	Luoyang
15S	28E	**156**	Lusaka
50N	25E	**146**	Lutsk
50N	60E	**145**	Luxembourg ■
47N	8E	**145**	Luzern
16N	121E	**151**	Luzon, I.
20N	121E	**150**	Luzon Strait
50N	24E	**147**	L'vov

57N 101W 83 Lynn Lake
45N 5E 145 Lyon
50N 121E 88 Lytton □
22N 113E 150 Macau □
9S 35W 139 Maceió
21S 149E 158 Mackay
22S 129E 157 Mackay, L.
55N 122W 88 Mackenzie
61N 115W 77 Mackenzie, District of □
67N 130W 77 Mackenzie R.
77N 110W 77 Mackenzie King I.
33N 83W 136 Macon
20S 47E 156 Madagascar ■
5S 145E 152 Madang
32N 17W 155 Madeira Is.
5S 61W 139 Madeira, R.
47N 61W 103 Madeleine, Îles de la
43N 89W 136 Madison
44N 97W 97 Madoc
13N 80E 154 Madras
11S 66W 139 Madre de Dios R.
40N 3W 143 Madrid
7S 113E 151 Madura, I.
10N 78E 154 Madurai
15S 168E 158 Maëwo, I.
59N 151E 148 Magadan
52N 11E 146 Magdeburg
46N 8E 145 Maggiore, Lago di (lake)
53N 59E 147 Magnitogorsk
76N 100W 78 Magnetic Pole, North
65S 140E 160 Magnetic Pole, South
45N 72W 98 Magog
15S 46E 156 Mahajanga
20N 86E 154 Mahanadi R.
50N 10E 146 Main R.
45N 69W 136 Maine □
34S 152E 158 Maitland
1S 118E 151 Makassar Strait
43N 47E 147 Makhachkala
21N 40E 153 Makkah / Mecca
4N 9E 155 Malabo
3N 101E 151 Malacca
3N 101E 151 Malacca, Straits of
36N 4W 143 Málaga
8S 112E 151 Malang
13S 34E 156 Malawi ■
12S 34E 156 Malawi, L.
4N 102E 151 Malaya □
5N 110E 151 Malaysia ■
16S 167E 158 Malakula, I.
15N 2W 155 Mali ■
39N 3E 143 Mallorca
55N 13E 146 Malmö
36N 14E 143 Malta ■
2S 138E 152 Mamberamo R.
14S 66W 139 Mamoré R.
54N 4W 145 Man, Isle of
1N 125E 152 Manado
12N 86W 137 Managua
3S 60W 139 Manaus
53N 2W 145 Manchester
22N 96E 151 Mandalay
13N 74E 154 Mangalore
22S 45E 156 Mangoky R.
51N 68W 84 Manicouagan, Réservoir
14N 121E 151 Manila
55N 97W 94 Manitoba □
51N 98W 94 Manitoba, L.
46N 76W 84 Maniwaki
5N 75W 139 Manizales
57N 117W 93 Manning
49N 120W 88 Manning Provincial Park
62N 80W 78 Mansel I.
19N 115W 137 Manzanillo
50N 109W 93 Maple Creek
26S 32E 156 Maputo
38S 57W 140 Mar del Plata
10N 71W 139 Maracaibo
9N 71W 139 Maracaibo, L.
10N 67W 139 Maracay
13N 8E 155 Maradi
5S 77W 139 Marañón R.
48N 86W 84 Marathon
21S 168E 158 Maré, I.
46N 15E 146 Maribor
80S 120W 160 Marie Byrd Land
42N 25E 146 Maritsa R.
44N 79W 97 Markham
44N 77W 97 Marmora
49N 4E 145 Marne R.
4N 54W 139 Maroni R.
10N 14E 155 Maroua
31N 8W 155 Marrakech
43N 5E 145 Marseille
14N 61W 138 Martinique □
38N 62E 147 Mary
39N 76W 136 Maryland □
52N 56W 104 Mary's Harbour
47N 55W 104 Marystown
35N 128E 150 Masan
12N 123E 151 Masbate
29S 27E 156 Maseru
36N 59E 153 Mashhad
46N 73W 98 Maskinonge
23N 58E 156 Masqat / Muscat
42N 72W 136 Massachusetts □
54N 132W 87 Masset
46N 73W 84 Mastigouche Provincial Park
6S 13E 156 Matadi
49N 77W 84 Matagami
25N 98W 137 Matamoros
49N 67W 103 Matane
49N 67W 103 Matane Provincial Park
23N 81W 138 Matanzas
48N 67W 103 Matapédia R.
8S 116E 151 Mataram
23N 58E 153 Matrah
49N 122W 88 Matsqui
33N 132E 150 Matsuyama
50N 81W 84 Mattagami R.
9N 63W 139 Maturín
21N 156W 135 Maui
46N 73W 84 Mauricie, La, National Park
21N 10W 155 Mauritania ■
67S 63E 160 Mawson (research station)
63N 136W 77 Mayo

23N 106W 137 Mazatlán
26S 31E 156 Mbabane
0 18E 156 Mbandaka
6S 23E 156 Mbuji Maya
24S 113E 157 McLeod, L.
72N 102W 77 M'Clintock Channel
77S 170E 160 McMurdo (research station)
52N 118W 88 McNaughton L.
54N 108W 93 Meadow Lake
54N 109W 93 Meadow Lake Provincial Park
44N 80W 97 Meaford
21N 40E 153 Mecca / Makkah
3N 98E 151 Medan
6N 75W 139 Medellín
50N 110W 93 Medicine Hat
24N 40E 153 Medina / Al Madīnah
26S 118E 157 Meekatharra
48N 57W 104 Meelpaeg L.
45N 71W 98 Mégantic, Lac
25N 100E 149 Mekong R. / Lancang R.
38S 145E 158 Melbourne
53N 104W 93 Melfort
49N 101W 94 Melita
51N 103W 94 Melville
11S 131E 157 Melville I. (Australia)
75N 112W 78 Melville I. (Canada)
53N 60W 84 Melville, L.
68N 84W 78 Melville Peninsula
9S 119E 151 Memboro
35N 90W 136 Memphis
45N 72W 98 Memphrémagog, Lac
33S 69W 140 Mendoza
3S 99E 151 Mentawai, Kepulauan (islands)
65N 64W 78 Mercy, Cape
11N 97E 151 Mergui
42N 27E 146 Meriç R.
20N 89W 137 Mérida
50N 120W 88 Merritt
38N 15E 143 Messina
5N 72W 139 Meta R.
49N 6E 145 Metz
32N 115W 137 Mexicali
20N 100W 137 Mexico ■
19N 99W 137 México City
25N 90W 137 Mexico, Gulf of
34N 64E 153 Meymaneh
65N 48E 147 Mezen R.
25N 80W 136 Miami
44N 85W 136 Michigan □
44N 87W 136 Michigan, L.
44N 80W 97 Midland
45N 9E 145 Milan / Milano
34S 142E 157 Mildura
43N 80W 97 Milton
43N 88W 136 Milwaukee
29N 104E 149 Min R.
45N 64W 103 Minas Basin
8N 125E 152 Mindanao □
13N 121E 151 Mindoro, I.
45N 93W 136 Minneapolis
46N 94W 136 Minnesota □
54N 27E 147 Minsk
46N 66W 103 Minto
45N 74W 98 Mirabel
47N 66W 103 Miramichi R.
66S 93E 160 Mirnyy (research station)
48N 21E 146 Miskolc
2S 130E 152 Misool, I.
32N 15E 155 Mişrātah
48N 83W 84 Missinaibi Lake Provincial Park
50N 83W 84 Missinaibi R.
43N 79W 97 Mississauga
33N 90W 136 Mississippi □
34N 91W 136 Mississippi R.
38N 92W 136 Missouri □
41N 96W 135 Missouri R.
49N 72W 84 Mistassini
51N 74W 84 Mistassini, Lac
50N 74W 84 Mistassini Provincial Park
43N 81W 97 Mitchell
16S 142E 158 Mitchell R.
72N 77W 78 Mittimatalik (Pond Inlet)
30N 88W 136 Mobile
15S 12E 156 Môcamedes
2N 42E 156 Mogadishu / Muqdisho
54N 30E 147 Mogilev
47N 28E 147 Moldavian S.S.R., I.
67S 45E 160 Molodezhnaya (research station)
1S 127E 152 Moluccas, I.
4S 124E 151 Molucca Sea
4S 39E 156 Mombasa
43N 7E 145 Monaco ■
50N 118W 88 Monashee Provincial Park
46N 65W 103 Moncton
47N 103E 149 Mongolia ■
42N 83W 136 Monroe
6N 10W 155 Monrovia
47N 110W 135 Montana □
18N 78W 138 Montego Bay
25N 100W 137 Monterrey
35S 56W 140 Montevideo
32N 86W 136 Montgomery
48N 68W 103 Mont-Joli
47N 75W 84 Mont Laurier
47N 70W 98 Montmagny
44N 72W 136 Montpelier
43N 4E 145 Montpellier
45N 73W 98 Montréal C.M.A.
16N 62W 138 Montserrat □
47N 71W 98 Mont Ste-Anne Provincial Park
46N 74W 84 Mont-Tremblant Provincial Park
22N 95E 151 Monywa
51N 80W 78 Moose Factory
50N 105W 94 Moose Jaw
49N 102W 94 Moose Mountain Provincial Park
51N 80W 84 Moose R.
51N 80W 84 Moosonee
29N 79E 154 Moradabad
44N 22E 146 Morava R.
58N 3W 145 Moray Firth
19N 101W 137 Morelia
32N 6W 155 Morocco ■

11S 42S 156 Moroni
2N 128E 152 Morotai, I.
45N 75W 98 Morrisburg
55N 37E 147 Moscow / Moskva
49N 7E 145 Moselle R.
55N 37E 147 Moskva / Moscow
43N 18E 146 Mostar
16N 97E 151 Moulmein
33N 5W 155 Moulouya R.
51N 115W 88 Mount Assiniboine Provincial Park
47N 67W 103 Mount Carleton Provincial Park
57N 130W 87 Mount Edziza Provincial Park
20S 139E 157 Mount Isa
51N 118W 88 Mount Revelstoke National Park
53N 119W 88 Mount Robson Provincial Park
19S 35E 156 Mozambique ■
20S 39E 156 Mozambique Channel
44N 129E 150 Mudanjiang
53N 7W 145 Mullingar
30N 71E 153 Multan
48N 11E 146 München / Munich
59N 125W 88 Muncho Lake Provincial Park
48N 11E 146 Munich / München
2N 42E 156 Muqdisho / Mogadishu
47N 15E 146 Mur R.
27S 114E 157 Murchison R.
38N 1W 143 Murcia
49N 65W 103 Murdochville
69N 33E 147 Murmansk
36S 144E 158 Murray R.
34S 147E 158 Murrumbidgee R.
23N 58E 153 Muscat / Masqat
43N 86W 136 Muskegon
2S 33E 156 Mwanza
21N 95E 151 Myingyan
25N 97E 151 Myitkyina
12N 76E 154 Mysore
13N 123E 151 Naga
32N 130E 150 Nagasaki
35N 137E 150 Nagoya
21N 79E 154 Nagpur
46N 17E 146 Nagykanizsa
26N 127E 150 Naha
61N 125W 77 Nahanni National Park
54N 132W 87 Naikoon Provincial Park
56N 61W 78 Nain
1S 36E 156 Nairobi
50N 86W 84 Nakina
50N 117W 88 Nakusp
41N 71E 147 Namangan
20N 106E 151 Nam-dinh
22S 18E 156 Namibia ■
15N 39E 156 Nampula
49N 124W 88 Nanaimo
28N 116E 150 Nanchang
30N 106E 149 Nanchong
48N 6E 145 Nancy
32N 118E 150 Nanjing / Nanking
22N 108E 149 Nanning
47N 1W 145 Nantes
42N 79W 97 Nanticoke
32N 121E 150 Nantong
44N 77W 97 Napanee
39S 177E 158 Napier
41N 14E 143 Naples / Napoli
2S 74W 139 Napo R.
41N 14E 143 Napoli / Naples
53N 22E 146 Narew R.
22N 74E 154 Narmada R.
30S 149E 158 Narrabri
33S 117E 157 Narrogin
68N 17E 146 Narvik
41N 75W 147 Naryn R.
36N 86W 136 Nashville
55N 129W 87 Nass R.
25N 77W 138 Nassau
23N 32E 155 Nasser, L.
5S 35W 139 Natal
50N 61W 84 Natashquan
12N 15E 155 N'Djamena
41N 100W 135 Nebraska □
54N 124W 88 Nechako R.
53N 97W 83 Negginan
39S 65W 140 Negro R. (Argentina)
1S 63W 139 Negro R. (Brazil)
10N 122E 152 Negros, I.
29N 105E 149 Neijiang
42N 112E 149 Nei Mongol □
49N 117W 88 Nelson (B.C.)
41N 173E 158 Nelson (N.Z.)
57N 95W 83 Nelson R.
49N 125E 150 Nen R.
28N 84E 154 Nepal ■
47N 66W 103 Nepisiguit R.
57N 4W 145 Ness, Loch
52N 5E 145 Netherlands ■
12N 69W 138 Netherlands Antilles □
66N 71W 78 Nettilling L.
54N 10E 145 Neumünster
39N 117W 135 Nevada □
40N 74W 136 Newark
47N 66W 103 New Brunswick □
21S 165E 158 New Caledonia □
33S 151E 158 Newcastle (Aust.)
47N 65W 103 Newcastle (N.B.)
44N 79W 97 Newcastle (Ont.)
54N 6W 145 Newcastle (U.K.)
28N 77E 154 New Delhi
53N 58W 103 Newfoundland □
45N 62W 103 New Glasgow
4S 136E 152 New Guinea □
43N 71W 136 New Hampshire □
40N 74W 136 New Jersey □
47N 79W 84 New Liskeard
23S 119E 157 Newman
44N 79W 97 Newmarket
34N 106W 135 New Mexico □
30N 90W 136 New Orleans
52N 91W 83 New Osnaburgh
39S 174E 158 New Plymouth
75N 142E 148 New Siberian Is. / Novosibirskiye Ostrova
33S 146E 158 New South Wales □

42N 76W 136 New York □
40N 74W 136 New York (city)
40S 176E 158 New Zealand ■
7N 13E 155 Ngaoundéré
12N 109E 151 Nha-trang
43N 79W 97 Niagara
13N 2E 155 Niamey
1N 97E 151 Nias, I.
11N 85W 138 Nicaragua ■
12N 85W 138 Nicaragua, L.
43N 7E 145 Nice
9N 93E 151 Nicobar Is.
35N 33E 144 Nicosia
13N 10E 155 Niger ■
16N 0 155 Niger R.
8N 8E 155 Nigeria ■
38N 139E 150 Niigata
47N 32E 147 Nikolayev
53N 140E 148 Nikolayevsk na Amure
30N 31E 155 Nile R.
44N 4E 145 Nîmes
30N 121E 150 Ningbo
38N 106E 149 Ningxia □
53N 104W 94 Nipawin
54N 104W 94 Nipawin Provincial Park
49N 88W 83 Nipigon, L.
43N 22E 146 Niš
58N 60E 147 Nizhniy Tagil
64N 95E 148 Nizhnaya Tunguska R.
64N 166W 133 Nome
51N 95W 83 Nopiming Provincial Park
46N 74W 98 Nora R.
48N 79W 84 Noranda, Rouyn
36N 76W 136 Norfolk
29S 168E 158 Norfolk I.
69N 88E 148 Noril'sk
65N 127W 77 Norman Wells
49N 58W 104 Norris Point
58N 16E 146 Norrköping
28S 114E 157 Northampton
53N 108W 93 North Battleford
46N 79W 84 North Bay
47N 60W 103 North, Cape
35N 80W 136 North Carolina □
49N 124W 88 North Cowichan
47N 100W 135 North Dakota □
80N 95W 148 North Land / Severnaya Zemlya
38S 175E 158 North I.
40N 127E 150 North Korea ■
76N 102W 77 North Magnetic Pole
42N 104W 135 North Platte R.
90N 159 North Pole
54N 110W 93 North Saskatchewan R.
56N 4E 145 North Sea
46N 64W 103 Northumberland Strait
53N 60W 84 North West River
54N 7W 145 Northern Ireland □
16S 133E 157 Northern Territory □
65N 100W 77 Northwest Territories □
67N 11E 143 Norway ■
54N 98W 83 Norway House
66N 1E 159 Norwegian Sea
52N 1E 145 Norwich
44N 78W 97 Norwood
53N 17E 146 Noteć R.
49N 55W 104 Notre Dame Bay
46N 73W 98 Notre-Dame-des-Prairies
46N 68W 103 Notre-Dame-du-Lac
44N 80W 97 Nottawasaga R.
53N 1W 145 Nottingham
21N 17W 155 Nouadhibou
18N 16W 155 Nouakchott
22S 166E 158 Nouméa
53N 78W 78 Nouveau Comptoir / Wemindji
45N 63W 103 Nova Scotia □
75N 56E 148 Novaya Zemlya, I.
45N 20E 146 Novi Sad
53N 87E 147 Novokuznetsk
71S 11E 160 Novolazarevskaya (research station)
55N 83E 147 Novosibirsk
75N 142E 148 Novosibirskiye Ostrova / New Siberian Is.
31N 95E 149 Nu R. / Salween R.
27N 99W 137 Nuevo Laredo
49N 11E 146 Nürnberg
64N 51W 159 Nuuk (Godthåb)
12N 25E 155 Nyala
22N 158W 135 Oahu
43N 79W 97 Oakville
17N 96W 137 Oaxaca
59N 80E 147 Ob' R.
67N 73E 147 Ob, Gulf of
1S 127E 152 Obi I.
55N 10E 146 Odense
53N 14E 146 Oder R.
46N 30E 147 Odessa
8N 4E 155 Ogbomosho
40N 84W 136 Ohio □
39N 82W 136 Ohio R.
49N 3E 145 Oise R.
50N 120W 88 Okanagan L.
50N 119W 88 Okanagan Mountain Provincial Park
34N 134E 150 Okayama
27N 81W 140 Okeechobee, L.
55N 145E 159 Okhotsk, Sea of
26N 128E 150 Okinawa
35N 97W 139 Oklahoma □
35N 97W 139 Oklahoma City
56N 16E 146 Öland, I.
68N 140W 77 Old Crow
50N 112W 93 Oldman R.
58N 122E 148 Olekma R.
68N 114E 148 Olenek R.
47N 123W 135 Olympia
41N 96W 136 Omaha
23N 58E 153 Oman ■
24N 58E 153 Oman, Gulf of
15N 32E 155 Omdurman
56N 126W 87 Omineca R.
7N 36E 155 Omo R.
65N 161E 148 Omolon R.
55N 73E 147 Omsk
62N 35E 147 Onega, L.
6N 6E 155 Onitsha
52N 88W 97 Ontario □
43N 78W 97 Ontario, L.

27S	135E	157	Oodnadatta
54N	126W	87	Ootsa L.
47N	22E	146	Oradea
35N	0	155	Oran
30S	20E	156	Orange R.
60S	47W	160	Orcadas (research station)
18S	128E	157	Ord R.
43N	44E	147	Ordzhonikidze
44N	121W	135	Oregon □
53N	36E	147	Orel
51N	55E	147	Orenburg
44N	79W	97	Orillia
8N	66W	139	Orinoco R.
19N	97W	137	Orizaba
59N	3W	145	Orkney Is.
46N	66W	103	Oromocto
54N	30E	146	Orsha
51N	58E	147	Orsk
18S	67W	139	Oruro
34N	135E	150	Ōsaka
44N	79W	97	Oshawa C.M.A.
45N	18E	146	Osijek
60N	10E	143	Oslo
50N	18E	146	Ostrava
57N	28E	146	Ostrov
51N	143E	148	Ostrov Sakhalin / Sakhalin I.
71N	180E	148	Ostrov Vrangelya / Wrangel I.
45N	76W	98	Ottawa R.
45N	75W	98	Ottawa-Hull C.M.A.
32N	5E	155	Ouargla
12N	1W	155	Ougadougou
34N	2W	155	Oujda
65N	25E	144	Oulu
54N	2W	145	Ouse R.
51N	107W	94	Outlook
43N	6W	143	Oviedo
44N	81W	97	Owen Sound
51N	1W	145	Oxford
55N	95W	83	Oxford House
0	140E	158	Pacific Ocean
49N	125W	87	Pacific Rim National Park
1S	100E	151	Padang
45N	12E	146	Padova
0	101E	151	Pakanbaru
30N	70E	153	Pakistan ■
7N	134E	152	Palau Is.
9N	118E	152	Palawan, I.
3S	105E	151	Palembang
38N	13E	143	Palermo
28N	18W	143	Palma
64S	65W	160	Palmer (research station)
44N	81W	97	Palmerston
3N	76W	139	Palmira
2N	109E	151	Paloh
42N	1W	145	Pamplona
8N	80W	138	Panama ■
9N	79W	138	Panama Canal
8N	79W	138	Panama, Golfo de
11N	122E	151	Panay, I.
2S	106E	151	Pangkalpinang
66N	66W	78	Pangnirtung
46N	75W	84	Papineau-Labelle
8S	145E	152	Papua New Guinea ■
23S	57W	140	Paraguay ■
25S	58W	140	Paraguay R.
6N	55W	139	Paramaribo
32S	60W	140	Paraná
30S	59W	140	Paraná R.
49N	2E	145	Paris (France)
43N	80W	97	Paris (Ont.)
43N	81W	97	Parkhill
49N	124W	88	Parksville
4S	42W	139	Parnaiba R.
27N	89E	154	Paro Dzong
45N	64W	103	Parrsboro
70N	124W	77	Parry, Cape
45N	80W	84	Parry Sound
55N	122W	88	Parsnip R.
25N	85E	154	Patna
69N	124W	77	Paulatuk
52N	77E	147	Pavlodar
16S	68W	139	Paz, La (Bolivia)
24N	111W	137	Paz, La (Mexico)
59N	114W	93	Peace R.
56N	117W	93	Peace River
42N	20E	146	Peć
66N	52E	147	Pechora R.
32N	106W	135	Pecos R.
46N	18E	146	Pécs
67N	135W	77	Peel R.
40N	116E	150	Peking / Beijing
62N	131W	77	Pelly R.
68N	90W	77	Pelly Bay
31S	52W	140	Pelotas
46N	77W	84	Pembroke
41N	78W	136	Pennsylvania □
30N	87W	136	Pensacola
15S	168E	158	Pentecost, I.
49N	119W	88	Penticton
53N	45E	147	Penza
40N	89W	136	Peoria
48N	64W	103	Percé
4N	75W	139	Pereira
58N	57E	147	Perm'
42N	3E	145	Perpignan
27N	50E	153	Persian Gulf
32S	116E	157	Perth (Australia)
45N	76W	84	Perth (Ont.)
8S	75W	139	Peru ■
34N	71E	154	Peshawar
46N	77W	84	Petawawa
44N	78W	97	Peterborough
65S	55W	160	Petrel (research station)
43N	82W	97	Petrolia
55N	69E	147	Petropavlovsk
53N	158E	148	Petropavlovsk Kamchatskiy
61N	34E	147	Petrozavodsk
40N	75W	136	Philadelphia
12N	123E	152	Philippines ■
12N	105E	151	Phnom Penh
33N	112W	135	Phoenix
44N	77W	97	Picton
45N	62W	103	Pictou
44N	10W	135	Pierre
44N	78W	97	Pigeon L.
52N	21E	146	Pilica R.
49N	13E	146	Pilsen / Plzeň
5N	100E	151	Pinang / George Town
22N	83W	138	Pinar del Rio
61N	114W	83	Pine Point
43N	81W	97	Pinery Provincial Park
22S	47W	140	Piracicaba
6S	37W	139	Piranhas R.
43N	10E	146	Pisa
45N	25E	146	Pitești
40N	80W	136	Pittsburgh
5S	80W	139	Piura
47N	54W	104	Placentia
47N	54W	104	Placentia Bay
47N	67W	103	Plaster Rock
35S	58W	140	Plata, La
41N	99W	135	Platte R.
46N	71W	98	Plessisville
43N	24E	146	Pleven
45N	26E	146	Ploiești
42N	24E	144	Plovdiv
50N	4W	145	Plymouth
49N	13E	146	Plzeň / Pilsen
45N	12E	145	Po R.
42N	82W	97	Point Pelee National Park
4S	12E	156	Pointe-Noire
46N	0	145	Poitiers
52N	20E	146	Poland ■
55N	85W	84	Polar Bear Provincial Park
56N	29E	146	Polotsk
49N	34E	147	Poltava
55N	160E	148	Poluostrov Kamchatka Kamchatka Peninsula
18N	66W	138	Ponce
52N	113W	93	Ponoka
0	109E	151	Pontianak
18N	74E	154	Poona
8S	148E	152	Popondetta
50N	98W	94	Portage-la-Prairie
49N	125W	88	Port Alberni
50N	127W	87	Port Alice
30N	94W	136	Port Arthur
50N	57W	104	Port au Choix
32S	138E	157	Port Augusta
18N	72W	138	Port-au-Prince
42N	80W	78	Port Burwell
50N	67W	84	Port-Cartier
42N	79W	97	Port Colborne
48N	65W	103	Port-Daniel
44N	81W	97	Port Elgin
34S	25E	156	Port Elizabeth
0	9E	156	Port Gentil
4N	7E	155	Port Harcourt
50N	127W	87	Port Hardy
45N	61W	103	Port Hawkesbury
20S	118E	157	Port Hedland
44N	78W	97	Port Hope
45N	122W	135	Portland
34S	136E	157	Port Lincoln
31S	152E	158	Port Macquarie
51N	128W	87	Port McNeill
9S	147E	152	Port Moresby
47N	72W	84	Portneuf Provincial Park
41N	8W	143	Porto
4S	52W	140	Pôrto Alegre
10N	61W	138	Port of Spain
6N	2E	155	Porto Novo
8S	64W	139	Pôrto Velho
44N	79W	97	Port Perry
33S	138E	157	Port Pirie
31N	32E	155	Port Said / Bûr Sa'îd
50N	1W	145	Portsmouth
42N	81W	97	Port Stanley
19N	37E	156	Port Sudan
40N	7W	143	Portugal ■
18S	168E	158	Port-Vila
60N	67W	78	Povungnituk
37N	110W	135	Powell L.
50N	124W	88	Powell River
52N	17E	146	Poznań
50N	14E	146	Prague / Praha
44N	75W	98	Prescott
64S	61W	160	Primavera (research station)
53N	106W	94	Prince Albert
54N	106W	94	Prince Albert National Park
67N	76W	78	Prince Charles I.
46N	63W	103	Prince Edward Island □
47N	63W	103	Prince Edward Island National Park
54N	123W	88	Prince George
73N	99W	77	Prince of Wales I.
77N	120W	77	Prince Patrick I.
54N	130W	87	Prince Rupert
49N	120W	88	Princeton
52N	28E	146	Pripyat' R.
42N	21E	146	Priština
54N	86E	147	Prokop'yevsk
42N	71W	136	Providence
52N	110W	93	Provost
70N	148W	133	Prudhoe Bay
57N	28E	146	Pskov
19N	98W	137	Puebla
38N	104W	135	Pueblo
15N	88W	137	Puerto Barrios
41S	73W	140	Puerto Montt
18N	66W	138	Puerto Rico □
48N	86W	84	Pukaskwa National Park
39N	9E	146	Pula
18N	74E	154	Pune / Poona
53S	71W	140	Punta Arenas
8S	65W	139	Purus R.
35N	129E	150	Pusan
38N	127E	150	P'yŏnyang
32N	65E	153	Qandahār
38N	85E	149	Qarqan
25N	51E	153	Qatar ■
36N	120E	150	Qingdao / Tsingtao
36N	98E	149	Qinghai □
40N	119E	150	Qinhuangdao
47N	124E	150	Qiqihar
35N	51E	153	Qom / Qum
51N	103W	94	Qu'Appelle R.
61N	69W	78	Quaqtaq
50N	70W	84	Québec □
46N	71W	98	Québec C.M.A.
53N	132W	87	Queen Charlotte Is.
51N	128W	87	Queen Charlotte Sound
76N	95W	77	Queen Elizabeth Is.
68N	102W	77	Queen Maude Gulf
86S	160W	160	Queen Maud Land □
22S	142E	158	Queensland □
18S	37E	156	Quelimane
53N	122W	88	Quesnel
52N	121W	88	Quesnel L.
48N	91W	83	Quetico Provincial Park
30N	67E	153	Quetta
15N	91W	137	Quezaltenango
26S	144E	158	Quilpie
0	78W	139	Quito
35N	51E	153	Qum / Qom
8S	119E	151	Raba
34N	6W	155	Rabat
4S	152E	152	Rabaul
46N	53W	104	Race, Cape
54N	78W	78	Radisson
51N	21E	146	Radom
49N	104W	94	Radville
62N	116W	83	Rae-Edzo
21N	82E	154	Raipur
35N	78W	136	Raleigh
51N	112W	93	Ralston
34S	71W	140	Rancagua
56N	10E	145	Randers
16N	96E	151	Rangoon
62N	93W	77	Rankin Inlet
44N	103W	135	Rapid City
37N	48E	153	Rasht
33N	73E	154	Rawalpindi
8S	35W	139	Recife
20N	106E	151	Red R. / Hong R.
50N	96W	94	Red R. (Man.)
48N	97W	136	Red R. (U.S.)
51N	56W	104	Red Bay
51N	113W	93	Red Deer
51N	111W	93	Red Deer R. (Alta.)
49N	57W	104	Red Indian L.
51N	94W	83	Red Lake
25N	36E	153	Red Sea
49N	12E	146	Regensburg
27N	0	155	Reggane
50N	104W	94	Regina C.M.A.
49N	4W	145	Reims
57N	102W	83	Reindeer L.
45N	76W	84	Renfrew
11S	161E	158	Rennell, I.
48N	1W	145	Rennes
39N	120W	135	Reno
44N	12E	146	Reno R.
45N	73W	98	Repentigny
66N	86W	78	Repulse Bay
48N	74W	84	Réservoir Gouin
51N	68W	84	Réservoir Manicouagan
27S	59W	140	Resistencia
48N	67W	103	Restigouche R.
51N	118W	88	Revelstoke
51N	118W	88	Revelstoke Mountain National Park
64N	22E	143	Reykjavik
51N	6E	145	Rhein R. / Rhine R.
41N	71W	136	Rhode I. □
36N	28E	144	Rhodes
44N	4E	145	Rhône R.
21S	48W	140	Ribeirão Prêto
44N	78W	97	Rice L.
46N	73W	98	Richelieu R.
37N	77W	136	Richmond
45N	76W	98	Rideau R.
51N	100W	94	Riding Mountain National Park
56N	24E	147	Riga
45N	14E	146	Rijeka
52N	114W	93	Rimbey
48N	68W	103	Rimouski
48N	68W	103	Rimouski Provincial Park
35S	58W	140	Rio de la Plata
30N	105W	135	Rio Grande R. / Rio Bravo del Norte
32S	52W	140	Rio Grande (city)
48N	69W	103	Rivière-du-Loup
24N	46E	153	Riyadh / Ar Riyād
37N	80W	136	Roanoke
37N	76W	136	Roanoke R.
48N	72W	84	Roberval
43N	77W	136	Rochester
42N	89W	136	Rockford
23S	150E	158	Rockhampton
45N	75W	98	Rockland
52N	115W	93	Rocky Mountain House
51N	56W	104	Roddickton
51N	117W	88	Rogers Pass
26S	148E	158	Roma (Aust.)
42N	12E	143	Roma / Rome (Italy)
47N	26E	146	Romania ■
42N	82W	97	Rondeau Provincial Park
55N	105W	94	Ronge, Lac la
78S	60W	160	Ronne Ice Shelf
79S	162W	160	Roosevelt I.
14S	135E	157	Roper R.
33S	61W	140	Rosario
15N	61W	138	Roseau
51N	108W	94	Rosetown
11S	155E	158	Rossel, I.
82S	180W	160	Ross Ice Shelf
74S	178E	160	Ross Sea
44N	65W	103	Rossignol, L.
54N	12E	146	Rostock
47N	39E	147	Rostov na Donu
67S	70W	160	Rothera (research station)
10S	123E	157	Roti, I.
38S	176E	158	Rotorua
52N	4E	145	Rotterdam
49N	1E	145	Rouen
46N	75W	98	Rouge R.
48N	56W	104	Round Pond
48N	79W	84	Rouyn, Noranda
50N	25E	146	Rovno
51N	105W	94	Rowan's Ravine Provincial Park
51N	78W	78	Rupert, Riv. de
44N	26E	146	Ruse
62N	95E	148	Russian Soviet Federated Socialist Republic □
75S	136W	160	Russkaya (research station)
8S	120E	151	Ruteng
11S	36E	156	Ruvuma R.
2S	30E	156	Rwanda ■
54N	39E	147	Ryazan'
58N	39E	147	Rybinsk
26N	128E	150	Ryukyu Is.
56N	34E	146	Rzhev
58N	22E	146	Saaremaa
43N	65W	103	Sable, Cape
44N	60W	103	Sable I.
72N	126W	77	Sachs Harbour
46N	64W	103	Sackville
38N	121E	135	Sacramento
11N	107E	151	Saigon / Ho Chi Minh
48N	56W	104	St. Albans
51N	55W	104	St. Anthony
46N	72W	98	St. Casimir
43N	79W	97	St. Catharines-Niagara C.M.A.
17N	62W	138	St. Christopher and Nevis □
42N	82W	97	St. Clair, L.
46N	4E	145	St. Étienne
48N	72W	84	Saint-Félicien
46N	71W	98	St-François, Lac
46N	72W	98	St-François R.
48N	59W	104	St. George, Cape
46N	72W	98	St. Georges
48N	58W	104	St. George's
48N	59W	104	St. George's Bay
52N	6W	145	St. George's Channel
38S	122W	156	St. Helena
46N	73W	98	Saint-Hyacinthe
45N	73W	98	St-Jean
48N	72W	20	Saint-Jean, Lac
46N	74W	98	St-Jérôme
45N	66W	103	Saint John C.M.A.
45N	66W	103	St. John R.
17N	62W	138	Saint John's (Antigua and Barbuda)
47N	52W	104	St. John's C.M.A. (Nfld.)
46N	71W	98	St-Joseph-de-Beauce
49N	66W	103	St. Lawrence R.
48N	62W	103	St. Lawrence, Gulf of
63N	170W	148	St. Lawrence I.
14N	61W	138	St. Lucia ■
43N	81W	97	St. Mary's
50N	116W	88	St. Mary's Alpine Provincial Park
46N	73W	98	St-Maurice, Riv.
47N	73W	84	St-Maurice Provincial Park
49N	2W	145	St. Malo
44N	66W	103	St. Mary's Bay
45N	93W	136	St. Paul
41N	80W	136	St. Petersburg
47N	56W	104	St-Pierre et Miquelon □
46N	73W	98	St-Pierre, Lac
48N	67W	103	St-Quentin
45N	67W	103	St. Stephen
54N	95W	83	St. Theresa Point
42N	81W	97	St. Thomas
13N	61W	138	St. Vincent and the Grenadines ■
46N	74W	98	Ste-Agathe-des-Monts
47N	72W	98	Ste-Anne R.
49N	66W	103	Ste. Anne-des-Monts
46N	71W	98	Ste-Marie
51N	143E	148	Sakhalin Island / Ostrov Sakhalin
45N	74W	98	Salaberry-de-Valleyfield
28S	64W	140	Salado R.
66N	66E	147	Salekhard
45N	123W	135	Salem
62N	74W	78	Salluit
54N	123W	88	Salmon R.
50N	119W	88	Salmon Arm
25S	65W	140	Salta
40N	112W	135	Salt Lake City
13S	38W	139	Salvador
16N	97E	151	Salween R.
47N	13E	146	Salzburg
12N	125E	151	Samar, I.
0	117E	151	Samarinda
39N	67E	147	Samarkand
50N	22E	146	San R.
15N	44E	153	Şan'ā'
70S	1W	160	Sanae (research station)
29N	98W	135	San Antonio
8N	73W	139	San Cristobal
10S	161E	158	San Cristobal, I.
6N	118E	151	Sandakan
32N	117W	135	San Diego
53N	131W	87	Sandspit
53N	93W	83	Sandy Lake
37N	122W	135	San Francisco
10N	84W	138	San José (Costa Rica)
37N	122W	135	San José (U.S.)
18N	66W	138	San Juan
22N	101W	137	San Luis Potosí
44N	12E	145	San Marino ■
68S	68W	160	San Martin (research station)
27S	65W	140	San Miguel de Tucumán
15N	88W	137	San Pedro Sula
13N	89W	137	San Salvador
14N	89W	137	Santa Ana
34N	119W	135	Santa Barbara
22N	80W	138	Santa Clara
17S	63W	139	Santa Cruz (Bolivia)
10S	166E	158	Santa Cruz Is.
50S	71W	140	Santa Cruz R.
31S	60W	140	Santa Fe (Argentina)
35N	106W	139	Santa Fe (U.S.)
29S	53W	140	Santa Maria
14S	165E	158	Santa Maria, I.
33S	70W	140	Santiago (Chile)
19N	70W	138	Santiago (Dominican Republic)
20N	75W	138	Santiago de Cuba
28S	64W	140	Santiago del Estero
18N	70W	138	Santo Domingo
24S	46W	140	Santos
15S	44W	139	São Francisco R.
23S	46W	140	São José dos Campos
2S	44W	139	São Luis
9S	56W	139	São Manuel R.
44N	5E	145	Saône R.
23S	46W	140	São Paulo
0	6E	156	São Tomé
0	6E	156	Sao Tome and Principe ■

43N 141E 150 Sapporo
44N 18E 146 Sarajevo
54N 45E 147 Saransk
51N 46E 147 Saratov
2N 113E 151 Sarawak □
40N 9E 143 Sardegna / Sardinia
43N 82W 97 Sarnia
49N 79W 84 Sarre, La
54N 106W 94 Saskatchewan □
54N 103W 94 Saskatchewan R.
50N 108W 94 Saskatchewan Landing Provincial Park
52N 106W 94 Saskatoon C.M.A.
40N 8E 143 Sassari
26N 44E 153 Saudi Arabia ■
44N 81W 97 Saugeen R.
46N 84W 84 Sault Ste. Marie
45N 17E 146 Sava R.
32N 81W 136 Savannah
34N 82W 136 Savannah R.
10S 122E 157 Sawu, I.
54N 67W 84 Schefferville
50N 55W 104 Scie, La
50N 6W 145 Scilly, Isles of
57N 4W 145 Scotland □
66S 100E 160 Scott Base (research station)
45N 71W 98 Scotstown
44N 79W 97 Scugog L.
43N 81W 97 Seaforth
47N 122W 135 Seattle
42N 1E 145 Segre, R.
13N 7W 155 Segau
49N 2E 145 Seine R.
49N 104E 149 Selenge R.
42N 80W 94 Selkirk
7S 110E 150 Semarang
50N 80E 147 Semipalatinsk
38N 141E 150 Sendai
14N 14W 155 Senegal ■
37N 127E 150 Seoul / Sŏul
4S 142E 152 Sepik R.
50N 66W 84 Sept-Îles
50N 66W 84 Sept-Îles-Port-Cartier
44N 33E 147 Sevastopol'
56N 87W 83 Severn R. (Ontario)
51N 2W 145 Severn R. (U.K.)
63N 44E 147 Severnaya R.
79N 100E 159 Severnaya Zemlya / North Land
37N 6W 143 Sevilla
10S 46E 156 Seychelles ■
34N 10E 155 Sfax
52N 4E 145 'S-Gravenhage / The Hague
35N 109E 149 Shaanxi □
38N 77E 149 Shache / Yarkant
47N 40E 147 Shakhty
36S 118E 150 Shandong □
31N 121E 150 Shanghai
31N 121E 150 Shanghai Shi □
52N 9W 145 Shannon R.
23N 116E 150 Shantou / Swatow
37N 112E 150 Shanxi □
27N 111E 150 Shaoyang
49N 108W 93 Shaunavon
46N 73W 98 Shawinigan
16N 16W 155 St. Louis (Senegal)
38N 90W 136 St. Louis (U.S.)
6N 44E 155 Shebele R.
45N 62W 103 Sheet Harbour
44N 80W 97 Shelburne
53N 106W 94 Shellbrook
41N 123E 150 Shenyang
17S 168E 158 Shepherd I.
45N 72W 98 Sherbrooke
60N 1W 143 Shetland Is.
38N 114E 150 Shijiazhuang
33N 133E 150 Shikoku □
25N 92E 154 Shillong
29N 52E 153 Shīrāz
35N 138E 150 Shizuoka
42N 19E 146 Shkodër
17N 76E 154 Sholapur
32N 94W 136 Shreveport
51N 119W 88 Shuswap, L.
1S 99E 151 Siberut, I.
31N 104E 149 Sichuan □
37N 16E 143 Sicily
9N 12W 155 Sierra Leone ■
60S 46W 160 Signy I. (research station)
50N 119W 88 Silver Star Provincial Park
43N 80W 97 Simcoe
44N 79W 97 Simcoe, L.
2N 95E 151 Simeulue, I.
45N 34E 147 Simferopol'
1N 104E 151 Singapore ■
42N 96W 136 Sioux City
43N 96W 135 Sioux Falls
50N 92W 83 Sioux Lookout
76S 82W 160 Siple (research station)
49N 57W 104 Sir Richard Squires Provincial Park
21N 93E 151 Sittwe / Akyab
55N 12E 146 Sjælland
57N 8E 145 Skagerrak
54N 129W 87 Skeena R.
42N 21E 144 Skopje
59N 113W 83 Slave R.
55N 115W 93 Slave Lake
54N 8W 145 Sligo
50N 28E 146 Sluch', R.
54N 63W 84 Smallwood Reservoir
54N 127W 87 Smithers
45N 76W 97 Smiths Falls
54N 32E 147 Smolensk
62N 140W 77 Snag
43N 116W 135 Snake R.
37S 148E 158 Snowy R.
12N 54E 153 Socotra
42N 23E 146 Sofia / Sofiya
7S 150E 152 Solomon Sea
7N 47E 155 Somalia ■
73N 93W 77 Somerset I.
46N 129E 150 Songhua R.
46N 73W 98 Sorel
23S 47W 140 Sorocaba
37N 127E 150 Sŏul / Seoul
46N 62W 103 Souris
49N 101W 94 Souris R.
30S 25E 156 South Africa ■
44N 81W 97 Southampton (Ont.)
51N 1W 145 Southampton (U.K.)
64N 84W 78 Southampton I.
32S 139E 157 South Australia □
41N 86W 136 South Bend
33N 81W 136 South Carolina □
10N 113E 151 South China Sea
45N 100W 135 South Dakota □
57N 98W 83 Southern Indian L.
62S 60E 157 Southern Ocean
55S 38W 160 South Georgia, I. □
44S 170E 158 South I.
36N 128E 150 South Korea ■
65S 140E 160 South Magnetic Pole
45N 75W 98 South Nation R.
63S 45W 160 South Orkney Is. □
62S 130W 160 South Pacific Ocean
90S 160 South Pole
51N 110W 93 South Saskatchewan R.
62S 59W 160 South Shetland Is. □
7N 5W 143 Spain ■
50N 115W 88 Sparwood
69N 93W 77 Spence Bay
34S 137E 157 Spencer Gulf
44N 10E 145 Spezia, La
56N 119W 93 Spirit River
43N 16E 146 Split
52N 96W 83 Split Lake
47N 117W 135 Spokane
42N 72W 136 Springfield
45N 64W 103 Springhill
53N 114W 93 Spruce Grove
49N 99W 94 Spruce Woods Provincial Park
49N 123W 88 Squamish
49N 57W 104 Squires, Sir Richard, Provincial Park
7N 81E 154 Sri Lanka ■
34N 75E 154 Srinagar
52N 2W 145 Stafford
51S 59W 140 Stanley
42N 25E 146 Stara Zagora
59N 5E 143 Stavanger
45N 42E 147 Stavropol'
44N 80W 97 Stayner
49N 96W 94 Steinbach
45N 62W 103 Stellarton
48N 58W 104 Stephenville
53N 56E 147 Sterlitamak
52N 112W 93 Stettler
56N 130W 87 Stewart
47S 168E 158 Stewart I.
63N 135W 77 Stewart R.
58N 132W 88 Stikine R.
44N 77W 97 Stirling
59N 18E 143 Stockholm
58N 125W 88 Stone Mountain Provincial Park
44N 78W 97 Stony L.
43N 81W 97 Stratford
50N 125W 87 Strathcona Provincial Park
48N 7E 145 Strasbourg
43N 81W 97 Strathroy
46N 80W 84 Sturgeon Falls
44N 78W 97 Sturgeon L.
48N 9E 145 Stuttgart
51N 25E 146 Styr R.
19S 65W 139 Sucre
15N 30E 155 Sudan ■
46N 81W 84 Sudbury C.M.A.
52N 8W 145 Suir R.
27N 69E 154 Sukkur
2S 126E 152 Sula, Kepulauan (islands)
6N 121E 151 Sulu Archipelago
8N 120E 151 Sulu Sea
46N 107W 151 Sumatra □
9S 119E 151 Sumba, I.
8S 117E 151 Sumbawa, I.
49N 119W 88 Summerland
46N 63W 103 Summerside
47N 87W 83 Superior, L.
22N 59E 153 Şur
7S 112E 151 Surabaya
21N 73E 154 Surat
9N 99E 151 Surat Thani
4N 56W 139 Suriname ■
45N 65W 103 Sussex
30N 73E 154 Sutlej R.
44N 79W 97 Sutton
31N 120E 150 Suzhou
78N 17E 147 Svalbard
57N 60E 147 Sverdlovsk
79N 97W 77 Sverdrup Is.
54N 115W 93 Swan Hills Provincial Park
51N 4W 145 Swansea
23N 116E 150 Swatow / Shantou
26S 31E 156 Swaziland ■
67N 15E 143 Sweden ■
50N 107W 94 Swift Current
53N 118W 93 Switzer, William A., Provincial Park
46N 8E 145 Switzerland ■
43N 82W 97 Sydenham R.
34S 151E 158 Sydney (Australia)
46N 60W 103 Sydney (N.S.)
46N 60W 103 Sydney Mines
69S 39E 160 Syowa (research station)
43N 76W 136 Syracuse
45N 65E 147 Syr Dar'ya (river)
35N 38E 153 Syria ■
53N 48E 147 Syzran'
53N 14E 146 Szczecin
46N 20E 146 Szeged
47N 20E 146 Szolnok
49N 112W 93 Taber
38N 46E 153 Tabrīz
28N 36E 153 Tabūk
47N 122W 139 Tacoma
58N 98W 77 Tadoule L.
36N 128E 150 Taegu
36N 127E 150 Taejŏn
11S 153E 158 Tagula, I.
15N 5E 155 Tahoua
50N 126W 87 Tahsis
23N 120E 150 T'ainan
25N 121E 150 T'aipei
24N 121E 150 Taiwan ■
38N 112E 150 Taiyuan
32N 120E 150 Taizhou
13N 44E 153 Ta'izz
39N 70W 147 Tajik S.S.R. □
17N 99E 151 Tak
34N 134E 150 Takamatsu
30N 84W 136 Tallahassee
59N 24E 144 Tallinn
9N 0 155 Tamale
23N 5E 155 Tamanrasset
52N 41E 147 Tambov
45N 20E 146 Tamiš R.
28N 82W 136 Tampa
61N 24E 144 Tampere
22N 98W 137 Tampico
45N 8E 145 Tanaro R.
6S 30E 156 Tanganyika, L.
36N 5W 155 Tanger
39N 118E 150 Tangshan
8S 132E 152 Tanimbar, Kepulauan (islands)
19S 168E 158 Tanna, I.
6S 34E 156 Tanzania ■
15N 92W 137 Tapachula
4S 55W 139 Tapajós R.
21N 76E 154 Tapti R.
32N 13E 155 Tarābulus / Tripoli
41N 82E 149 Tarim R.
41N 69E 147 Tashkent
36S 160E 158 Tasman Sea
42S 146E 158 Tasmania □
57N 127W 87 Tatlatui Provincial Park
14N 98E 151 Tavoy
67N 82E 147 Taz R.
41N 45E 147 Tbilisi
14N 87W 137 Tegucigalpa
35N 51E 153 Tehrān
16N 95W 137 Tehuantepec, Golfo de
32N 34E 153 Tel Aviv-Yafo
5S 105E 151 Telukbetung
19S 134E 157 Tennant Creek
36N 86W 136 Tennessee □
34N 87W 136 Tennessee R.
21N 105W 137 Tepic
5S 42W 139 Teresina
45N 137E 148 Terney
49N 25E 146 Ternopol'
54N 128W 87 Terrace
48N 54W 104 Terra Nova National Park
61N 134W 77 Teslin R.
41N 12E 146 Tevere R. / Tiber R.
31N 98W 135 Texas □
16N 102E 151 Thailand ■
10N 101E 151 Thailand, Gulf of
42N 82W 97 Thames R. (Ont.)
51N 0 145 Thames R. (U.K.)
52N 4E 145 The Hague / s'Gravenhage
62N 104W 77 Thelon R.
53N 101W 94 The Pas
40N 23E 144 Thessaloníki
46N 71W 98 Thetford Mines
27N 89E 154 Thimphu
50N 121W 83 Thompson
50N 121W 88 Thompson R.
25S 142E 158 Thomson R.
51N 113W 93 Three Hills
48N 89W 83 Thunder Bay C.M.A.
39N 117E 150 Tianjin / Tientsin
39N 117E 150 Tianjin Shi □
41N 12E 146 Tiber R. / Tevere R.
32N 88E 149 Tibet / Xizang □
45N 8E 145 Ticino R.
35N 44E 153 Tigris R. / Dijlah R.
32N 117W 137 Tijuana
42N 82W 97 Tilbury
44S 171E 158 Timaru
17N 3W 155 Timbuktu / Tombouctou
45N 21E 146 Timişoara
45N 21E 146 Timiş R.
48N 81W 84 Timmins
9S 125E 152 Timor
27N 8W 155 Tindouf
41N 19E 143 Tiranë
46N 24E 146 Tîrgu-Mureş
10N 78E 154 Tiruchirappalli
15S 69W 139 Titicaca, L.
42N 19E 146 Titograd
18S 49E 156 Toamasina
47N 67W 103 Tobique R.
56N 65E 147 Tobol R.
4S 49W 139 Tocantins R.
53N 49E 147 Togliatti
6N 1E 155 Togo ■
35N 139E 150 Tōkyō
41N 83W 136 Toledo
23S 43E 156 Toliary
17N 3W 155 Tombouctou / Timbuktu
56N 85W 147 Tomsk
34N 96E 149 Tongtian R. / Yangtze R.
20N 108E 150 Tonkin, Gulf of
13N 104E 151 Tonle Sap (lake)
27S 152E 158 Toowoomba
39N 95W 136 Topeka
49N 115W 88 Top of the World Provincial Park
45N 7E 145 Torino / Turin
43N 79W 97 Toronto C.M.A.
31S 138E 157 Torrens, L.
13S 166E 158 Torres I.
53N 18E 146 Torun
43N 1E 145 Toulouse
19N 96E 151 Toungoo
47N 0 145 Tours
19S 146E 158 Townsville
47N 65W 103 Tracadie
49N 117W 88 Trail
44N 78W 97 Trent R.
40N 74W 136 Trenton (New Jersey)
44N 77W 97 Trenton (Ont.)
46N 53W 104 Trepassey
45N 13E 146 Trieste
8N 81E 154 Trincomalee
10N 61W 138 Trinidad and Tobago ■
48N 53W 104 Trinity Bay
32N 13E 155 Tripoli / Tarābulus
8N 77E 154 Trivandrum
46N 72W 98 Trois-Rivières C.M.A.
69N 19E 143 Tromsø
63N 10E 143 Trondheim
48N 4E 145 Troyes
8S 79W 139 Trujillo
45N 63W 103 Truro
51N 71E 147 Tselinograd
36N 120E 150 Tsingtao / Qingdao
32N 111W 139 Tucson
69N 133W 77 Tuktoyaktuk
54N 37E 147 Tula
36N 96W 136 Tulsa
42N 130E 150 Tumen R.
16N 76E 154 Tungabhadra R.
62N 128W 77 Tungsten
37N 10E 155 Tunis
33N 9E 155 Tunisia ■
47N 73W 84 Tuque, La
45N 7E 145 Turin / Torino
3N 36E 156 Turkana, L.
39N 36E 153 Turkey ■
43N 80W 97 Turkey Point Provincial Park
39N 59E 147 Turkmen S.S.R. □
21N 71W 138 Turks and Caicos Is.
60N 22E 144 Turku
43N 89E 149 Turpan
49N 100W 94 Turtle Mountain Provincial Park
17N 93W 137 Tuxtla Gutiérrez
44N 77W 97 Tweed
53N 126W 87 Tweedsmuir Provincial Park
57N 65E 147 Tyumen'
2N 18E 156 Ubangi R.
20S 48W 139 Uberaba
19S 48W 139 Uberlândia
15N 105E 151 Ubon Ratchathani
9S 74W 139 Ucayali R.
49N 126W 88 Ucluelet
46N 13E 146 Udine
54N 56E 147 Ufa
2N 32E 156 Uganda ■
5S 119E 151 Ujung Pandang
50N 30E 147 Ukrainian S.S.R. □
48N 107E 149 Ulaanbaatar / Ulan Bator
51N 107E 148 Ulan Ude
48N 10E 145 Ulm
47N 88E 149 Ulungur R.
54N 48E 147 Ul'yanovsk
45N 17E 146 Una R.
59N 67W 78 Ungava Bay
60N 100E 148 Union of Soviet Socialist Republics / U.S.S.R. ■
24N 54E 153 United Arab Emirates ■
55N 3W 145 United Kingdom ■
37N 96W 135 United States ■
52N 109W 93 Unity
50N 117W 88 Upper Arrow L.
49N 51E 147 Ural R.
59N 108W 83 Uranium City
19N 102W 137 Uruapan
32S 56W 140 Uruguay ■
43N 87E 149 Ürümqi
60N 100E 148 U.S.S.R. / Union of Soviet Socialist Republics ■
50N 82E 148 Ust'Kamenogorsk
40N 112W 135 Utah □
36N 140E 150 Utsunomiya
21S 167E 158 Uvéa, I.
44N 79W 97 Uxbridge
41N 65E 147 Uzbek S.S.R. □
29S 26E 156 Vaal R.
63N 21E 144 Vaasa
22N 73E 154 Vadodara
47N 9E 145 Vaduz
48N 18E 146 Váh R.
61N 146W 133 Valdez
40S 74W 140 Valdivia
48N 77W 84 Val-d'Or
39N 0 143 Valencia (Spain)
10N 68W 139 Valencia (Ven.)
41N 4W 143 Valladolid
46N 71W 98 Valleé-Jonction
36N 14E 143 Valletta
55N 117W 93 Valleyview
33S 71W 140 Valparaiso
49N 123W 88 Vancouver C.M.A.
49N 126W 87 Vancouver I.
54N 124W 88 Vanderhoof
58N 13E 146 Vänern (lake)
45N 74W 98 Vankleek Hill
14S 168E 158 Vanua Lava, I.
15S 165E 158 Vanuatu ■
25N 83E 154 Varanasi
43N 28E 146 Varna
58N 14E 146 Vättern (lake)
53N 112W 93 Vegreville
56N 30E 146 Velikiye Luki
45N 12E 146 Venezia / Venice
8N 65W 139 Venezuela ■
45N 12E 146 Venice / Venezia
19N 96W 137 Vera Cruz
47N 77W 84 Vérendrye, La, Provincial Park
43N 73W 140 Vermont □
50N 119W 88 Vernon
45N 11E 146 Verona
18N 102E 151 Viangchan / Vientiane
64S 57W 160 Vicecomodoro Marambio (research station)
46N 3E 145 Vichy
38S 147E 158 Victoria (Australia) □
48N 123W 88 Victoria C.M.A. (B.C.)
22N 114E 150 Victoria (Hong Kong)
71N 111W 77 Victoria I.
1S 33E 156 Victoria, L.
17S 131E 157 Victoria R.
48N 16E 146 Vienna / Wien
46N 0 145 Vienne R.
18N 102E 151 Vientiane / Viangchan
19N 106E 151 Vietnam ■
42N 8W 143 Vigo
46N 14E 146 Villach
18N 93W 137 Villahermosa
54N 25E 147 Vilnius
64N 122E 148 Vilyuy R.
49N 28E 147 Vinnitsa
18N 64W 138 Virgin Is., □
37N 78W 136 Virginia □
74N 108W 77 Viscount Melville Sound
17N 83E 154 Vishakhapatnam
52N 19E 146 Vistula R. / Wisla R.
55N 30E 147 Vitebsk

SOURCES

Information for the map plates and World Statistics was adapted from the following sources. A full reference is given the first time a source is listed. An abbreviated version is given thereafter.

1/2 United States Department of Commerce, National and Atmospheric Administration. Map #3042.

3/4 Cappon, Lester J., ed.-in-chief. *Atlas of Early American History: The Revolutionary Era, 1760-1790*. Princeton: Princeton University Press, 1976.

Department of Energy, Mines, and Resources. *The National Atlas of Canada*, 4th ed. Toronto: Macmillan of Canada, 1974.

Kerr, D.G.G. *A Historical Atlas of Canada*. Toronto: Thomas Nelson and Sons Canada Ltd., 1966.

5/6 *The National Atlas of Canada*, 4th ed., 1974.

Statistics Canada (Canadian Census, 1941).

7/8 Department of the Environment, Canadian Hydrographic Service. Map #400, 1974.

Statistics Canada (Canadian Census, 1981).

9/10 Statistics Canada (Canadian Census 1871, 1911, 1981).

Warkentin, John, ed. *Canada: A Geographical Interpretation*. Toronto: Methuen Publications, 1968.

11/12 *Great International Atlas*. Englewood Cliffs: Prentice-Hall Inc., 1981.

Murphy, Elaine M. "World Population: Towards the Next Century". Washington: Population Reference Bureau Inc., 1981.

Statistics Canada (Canadian Census, 1981).

13/14 Department of Energy, Mines, and Resources. "Indian Treaties" map. 1977.

Department of Indian and Northern Affairs.

The National Atlas of Canada, 5th ed. "Reserves and Trusts: Indian and Inuit Affairs Program" map. 1980.

15/16 Ministry of Citizenship and Culture.

Perspectives Canada III. Statistics Canada, 1980.

Statistics Canada, 1977-1981.

17/18 *The Atlas of Canada*. The Reader's Digest Association (Canada) Ltd., 1981.

Environment Canada.

National Geographic. "Atlantic Ocean Floor", map published in Vol. 147 No. 6 (June 1968).

19/20 *The National Atlas of Canada*, 4th ed., 1974.

21/22 *The National Atlas of Canada*, 4th ed. 1974

23/24 *The National Atlas of Canada*, 4th ed., 1974.

25/26 *British Palaeozoic Fossils*. London: British Museum, 1974.

The Canadian Oxford School Atlas, 4th ed. Toronto: Oxford University Press (Canada), 1977.

Life Nature Library. *The Fishes*. New York: Time Inc., 1963.

Life Nature Library. *The Mammals*. New York: Time Inc., 1963.

The National Atlas of Canada, 4th ed., 1974.

27/28 *The Atlas of Canada*, 1981.

Department of Energy, Mines, and Resources. "Principal Mineral Areas of Canada", map 900A. 1980.

The National Atlas of Canada, 4th ed., 1974.

Statistics Canada, 1981.

29/30 "The Coal Option". Shell Canada, 1981.

Indal Technologies Inc., Mississauga, Ont.

The National Atlas of Canada, 5th ed. "Energy" map. 1978. "Coal" map. 1982.

31/32 Drilling in the Foothills". Shell Canada, 1981.

"Enhanced Recovery of Oil". Shell Canada, 1981.

Gerlach, Arch C., ed. *The National Atlas of the United States*. Washington: U.S. Department of Interior Geological Survey, 1970.

The National Atlas of Canada, 4th ed., 1974.

The National Atlas of Canada. 5th ed. "Energy" map. 1978.

"World Oil and Gas Production". Shell Canada, 1983.

33/34 *Canada Gazetteer Atlas*. Toronto: Macmillan of Canada in cooperation with Energy, Mines, and Resources Canada, 1980.

Department of Energy, Mines, and Resources. "Oceanic Regions Adjacent to Canada", map 800A. 1971.

Gallagher, J.P. "Crude Oil Self-Sufficiency for Canada by 1990?" Address to Toronto Board of Trade, January 1981.

"Offshore Technology". Münich: Müncheyer Rückversicherungs – Gesellschaft, 1981.

"Oil Products in Canada". Shell Canada, 1980.

Oilweek Publication (map supplements). Toronto: Maclean-Hunter, May 10 1982 and June 14 1982.

35/36 Ontario Hydro.

Sociète d'Énergie de la Baie James.

United States Department of Energy.

37/38 Hare, F. Kenneth and Thomas, Morley K. *Climate Canada*. Toronto: John Wiley and Sons Canada, 1975.

The National Atlas of Canada, 4th ed., 1974.

The National Atlas of Canada, 5th ed. "Energy" map. 1978.

39/40 *The Atlas of Canada*, 1981.

Atlas of the World. Washington: The National Geographic Society, 1981.

"Mapping Weather". Environment Canada, 1978.

Wright, Peter. *The Prentice-Hall Concise Book of the Weather*. Toronto: Prentice-Hall Canada Inc., 1981.

41/42 *Great International Atlas*, 1981.

The National Atlas of Canada, 4th ed., 1974.

"Still Waters: The Chilling Effects of Acid Rain. Ottawa: Ministry of Supply and Services, 1981.

43/44 Bridges, E.M. *World Soils*. London: Cambridge University Press, 1970.

The National Atlas of Canada, 4th ed., 1974.

45/46 *The National Atlas of Canada*, 4th ed., 1974.

Statistics Canada, 1981, 1982, 1984.

47/48 *The National Atlas of Canada*, 4th ed., 1974.

Statistics Canada, 1976, 1984.

49/50 Agriculture Canada, 1982. (Selected statistics.)

"Agriculture Facts". Agriculture Canada, 1981.

McCool, Nydia. *Canadian Facts and Figures*. Edmonton: Hurtig Publishers Ltd., 1982.

Statistics Canada, 1980, 1984.

51/52 *The National Atlas of Canada*, 4th ed., 1974.

Environment Canada, Forestry Service. "Wildland Fire Occurrence in Canada" map, 1975.

53/54 Environment Canada, Forestry Service. "Forest Fire Weather Zones of Canada" map, 1973. "Canada's Eight Forest Regions" map, 1974. "Canada's Forests" map, 1979.

"Forests for the Future". Canadian Pulp and Paper Association, 1981.

Statistics Canada, 1981.

"Trees and Forests of Canada". Published by *Maclean's Magazine* for The Canadian Pulp and Paper Association, 1981.

55/56 "The Forest Industry of British Columbia". MacMillan-Bloedel Ltd., 1976

"Reference Tables 1982". Canadian Pulp and Paper Association, 1982.

57/58 Department of Fisheries and Oceans, 1982.

Farley, Albert L. *Atlas of British Columbia*. Vancouver: University of British Columbia Press, 1979.

Life Nature Library. *Ecology*. New York: Time Inc., 1963.

The National Atlas of Canada, 4th ed., 1974.

Statistics Canada, 1981.

Yearbook of Fishery Statistics: Catches and Landings. Food and Agriculture Organization of United Nations, Vol. 54 (1982).

59/60 *Canadian Facts and Figures*, 1982.

Canadian Manufacturer's Association.

The Financial Post 500. Vol. 78 No. 21 (June 1984).

Statistics Canada, 1981.

"Woods Gordon Long Range Forecast". Woods Gordon.

61/62 *Canada Year Book 1980-1981*. Statistics Canada, 1981.

Statistics Canada, 1981.

Statistics Canada "Update", 1983.

63/64 *The Bank of Canada Review*.

Canada Mortgage and Housing Corporation.

The Canadian Bankers' Association.

The Financial Post 500. Vol. 77 No. 25 (June 1983).

Statistics Canada, 1981.

"Woods Gordon Long Range Forecast". Woods Gordon.

65/66 Bank of Canada.

Statistics Canada, 1981.

The Financial Post, February 13, 1983.

67/68 Health and Welfare Canada.

Statistics Canada, 1981.

Statistics on Alcohol and Drug Use in Canada and Other Countries. Toronto: The Addiction Research Foundation, 1983.

69/70 Ministry of Transportation.

The National Atlas of Canada, 4th ed., 1974.

Statistics Canada, 1981.

71/72 *Airport Classification System*. Transport Canada, June 1981.

Statistics Canada, 1981.

73/74 Statistics Canada, 1981.

75/76 Alberta Bureau of Statistics.

Calgary In Fact. City of Calgary Department of Business Development, 1982.

Calgary Market Facts. City of Calgary Department of Business Development, 1982.

The Calgary Plan. City of Calgary Planning Department, May 1973.

City of Calgary Planning Department. Maps of Calgary dated September 1981 and July 1982.

Financial Post.

"Residential Land and Housing Survey Report". City of Calgary Planning Department, 1981.

77/78 83/84 87/88 93/94 97/98 103/104 *The Gazetteer Atlas of Canada*. 1980.

Statistics Canada, 1981.

79/80 *Climate Canada*, 1979.

The National Atlas of Canada, 4th ed., 1974.

81/82 91/92 101/102 These topographic maps are reproduced from the National Topographic System map sheets 21 A/14 © 1976, 31 F/15 © 1974, 42 I/10 © 1980, 83 C © 1962, 31 H © 1974, 106 M © 1974 Her Majesty the Queen in Right of Canada, with permission of Energy, Mines and Resources Canada.

85/86 Bickerstaff, A., Wallace, W.L., and Evert, F. *Growth of Forests in Canada – Part 2*. Environment Canada, Canadian Forestry Service, 1981.

Climate Canada, 1979.

Corporation Touristique de Sept-Îles.

Matthews, Geoffrey J. *The Ontario Economic Atlas*. Toronto: University of Toronto Press, 1967.

The National Atlas of Canada, 4th ed., 1974.

89/90 *Climate Canada*, 1979.

Atlas of British Columbia, 1979.

95/96 *Canada: A Geographical Interpretation*, 1968.

Climate Canada, 1979.

Statistics Canada, 1981.

Weir, Thomas R. *Atlas of Winnipeg*. Toronto: University of Toronto Press, 1978.

99/100 *Climate Canada*, 1979.

Environment Canada, Canada Land Data Systems Divison. *Land Directorate*.

Statistics Canada, 1981.

105/106 *Climate Canada*, 1979.

"Farming Facts". Statistics Canada, 1982.

The National Atlas of Canada, 4th ed., 1974.

The Oceanographic Atlas of the North Atlantic Ocean. Washington: U.S. Naval and Oceanographic Office, 1965.

107/108 Chief electoral officer for each province and territory.

The Globe and Mail

109/110 Chief electoral officer for each province and territory.

The Toronto Star

111/112 *CIDA's Year in Review*. "Canadians in the Third World: 1981-82" (statistical annex, 1981-82). Ministry of Supply and Services, 1983.

Food Outlook. Food and Agriculture Organization of the United Nations, 1983.

113/114 CIDA. "A Developing World" map, 1982.

External Affairs Canada.

En Route, Vol. 12 No. 9 (1984). Published by Airmedia for Air Canada.

Ka'na'ta, Fall Issue (1984). Published by Aircom Publishing for CP Air.

The 1984-85 Statesman's Yearbook. London: Macmillan Press, 1984.

Teleglobe Canada corporate brochure. Toronto: 2nd ed., 1983.

115/116 Banks, A.S. and Overstreet, W., eds. *The Political Handbook of the World*. New York: McGraw Hill Book Co., 1980.

The 1984-85 Statesman's Yearbook. London: Macmillan Press, 1984.

117/118 *Great International Atlas*, 1981.

"World Population: Towards the Next Century", 1981.

119/120 "World Population: Towards the Next Century", 1981.

121/122 *The New International Atlas*. Chicago: Rand McNally and Co., 1980.

The Times Atlas of the World. Boston: Houghton-Mifflin, 1967.

123/124 *The New International Atlas*, 1980.

Strahler, Arthur N. *Introduction to Physical Geography*. New York: John Wiley and Sons, 1965.

World Soils, 1970.

Yearbook of Fishery Statistics, 1982.

125/126 Sivard, Ruth Leger. *World Military and Social Expenditures 1981*. © World Priorities, Leesburg, VA 22075, U.S.

World Development Report 1982. New York: Oxford University Press for The World Bank, 1982.

127/128 "Food and Agriculture Organization of the United Nations". United Nations Annual Report, 1981.

World Development Report 1982.

World Military and Social Expenditures 1981.

"World Population: Towards the Next Century", 1981.

129/130 *World Development Report 1982*.

Yearbook of Labour Statistics. Geneva: International Labour Office, 1983.

131/132 *Stockholm International Peace Research Institute Yearbook 1983*. London: Taylor and Francis Ltd., 1983.

World Military and Social Expenditures 1981.

World Statistics

Demographic Yearbook. United Nations, 1982.

Encyclopedia Britannica 1984 Yearbook. Chicago.

The Europa Yearbook 1982: A World Survey. New York.

Population and Vital Statistics Report. United Nations, 1984.

The World Almanac 1984. New York

World Bank Atlas. World Bank, 1983.

World Development Report 1982.

"World Population: Towards the Next Century", 1981.

World Population Trends. New York: Population Reference Bureau, 1983.

Cover Photo: Bill Brooks/Masterfile

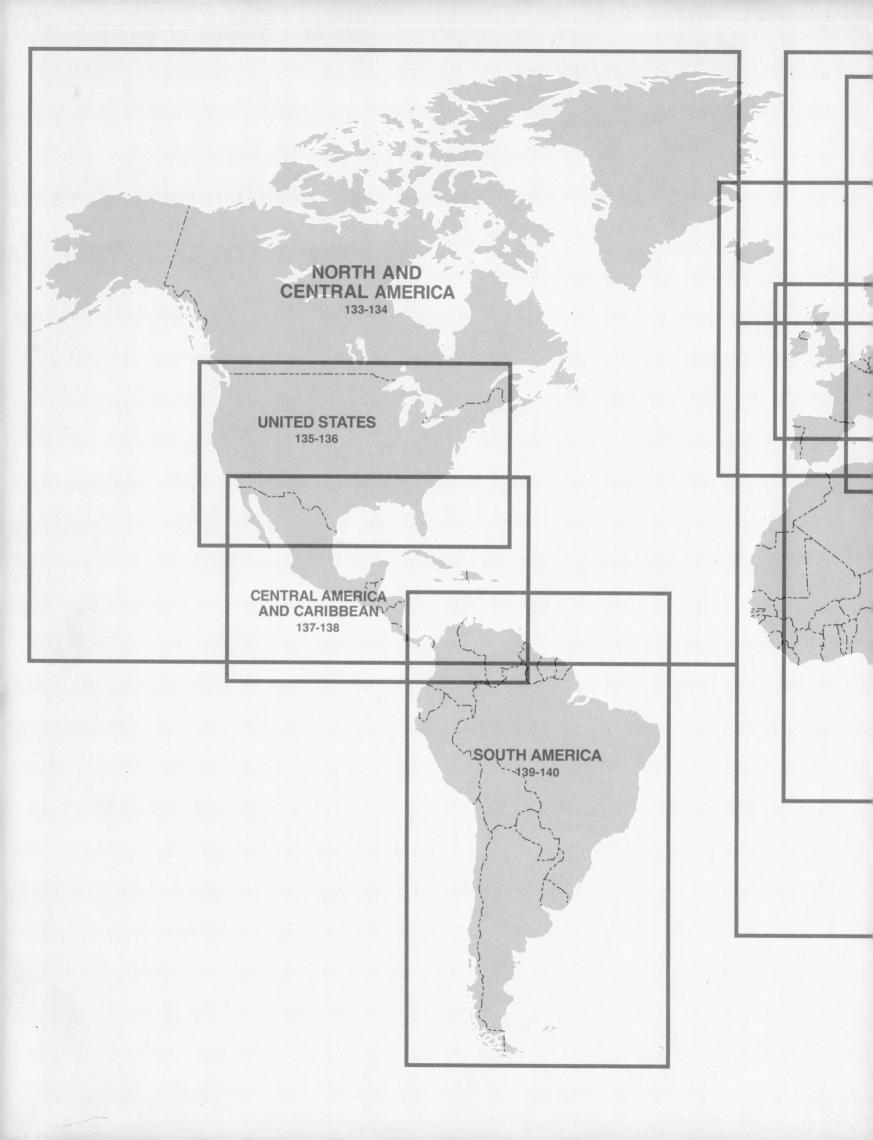

NORTH AND
CENTRAL AMERICA
133-134

UNITED STATES
135-136

CENTRAL AMERICA
AND CARIBBEAN
137-138

SOUTH AMERICA
139-140